Principles of
Public Speaking

FOURTEENTH EDITION

Principles of
Public Speaking

KATHLEEN GERMAN

Miami University • Oxford, Ohio

BRUCE E. GRONBECK

The University of Iowa

DOUGLAS EHNINGER

ALAN H. MONROE

Longman

New York • San Francisco • Boston
London • Toronto • Sydney • Tokyo • Singapore • Madrid
Mexico City • Munich • Paris • Cape Town • Hong Kong • Montreal

Publisher: Priscilla McGeehon
Acquisitions Editor: Michael Greer
Development Director: Lisa Pinto
Development Manager: Betty Slack
Marketing Manager: Megan Galvin-Fak
Supplements Editor: Kristinn Muller
Production Manager: Denise Phillip
Project Coordination, Text Design,
    and Electronic Page Makeup: Thompson Steele, Inc.
Cover Design Manager: Nancy Danahy
Cover Designer: Joel Zimmerman
Cover Illustration: "Person Giving Presentation" © Ryoichi Yotsumoto/SIS
Photo Researcher: PhotoSearch, Inc.
Senior Manufacturing Buyer: Dennis J. Para
Printer and Binder: R.R. Donnelley & Sons Company
Cover Printer: Coral Graphics Services, Inc.

For permission to use copyrighted material, grateful acknowledgment is made
to the copyright holders on pp. 319–320, hereby made part of this copyright page.

Previously published as *Principles of Speech Communication, Brief Edition.*

Library of Congress Cataloging-in-Publication Data

Principles of public speaking / Kathleen German . . . [et al.].—14th ed.
        p. cm.
      Rev. ed. of: Principles of speech communication / Bruce E. Gronbeck . . . [et al.].
13th brief ed. 1997.
      Includes index.
      ISBN 0-321-07015-1
      1. Public speaking. I. German, Kathleen M. II. Gronbeck, Bruce E. III. Title:
Principles of public speaking.

PN4121 .E36 2000
808.5' 1—dc21   00-035588

Please visit our website at http://www.awl.com/german

ISBN 0-321-07015-1

4 5 6 7 8 9 10—DOC—03 02

Brief Contents

Contents

PART 4   Types of Public Speaking

Preface

A TRADITION OF EXCELLENCE

Principles of Public Speaking, Fourteenth Edition, (which was previously published as *Principles of Speech Communication, Brief Edition*), presents the fundamental principles that have helped thousands of students gain the expertise and confidence to speak in public. It combines the latest research of scholars in rhetorical and communication theory with practical advice to students on how to speak effectively in a culturally diverse society. It retains the core concepts that have been its trademark from its inception—(e.g., Monroe's Motivated Sequence) while it also explores the latest developments in adapting electronic resources and technology to public speaking. Three keynote statements describe the basic approach of the book:

1. **This textbook gets you on your feet quickly.** While you will need a communication vocabulary to prepare and critique speeches, you must also put concepts into practice early. Chapter 2, "Getting Started," will get you on your feet and speaking to your classmates. Later chapters will develop ideas in more detail to help you increase your expertise as a public speaker and critical listener.

2. **This textbook focuses on communication in your college life but also includes examples from the worlds of work, politics, and social activism.** We recognize that your college environment probably commands your immediate attention, but we're sensitive to the fact that you're preparing for a lifetime of public participation. So we've incorporated applications and examples from both the college world and the world beyond.

3. **This textbook challenges you technically, intellectually, and morally.** Throughout your life, you will be expected to know how to accomplish goals (technical skills), how to analyze situations and propose courses of action (intellectual skills), and how to lead your social and professional life in trustworthy ways (moral development). The textbook challenges you not only to develop your skills and thought processes through public speaking and critical listening but also to understand your responsibilities as a speaker and listener.

THE PLAN OF THE BOOK

Principles of Public Speaking, Fourteenth Edition, is organized into four parts, reflecting the four major emphases of most contemporary courses in public speaking.

✓ Part 1: "Public Speaking and Critical Listening" provides you with *an orientation to the communication process.* Here you will encounter the conceptual underpinnings of communication theory, examine the public speaking skills that will enhance your success in school, at work, and in society, and learn how to adapt your ideas to the folks who make all the difference—the people in your audience. In Chapter 4, "Public Speaking and Cultural Life," you will consider the connection between culture and public speaking so that you will recognize the importance of attending to cultural differences. The chapters in Part 1 introduce important ways to think about speechmaking even as, with the help of Chapter 2, you give your first classroom speeches. Numerous examples show you how the particular skills involved in public speaking apply to a variety of real-world contexts.

✓ Part 2: "Planning and Preparing Your Speech" offers *a step-by-step approach to speech preparation.* You will learn how to confront and conquer your fears of public speaking by breaking down the complex task of public speaking into its component parts: setting your purposes, articulating central ideas, finding and assessing supporting materials, organizing and outlining these materials, and building effective introductions and conclusions.

✓ Building a speech is the first half of the speechmaking process. The other half is actually delivering your speech—*putting your presentation into words, gestures, bodily actions, vocal patterns, and visual aids.* That's what Part 3, "Presenting Your Speech" is all about. Every time you speak, you're communicating by way of four channels: language, sounds, movements, and visuals. The chapters in Part 3 will help you master how to send and control the message flowing through each channel.

✓ There are many different kinds of speeches, each with its own demands and conventional rules. In Part 4, "Types of Public Speaking," you will learn about three broad categories of speeches—speeches to inform, speeches to persuade, and argumentative speeches. Studying the characteristics of each of these types of speeches will help you refine your speechmaking skills and learn how to adapt them to particular speaking occasions.

✓ The Appendix, "Speaking at Community- and Group-Centered Events" is new to this edition. Here you will examine the particular characteristics of speeches of introduction, speeches of courtesy, and speeches to entertain—three types of special occasion speeches that are particularly sensitive to community needs and expectations. Understanding the responsibilities of participants in group discussions will help increase your effectiveness in speaking in such group-centered events.

FEATURES OF THE BOOK

With each new edition we strive to keep the text up-to-date and lively by rewriting material, reorganizing sections, and refining the features that complement the presentation. Features in the Fourteenth Edition include the following:

1. **New! Expanded coverage of electronic and World Wide Web databases.** Chapters 6 and 9 in particular will guide you in using these new technologies to

find and assess supporting materials and evaluate the types and use of computer-generated visual aids.

2. **New! Surfing the Web activities.** These exercises at the end of each chapter will familiarize you with how to use the Internet as a research tool.

3. **New! Web Exploration icons link the text presentation to the companion Web site.** The book Web site includes links to additional electronic resources and interactive tools integrated with core concepts presented in the book.

4. **New! Speech Writer's Workshop CD-ROM icons.** These icons in the text margins direct students to appropriate parts of the Speech Writer's Workshop CD-ROM where they engage in interactive worksheets and find extra help on topics.

5. **Appreciation of diversity.** Serious attention to the role of cultural practices reflects the fact that we live and interact in an increasingly diverse society. Successful public speakers recognize the connections between culture and public speaking and are able to adjust their styles and presentations to their audience. Chapter 4, "Public Speaking and Cultural Life," focuses specifically on the role of culture in communication.

6. **Critical thinking emphasis.** Critical thinking is an important part of overall education, including speech instruction. We cover critical thinking throughout the chapters and highlight the topic with special emphasis in Chapter 3, "Critical Listening" and Chapter 15, "Argumentation and Critical Thinking."

7. **Attention to ethics in public speaking.** We discuss speech ethics in the first chapter of the book and in a series of boxed features, "Speaking of . . . Ethics." These boxes examine the moral consequences of communicating and help you explore your own thinking about ethical choices in speechmaking. Box topics include "Considering Cultural Practices" in Chapter 4 and "Name-Calling" in Chapter 15.

8. **Focus on practical applications to speechmaking in society.** Boxed features entitled "Speaking of . . . Apprehension" and "Speaking of . . . Skills" examine questions and fears of public speakers. The boxes describe speaking situations in which you might find yourself and ask you to look beyond the classroom to consider the role of public speaking in society. Box topics include "First-Time Fears" in Chapter 1 and "Handling Hostile Audiences" in Chapter 5.

9. **Sample outlines and speeches.** Sample outlines and speeches demonstrate the application of speechmaking principles. Annotations on many of the outlines and speeches alert you to the rhetorical principles being used in them.

10. **Refining the central concepts developed by Monroe and Ehninger.** Alan Monroe (1903–1975) and Douglas Ehninger (1913–1979) worked with students and teachers to develop strategies for teaching public speaking to students of varied backgrounds and talents. With this textbook, you are heir to the pedagogy they built:

   ✓ Monroe's motivated sequence, the greatest formula for putting together a speech. Others have copied it, but none have topped it.

   ✓ A critical examination of the forms of supporting materials.

✓ Exploration of types of language use, including imagery.

✓ Exploration of various kinds of introductions, organizational patterns, and conclusions.

✓ Discussion of the factors of attention that help you capture and keep your listeners' interest.

✓ Focus on argumentation that teaches you how to build an argumentative speech and analyze the arguments of others.

Principles of Public Speaking has guided students for over half a century by setting the standard for education in the basic speech course. Commitment to this standard combined with coverage of the latest research in communication theory and recognition and understanding of contemporary issues and challenges makes this textbook as useful today as it has been through all its editions.

RESOURCES FOR INSTRUCTORS

The latest in ancillary support for instruction is available to make your classroom even more challenging. The resources program for *Principles of Public Speaking*, Fourteenth Edition, includes the following instructional supplements:

1. **New! Companion Website at http://awl.com/german.** An online study guide—and much more—this new site is tied to the text and provides enriching chapter-by-chapter resources. *For instructors:* Syllbus Manager (just fill out some forms and your course goes online!); links of professional interest, innovative teaching suggestions; downloadable graphics; PowerPoint® presentation.

2. **Instructor's Resource Guide.** This is an extensive guide to teaching the course written by Kathleen German of Miami University, Ohio. For each chapter, it includes an outline of key concepts, questions to check student comprehension and to encourage critical thinking, detailed descriptions of classroom activities, impromptu speaking exercises, and a bibliography for further reading.

3. *Teaching Public Speaking.* Also written by Kathleen German, this introduction to teaching the basic course in public speaking offers suggestions for everything from lecturing to designing assignments and examinations to incorporating cultural diversity in the classroom. Essential for graduate teaching assistants and first-time instructors, it may also provide new ideas for the experienced instructor. An extensive general bibliography and list of references for media resources is also included.

4. **Test Bank.** A comprehensive test bank including over 3000 test items: true/false, multiple choice, short answer, and essay questions written by Terry Perkins at Eastern Illinois University, is available to instructors upon adoption.

5. **Computerized Testing.** This printed Test Bank is also available on a cross-platform CD-ROM through our fully networkable computerized testing system, TestGen-EQ. The program's friendly graphical interface enables instruc-

tors to view, edit, and add questions; transfer questions to tests; and print tests in a variety of fonts and forms. Search and sort features help instructors locate questions quickly and arrange them in a preferred order. Six question formats are available, including short-answer, true-false, multiple-choice, essay, matching, and bimodal.

6. ***Great Ideas for Teaching Speech (GIFTS).*** Written by Raymond Bud Zeuschner of California Polytechnic State University, this book provides descriptions and guidelines for assignments successfully used by experienced public speaking instructors in their classrooms.

7. **PowerPoint Presentation CD-ROM.** Written and designed by Jane Flesher of Chippewa Valley Technical College, this set of PowerPoint presentation slides provides instructors with ready-made lecture outlines and visuals for class presentations that they can adapt to suit their needs.

8. **Transparencies.** Seventy-five four-color transparencies of diagrams and outlines from the text are available upon adoption to qualified college adopters.

9. **Longman's Public Speaking Video Library.** Three professionally produced videos are available to qualified college adopters and are accompanied by an **Instructor's Video Guide,** written by Kathleen German of Miami University. The Instructor's Guide offers suggestions for classroom exercises, discussion, and applications.

   ✓ **Speaker Apprehension Video.** This video addresses student speech apprehension and provides students with methods for overcoming anxiety in speaking.

   ✓ **Audience Analysis Video.** This video offers strategies and suggestions for students on how best to plan speech delivery based on the demographics of an audience and the context in which a speech is presented.

   ✓ **Student Speech Video.** This video features three complete student speeches and special analysis sections on key speech components such as introductions and conclusions. Outlines of each presentation are available in the accompanying **Instructor's Video Guide.**

10. **New! Student Speeches 2000.** This new video presents nine different speeches given by students and is packaged with a brief video guide for instructors and students. Sample topics include: Censorship and the Internet, Drumming and Singing in African Culture, and Salat-Prayer.

RESOURCES FOR STUDENTS

1. **New! Companion Website at http://awl.com/german.** An online study guide—and much more—this new site is tied to the text and provides enriching chapter-by-chapter resources. *For Students:* "Web Exploration" links and activities; "Surfing the Web" exercises; practice tests; Online Research and Citation Guide; and a Chatroom and Bulletin Board.

2. **New! Interactive Edition CD-ROM.** Taking readers beyond the printed page, this exciting new CD-ROM contains the full text of the book with hyperlinks to: video clips (a multitude of speeches by both students and public figures that students can watch and analyze!); Web links and exercises; practice tests and study questions; photos, figures, and much more!

3. **The Speech Writer's Workshop CD-ROM.** This fully revised interactive software will assist students with speech preparation and enable them to write better speeches. It contains a topic dictionary and powerful documentation tools that include coverage of how to cite new bibliographic types like online sources and e-mail correspondence.

4. **New!** *Outlining Workbook for Public Speaking.* This unique new workbook will help students develop and master the critical skill of outlining.

5. **New! StudyWizard CD-ROM.** Written by Glynis Holm Strause of Coastal Bend College, this computerized student tutorial program, now available on CD-ROM, helps students review and master key concepts in the text. Using chapter and topic summaries, practice test questions, and a comprehensive glossary, *StudyWizard* supplements the text by allowing students the opportunity to explore new topics and test their understanding of terms and ideas already presented in the reading assignments. Students receive immediate feedback on test questions in the form of answer explanations and page references to the text. In addition, the program allows students to print chapter outlines, difficult vocabulary, missed test questions, or a diagnostic report, which includes suggestions for further study.

6. **New! Study Guide.** Also written by Glynis Holm Strause, the Study Guide helps students reinforce themes and concepts they encounter in the text. The Study Guide also includes chapter summaries, practice test questions to aid the students in preparation for exams, and a comprehensive glossary.

7. **Student Guide to PowerPoint.** This short, but thorough guide by Karla Tonella of the University of Iowa gets students involved with using PowerPoint computer applications. It provides clear, step-by-step instructions. Even first-time users will be able to generate slides, graphs, and presentation shows easily.

8. **Assessment Guide for Public Speaking.** Written by Bruce Gronbeck of the University of Iowa and Ray McKerrow of Ohio University, this manual provides chapter-by-chapter objectives and activities that help students focus on assessing their own progress through the course and techniques and resources for assessing their peers. Based on the National Communication Association guidelines for "Assessing College Student Competency in Speech Communication," this is an invaluable student resource for classrooms, departments, and institutions who are focused on assessment.

Faculty can order these student supplements packaged with the textbook or in bulk for classroom use through a campus bookstore. For order and price information, please contact the local Longman representative, call us at 1-800-322-1377, or visit us on the Web at http://www.awl.com.

ACKNOWLEDGMENTS

We owe a great debt to instructors who took the time to review the previous edition and offer feedback and suggestions for the preparation of this edition:

- David Airne, University of Missouri–Columbia
- Robert Arend, Miramar College
- Eugenia E. Badger, University of Louisville
- Arlene Badura, Schoolcraft College
- George Bang, University of Cincinnati
- Rita Bova, Columbus State Community College
- Martin Brodey, Montgomery College
- Michael Butterworth, College of Lake County
- Mina Casmir, Pepperdine University
- Rick Casper, Dawson Community College
- Dennis Fus, University of Nebraska–Omaha
- Carla Gesell-Streeter, Cincinnati State Technical and Community College
- Richard Harrison, Kilgore College
- Richard Katula, Northeastern University
- Michael Leal, Cameron University
- Linda Gentry Martin, Florida Community College at Jacksonville
- Barry Morris, State University of New York College–Cortland
- Rhonda Parker, University of San Francisco
- Renee Reeves, Rose State College
- Sam Walch, Pennsylvania State University, Main Campus

A special thank you is also due to the thousands of students and instructors who have used this textbook. Their support and suggestions over the years have helped to make *Principles of Public Speaking* comprehensive and enduring. In this way, this textbook belongs to all those who have shared it.

Kathleen German
Bruce E. Gronbeck

Speechmaking in an Age of Diversity

Chapter 1

Y ou've been speaking most of your life. From the time you started gurgling in your crib, you have used speech to interact with others. Since speaking with others has been a part of your life for such a long time, you're probably asking yourself, "What am I doing in a public speaking class?"

You're in this class because public speaking is something that you must be able to do well if you hope to contribute to society. Since the first schools of public speaking opened in ancient Greece in the sixth century B.C., training in the art of public discourse has held a special place in education. It will prepare you to add your voice to the chorus of public conversation.

THE FUNCTIONS OF
SPEECHMAKING IN SOCIETY

As a member of society, you have an opportunity to help build your community. As an individual, you also have a responsibility to contribute your viewpoint to the public conversation. When you articulate your perspective, you help others broaden their understanding of society.

Individual Diversity

Throughout history, people with ideas have presented them in the public forum for consideration by others. For example, following the lead of Frederick Douglass, a former slave who urged the abolition of slavery, African Americans demanded the right to speak for themselves. They asserted their selfhood in public. In the language of his times, Douglass said, "Men may combine to prevent cruelty to animals, for they are dumb [mute] and cannot speak for themselves; but we are men and must speak for ourselves, or we shall not be spoken for at all."[1] Similarly, the women attending the Seneca Falls, New York, convention for women's rights in 1848 argued that they should be allowed to talk publicly. Originally, they had been assigned only to watch the proceedings from the gallery, but they were determined to define their own rights by exercising the freedom to speak afforded in the First Amendment to the Constitution.

As you see, you have inherited this tradition of public speaking. Today, speaking in public is still a measure of your individuality, a recognition of your uniqueness in society. There is an important connection between being heard publicly and being accepted as a human being. It is this very need for recognition that often calls for public speaking as we try to create understanding and respect for **human diversity**—that is, the variation of backgrounds and experiences among human beings. Public speaking is a primary vehicle for representing individual identity. However, because we are all constrained by social groups, our individual voices must be understood in terms of the community.

Community Building

Like individuals, communities are also defined by public dialogue. The words *community* and *communication* both come from common Latin root words—*cum,* meaning "with," and *munis,* denoting "public work." Communicating is doing public work—defining, exercising, maintaining, or saving communities—groups of individuals with shared characteristics and goals. These groups are created and maintained symbolically, largely through public talk. Boy Scouts take their oaths together; churchgoers pray aloud and together offer public declarations of shared beliefs; the Pledge of Allegiance echoes through American schoolhouses every weekday; during lunch breaks, work groups share their corporate culture; Olympic athletes pledge to uphold the common ideals of international competition.

Your sense of community is created in large part through public address. Social communities take shape from the sharing of common interests through public discussion. Most of the groups you value influence your life through public talk. We

Web Exploration

To learn more about the writings of Frederick Douglass go to

http://awl.com/german

become bonded together in a community as we discover common interests through public discourse. We learn that we are related by blood, locale, nationality, race, occupation, gender, or other shared experiences and attributes. Senator Ben Nighthorse Campbell of Colorado, a Native American, expresses this idea when he speaks of the "Indian way." He explains, "To Indians . . . success isn't what you have, it's what you've given away. The most revered member of the tribe may be the poorest, because giving away increases your stature. We should place greater value on what we contribute to society rather than on what we accumulate."[2]

Public speech serves both to maintain and to change our communities. You'll even end up creating a small community in your speech classroom. You'll see first-hand the power of public speech to build a community from a collection of strangers as you develop a classroom atmosphere for learning together.

THE ADVANTAGES OF SPEECH TRAINING TO THE RESPONSIBLE SPEAKER

Let's turn back to the question of why you are taking this course. You probably realize that public speaking skills are different than the interpersonal skills that you have already extensively practiced. You're taking this course because you need to become

To Senator Ben Nighthorse Campbell of Colorado, the "Indian Way" places greater value on contributions to society than on ownership of material possessions.

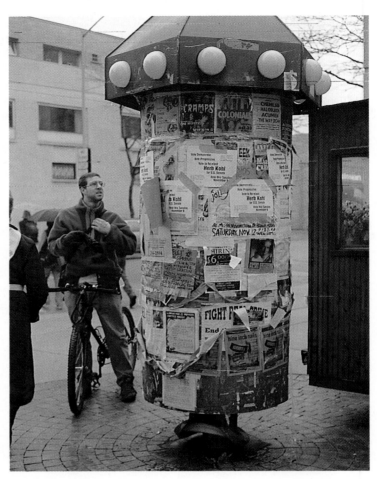

Studying communication helps you become a more shrewd consumer of messages.

more skilled in the kind of communication that goes on publicly. It is important for you to be able to express your ideas to others effectively, especially in situations in which you address many people at once.

For now, you'll talk in your classes and in other familiar settings. Later, you will encounter even more occasions for public talk: meetings of parent groups, church organizations, your kid's scout troop, professional presentations, weddings, neighborhood get-togethers, city government hearings.

As a society, Americans traditionally have thought that self-expression is important enough to merit special legal protection in the First Amendment to the Constitution. And, following the Western heritage of training in public speaking, we have placed special emphasis on it in our educational systems. Specifically, you will gain these benefits from your class:

SPEAKING OF . . . *Apprehension*

First-Time Fears

When you get up to speak for the first time, if you haven't already, the biggest thing on your mind will most likely be stage fright. Some fears can be overwhelming, interrupting good ideas and stopping otherwise great talks dead in their tracks.

The key is to use your anxiety to energize your performance. Expect that you'll be anxious, but don't let it get the best of you. The rush of adrenaline that comes just before you get up to speak should be used to fuel your speech. Below are some tips to help you cope with stage fright.

1. Prepare ahead of time. Uncertainty about what you're going to say just adds to the anxiety. You don't need that.
2. Breathe slowly and deeply. You can't expect to support your voice and movement without oxygen.
3. Think about your ideas. Concentrate on what you're sharing with your listeners, not on how you're feeling.
4. Don't let your imagination run wild. A listener who yawns probably didn't get enough sleep last night. Make it your goal to keep him awake during your speech.
5. Brace yourself for the natural physical symptoms of adrenaline. Expect damp palms, a dry throat, or your own peculiar symptoms.

Above all, give yourself a break. Don't expect perfection the first time you speak—or even the second. Speaking well sometimes takes years of practice. Give yourself a chance and take every opportunity to develop and polish your skills.

1. *Your speech classroom is a laboratory, an ideal place for experimentation.* You can try out new skills in the safety of the classroom. Use your classroom as a lab to develop your repertoire of speaking skills.

2. *As you plan, prepare, and deliver speeches, you will learn the techniques that will help you be a more effective communicator.* You will discover what works and what doesn't work.

3. *Becoming audience-centered is a key to becoming a more powerful speaker.* Your speech classroom is a great place to learn how to do that. As you get to know your classmates, you can focus on them as listeners, learning to work with them to accomplish your speech goals.

4. *You can learn from the feedback of your classmates.* They can provide you with valuable feedback on the effectiveness of your speaking skills. As you become more adept as a speaker, they can help you assess your progress.

5. *Studying oral communication helps you to become a more shrewd consumer of messages.* In your lifetime, you'll be exposed to thousands of messages. To protect yourself, you'll need to become a critical listener and thinker. You can practice those skills as you listen to your classmates' speeches and evaluate their ideas.

6. *Adapting to listeners helps you cope in an increasingly diverse society.* Predictions suggest that in the next fifty years, the United States will undergo a profound ethnic shift. As our society becomes increasingly diverse, your understanding of the complexity of the communication process can help you appreciate differences among people, their lifestyles, and ideas.

By learning to speak in public, you can acquire the basic skills to voice your opinions effectively in an age of diversity and change. Your speechmaking skills will enhance your ability to influence others in your neighborhood, in the coffee room at work, in government meetings, and in the associations and clubs to which you belong. Speechmaking will prepare you to participate more fully in our changing society.

BASIC ELEMENTS IN THE SPEECHMAKING PROCESS

Web Exploration
For more information on the four basic elements of public speaking go to http://awl.com/german

Public speaking is an **interactive process.** That is, it is a transaction or exchange among people in public, rather than interpersonal, settings. Four basic elements of speaking work together to create the speech process—a speaker, a message, listeners, and the context. Let's consider each of these four basic elements:

The **speaker** is the source of the message. As the primary communicator in the public speaking situation, the speaker brings an individual perspective and experiences to the communication transaction.

The **message** is comprised of both the factual content of the speech and the speaker's attitudes and values on the topic. The message is transmitted by selecting words and ideas then arranging them in a particular pattern.

The **listener** (someone who receives and interprets your message) is also a partner in the speech transaction. You may think of public speaking as communication flowing in only one direction from speaker to listener, but that is not an entirely accurate picture. Listeners bring prior knowledge, attitudes, and interests to the speech situation. They also provide verbal and nonverbal **feedback** such as frowns, laughter, yawns, or questions. Feedback refers to messages your listeners send to you before, during, and after your speech.

Speakers and listeners engage each other in a **context.** Some parts of the communication context are obvious, such as the physical setting in which the speech takes place. Other elements, however, are more subtle. The context of the speech also includes the social expectations and cultural rules that come into play when speakers and listeners interact.

To understand how the basic elements function in the communication process, consider actor Christopher Reeve's appeal to a congressional subcommittee. Reeve offered his perspective as a paraplegic when he spoke on behalf of increased research funding for spinal cord injuries. Members of the subcommittee probably recognized Reeve from his movie role as "Superman" or from news bulletins about his riding accident. During his speech, they listened with looks of concern, encouragement, and interest. Afterward, they asked questions. The context was defined by the formal

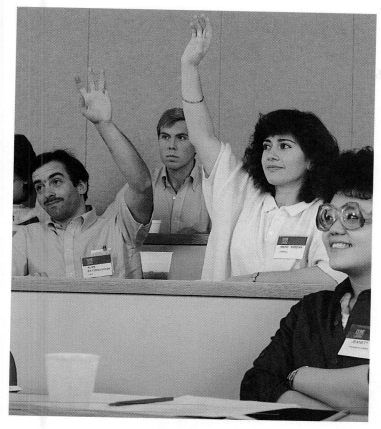

Listeners react to the speaker with verbal feedback such as questions or comments and nonverbal feedback such as frowns, puzzled looks, or laughter.

room and format of the hearing. You can easily identify the basic elements of speechmaking in this transaction. Each element is an integral part of the process. If any single part of the process is changed, the entire transaction is altered.

ETHICAL RESPONSIBILITIES FOR SPEAKERS

Because public speaking is an interactive process, you have certain responsibilities to your listeners. Each time you speak publicly, you are contributing to the process of community building and affecting the lives of others. Because of this, the act of speaking involves making ethical choices. Ethical choices pivot on questions of justice and injustice, goodness and badness, rightness and wrongness. As a speaker, you might ask yourself questions like these: Should you tell both sides of the story when giving people information about a new wonder drug? Is it ethical to make explicit racial references when describing an individual or a group? Should you suppress certain kinds of information when trying to change people's minds? Is it fair to use language that you know will trigger emotional reactions in your listeners? These and

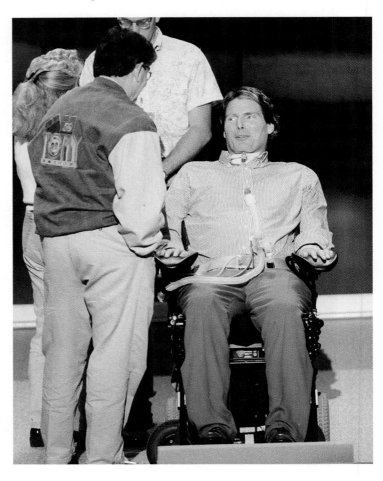

As a speaker, you contribute your unique perspective to the communication interaction. Christopher Reeve often speaks on behalf of the handicapped.

Web Exploration
For additional coverage of the ethical dimensions of public speaking go to
http://awl.com/german

other ethical questions will surface as you prepare and deliver your speeches. While no one can presume to tell you precisely what ethical codes you ought to adhere to when giving a speech, acknowledging the role of **ethics** in public speaking and working through ethical dilemmas will make you a more thoughtful speaker. Ethics provide the system of moral principles that guide your choices and conduct.

Achieving Credibility

Your reputation for reliability and truthfulness is a powerful means of influencing others because it expresses your concern for your audience. Integrity is important, especially in an age of diversity, when fragmented groups may not understand each other's intentions. Listeners who have no personal experience with a particular subject seek information and advice from speakers they trust. Ancient writers recognized the importance of the speaker's reputation as seen by the audience and labeled it ethos. **Ethos,** sometimes referred to as *credibility,* is attributed to you by your listeners based on their perceptions of your honesty and intentions in the speech.[3]

Demonstrating expertise is an essential quality contributing to credibility. So, even though you may know a lot about a topic through personal experience, take time to do some extra reading, talk with experts, and find out what aspects of the topic will engage your listeners. You must know both what you're talking about and how to demonstrate your expertise to your listeners.

Fluency, poise, and vocal control also contribute to your credibility because they mark you as a skilled speaker. These oral skills are achieved through practice. Such practice is a matter of rehearsing both inside and outside your classroom, aiming at becoming an animated, self-confident, and conversational speaker. You'll have many opportunities in your classroom to sharpen these skills.

Recognizing Human Diversity

For many centuries since the rise of Western oratory in ancient Greece, public speaking was reserved for privileged members of society. Social and political revolutions of the ensuing centuries have given public voices to previously silenced segments of society. While progress toward public empowerment continues, we've come far enough toward the goals of justice and equality to demand that public speakers keep human diversity in mind while preparing to speak. Many segments of American society will undoubtedly be represented in your audiences—whites and people of

SPEAKING OF . . . *Ethics*
Ethics and Public Speaking

Occasionally, we'll include a boxed area devoted to "ethical moments"—ethical decisions public speakers must make in preparing and delivering their talks. We hope that you'll take a moment to think about the problems presented and their solutions in your life. You might discuss some of these problems with others to get alternative perspectives.

Here are some typical ethical questions that you might face in the speeches you'll give this term:

1. You read a fascinating article about fund-raising ideas for organizations. Should you borrow these ideas and present them as your own at your next club meeting? Do you need to acknowledge everything you learn from others? Must you always cite sources?
2. An article says exactly what you intended to say about the use of tanning beds. Then you find a more recent article claiming that new research contradicts the first article. Should you ignore the new evidence?
3. An authority whom you wish to cite uses the words *perhaps, probably, likely,* and *often.* Should you strike these words from the quotation to make it sound more positive? After all, you're not tinkering with the ideas, only the strength of assertion.

Ethical decisions such as these will confront you regularly, both in your speech classroom and throughout the rest of your life. Take a few moments now to consider such situations and to articulate your position. Identify your moral standards before you face ethical dilemmas on the platform.

color, the economically advantaged and disadvantaged, men and women, the elderly as well as the young, gays and lesbians, conservatives and liberals.

As a speaker, you must recognize that human diversity will affect your public messages. Most successful speakers are "other-directed," concerned with meeting their listeners' needs and solving their problems. The best speakers recognize and respect listeners and their needs; they are rhetorically sensitive. **Rhetorical sensitivity** refers to speakers' attitudes toward listeners during the speech preparation and delivery process.[4] Rhetorical sensitivity is the degree to which speakers:

1. *Recognize that their listeners are different and complex.* To treat them as a uniform mass instead of as people with individual heritages and needs is to dehumanize them. A speaker can't really talk to each member of the audience individually, but he or she can convey respect for their opinions.

2. *Adapt their messages to particular audiences.* Sensitive speakers work at clearly conveying their ideas to each group of listeners. They draw supporting materials out of their listeners' experiences and employ language that is suitable to the group being addressed. Political candidates, for example, talk about local issues and problems.

3. *Consciously seek and react to audience feedback.* In responding with clarification to puzzled looks or laughter and clapping, speakers recognize the interactive nature of communication. They acknowledge that their listeners are an important part of the speech transaction process.

4. *Understand that words sometimes cannot bridge the differences between people.* There are limitations of talk. Speech sometimes cannot express the inexpressible. You must recognize that you can't always represent everyone as you speak. To pretend to do so is to ignore the humanity and individuality of people. In the face of utter personal tragedy, for example, perhaps the best we can do is to hug the victims, hold their hands, and say "I'm sorry"; more words may be insensitive.

Being rhetorically sensitive does not mean saying only what you think others want to hear. Rather, it is a matter of respecting your listeners by conducting careful audience analysis and making responsible decisions. What are your reasons for speaking? To what degree will those reasons be understood and accepted by others? Can you maintain your integrity while adapting your purposes to your audience's preferences? Do your listeners respect you and your ideas? These questions demand your sensitivity for your audience members as individuals.

YOUR FIRST SPEECH

Now, it's time to get you started—up on your feet and ready to speak. Your first speech should follow a few simple guidelines.

Structuring the speech in three main parts works well—the introduction, the body, and the conclusion. Begin by stating your main idea clearly in your introduction. Doing so will help listeners follow your ideas through to the end of your speech. Likewise, your last few sentences should recapture the main idea of your speech to wrap it up and give it a sense of finality. Most speakers draw on their own knowledge as they develop their ideas. Notice how a beginning student, Delores Lopez, used her own experiences in her first speech assignment "Who Am I?" Delores explains why she is in a public speaking class:

One word that describes my life is "change." Ever since I can remember, things around me have constantly changed. I'm forty-two years old and as I look back, I see lots of change.

When I was a kid, a high school education was enough. My parents didn't go to college; no one in my family did. Although education was respected in my family, there wasn't enough money for us to go on to school. My dad was partially disabled in an industrial accident and we depended on my mom's job to support us. While I was in high school, I had a weekend job and after graduating, I found a full-time job to help support my younger brothers and sisters. At the time, I never considered going to college. It wouldn't have mattered if I had wanted to go. I didn't have the time or money. But things have changed. After I had my oldest son, my mom took care of him and I went back to work. Now he's seventeen and I want him to go to school—to have an opportunity I didn't have. I want his life to be different than mine has been.

My life has changed too. The corporation where I work has been downsizing and looking for leadership within the ranks. My supervisor has encouraged me to go back to school. She thought I was smart enough to make it, and I know I can study hard. The company is even paying part of my tuition. In this economic climate I realize that to be without higher education is to be more disadvantaged than ever. Maybe those of you who don't have kids don't realize the financial pressures of raising kids.

There is one skill that is in demand in my company. They're looking for leadership qualities in their employees—especially the ability to present oneself and communicate well with others. That's why I decided to take this class in public speaking. As you can see, there has been a lot of change in my life. Some of those changes have come from outside—my job, my family. But, I'm changing inside too. I am more confident about what I want in my life and I'm finding ways to meet my goals. I'm looking forward to working with all of you; I think we can learn from each other.

Notice how Delores's speech was divided into three main sections. In the introduction she mentioned the theme of change. She elaborated on that idea by tracing changes in her own life, building on what she knew best, her own experiences. Examples from her family supported and elaborated the theme. Delores answers the question "Who Am I?" by explaining how she has come to be in her public speaking class. The final sentences of the speech summarize the main theme of change. Of course, there's more to consider as you develop your skills in public speaking. Chapter 2 will give you additional advice to get you started.

ASSESSING YOUR PROGRESS

Chapter Summary

1. Public speaking offers special opportunities for expressing individual diversity and building communities.

2. Your speech classroom gives you a unique opportunity to practice your skills on a live audience, get feedback from your listeners, become a better consumer of oral messages, and cope in an increasingly diverse society.

3. Speaking is a transaction involving a speaker, listeners, and a message within a context.

4. Listeners attribute ethos, or credibility, to a speaker based on their perceptions of the speaker's honesty and intentions.

5. Rhetorical sensitivity refers to the speaker's attitudes toward listeners during the preparation and delivery of a speech.

6. Your first speech should have an introduction, body, and conclusion that develop a main idea.

Key Terms

context (p. 6)   interactive process (p. 6)

ethics (p. 8)   listener (p. 6)

ethos/credibility (p. 8)   message (p. 6)

feedback (p. 6)   rhetorical sensitivity (p. 10)

human diversity (p. 2)   speaker (p. 6)

Assessment Activities

1. Interview a representative of a local group that schedules public lectures, the director of the campus speakers' bureau, or someone in a position to discuss the speech skills that are characteristic of professional speakers. Bring a list of those skills to class and be prepared to share your notes with others. Identify the basic competencies of effective speakers.

2. Make a list of the times you've had to express your viewpoint about an idea or issue during the last week. How well did you phrase your viewpoints? What were your listeners' reactions? How could you improve your responses?

3. Prepare an inventory of your personal speaking abilities. (Your instructor may make this an assignment in a journal that you will maintain throughout the term.) What is your ethical standard for speaking? How does your speaking reflect respect for human diversity? Assess your integrity as a speaker.

Surfing the Web

1. You can learn more about the history of public discourse and its impact on our lives by searching the Web, using "rhetoric" as your key word. You might refine your search by looking for "rhetoric in ancient Greece and Rome."

2. The National Speakers Association maintains a Web page describing its activities and resources. Access this page to discover more about opportunities as a professional speaker.

3. Individuals have made outstanding contributions to our society through public speaking. Search the Internet for their biographies and texts of their speeches. Some individuals you might look for are Elizabeth Cady Stanton, Red Cloud, George Washington Carver, Booker T. Washington, Emma Goldman, Stephen Douglas, John C. Calhoun, Abraham Lincoln, Madame Curie, and Eleanor Roosevelt.

References

1.   Frederick Douglass, "Speech at the National Convention of Colored Men [1883]," reprinted in *The American Reader: Words That Moved a Nation,* edited by Diane Ravitch (New York: HarperCollins, 1990), 172.

2.   Quoted by Wallace Terry, "Success Isn't What You Have—It's What You've Given Away," *Parade,* June 2, 1996, p. 17.

3.   William L. Benoit, "A Cognitive Response Analysis of Source Credibility," *Progress in Communication Sciences,* 10 (1991): 1–19.

4.   See Roderick P. Hart and Don M. Burks, "Rhetorical Sensitivity and Social Interaction," *Speech Communication Monographs,* 47 (1980): 1–22.

Chapter 2

Getting Started

Y ou learned about your role as a public speaker in our society in Chapter 1. While there's a lot to discover about the intricacies of speech preparation and speechmaking, you can learn enough about the basics to begin speaking right away. As you prepare to speak, you'll probably ask questions like:

- ✓ How do I choose a topic?
- ✓ How do I make ethical choices for the content of my speech?
- ✓ What will my listeners want to hear?
- ✓ Where do I find the material for my speech?
- ✓ What kind of notes should I make?
- ✓ What's the best way to practice delivering my speech?

These may seem like a lot of decisions, but by thinking about them now you'll be well on your way to success. The key to effective speechmaking is planning. You can save time and effort by planning carefully instead of wandering aimlessly through the library or sitting at your desk hoping for inspiration.

There's no magical formula for speaking. However, if you follow the seven steps offered in this chapter—either as they are presented here or in another order that works for you—you'll be ready for your audience. By the end of this chapter, you'll have mastered the basic steps for delivering your first speeches.

SELECTING AND NARROWING YOUR SUBJECT

Web Exploration

For more on selecting a topic go to

http://awl.com/german

The most difficult task for many speakers is to choose a subject. Sometimes the subject is chosen for you, but often you will choose your own topic for classroom speeches. You might begin the process of choosing a topic by asking yourself questions: What do you know something about? What are you interested in talking about? What topics will interest your listeners? Does the occasion or situation suggest a topic for discussion? It's important to answer these questions carefully. Your answers will help you select and narrow your subject. A well-chosen speech topic is the first step to a successful speech. Let's examine in more detail the processes of choosing and narrowing a topic.

It's a good idea to begin selecting a topic by listing those subjects that you already know something about, choosing the ones you'd like to share with others, and thinking about ways you can relate them to your listeners. If the purpose of your first

SPEAKING OF ... *Skills*

Brainstorming to Generate Topics

Having trouble coming up with possible speech topics? Try this brainstorming exercise:

1. Get a large blank sheet of paper and a pencil.
2. On the left-hand side of the paper, write the letters of the alphabet in a column.
3. Then, as quickly as you can, write down single words beginning with each of the letters. Write down any word that comes to your mind. Repeat until you have the entire sheet filled. You might begin like this: A—apples, alphabet, alarm, alimony; B—bazaar, balsa, baboon, bassoon, balloon; C—comics, cologne, colors, confetti.
4. Next, consider each of the words as a key to potential topics. For example, *apples* might suggest apple pie recipes, Johnny Appleseed and other early American legends, pesticide controversies, fruit in our diets, farm and orchard subsidies, or government price controls of farm produce. This is just the beginning. From one key word, you can derive many possible speech topics.
5. Obviously, not all of these topics would be great speech topics, but this exercise gives you a creative and quick way to generate lots of ideas.

classroom speech is to inform your classmates about a subject, you might come up with the following list of things you know something about:

High school baseball (you played baseball)

Sharks (you did a science project on this subject)

Halloween (it's your favorite holiday and you love to make costumes)

The Internet (you like to surf)

Soap operas (you watch them)

Smoking (you quit two years ago)

Careers in accounting (you're considering them now)

Photography (you like taking amateur photos)

Skin cancer (you're worried about suntanning)

Next, you need to consider the people who make up your audience. Which topics would interest them most? When you ask yourself this question, you realize that several topics such as making Halloween costumes, careers in accounting, and photography are mainly of interest to you. Members of your audience have made career choices and they already have hobbies. Unless you can come up with ways to involve your listeners in your career or your hobbies, you should probably cross these topics off your list.

You should also think about your listeners' expectations. What do they already know, and what do they expect to learn? They may already know more than you do about the Internet and soap operas. You'll certainly need to eliminate these topics from your list unless you plan to do a lot of research. Now you have a narrower list of potential topics—those that will interest your audience and meet your listeners' expectations.

After some additional thought, you decide to inform your classmates about sharks because you've done a lot of research on this subject and know you can arouse their interest. Once you've determined your general subject, you can generate subtopics, including:

The types of sharks

The life cycle of the shark

Endangered species of sharks

Shark habitats and habits

Famous shark stories

Sharks as a source of human food

Movies about sharks

Shark cartilage as a potential cure for cancer

Shark attacks and how to prevent them

The historical evolution of the shark

From this list of subtopics, ask yourself additional questions to narrow the topic even further. How much time do I have to deliver this speech? What do my classmates already know about my topic? Can I group some of these ideas together? After you answer these questions, you may end up with an informative speech focusing on three topics that cluster around the characteristics of sharks:

**Speech
Writer's
Workshop**
Use the Topics
Dictionary to generate
ideas and refine speech
topics.

The types of sharks

The life cycle of the shark

Shark habitats and habits

As you can see from this example, you begin with a broad list of potential topics. Then, you select those that reflect your knowledge, the expectations of your listeners, and the requirements of the occasion. Finally, you consider the possible subtopics and choose several that fit the time limits and go together naturally. This kind of systematic topic selection is the first step in successful speaking. The next step is to identify your speaking purposes and central idea.

DETERMINING YOUR PURPOSES AND CENTRAL IDEA

**Web
Exploration**
To analyze general and
specific purposes of your
speech go to
http://awl.com/german

Once you know what you want to talk about, you need to ask yourself still more questions: Why do you wish to discuss this subject? Why might an audience want to listen to you? Is what you're discussing appropriate to the occasion? To answer these questions you must analyze the reasons for your speech. First, think about the **general purpose,** the primary reason you will speak in public. Next, consider your **specific purposes,** the concrete goals you wish to achieve in a particular speech. Finally, focus your thoughts on a central idea, the statement guiding the thoughts you wish to communicate.

General Purposes

If you examine most speeches, you'll identify one of three *general purposes:* to inform, to persuade, and to entertain. This chart summarizes the general purposes for speaking:

General Purpose	Audience Response Sought
To inform	Clear understanding
To persuade	Acceptance of ideas or behaviors
To entertain	Enjoyment and comprehension

Throughout this book, we will emphasize speeches to inform and speeches to persuade. These types of speeches dominate the speaking occasions you'll face in life.

Speaking to Inform   When you speak *to inform,* your general purpose is to help your listeners expand their knowledge—of an idea, a concept, or a process. This is the aim of scientists who gather at the International AIDS Conference to report their research results to colleagues, of presidential press secretaries who make public announcements, of job supervisors who explain the operation of new equipment, and of your professors in college classes.

To create understanding, you must change the level or quality of information possessed by your listeners. They should leave your speech knowing more than they did before they heard it. For example, you might inform your classmates about herbal medicine, photographic composition, laser surgery, Web page construction, tornadoes, Individual Retirement Accounts, anorexia nervosa, the Tet Offensive, or any number of topics. If you talk about laser surgery, for instance, assume that they may already have some knowledge. To increase their understanding, you will need to focus on innovative surgical techniques using lasers, such as radial keratotomy. You might even speculate about how lasers will change standard surgical procedures in the future. By providing explanations, examples, statistics, and illustrations, you expand your listeners' knowledge.

Not only must an informative speech provide new knowledge, but it must also be structured so that listeners can easily understand and remember those facts. For example, an informative speech on how to design a Web page must include the necessary instructions in the correct sequence of steps. Your goal as an informative speaker is to impart both knowledge and overall understanding. Understanding how to prepare a Web page depends not only on learning what to do, but also on knowing when to do it and why.

Speaking to Persuade   If you seek to influence listeners' beliefs and actions, then your purpose is *to persuade.* Celebrities sell us on the benefits of cars and shampoos; lawyers convince jurors to recommend the death penalty; activists exhort tenants to stand up to their landlords; politicians debate taxes.

As a persuasive speaker, you usually seek to influence the beliefs and attitudes of your listeners. You might want to convince them that John F. Kennedy was shot by several assassins, that education is the cornerstone of freedom, or that life exists after death. In these cases, you are attempting to alter beliefs or attitudes. Sometimes, however, you will want to persuade your listeners to act. You may want them to contribute money to the Humane Society, sign a petition against a landfill project, vote for a new tax levy, or boycott a local grocery store. In this type of persuasive speech, called a speech *to actuate,* you ask your listeners for specific actions. You might ask your classmates to quit watching television, cut back on caffeine consumption, donate blood, sign prenuptial agreements, start stock portfolios, or register to vote.

Speaking to Entertain   Sometimes a speaker's general purpose may be *to entertain.* The goal is to amuse and divert listeners so that they relax and enjoy themselves. After-dinner speeches, travel lectures, and even commencement addresses can be highly entertaining. Gatherings of friends and associates may provide the occasions for such speeches to entertain.

Humor is often used, although speeches to entertain are not simply comic monologues. While a lecture on the customs of another culture may entertain an audience with amusing anecdotes, a great deal of information can be presented. As you can see, the skills required are subtle and often difficult to master because they combine enjoyment with comprehension.

To inform, to persuade, and to entertain are the general purposes of speaking. By thinking about general purposes, you begin your orientation process and assessment of the task ahead. The next step is to focus on the specific purposes of your speech.

Specific Purposes

Your *specific purpose* combines your general purpose for speaking with your topic. For example, if your topic is aircraft and your general purpose is to inform, then your specific purpose might be to inform your audience about the role of aircraft in military combat or to provide them with a history of aircraft design. If your general purpose is to persuade, then your specific purpose might be to persuade your listeners that safety regulations governing air travel ought to be raised. The specific purpose provides a focus for your speech by combining your general purpose with the topic of your speech.

While some specific purposes are public, some are private—known only by you. For example, you probably hope you'll make a good impression on an audience, although you're not likely to say that aloud. Some purposes are short-term; others are long-term. If you're speaking to members of a local organization on the importance of recycling, your short-term purpose might be to convince them to save their aluminum cans, while your long-term purpose could be to gather support for a citywide recycling program.

While you may have several private and public short-term and long-term specific purposes whenever you speak, you need to identify a dominant one. It is important to identify one dominant specific purpose to guide your speech preparation. A single specific purpose, one that you can articulate for an audience, focuses you on precisely what you want your audience to understand, believe, or do.

Suppose that you wanted to take on the challenge of getting more of your classmates to use electronic databases. Consider various ways of wording your specific purpose:

✓ "The purpose of my speech is to explain how electronic retrieval systems can put the resources of other libraries at your fingertips" (understanding).

✓ "The purpose of my speech is to show my listeners that computers are good for much more than playing games" (beliefs).

✓ "The purpose of my speech is to get my classmates to search electronic databases for their next speech" (action).

All these purposes involve electronic databases, yet each has a different specific focus, making it a different speech. Locking onto a specific purpose allows you to zero in on your primary target.

Central Ideas

Web Exploration
For more examples of central ideas for your speech go to
http://awl.com/german

Once you've settled on a specific purpose for your speech, you're ready to compose a sentence that captures it. You need to capture the controlling thought of your speech to guide your development of it. This **central idea** (sometimes called a *thesis statement*) is a statement that captures the essence of the information or concept you wish to communicate to an audience, usually in a single sentence. For example, your

TABLE 2.1   Speaking Purposes

This table provides a guide to the relationships between the general purpose, specific purpose, and central idea of your speech.

General Purpose	Specific Purpose	Central Idea
To help your listeners understand an idea, concept, or process (to inform)	To teach your listeners about the Federal Reserve Board	"The most important influence on interest rates in this country is the Federal Reserve Board."
To influence your listeners' actions (to actuate)	To get your listeners to walk to classes this week (short-term goal) To get your listeners to develop a fitness program (long-term goal)	"You should start a fitness program today to improve the quality of your life."
To influence your listeners' thoughts (to persuade)	To increase your listeners' appreciation of the role of pure scientific research	"While science doesn't always yield a better mousetrap, it is still an important human activity."

central idea for a speech on diamonds might be: "The value of a diamond is largely determined by four factors—color, cut, clarity, and carat."

In a persuasive speech, the central idea phrases the belief, attitude, or action you want an audience to adopt. Your central idea for a persuasive speech on dieting might be: "Avoid fad diets because they create dangerous imbalances in essential nutrients and break down muscle tissue."

The precise phrasing of central ideas is very important because wording conveys the essence of your subject matter, setting up audience expectations. Examine Table 2.1 for examples of ways to word speech purposes. Then consider this example—assume that you've decided to give an informative speech on fixing a leaky faucet. You might phrase your central idea in one of three ways:

✓ "With only minimal mechanical skills, anyone can fix a leaky faucet."

✓ "With a few simple supplies, you can fix a leaky faucet for less than $10."

✓ "Fixing a leaky faucet yourself will give you a sense of accomplishment as well as free you from depending on plumbers for making home repairs."

Note that the phrasing of the central idea controls the emphasis of the speech. The first version stresses the individual audience member's ability to complete the task. Presumably, the speech would offer a step-by-step description of the repair process. The second version suggests a quite different speech, focused on securing the inexpensive supplies. In contrast, the third version concentrates on benefits to the listener.

The process of selecting your subject, determining your general and specific purposes, and phrasing your central idea is the process of narrowing. When you put it all together, here is the result for an informative speech:

> **Subject:** Plumbing repair
>
> **General Purpose:** To inform
>
> **Specific Purpose:** To explain how you can fix a leaky faucet.
>
> **Central Idea:** Most leaky faucets require a new washer that you can install in less than an hour for about $2.00.

Work on your general and specific purposes before constructing your speech. Your speaking purposes clarify your relationship to your audience. They also guide your search for speech materials.

ANALYSIS OF THE AUDIENCE AND OCCASION

Communication is a two-way street. That means you need to consider your listeners when you are preparing to speak. It's tempting to focus only on yourself—your goals, your fears, and your own interests. However, if you want to speak so that others will know what you know, believe what you believe, feel what you feel, and do what you believe is in their best interests, then you've got to construct the speech from your listeners' viewpoint.

Responsible speakers regularly ask questions such as: "How would I feel about this topic if I were in their place?" or "How can I adapt this material to their interests and habits, especially if their experiences or understandings are different from mine?" Putting yourself in your listeners' shoes is what researchers call **audience orientation,** an ability to understand the listener's point of view. Being audience-oriented will push you to construct speeches from the receiving end of the communication process, investigating aspects of the audience's demographic and psychological background that are relevant to your speech. Chapter 5 takes up the topic of audience orientation in detail.

For now, you should find out how much your listeners already know about your subject so that you can adjust to their level of understanding. You should also discover their attitudes toward your subject. If they are apathetic, you must create interest; if they are hostile or favorable, you must adapt what you say. In a public speaking class, this type of investigation is easy enough to conduct—start asking questions. After all, your whole purpose in speaking is to connect with your listeners!

It is also important to consider the occasion on which you're speaking. The occasion is what brings people together, and, consequently, it often determines listeners' expectations. Do they expect to hear a comic monologue? Does the situation demand a serious approach such as a lecture? Will your listeners be tired, wide awake, or distracted by outside noises?

In addition to answering these questions, you should consider the nature and purpose of the occasion. Is this a voluntary or captive audience? How many people will attend? Will the speech be delivered indoors or outdoors? Will the audience be sitting or standing? Will there be other speakers? Will you need to make special arrangements for equipment such as a public address system or an overhead projector?

Throughout the process of developing your speech, consider your listeners and the occasion. Your listeners' expectations and the reasons they have gathered to hear you will influence your choice of topic and the focus of your speech. As you examine the remaining steps in the process of speech development, remember that your ultimate goal is to communicate with your listeners.

GATHERING YOUR SPEECH MATERIAL

Once you've considered the subject and purpose of your speech and analyzed the audience and occasion, you'll be ready to gather the materials for your speech. Ordinarily, you'll start by assembling what you already know about the subject and deciding which ideas you want to include. Nearly always, however, you'll find that what you already know is not enough. You'll need to supplement what you know with additional information—facts, illustrations, stories, and examples. You can gather some of this material from newspapers, magazines, books, government documents, or radio and television programs. You can acquire other information through interviews and conversations with people who know something about the subject that you do not know. And, more and more information is becoming available through electronic databases.

As you search for materials, if you plan to deal with a current question of public interest, you should consult such sources as the "The Week in Review" section of the *Sunday New York Times, U.S. News and World Report, The Wall Street Journal, Harper's,* and *The Observer.* Many magazines of general interest are indexed in the *Readers' Guide to Periodical Literature* or can be accessed via electronic database searches and the Internet; numerous encyclopedias, yearbooks, government reports, almanacs, and other reference materials can be found in your college library. This important topic—locating supporting materials—will be covered in detail in Chapter 6.

MAKING AN OUTLINE

Early in your preparation, make a rough sketch of the points you wish to include in your speech. A complete outline can be drawn up once you've gathered all of the necessary material. When this material is at hand, set down in final order the principal points you expect to present, together with the subordinate ideas that will be necessary to explain or prove these points. Flesh out your ideas with supporting materials such as examples, statistics, and quotations.

In Chapter 8, you'll find a number of specific organizational patterns for arranging the ideas in a speech. There, too, you'll find the form that a complete outline should take. For the present, remember two simple but important rules: (1) arrange your ideas in a sequence that is clear to your listeners and (2) make sure that each point is directly related to your specific purpose. If you follow these rules, your speech should be coherent. To make sure your listeners can follow your ideas easily, use linking statements or transitions to guide them. You might say, "Now that we've examined Mayan art uncovered by archaeologists, let's look at its influences on contemporary Mexican art" or "Once you've mastered the three essential features of good writing—clarity, coherence, and creativity—you may wonder where to find a publisher for your first novel. Let's answer that question."

PRACTICING ALOUD

When you have completed your outline, you're ready to practice your speech (see Figure 2.1). Even though you may feel silly talking to yourself, practice aloud to refine the ideas and phrasing of your speech and to work on delivery skills.

Give practice a chance. It can mean the difference between an adequate effort and an outstanding speech. Repeatedly read through the outline until you've made all the changes that seem useful and until you can express each idea clearly and smoothly. Then write out a notecard with brief cues for each of your main ideas. Next, try to talk through the speech by looking at your notecards. As you practice aloud, you may inadvertently leave out some points; that's okay. Practice until all of the ideas come out in their proper order and the words flow easily. Talk in a normal voice to get used to the sound—don't mumble. Finally, if possible, get a friend to listen to your speech, give you direct feedback, and help you practice making eye contact with a real person.

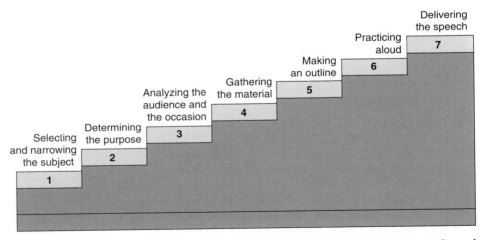

FIGURE 2.1 The Essential Steps in Planning, Preparing, and Presenting a Speech

Systematic planning and preparation will save you time and frustration as you develop your speeches. These are the seven basic steps involved in effective speech preparation. Do you usually prepare your speeches in this order? Which steps are the easiest and which are the most difficult for you?

Many people practice alone, sometimes in front of a mirror, before delivering their first speech to an audience.

DEVELOPING CONFIDENT DELIVERY

Now you're ready to present your speech. Even if you've prepared fully, you still might be asking, "How can I deal with my nervousness? If I'm anxious, how can I convey a sense of self-confidence to my listeners?" If you have thought about some strategies for coping with anxiety, you'll be ready to deal with it. Although there's no foolproof program for developing self-confidence, there are some practical ways to communicate confidently:

Speech Writer's Workshop
The Speech Handbook has more information to help overcome speaker anxiety.

1. *Realize that tension and nervousness are normal.* They can even benefit you. Remember that tension can provide you with energy. As adrenaline pours into your bloodstream, you experience a physical charge that increases bodily movement and psychological alertness. A baseball pitcher who's not pumped up before a big game may find that his fastball has no zip. Similarly, a speaker who's not pumped up may come across as dull and lifeless. Practice speaking often so that you learn how you react to stress and develop strategies for coping with it.[1]

SPEAKING OF . . . *Apprehension*

State and Trait Apprehension

Research distinguishes between two kinds of speech anxiety: state apprehension and trait apprehension. **State apprehension** refers to the anxiety you feel in particular settings or situations. For example, perhaps you can talk easily with friends but are uncomfortable when being interviewed for a job. This sort of apprehension is also known as *stage fright,* because it's the fear of performing that leads to your worries about failure or embarrassment.

Stage fright has physiological manifestations that vary from one person to another. You can probably list your own symptoms—clammy hands, weak knees, dry mouth, and a trembling or even cracking voice. Its psychological manifestations include mental blocks (forgetting what you're going to say), vocal hesitation and nonfluency.

While some aspects of nervousness are characteristic of the situation, others are a part of your own personality. This kind of apprehension, called **trait apprehension**, refers to your level of anxiety as you face any communication situation. A high level of anxiety leads some people to withdraw from situations that require interpersonal or public communication with others.

2. *Focus on your ideas.* Think about what you want to communicate to your listeners. When you speak, you want their minds to be focused on your ideas, not on the way you're presenting them. Speech anxiety arises in part because of self-centeredness; sometimes you're more concerned with your personal appearance and performance than with your topic. One means of creating confidence is to select topics that you are interested in and know a lot about. By doing this, you make the situation topic-centered rather than self-centered. Have you ever wondered why you can talk at length with friends about your favorite hobby, sports, or political interests without feeling anxious? Talking about a subject that interests you may be part of the answer.

3. *Look at your listeners.* Americans tend to mistrust anyone who doesn't look them in the eye. If you look at your notes rather than at your listeners, they may get the impression that you don't care about them or that you aren't interested in their reactions to your message. Eye contact with members of your audience will signal your eagerness to communicate with them. In addition, you can watch your listeners' faces for feedback and make minor adjustments as you speak. If you notice looks of puzzlement, for example, you'll certainly want to adjust by further explaining your ideas.

4. *Remember to breathe.* Although this seems like unnecessary advice, research shows that stress can interfere with your breathing. To counter the effects of stress, breathe deeply using your diaphragm. Your chest should expand, pushing down and out against your waistband. An adequate supply of oxygen

will help calm your anxiety and support your vocal apparatus as you speak, so remember to breathe!

5. *Relax your body.* Realize that you are being seen as well as heard and that your body can communicate confidence. In addition, bodily movements and changes in facial expression can help clarify and reinforce your ideas. You might smile as you refer to humorous events or step toward your listeners as you take them into your confidence. Keep hands free at your sides so that you can gesture easily. As you say, "On the other hand," you might raise one hand to reinforce your statement. As you speak, your body uses up the excess adrenaline it generates. The very act of talking aloud reduces fear.

6. *Speak in public as often as you can.* Public speaking experience will not eliminate your fears, but it will help you to cope. Speaking frequently in front of your classmates is a great way to practice coping with anxiety. Then, as you gain confidence and poise, you'll want to try speaking to different audiences and in different settings. So speak up in class discussions, join in conversations with friends, and contribute to public meetings. You might even decide to run for office!

There are no shortcuts to developing speaking confidence. For most of us, gaining self-confidence results from experience and from understanding the process of communication. The uneasy feeling in the pit of your stomach may always be there, but it need not paralyze you. As you gain experience with each of the essential steps—from selecting a subject to practicing the speech—your self-confidence as a speaker will grow.

SPEAKING OF . . . *Skills*
Practicing Your Speech

If you're ever learned to play the piano or drive a car with a standard transmission, you know that you can't do it all at once. You must practice to improve. The same principle can be applied to improving your public speaking skills. Practice repeated over time will result in more improvement than a single practice session. In addition, remember these guidelines:

1. Keep practice sessions brief. It's better to practice your speech for a few minutes at a time over the course of several days than to go through it repeatedly for two hours the day before it's due.
2. Practice in different settings. Deliver your speech as you walk to classes, in front of your friends, or in an empty classroom. This kind of varied practice encourages flexibility.
3. After you start your speech, finish it without stopping to correct errors or to restart it. You aren't going to deliver your speech exactly the same way every time you give it. Expect some changes in your speech delivery and phrasing.

You should practice your speaking skills whenever the opportunity arises.

SAMPLE SPEECH

The following speech was given by David Mellor of Southern Connecticut State University at a speech contest. It's a comparatively simple, thought-provoking talk about diversity of educational goals. David opens with some reflections on the current job market and successful preparation for it. Then, he turns his attention to diversity. Using the unique life of Bill Veeck, David elaborates on his theme. Notice how the specific examples David uses make this speech interesting. The speech is easy to follow, thoughtful, and well adapted to student listeners. The speaker uses supporting material to show the challenges in the current job market for college graduates. The answer he proposes is to take chances by choosing creative careers. Bill Veeck is an example.

Bill Veeck[2]   David Mellor

By parents, peers and professors, we, as college students are pressured to succeed. This pressure is now at an all-time high. According to an April 19th article in the *New York Times,* "the job search for this year's graduates is the worst ever." Regardless of this hindrance, we see that in order to be successful, one must not only be intelligent but innovative and unique. In short, one must be creative. According to *The Journal of Higher Education,* we college students are anything but that. Over 33 percent of 1990 college graduates received business-oriented degrees. Of the remaining students, over half were divided between communications, political science, and computer studies. The problem is obvious: we need diversity. The solution is simple. We should not look to these overcrowded areas, but direct our attention towards individuals; people who chase chances rather than rest in routines. Baseball's business executive Bill Veeck was such a person. Of course, being a corporate baseball boss is not the only avenue to success. But the example shown to us by Veeck is an enlightening one. An amputee with . . . impaired vision and hearing, Bill Veeck far exceeded all expectations of him. It has been said ". . . when life gives you lemons, make lemonade." Bill Veeck did just this with his product: the game of America, the game of baseball; with his employees; our heroes, our idols, the players; and finally, with his patrons, all of us. We'll first see how Bill Veeck's creative product innovation made baseball the creative successful game that it is today. Next, we'll see how Bill Veeck's employee relations are not only the epitome of employee relations for baseball coaches, but for business executives everywhere. We'll finally see how Bill Veeck's patron appreciation has made him a man worthy of our admiration and praise. Unique, innovative individuals are hard to come by, as is success. Bill Veeck embodies a lesson we can all learn from./1

From his autobiography *Veeck as in Wreck,* Bill Veeck stated ". . . baseball's greatest asset is the long sense of continuity that comes with a deep personal affiliation." Indeed Bill Veeck had long been affiliated with baseball. He merely followed in his father's footsteps when he purchased his first team. However, Bill Veeck was by no means a follower. His creative innovations upon baseball had never been seen before and may never be duplicated again. A typical day at the ballpark we'll hear, ". . . a deep drive to the center field fence, it's going, it's going, it's gone for a homerun. The scoreboard is exploding with light and a pitching cart will be out of the bull pen soon with relief help." We hear that and it is commonplace, but we hear that courtesy of Bill Veeck. The exploding scoreboard was one of the many in-Veeck-ions that ignited both the crowd and the game of baseball. The pitching cart: a means by which the pitcher can make his grand tour of the stadium before taking to the mound—not quite. Bill Veeck created the pitching cart as a means by which to avoid lulls in the game and keep the action continuous by getting the pitcher from the bullpen to mound quicker. From the highly acclaimed business book, *Swimming with the Sharks without Being Eaten,* we see that Bill Veeck was correct in saying ". . . promotion is a state of mind long before it becomes a state of action." It was these creative innovations that brought us to Comiskey and ballparks all over the nation. This is because Bill Veeck

The speaker uses supporting material to show the problems in the current job market for college graduates. The answer he proposes is to take chances by choosing creative careers. Bill Veeck is an example.

The speaker develops his first point. Bill Veeck introduced innovations to baseball, including the exploding scoreboard and the pitching cart.

owned several teams as a major league executive: the St. Louis Browns, the Chicago White Sox, and the Chicago Cubs just to name a few. Now some may see hints of inconsistency in wandering from team to team. Such is not present with Bill Veeck. What is present is his means by which to adopt an ailing franchise and help it achieve success. How was this done? By dealing all employees the same policy, honesty./2

In 1977, pitcher Steve Stone started out with Veeck's Chicago White Sox. After winning 18 games his rookie season, his demand throughout the league skyrocketed. Bill Veeck could not keep up with Stone's comparable offers. Though Stone wished to stay in Chicago, Bill Veeck referred him elsewhere. Now, Bill Veeck could have easily taken advantage of Stone's success and allegiance but did not. Steve Stone went on to win 25 games and the Cy Young Award in 1980, but went on to praise Bill Veeck as being the person who opened the door to his stellar career. Events such as this earned Veeck respect and admiration throughout the league. In his book, *A Hustler's Handbook,* coauthor Ed Linn cites, ". . . if wealth could be measured by admiration Bill Veeck is indeed the richest man in the world." We see that Bill Veeck did have a rich reputation. But his treatment of Stone was not exceptional. Bill Veeck treated all players, major and minor leaguers, to that same honest policy and so strived to refine the echelons of his own business before intruding upon others. Such is seen with his treatment of the minor league teams. According to a 1989 *Sporting News* article, ". . . most today are mere drop-offs for hero has-beens." This was not the view of Bill Veeck, who looked to minor league teams as a means by which to recruit young talent, refine young ball players, and so set up a steady chain of progression from the minors to the majors. With Bill Veeck, few if any players were considered to be in the "minor league." The story of Eddie Gadell proves this fact. In 1951, Veeck sent the 3-foot 11-inch Gadell to the plate for the St. Louis Browns. Equal opportunity was provided at all levels of business under Bill Veeck. In turn, business was attracted to Bill Veeck./3

The second point is expanded. Veeck earned respect from his employees by treating them honestly and equally. Examples of specific instances and testimony provide support for this point.

Again from his autobiography *Veeck as in Wreck,* Bill Veeck stated ". . . baseball consists of three dimensions, the customer brings a fourth." We all know that customers are the business to any business, but no one acknowledged this commonsense theory more than Bill Veeck. Most sports corporations today, be it Nike with the Air Jordan Shoe or Starter with the Pro-Line Jacket, offer a glitzy product but for a glitzy price. Bill Veeck took his product, the game of baseball, and not only made it affordable and accessible but enjoyable to all. An old archive rule in baseball states the pitcher must release the ball 20 seconds after it has been returned to him with the bases empty. Now some may protest this foolish rule, but Bill Veeck took full advantage of it. He went as far as to install a 20-second pitchometer that would bleep, scream, and siren every time the opposing pitcher exceeded

20 seconds. Baseball often falls victim to the weather. But rain did not foil the fun for the fan or Bill Veeck. Any day rain was expected fans would be given a team-emblemmed poncho upon entering the ballpark. Should the rain continue, the tarp that was rolled out onto the infield was also a chess/checkerboard on which the ground crew would be the pawns. Two lucky fans would then be recruited up into the press box and announce their moves over the public address system to the ground crew. Should chess or checkers not be the choice, the exploding scoreboard was also a movie screen that would show past highlights. We see that Bill Veeck confronted life's handicaps as he would hurdles, clearing them all. Be it with the exploding scoreboard, the checkerboard, or the complimentary ponchos, Bill Veeck has adopted all of life's abandoned apples and made a pie to please all. Eventually fans do have to leave the ballpark, but not without the continued gratuity and respect of Bill Veeck. Annually, he donated hundreds of thousands of dollars to clean up the communities beyond the stadiums. So be it in the ballpark or our own backyards, Bill Veeck is indeed worthy of our admiration and praise./4

Veeck upheld many high traits. He was genuine, a true fan and follower of the game. He was grateful to have long been affiliated with baseball, and he was generous with his product, the game of baseball, to all of us, all of his patrons. Chances are many of us may have never made it to Comiskey. But Jerry Reinsdorf, owner of the Chicago White Sox, in the *New York Times* stated, ". . . memories won't leave, just the building is coming down." How true this is since the memory of the man who brought ivy greens to Wrigley Field and a midget to the plate in Eddie Gadell is everlasting. His employee relations, customer courtesy and creative innovations have made him a man of unequal imitation. Unfortunately college students today live in a world of imitation. It is time we seek alternatives. In this case, we need not address our congressman but rather the idea of our own originality and ingenuity. We need look no further than Bill Veeck./5

The final point extends the central ideas of the speech, Veeck never forgot that the customer was the heart of the game of baseball. Examples of the pitchometer, team ponchos, checkerboard tarps, and other baseball fan involvement support this point.

The speaker summarizes the three main points of the speech, then returns to the idea of creativity that introduced this speech.

ASSESSING YOUR PROGRESS

Chapter Summary

1. Select and narrow your subject, making it appropriate to you and your listeners.

2. Determine your general and specific purposes, then word the central idea to guide your development of the key ideas.

3. Analyze your audience and the occasion to discover what you might say and how you might say it.

4. Gather your material, beginning with what you already know and supplementing it with additional research.

5. Arrange and outline your points to package your ideas clearly and coherently.

6. Practice your speech aloud, working from outlines and then notecards, first alone and then with an audience.

7. Recognize that self-confidence can be developed by understanding the communication process and through public speaking experience.

Key Terms

audience orientation (p. 22)

central idea (p. 20)

general purposes (p. 18)

specific purposes (p. 18)

state apprehension (p. 26)

trait apprehension (p. 26)

Assessment Activities

1. Go to the library or log on to the Internet and read several popular magazines and newspapers from the week that you were born. Sort out the events of that week and write a clear central idea for a brief informative speech. Organize your ideas and use some illustrations or perhaps some expert testimony from the sources you examined. Follow the rest of the steps suggested in this chapter for developing a speech; then deliver it to your classmates. After the speech, ask for feedback. Was the central idea clear? Did your listeners follow the structure of the speech easily? Did your delivery convey confidence?

2. Rewrite each of the following statements, making it into a clear and concise central idea for a speech to inform:

   a. "Today I would like to try to get you to see the way in which the body can communicate a whole lot of information."

   b. "The topic for my speech has to do with the high taxes people have to pay."

   c. "A college education might be a really important thing for some people, so my talk is on college education."

   Be ready to present your central ideas in a class discussion.

3. For each of the following statements, write a central idea for a persuasive speech that incorporates the three ideas. Compare your phrasing of the central ideas with those of your classmates.

   a. Many prison facilities are inadequate.

   b. Low rates of pay result in frequent job turnover in prisons.

   c. Prison employees need on-the-job training.

   a. Few doctors practice general medicine; most doctors specialize in one or two areas.

   b. The present system of delivering medical service is excellent.

   c. Rural areas have a shortage of doctors.

4. To learn brainstorming, you must practice it. Form groups, appoint a recorder to jot down all ideas, then practice brainstorming with the questions listed below. Don't evaluate or editorialize until the brainstorming session has stopped. The goal is to list as many ideas as possible. To evaluate the success of the brainstorming session, compare the number of ideas generated.

   a. How can an egg be packaged so that it will not break when dropped from the top of a twenty-foot ladder?

   b. What can we do with all the disposable diapers clogging our landfills?

   c. What adjustments would our society have to make if there were three sexes instead of two?

   d. Imagine that aliens have been spotted hovering over our cities in spacecraft. How can we communicate with them?

   e. You are a scientist who has just discovered how to double a person's IQ. Should you share your discovery?

Surfing the Web

1. There are many places to find excellent examples of speeches on the Internet. You might locate the home page for The History Channel: Great Speeches, Douglass: Archives of American Public Address, and Columbia University's Inaugural Addresses of the President of the United States.

2. Having trouble finding a speech topic? Visit reputable media sites on the Internet like CNN, ABC, CBS, NBC, or PBS. You can also find regional newspapers on the Internet. These sources will give you an idea about what's current. Use your search engine to locate The Internet Public Library or Electronic Newsstand. Browse through thousands of publications from all over the world. These should give you some good ideas for speeches.

References

1. Michael Neer, "Reducing Situational Anxiety and Avoidance Behavior Associated with Classroom Apprehension," *Southern Communication Journal,* 56 (1990): 49–61; John Gorhis and Mike Allen, "Meta-Analysis of the Relationship Between Communication Apprehension and Cognitive Performance," *Communication Education,* 41 (1992): 68–76; James McCroskey, "Oral Communication Apprehension: A Summary of Current Theory and Research," *Human Communication Research,* 4 (1977): 78–96.

2. David Mellor, "Bill Veeck," Winning Orations, 1991 (the Interstate Oratorical Association). Reprinted by permission of Larry Schnoor, Executive Secretary, Interstate Oratorical Association, Mankato State University, Mankato, MN.

Chapter 3

Critical Listening

In your daily life, you spend more time listening than you do reading, writing, or speaking. Listening accounts for over 40 percent of your communicative time.[1] While you may assume that you're a good listener from all that practice, you really don't know until you discover you've missed something important. The fact is, you've probably never had any training in listening, especially for situations such as class lectures where you're expected to acquire technical or abstract materials primarily through listening.

Conversations, classroom lectures, group meetings, and electronic media expose you to an amazing amount of information every day. If you are to make the best use of all that information, you must hone your listening skills.

Both speaker and listener are active partners in the communication process. As a speaker, you reach out to your audience; and in turn, as a listener, you respond. Listening is a central part of the communication process.

After a more detailed introduction to the idea of listening, this chapter will focus on practical listening techniques you can use in almost any listening situation. We'll finish by suggesting how you can put new listening skills to work in your classes.

HEARING AND LISTENING

Hearing is the first step in the listening process. To listen to a message, you first must hear it. **Hearing** is the physiological process of receiving sound waves. Sound waves travel through the air and set up vibrations on the eardrum; these vibrations, in turn, are transmitted to the brain. Hearing is affected by the laws of physics and the neurophysiology of the body. Any number of factors can interfere with hearing—distracting noises, sounds that are too soft, or hearing loss. Some of these conditions can be improved. The speaker can change speaking volume and audience members can move to better seats in order to facilitate hearing. Listeners can provide feedback to the speaker if their hearing is blocked.

Web Exploration
To test your listening skills go to
http://awl.com/german

Listening, on the other hand, involves thinking. After sound waves are translated into nerve impulses by the middle ear and the auditory nerve, they're sent to the brain for interpretation. This process of interpretation—registering impulses, assigning them to meaningful contexts, and evaluating them—constitutes listening. **Listening** is the thinking process whereby people attach meanings to sounds.

BARRIERS TO GOOD LISTENING

Listening is easy to define but hard to practice. You've probably developed some barriers to good listening. You'll have to recognize and remove them if you're going to become a better listener. At one time or another, most of us experience these five barriers to good listening:

1. *Passive listening.* Many of us are just plain lazy listeners, tuning in and out as our attention dictates. As a result, we often miss important facts and ideas. Because we are partners in the communication transaction, we need to become active listeners, identifying our purposes for listening, taking notes, and evaluating the ideas in the message.

2. *Drifting thoughts.* You can comprehend many more words per minute than someone can utter; you probably can process about 400 words per minute, while most speakers produce only about 125 to 175 words per minute. As a result, you may fill the time lag with other thoughts. Your **internal perceptual field** is the world of your own thoughts. While someone is speaking, you may be remembering a television show you saw last night or planning the menu for supper or thinking about a topic for your next term paper.

3. *Physical distractions.* Sometimes your attention may be diverted by elements outside your own thoughts. Your **external perceptual field** is those things in

The speaker receives verbal and nonverbal feedback both during and after the communication transaction. Immediate feedback occurs during the speech. Delayed feedback happens after the communication transaction.

your physical environment such as the buzz of overhead lights, the sun's glare off your teacher's glasses, or a banging radiator that can distract you. Our attention can be sidetracked by physical interference, so that we hear and process only part of a spoken message.

4. *Trigger words.* We often bring our beliefs and feelings into the speech setting. Memories of past events or strong feelings can be triggered by a word or a reference. Many people spend time mentally debating with speakers and remain stuck on one idea while the speaker moves ahead to others. For example, some listeners become hostile when they hear a speaker refer to a secretary as "my girl." They may spend several minutes fuming and miss the next part of the speaker's message.

5. *Self-fulfilling prophecies.* Preset ideas can get in the way of good listening. If you've heard that Professor Rogers is a dull lecturer, you probably enter the class expecting to be bored. Sometimes previous encounters with a speaker can color your expectations.

Like most people, you probably have beliefs and feelings about topics and people. If you let these predispositions get in the way of careful listening, you're likely to miss important parts of speeches. It is important to overcome these barriers to become an active listener and a better participant in the communication transaction. Here are some suggestions for developing your listening skills.

PRACTICAL LISTENING TECHNIQUES

While hearing is a natural physiological process for most people, listening is another matter. You've got to work hard to listen well. The good news, though, is that you can train yourself to listen better. You can begin to practice better listening habits in three ways: (1) determine your purposes for listening; (2) develop techniques that help you comprehend speeches; and (3) design questions that help you evaluate or assess speeches on criteria that matter to you.

Know Your Purposes

The first thing good listeners must do is figure out why they're listening. This is not as obvious as it seems, because, if you think about it, you engage in many different kinds of listening. On any given day, you may listen intently to your instructors in order to learn new concepts, you may listen to your favorite music to relax, and you may listen attentively to be sure that a car salesperson isn't skipping over essential features of the dealer's guarantee.

Researchers have identified five kinds of listening that reflect purposes you may have when communicating with others:[2] appreciative, discriminative, empathic, comprehension, and critical.

Appreciative listening focuses on something other than the primary message. Some listeners enjoy seeing a famous speaker. Others relish a good speech, a classic movie, or a brilliant performance. On these occasions, you listen primarily to entertain yourself.

Discriminative listening requires listeners to draw conclusions from the way a message is presented rather than from what is said. In discriminative listening, people seek to understand the meaning behind the message. You're interested in what the speaker really thinks, believes, or feels. You're engaging in discriminative listening when you draw conclusions about how angry your parents are with you, based not on what they say but on how they say it. You draw inferences from the presentation of the message rather than from the message itself.

Empathic or therapeutic listening is intended to provide emotional support for the speaker. Although it is more typical of interpersonal than public communication, empathic listening does occur in public speaking situations, for example, when you hear an athlete apologize for unprofessional behavior, a religious convert describe a soul-saving experience, or a classmate reveal a personal problem to illustrate a speech. In each case, your role is supportive.

Listening for comprehension occurs when you want to gain additional information or insights from the speaker. You are probably most familiar with this form of listening because you've relied heavily on it for your education. When you listen to a radio newscast, to a classroom lecture on the principal strategies in an advertising campaign, or to an elections official explaining new registration procedures, you're listening to understand—to comprehend information, ideas, and processes.

Critical listening is the most difficult kind of listening because it requires you to both interpret and evaluate the message. It demands that you go beyond understanding the message to interpreting it and evaluating its strengths and weaknesses. You'll practice this sort of listening in class. A careful consumer also uses critical listening to evaluate television commercials, political campaign speeches, advice from talk show guests, or arguments offered by salespeople. When you are listening critically, you decide whether to accept or reject ideas and whether to act on the message.

You may have many different purposes for listening, and that's why the first question you ought to ask yourself is: "What's my purpose in listening?" Do you expect to gain information and insight to make a decision? Or are you listening to enjoy yourself, to understand the feelings of another human being, to assess someone's state of mind, or to test ideas? Knowing why you're listening will help you listen more efficiently and effectively. In the rest of this chapter, we'll focus on listening for comprehension and critical listening because those are the kinds of listening you use primarily in a public speaking situation.

SPEAKING OF . . . *Skills*
Good Note Taking and Active Listening

One of the easiest ways to practice your listening skills while in college is to work on note taking. As you become a better note taker, you'll also become a better listener. Here are some tips for improving your note-taking skills.

1. *Get organized.* Develop a note-taking system like a loose-leaf notebook so you can add, rearrange, or remove notes. Use separate notebooks for different subjects to avoid confusion.
2. *Review your notes regularly.* This will prepare you to ask questions while the lecture or readings are still fresh in your mind and will help to keep you oriented to the class. Research shows that students who review their notes achieve significantly more.
3. *Leave a 2- to 3-inch blank margin.* Later, you can add facts, clarification, reactions, and other alterations after comparing your notes with other students' or after doing related reading. Such critical commentary is an important stage in merging the material in the notes with your own thoughts.
4. *Write more.* Making a conscious effort to record more ideas and more words related to a speech or lecture will help you to remember the important ideas, structure, and supporting evidence. Research shows that most students don't take enough notes. The problem is compounded with long messages; students take even fewer notes as the speech or lecture continues.
5. *Develop a note-taking scheme.* Consider using abbreviations such as the ampersand (&) for *and, btwn* and *w/o* for *between* and *without* or specialized notations like *mgt* and *acctg* for *management* and *accounting.* Color-code your notes or use highlighter pens to remind yourself of the most important parts of the material.

By taking these steps, you can become an active listener who's engaging in a two-way communication channel.

See: Kenneth A. Kiewra, "Note-taking and Review: The Research and Its Implications," *Instructional Science,* 16 (1987): 233–249.

Listening for Comprehension

Listening for comprehension is the kind of listening you usually do in class lectures. Fully comprehending what's being said requires that you understand the three essential aspects of speech content: *ideas, structure,* and *supporting materials.* You've got to understand clearly what ideas you're being asked to accept, how they're related to each other, and what facts and opinions underlie them. Asking three questions will help you comprehend a message:

1. *What are the main ideas of the speech?* Determine the central idea of the speech and look for the statements that help develop it. These main ideas should serve as the foundation on which the speaker builds the speech. The next time you listen to a soap commercial, listen for the main ideas: Are you encouraged to buy it because of its cleaning power, smell, sex appeal, or gentleness to your skin? Before you decide to buy a new brand of soap, you ought to know something about its characteristics. Now transfer this listening behavior to a speech. Always know what ideas you're being sold.

2. *How are the main ideas arranged?* Once you've identified the main ideas, you should figure out the relationships between them. In other words, identify the structure of ideas and then examine it. If a speaker is explaining affirmative action laws, which ideas are highlighted? Does the explanation seem reasonable? Is the speaker limited only to one perspective? Who is defined as the victim? Does the speaker express sympathy for one point of view over another?

3. *What kinds of materials support the main ideas?* Consider the timeliness, quality, and content of the supporting materials. Are facts and opinions derived from sources too old to be relevant to current problems? Is the speaker quoting recognized authorities on the subject? Ask yourself whether the materials clarify, amplify, and strengthen the main ideas of the speech. For example, if a speaker claims that the murders at Columbine High School in Littleton, Colorado, in 1999 show that school violence is a growing national problem, ask yourself several questions: How many episodes of school violence occurred during the entire year? Over the past decade, have incidents of school violence increased or decreased? Is this example typical of the kinds of violence in schools?

Web Exploration
For more analysis of the RRA technique go to
http://awl.com/german

In other words, to comprehend the content, make sure you know what ideas, relationships, and evidence you're being asked to accept. To be an active listener, you should constantly employ the **RRA Technique:** *review, relate,* and *anticipate.*

Take a few seconds to *review* what the speaker has said. Mentally summarize key ideas each time the speaker initiates a new topic for consideration.

Relate the message to what you already know. Consider how you could use the information in the future.

Anticipate what the speaker might say next. Use this anticipation to focus on the content of the message.

By reviewing, relating, and anticipating, you can keep your attention centered on the message. Using the RRA Technique keeps you actively engaged in the listening process.

Listening well has been a human (and canine) concern for a long, long time.

Critical Listening

Once you've figured out why you're listening, how the ideas are arranged, and what supporting materials are being presented, you're in a position to form some opinions. You, after all, are the reason the speech is being given, so you're the one who must decide whether the speaker's ideas are worth accepting. Making such a judgment is a good way to protect yourself from inflated claims, dated information, and unethical speakers. Completely assessing a speech could include asking yourself about the situation, the speaker, and the message. The following questions will help you listen critically:

1. *How is the situation affecting this speech and my reception of it?* What is the reason for the speech? Is the speaker expected to deal with particular themes or subjects? Am I in sympathy with this speech occasion? Speeches in churches, basketball arenas, and Rotary Clubs are very different from one another, and you must adjust your evaluation criteria to each situation.

2. *How is the physical environment affecting the speaker and my listening?* Is the room too hot or too cold? Too big or too small? What other distractions exist? The physical environment can have an important impact on your listening. In uncomfortable environments, you might have to compensate: lean forward, move up, or concentrate more closely.

3. *What do I know about the speaker?* The reputation of this person may influence you, so think about it. Are you being unduly deferential or hypercritical of the speaker just because of his or her reputation? Do you think the speaker will be fair and honest because he or she represents your interests or is similar to you? Don't let your assumptions about the speaker get in the way of critical listening.

4. *How believable do I find the speaker?* Are there things about the speaker's actions, demeanor, and words that seem either pleasing or suspicious? Does the speaker use adequate and compelling supporting material to reinforce the message? Try to figure out why you're reacting positively or negatively and then ask yourself whether it's reasonable for you to believe this speaker.

5. *Is the speaker adequately prepared?* Imprecise remarks, repetitions, backtracking, vague or missing numbers, and the lack of solid testimony are all signs of a poorly prepared speaker. For example, a speaker talking about how audiences influence TV programming decisions should discuss, among other things, the networks' use of focus groups. If the speaker doesn't discuss this, you'll know that he or she hasn't gotten very far into the topic. Similarly, if the speaker can't clearly explain the different rating systems, you should question the reliability of other information in the speech.

6. *What's the speaker's attitude toward the audience?* How is the audience being treated: cordially or condescendingly, as individuals or as a general group, as inferiors or as equals? Answering these questions will help you not only to assess your experience but also to form some questions for the speaker after the speech.

7. *How solid are the ideas being presented?* We've been stressing this point throughout the chapter because it's crucial for you to assess the ideas in terms of your own knowledge and experience. Just one warning: You could be mistaken yourself, so don't automatically dismiss new ideas. But listen more carefully to ideas that are new and different or seem strange, making sure that you understand them and that they're well supported.

8. *Are the ideas well structured?* Are important concepts missing? For example, anyone who talks about the branches of the federal government but then ignores the Supreme Court has an incomplete set of ideas. Are logical links apparent? The comparisons must be fair; the cause-and-effect links clear and logical; and the proposals for correcting social wrongs both feasible and practical. Structural relationships between ideas are what give them their solidity and coherence as a package.

9. *Is sufficient evidence offered?* The world is filled with slipshod reasoning and flawed evidence. Bad reasoning and a refusal to test the available evidence, after all, led the American high command to believe that Pearl Harbor was an impregnable port in 1941. Listen for evidence; write down the key parts of the evidence so you can mull it over, asking yourself if it's good enough to use as a basis for changing your mind. Be demanding; adopt a "show me" attitude. Insist on adequate evidence and logical reasons when a speaker asks you to make crucial decisions.

You may not ask all of these questions every time you hear a speech, because your listening purposes vary considerably from occasion to occasion. However, you will want to ask yourself most of these critical listening questions before you make important decisions such as whom to vote for, whether to take the job offer, or if you should make a major purchase. To practice critical listening you can begin now in your classes.

SPEAKING OF . . . *Ethics*

Deliberately Misguiding Listeners

Some advertisers, politicians, sales representatives, and even friends have learned how to misguide their listeners without actually lying. They hope, of course, that you'll draw the conclusions they want you to on the basis of distracting or misdirective statements. You can recognize these situations by thinking and listening critically. Here are some things to listen for:

1. *Percentages rather than absolute numbers.* You're told that women's salaries went up 50 percent more than men's last year. Should you cheer? Maybe not. Even if women got a 3 percent raise when men got 2 percent, there's such a differential in their salaries that the actual dollar amount of women's and men's raises was probably about the same.
2. *Characteristics of the sample.* Beware when the manufacturer tells you that "Four out of five of the dentists surveyed preferred the ingredients in Smiles-Aglow toothpaste." How big was the sample? Were the dentists surveyed working in Smiles-Aglow labs or were they in private dental practice? You need to know more about them to know whether this claim is solid.
3. *Hasty generalization.* The neighbor who tells you that "Most folks on this block are against the widening of our street" may have talked to everyone, although that's not likely. He probably means "most folks I know on this block"—and then you'd better find out how many that it is. Press him for details before you accept or reject his judgment.

Are speakers lying when they use these distracting or misguiding techniques? Are they acting unethically? Where does ethical responsibility lie—with the speaker or with the audience?

Source: Andrew Wolvin and Carolyn Coakley, *Listening,* 5th ed. (Dubuque, IA: Brown and Benchmark, 1995), pp. 3–11 and chaps. 4–8.

DEVELOPING SKILLS FOR CRITICAL LISTENING

Your speech classroom is set up to teach skills that you can use for the rest of your life. Listening is one of the skills you'll need to survive in your career, your community, and your social life. You'll have to listen to understand your employer's explanation of a new computer system, to make reasonable decisions between two political candidates who offer different views of health care reform, and to follow a neighbor's instructions as she tells you how to rewire a light fixture. The ability to listen can help you make money, be a good citizen, and keep you from frying your fingers on a 110-volt circuit!

Your classes are excellent settings for practicing new listening skills and refining old ones. Use the Speech Evaluation Form in Table 3.1 as a checklist when listening to speeches. It will challenge your listening skills. During this term, we also suggest that you improve your listening in the following ways:

1. *Practice critiquing the speeches of other students.* Practice note-taking techniques; ask questions of the speaker; take part in post-speech discussions. You can learn as much from listening well as from speaking yourself.

TABLE 3.1 Speech Evaluation Form

Use this form to evaluate your own speeches.

The Speaker	The Audience
☐ Poised?	☐ All listeners addressed?
☐ Positive self-image?	☐ Their presence recognized and complimented?
☐ Apparently sincere?	☐ Their attitudes toward subject and speaker taken into account?
☐ Apparently concerned about the topic?	
☐ Apparently concerned about the audience?	
☐ Apparently well prepared?	**The Speech as a Whole**
The Message	Audience's expectations met?
☐ Suitable topic?	_____
☐ Clear general purpose?	_____
☐ Sharply focused specific purpose?	_____
☐ Well-phrased central idea or proposition?	_____
☐ Adequately supported (enough, varied, trustworthy sources)?	Short-range effects of the speech?
☐ Supporting materials tailored to the audience?	_____
☐ Introduced adequately?	_____
☐ Concluded effectively?	_____
☐ Major subdivisions clear, balanced?	Long-range effects?
☐ Use of notes and lectern unobtrusive?	_____
The Channel	_____
☐ Voice varied for emphasis?	_____
☐ Voice conversational?	_____
☐ Delivery speed controlled?	_____
☐ Body alert and nondistracting?	Possible improvements?
☐ Gestures used effectively?	_____
☐ Face expressive?	_____
☐ Language clear (unambiguous, concrete)?	_____
☐ Language forcible (vivid, intense)?	_____

2. *Listen critically to discussions, lectures, and student-teacher interactions in your other classes.* You're surrounded with public communication worth analyzing when you're in school. You can easily spot effective and ineffective speech techniques in those classes.

3. *Listen critically to speakers outside of class.* Attend public lectures, city council meetings, religious rallies, or political caucuses. Watch replays of presidential or

congressional speeches on C-SPAN. You'll be amazed by the range of talent, techniques, and styles exhibited in your community every week.

4. *Examine the supporting materials, arguments, and language used in newspapers and magazines.* Refine your critical listening skills by practicing critical reading. Together, they represent the skills of critical thinking you need to survive in this world. **Critical thinking** is the process of consciously examining the content and logic of messages to determine their bases in the world of ideas and to assess their rationality. Critical thinking is the backbone of evaluation. It's what happens when you actively listen and read others' messages.

Overall, then, listening makes public speaking a reciprocal activity. Listeners seek to meet their diverse needs, ranging from personal enjoyment to crucial decision making, through specialized listening skills designed for each listening purpose. When both speakers and listeners work at making the speech transaction succeed, public speaking reaches its full potential as a partnership in communication.

ASSESSING YOUR PROGRESS

Chapter Summary

1. Both the speaker and listener are critical participants in the communication transaction.

2. Hearing is a physiological process; listening is a psychological process by which people seek to comprehend and evaluate sounds.

3. There are five purposes for listening: appreciative listening, discriminative listening, empathic (therapeutic) listening, listening for comprehension, and critical listening.

4. To improve your listening skills sort out the essential aspects of speech content: ideas, structure, and supporting materials.

5. The RRA Technique—review, relate, and anticipate—can help you listen more efficiently.

6. To improve your speech evaluation skills, practice assessing the situation, the speaker, and the message.

Key Terms

appreciative listening (p. 38)

critical listening (p. 38)

critical thinking (p. 45)

discriminative listening (p. 38)

empathic listening (p. 38)

external perceptual field (p. 36)

hearing (p. 36)

internal perceptual field (p. 36)

listening (p. 36)

listening for comprehension (p. 38)

RRA technique (p. 40)

Assessment Activities

1. Conduct a class discussion on a controversial topic, for example, doctor-assisted suicide, multiculturalism and political correctness, the rights of smokers, or health care reform. Establish the rule that before anyone can speak, he or she first must summarize to the satisfaction of the previous speaker what that person said. What conclusions can you draw about people's ability to listen and provide feedback? How do good listening and feedback reduce the amount and intensity of disagreement?

2. Keep a listening log. For two or three days, record your oral communication interactions noting (a) to whom you were speaking, (b) what were your listening purposes, and (c) how effectively you listened. After completing the log, do a self-assessment: What are your strengths and weaknesses as a listener? What changes would make you a better listener?

Surfing the Web

1. Locate the Web site of the International Listening Association (http://www.listen.org). You'll discover numerous exercises for testing and improving your listening skills in public speaking and interpersonal situations.

2. Visit a chat room and observe the listening skills of individuals participating in the discussion. Can you identify barriers to good communication? How did these barriers affect other participants? Suggest some ways to overcome these barriers.

References

1. Steven Rhodes, "What the Communication Journals Tell Us About Teaching Listening," *Central States Speech Journal,* 36 (1985): 24–32.

2. Andrew Wolvin and Carolyn Coakley, *Listening,* 5th ed. (Dubuque, IA: Brown and Benchmark, 1995).

Public Speaking and Cultural Life

Chapter

Chapter

4

At its simplest, a **culture** is a social group's system of meanings. You are part of a culture because you've been taught since you were an infant to attach meanings to persons, places, ideas, rituals, things, routines, and communication behavior. Think of what you've absorbed from your culture—not to talk to strangers (persons), how to act on the playground (places), what's true about the world (ideas), how to greet friends (rituals), what's valued (things), what's safe to talk about at parties (routines), and the most effective ways to get favors from your parents (communication behavior). Your culture is comprised of social knowledge that you've been taught. It enables you to comprehend and act effectively within the world.

What's true of you and your life, of course, is true for everyone else as well. We've all been taught about persons, places, rituals, ideas, and the rest. But, of course, your experiences are different from those of others. In some important ways we have all been given different social educations—men differ from women, whites from Hispanics, rich people from poor people, sighted from visually challenged people. All of our differences can cause speakers some serious problems.

> *"I can't go out there and speak!" Melissa was distraught. She was a delegate from the Panhellenic Council about to speak to a gathering of the campus African American, Hispanic, and international students' associations on coordinating a weekend of fun and games for everyone. "Here I am, a white sorority member born in Iowa, a state that's ninety-seven and a half percent white. And there they are, from places and countries totally different from mine. They'll resent me. What do we have in common?" "That's the question you must answer," replied her best friend, Sherri. "What do you have in common? You're all students here, you all need a break from studies to celebrate spring, you all enjoy group competition, you'll all dance the night away—you have a lot in common!" "Well, I guess we do, but . . ." "'But' nothing!" said Sherri. "Quit emphasizing your differences as barriers to a successful spring celebration. Think of what you share. That's what to talk about."*

Like Melissa, when you face diverse audiences you'll want to follow her friend Sherri's advice, looking for the common ground that turns a group of listeners toward a collective goal. In this chapter, we'll discuss relationships between public speaking and cultural life by first examining the components of culture more specifically and then reviewing some strategies that you can use in your speeches.

UNDERSTANDING CULTURAL PROCESSES

Before you can think about public speaking strategies that you'll need to manage cultural diversity, you'll want to think more about how culture affects your everyday life. As we've defined it, culture is a social group's system of meanings. Since this is still a broad concept, let's focus on three dimensions of social life: culture as lived, thought, and performed.

Culture as Lived

One way to examine cultural life is by examining the demographic categories that organize our social lives. You have learned to define yourself by gender (male, female, transsexual), ethnic background (Norwegian American, Mexican American), age (young, old), sexual orientation (straight, gay), nationality (Slovene, Chinese), educational background (high school dropout, college grad), disability (hearing impaired, visually challenged), socioeconomic status (welfare recipient, upper-bracket taxpayer). These demographic categories become amazingly important in your relationships with people. Melissa, for example, thought about herself in terms of race, gender, and reference group. Such categories can become determinative of **culture as lived.**[1]

SPEAKING OF . . . *Apprehension*

Xenophobia

As the story of Melissa indicates, people can become terrified when talking to listeners whom they perceive to be significantly different from themselves. Men can stammer when facing female listeners, African Americans can fear that no white will accept what they have to say, and most people are convinced that they'll be misunderstood by or even offend foreigners—*xenophobia* is a word whose meaning should be expanded to include fear of all kinds of "different" people. How can you overcome or at least control such fears and misgivings?

1. Engage in conversation members of the groups you fear so as to explore the bases of your fears. Get to know some African Americans or Mexican Americans well enough to discuss your concerns. The more men and women talk informally about their relations, the less likely their differences will affect public speaking.
2. Talk with members of groups you fear after you've spoken to see what their reactions were. Don't take a simple "You were fine!" or "You're great!" from them. Ask specific questions about specific things you said and did in order to force particular judgments about your speaking skills and strategies.
3. Accentuate the positive. When talking to a diversified audience, concentrate on your shared values and outlooks, not your differences. That was Sherri's advice to Melissa. It's good advice.
4. Focus on actions, not beliefs, attitudes, values, and ideologies. Getting people to act together—to work together for a cause—often can be advocated without exploring too many of their cultural differences. Even people who outrightly dislike each other will work together if there's a gain for all of them.

Take the demographic category of gender. Its influence on each of us is considerable. Gender identification starts at a young age. As a little boy or little girl, you probably learned how to play and what to wear based on your sex. Even your name may indicate your gender. Gender identification became more and more important as you matured, governing your sexual orientation (straight or gay), social relations (the dating game), extracurricular activities (different high school sports for females and males), and even work (women paid less for comparable work than men). In a similar way, ethnic background can produce differences, especially because whites tend to have much easier access to social-economic-educational institutions than people of color, other things being equal. But, of course, they're not equal, so one's economic status can neutralize or exacerbate racial differences. As well, age can enter in, for racial prejudices tend to harden with age.

And so it goes: culture as lived, especially as you move out of your immediate family and neighborhood, becomes increasingly focused on cultural differences. **Multiculturalism**—the recognition that a country such as the United States possesses a mosaic of cultures that interpenetrate yet are separate from each other—is a fact of life.[2] And its effect on public speaking, as we'll see, is considerable.

The ability to communicate across gender, racial, and class lines is an essential skill for all members of diverse communities.

Culture as Thought

Not only have you been socialized to act in particular ways through lived experiences, but you've also been conditioned to think in particular patterns as well. You've been conditioned to think, perhaps, that freedom is worth dying for, that potatoes taste better than jicama roots, that your personal safety is affected by the skin color of people around you, that with hard work anyone can succeed in life. That is, you've learned to think that certain values (freedom) are positive, and others (slavery) are negative; that personal tastes (such as for potatoes) are grounded in real differences between things rather than in mere preference; that people can be usefully stereotyped by such accidental characteristics as skin color; that rules for succeeding in your own society (hard work) hold true everywhere.[3]

A system of thought that represents social values and orientations to the world is called an **ideology.** The key to ideology's power in your life is that it is "naturalized."[4] That is, it's merely "what everyone knows" or "how things are done around here." These thoughts have been unquestioned and regularly reinforced by those around you—your parents, siblings, friends, authority figures in your community and schools. A person in your locale who doesn't believe in freedom will be thought deviant; someone who prefers jicama to all-American vegetables will be regarded as a little strange; and someone who leaves his or her family (blood ties) to join a Hare Krishna community might even be chased down by deprogrammers.

Ideologies are powerful not only because familial, religious, social, and political institutions support them; they're also powerful in your life because you reinforce them. Not only do you seldom question fundamental tenets of living with like-minded others, but you even strengthen them in your own talk to others. You're liable to try to rein in a child running off to school without eating breakfast by saying "That's not the way we do things around here, kid." If you were raised in a small mill town where working families gathered on Labor Day for a community picnic, you probably assumed that all working-class families were pretty much alike everywhere. And, when you decided to enroll in college, you might have assumed that everyone had the same opportunity to go to school. In all of these instances you internalized a series of cultural rules and beliefs and made them a part of your thinking.

Hegemony is a word that refers to power relationships, usually in a hierarchy. It explains why cultures are so difficult to change—they're based on power. Hegemonic relationships are often signaled by such phrases as "That's the way we do things," or "That's the way it goes," or "That's a fact of life." Relationships between classes (rich and poor), between racial groups (white and nonwhite), even between the sexes (male and female) often are maintained as much by acceptance of one's status as by direct force. The idea of hegemony in part accounts for why it's so difficult to change social relations quickly; even when women or Hispanics or gays have been "liberated" from some dimensions of their oppression by others, not all of them join in the singing of a chorus of "Free at last! Free at last! Thank God Almighty, we're free at last!" There still are women who sneer at feminist thought, Mexican Americans who don't look forward to the revolution, and gays, lesbians, and bisexuals who haven't come out of the closet. Naturalized attitudes and social relations resist alteration. **Culture as thought** has a lock on many of our minds, thanks to the forces of ideology and hegemony.[5]

Culture as Performed

The rules and thoughts governing life can be put into words, as when you recite the Pledge of Allegiance, promise to tell "the truth, the whole truth, and nothing but the truth" in court, or warn a friend that "Haste makes waste." Cultural rules and the social roles are not only heard but also seen. **Embodiment** is the process whereby ideas, attitudes, values, and social character are incorporated in communication acts.[6]

You come to understand what a "governor" is by watching your governor on TV. A television show such as *Mad About You* exaggerates husband-wife gender talk. In *ER* we see how the personal and the professional aspects of people's lives actually are inseparable. You come to understand what education is by watching your instructors teach. And, the idea of police brutality came to be understood by Americans who watched the use of police dogs and water hoses on civil rights demonstrators in the early 1960s and the arrest of Rodney King in Los Angeles in the 1990s. You learn many—probably most—of the cultural rules you know because others embody them in their activities.

In turn, then, you work to enact them. **Enactment** is a communication process whereby a person behaves in a manner consistent with society's cultural rules. Insurance agents go to school to learn how to sell policies; they learn to talk like insurance agents are expected to talk in the United States. Athletes often describe their achievements with such phrases as "I couldn't have done this without my teammates!" Such modest behavior is consonant with rules for sports etiquette. In this course, you practice giving speeches with introductions, bodies, and conclusions on the assumption that your listeners expect it. Rules for speaking are grounded in audience expectations, which you try to enact so others will judge you to be a competent speaker.[7]

Culture as performed, therefore, takes us to the heart of the matter of this book: how we communicate with each other. The forms of public talk (introductions, bodies, conclusions), the substance of public talk (accepted ways of thinking), the relationships between speaker and audience (grounded in lived experiences), and even the outcomes of public speeches (who'll listen to whom) are affected by your skills in "performing" those speeches in culturally accepted ways. In different societies, you'll likely have to learn different forms of talk.[8]

An important question now arises: Can you respect individual differences and cultural diversity even while attempting to get a group of people to think alike and work together? Yes, we think you can. We think that you can embody in your speaking some generally accepted cultural standards for interpersonal relationships. What those standards are and ways in which you can embody them are the next topics we address.

STRATEGIES FOR COMMUNICATING UNITY THROUGH DIVERSITY

As a speaker, you can make a group of individuals feel unified in many different ways. Rather than catalog every rhetorical technique you might use, we will concentrate on five strategies in this chapter. These have been chosen for analysis because each respects diversity while recognizing the importance of collective action.

TABLE 4.1   What's Your Conversational Style?

There are cultural preferences for varied conversational styles. Researchers have identified four dimensions that govern these preferences. See which of the following is most comfortable for you.

Direct/Indirect	1. "Can I borrow your pen?" (direct) 2. "I didn't bring a pen to class today." (indirect)
Elaborate/Succinct	1. "Your eyes have a blue tone that picks up the color in your blouse." (elaborate) 2. "You look good in blue." (succinct)
Personal/Contextual	1. "I think it's your fault." (personal) 2. "The time limits for the meeting won't allow for further discussion." (contextual)
Instrumental/Affective	1. "When I finish my homework, I'll be able to watch television." (instrumental) 2. "I hate Mondays!" (affective)

For additional information, see: William Gudykunst and Stella Ting-Toomey, *Culture and Interpersonal Communication* (Newbury Park, CA: Sage, 1988), pp. 99–116.

Recognizing Diversity

Most fundamentally, speakers should acknowledge the different cultural experiences of their listeners and yet call for unified thought and action. Even in their differences, members of a group must learn to think alike on particular matters and to find ways of acting together. Perhaps the most famous speaker of our time who uses this strategy often is Jesse Jackson. His 1988 speech to the Democratic National Convention illustrates his skill. First, he recognized the diversity of American political audiences:

Web Exploration

For more on Jesse Jackson and diversity in public speaking go to http://awl.com/german

> *America's not a blanket woven from one thread, one color, one cloth. When I was a child growing up in Greenville, South Carolina, and Grandmother could not afford a blanket, she didn't complain and we did not freeze. Instead, she took pieces of old cloth—patches, wool, silk, gabardine . . . barely good enough to wipe off your shoes with.*

Having recognized the fundamental fact of diversity through the cloth metaphor, Jackson then calls for unified action:

> *But they didn't stay that way very long. With sturdy hands and a strong cord, she sewed them together into a quilt, a thing of beauty and power and culture.*
>
> *Now, Democrats, we must build such a quilt. Farmers, you seek fair prices and you are right, but you cannot stand alone. Your patch is not big enough. Workers, you fight for fair wages. You are right. But your patch, labor, is not big enough. Women, you seek comparable worth and pay equity. You are right. But your patch is not big enough. Women, mothers, who seek Head Start and day care and prenatal care on the front side of life, rather than jail care and welfare on the back side of life, you're right, but your patch is not big enough.*

Jesse Jackson's speech rhythms come in part from his experiences in African American churches, also in part from his personal goals—to give hope and inspiration to the downtrodden.

Students, you seek scholarships. You are right. But your patch is not big enough. Blacks and Hispanics, when we fight for civil rights, we are right, but our patch is not big enough. Gays and lesbians, when you fight against discrimination and [for] a cure for AIDS, you are right, but your patch is not big enough. Conservatives and Progressives, when you fight for what you believe, right-wing, left-wing, hawk, dove—you are right, from your point of view, but your point of view is not enough.

But don't despair. Be as wise as my grandmama. Pool the patches and the pieces together, bound by a common thread. When we form a great quilt of unity and common ground we'll have the power to bring about health care and housing and jobs and education and hope to our nation.

We the people can win.[9]

This is a prime example of recognizing diversity because Jackson also hammers at the consequences of failing to do so—"your patch is not big enough" becomes the refrain. By finishing with a list of common goals, he gives his listeners reasons for working together to benefit everyone.

Inventorying diversity is a technique you can quickly learn to use. For example, in a speech on why students in your school's Study Abroad program should consider going to school in Malta, you might say: "Malta has earned its reputation as 'The Crossroads of the Mediterranean,' and that fact can be highly significant for you. You'll be educated in English, but will hear a dozen languages spoken on the streets. You'll experience the mixing of Christian and Islamic cultures. You'll vacation in both Europe and Africa, eating scampi in Slovenia and cous cous in Morocco. Your palate—and your mind—will be opened to a dozen cultures on Malta."

Even if the topic you're addressing doesn't seem inherently multicultural, you'll want to be sensitive to diversity. In mentioning dating in a speech on urban teenagers' lifestyles, avoid talking only about heterosexual relationships or traditionally American dating practices. Members of your audience may be homosexual or recent immigrants with their own well-established courtship rituals. When talking about the crisis in medical practice in this country, be careful you don't ascribe gender to the professions, calling doctors "he" and nurses "she." And, don't assume that only older listeners will be interested in your explanation of Individual Retirement Accounts or pension plans.

Negotiating Diverse Values

Often, you must help your listeners realize that they see the world in different ways before you can move them to action. While they may use some of the same words, their meaning is quite different because of varied value orientations. Consider, for example, how much the phrase "family values" has been knocked around in the 1990s. Everyone supports family values, but varied ideologies lie behind uses of that label (Table 4.2).[10]

The ideologies described in Table 4.2 are, of course, simplified positions, but when many people talk about values in public, they in fact deal in such simplicities. That "family values" can mean such different things to people should not be sur-

Web Exploration
For links to other readings on diversity go to
http://awl.com/german

TABLE 4.2   The Diversity of "Family Values"

Conservative Ideology	• America is in moral decline and must return to older family values. • We've become a permissive society characterized by divorce, illegitimacy, and juvenile crime. • We must bolster the traditional two-parent, heterosexual family as the best environment for children. • Governmental (including school) interference with families should be stopped.
Liberal Ideology	• America has to give parents more aid in raising their children. • Everyone, not just parents, has a stake in making sure that children are cared for, supported, and raised to be good citizens. • Because of inequities in financial resources, local, state, and national government must help parents with child care, health care, paid parental leave, and other forms of financial assistance. • All forms of family should be helped—single- and dual-parent, traditional and nontraditional couples—or we will have to deal with juveniles in prisons later.
Middle-of-the-Road Ideology	• Parents should be primarily responsible for raising their children but with governmental safety nets in place. • Parents must be made more responsible for the growth and actions of their children, yet should have help available in the form of family planning agencies, subsidized adoption and abortion services, and sex education in the schools. • The state should rescue children from abusive families; otherwise parents should be responsible for the care, feeding, and nurture of their children.

prising, for our culture is strongly divided on this issue, and what constitutes a family unit can affect a full range of public actions. The divisions are so deep that, as a speaker, you cannot ignore them. Rather, you're better advised to recognize those differences, identifying various definitions of a phrase like "family values" so every listener understands that the meaning of family is disputed in this country. You might say, for example, "Even though others may disagree, to me family values mean honesty, hard work, and patriotism." Only after recognizing such diversity of opinion can you ask your audience, "All right, then, on what do we agree? Together, how can we help parents raise their children?" It was precisely that kind of thinking that brought liberals, conservatives, and middle-of-the-roaders together in 1993 to form a coalition in Congress. That coalition passed the Family and Medical Leave Act to foster traditional families (by requiring businesses to allow parents to stay at home with their infants) while recognizing a child's needs (by guaranteeing him or her parental support in the earliest stages of social life). The middle-of-the-roaders saw the act as a perfect example of family-business-government cooperation. Speakers found common goals in the political debates surrounding the hot-button issue of family values.

The tricky part of negotiating across valuative differences is ensuring that negotiation doesn't turn into erasure. Remember Rodney King's plea, "Can't we all just get along?" Make sure you don't interpret that as meaning that blacks must learn to think and act like whites. Getting along doesn't mean becoming all the same, but rather looking for solutions that respect differences and yet achieve aims common to multiple groups in society.

Accepting Multiple Paths to Goals

Another challenge is to convince people that there are many ways for them to reach a shared goal. Doing so can be a highly useful tactic for bringing together a diverse audience. Thus, some colleges and universities allow their students to meet a physical education requirement in varied ways: a demonstration of skills (playing a set of tennis well with an advanced beginner), life experiences (having a record of having played tennis in a city league for three years), and in-class instruction (taking a class). Likewise, you can urge smokers to try quitting with the help of hypnosis and psychotherapy, the "patch" or nicotine gum, group programs, or cold-turkey regimens.

Difficulties occur when goals traditionally have been pursued only in one way. People may not recognize that there can be other means to the same end. Many's the child who's heard a parent say, "There's only one way to do this: the *right* way!" (that is, *my* way!). So, how can speakers create a sense of tolerance and acceptance of multiple paths leading to common goals?

Metaphors and allegories (see Chapter 10) are useful ways for letting people see the utility of allowing multiple paths to lead to common goals. In his speech to the Atlanta Exposition in 1894, African American educator and social activist Booker T. Washington used the metaphor of the hand, depicting individual ethnic groups (the fingers) as part of the same social system (the hand). In urging the U.S. Forest Service to hire a more culturally diverse workforce, Native American woman Henri Mann Morton used the metaphors of a former chieftain to argue that multiple paths can lead to the same goal:

> *Finally, I would like to leave you with the words of one of our Cheyenne philosophers, High Chief, who said:*
>
> > *In this land there are many horses—red, white, black, and yellow. Yet, it is all one horse.*
> > *There are also birds of every color, red, white, black, and yellow. Yet, it is all one bird. So it is with all living things.*
> > *In this land where once there were only Indians, there are different races, red, white, black, and yellow. Yet, it is all one people.*
> > *It is good and right.*
>
> *High Chief was a wise man. He knew that cultural uniquenesses have a strength of their own. At the same time he recognized our common humanity.*

Native American speaking styles often combine characteristics learned in tribal experiences with those needed for talking to broader cultural audiences.

You, too, know this, as indicated by your powerful theme of "Strength Through Cultural Diversity."[11]

The metaphor of colors—Jesse Jackson even called his political organization the Rainbow Coalition in the 1980s—is useful because it suggests how differences can be focused into a whole, just as the color spectrum is blended together to make "light." Thus, the metaphor works to make multiple paths to shared goals seem sensible.

Giving historical examples can be equally useful: for example, pointing to the success of multinational forces in times of war (the Allies of World War II), multinational cooperation in times of peace (UNICEF programs in the United Nations), interpersonal and group efforts in times of disaster (people-to-people support programs in Southeast Asia), and the overcoming of differences in times of celebration (the building of the multiracial South African Olympic team for the first time in 1996). Teaching people to accept multiple paths to shared goals is a technique you must learn to use if you're going to transform distrustful listeners into cooperative groups.

So, think about using such speaking techniques as these:

✓ *In a speech on getting people to vote:* "So, register to vote. Those of you who aren't American citizens still can participate by working in voter-registration booths or by providing rides to voters who need them on election day. This country can use everyone's help in making it a truly participatory democracy."

✓ *In a speech on allowing prayer in public schools:* "I realize this is a difficult issue for many, especially non-Christians and atheists. The question, though, is not whether everyone should pray a prayer together—they should not. The question is not whether everyone even has to pray during a time set aside for prayer—of course not. Rather, the question is, can children with various religious convictions be allowed a time for self-reflection during the school day? Some will pray, some will think about their life at home. Some will pray, others will play. Some will pray to God, some to Allah. It is the concept, not the words, that is important."

Working Through the Lifestyle Choices of Others

An old saying recommends that "When in Rome, do as the Romans do." Often, you do. You might eat with chopsticks and a flat-bottomed spoon when in a Chinese restaurant, remove your shoes when entering the home of a Finn, greet a Romanian with a kiss on both cheeks, or take a siesta after lunch when visiting the Patagonian region of South America. Urging people to accommodate the lifestyles of others is something you'll need to do on occasion, particularly if that's the only way to come together, and if coming together is important to you.[12]

So, in urging your classmates to put pressure on Congress to pass a more aggressive policy on protecting gays in the military, you might say: "Now, for many—probably even most—people in this class, the issues of gays in the military seems irrelevant. You're not gay, right? So, why worry? Well, there are plenty of reasons to worry. If the military can dictate sexual lifestyle, then it can dictate other aspects of lifestyle as well. If the military drives out gays who 'tell,' then it's weakening civil rights in this country as well as closing employment doors to about ten percent of our population.

SPEAKING OF . . . *Skills*
What Others Are Saying: Oral Culture

Oral specialists in many ancient societies composed and recited poems that served as encyclopedias long before written languages were invented. Those societies with oral specialists were able to preserve more information than those without them. A few of those societies that developed elaborate oral technologies evolved into civilizations.

An interesting area of contemporary studies is the orality-literacy distinction—the notion that information and ideas organized and stored orally are quite different from those organized and stored in writing, that is, literately. Oral cultures existing before literate cultures had to preserve history, laws, and literature in devices built into oral codes. While you of course live in a society that has available not only oral but also literate and electronic communication technologies, you don't need a lot of oral encyclopedias, though you have some oral mnemonics you learned before you could write: "Thirty days hath September, April, June, and November . . . ." "'Do,' a deer, a female deer; 're,' a drop of golden sun; 'mi,' a name I call myself . . . ." "'I' before 'e,' except after 'c,' or when sounded as 'ay' as in 'neighbor' or 'weigh.'" You still can help your audiences store information in their orally conditioned memories through wording and rhythm choices.

Source: Carl Couch, *Information Technologies and Social Orders* (New York: Aldine de Gruyter, 1996), 29.

If the military drives out gays, it prejudices the remaining military personnel against them. Even those of you who are straight, therefore, should have important social and legal questions on your mind. Your life may not be directly affected by the 'don't ask, don't tell' policy, but you sacrifice little or nothing by trying to help a marginalized group in society find self-respect and legal standing in this country."

Maintaining Self-Identity When Facing Difference

Most of the time, however, you're probably not willing to surrender your self-identity, your unique life experience and culture, to others. So then you're in a pickle: how can you be true to yourself even while managing to work effectively with others?

One technique you can use is acknowledging your similarities with others even while maintaining a separation of yourself from them. Supreme Court Justice Clarence Thomas did this in 1998 when he spoke to the annual meeting of the National Bar Association, an organization representing African American attorneys and judges. Thomas squarely confronted his critics after weeks of protest against his appearance. After recalling the struggle to attain equality in a predominantly white world and the values of individuality held in common with his audience, Thomas concluded with these words:

> *I have come here today not in anger or to anger, though my mere presence has been sufficient, obviously, to anger some. Nor have I come to defend my views,*

SPEAKING OF . . . *Ethics*
Considering Cultural Practices

There may well be times when you run into cultural tenets or practices that you don't understand or that you find unappealing. Then what?

1. Suppose you're an African American who runs into a white person discussing the "Bell Curve," the research that suggests African Americans are intellectually inferior to whites and hence unable to achieve as much success as whites. How tolerant can and should you be of that opinion? Is it possible to approach such a person openly on the matter of race, intelligence, and success?
2. As a woman, you have a boss who regularly puts his arm around your shoulders while telling you that he's glad you're here and that the company wants to do everything it can to help you grow and prosper. You don't like the paternalism and even the sexual innuendo suggested by that arm on your body, though you have no reason to believe it's an aggressive move on his part. What can you say?
3. You're giving a speech on children's rights. In your audience are many international students from Arab countries that practice the circumcision of teenaged boys—a ritual you find revolting. Can you handle this issue reasonably for the Arab students as a question of children's rights?

The relationships between your personal feelings or moral standards and the cultural practices of your listeners can lead to serious ethical dilemmas. You must learn to think through them before opening your mouth in public.

> *but rather to assert my right to think for myself, to refuse to have my ideas assigned to me as though I was an intellectual slave because I'm black.*
>
> *I come to state that I'm a man, free to think for myself and do as I please. . . .*
>
> *Isn't it time that we respect ourselves and each other as we have demanded respect from others?*
>
> *Isn't it time to ignore those whose sole occupation is sowing seeds of discord and animus? That is self-hatred.*
>
> *Isn't it time to continue diligently to search for lasting solutions?*
>
> *I believe that the time has come today. God bless each of you, and may God keep you.[13]*

Notice how Thomas declared his identity as an individual in spite of audience hostility. While his audience didn't agree with him, they listened.

Identity can become a complicated issue when speakers see themselves as having multiple identities that come into conflict. So, speaking to the 1996 Republican National Convention, Mary Fisher had a potential identity problem: she had AIDS and was speaking as an AIDS advocate, yet to an audience in which the more conservative members especially wanted little to do with AIDS patients and with federal programs for help. Fisher phrased the potential identity problem early in her speech: "I mean to live, and to die, as a Republican. But I also live, and will die, in the AIDS community—a community hungry for the evidence of [political] leadership and desperate for hope." To make use of that distinction—and to overcome it—Fisher chose to strip away the conservative political culture of her listeners in order to demand their action: "The question is not political. It's a human question, sharpened by suffering and death, and it demands a moral response." By the end of her speech, she could argue that political action should be undertaken, not for ideological reasons, but for social and cultural ones. Hugging a 12-year-old African American girl, Heidia, who was born with AIDS, Fisher concluded her speech in this way:

> *The day may come when AIDS will have its way with me, when I can no longer lift my sons to see the future or bend down to kiss away the pain. At that moment Max and Zack will become the community's children more than my own, and we will be judged not through the eyes of politics but through the eyes of children. I may lose my own battle with AIDS, but if you would embrace moral courage tonight and embrace my children when I'm gone, then you and Heidia and I would together have won a greater battle, because we would have achieved integrity.[14]*

To find ways of affirming your own self while also recognizing your listeners' sense of self is a search you will continue throughout your lifetime when you speak publicly. To find ways of achieving unity through social diversity is a central challenge to all who would inform and persuade others. You'll often find yourself saying such things as:

✓ "Well, now, I'm not a Mexican American, but I think I can understand something of the community's concern about racial stereotyping in the film *La Bamba* because . . ."

✓ "You may not be poor, but your life is directly affected by those who aren't as fortunate. They deserve more than a pat on the head, a dime in a tin cup, and a little contribution to your local Salvation Army shelter . . ."

✓ "Consider the daily life of a football player during the season. You may think it's a gravy train, but you're wrong. Every fall, football players face a juggling act that you've never experienced. They've got to learn to handle their classes, daily practice, and weekends on the road if they're going to survive at this university. Instead of contempt, give them your understanding and personal support."

One final point: just as you'll often maintain your own identity in the face of others who are different, so also will you want to urge others to act from a conviction that their own cultural identities provide the grounds for actions. Karl Marx began his treatise on the proletarian revolution with the call, "Workers of the World, Unite!" His very first sentence signaled his argument that workers as a class had to take control of their own destinies because certainly the other classes of society weren't serving worker interests. In the 1960s, the phrase "Sisterhood is powerful" likewise was a call to recognize that gender could empower women. Similarly, "Black power" and "Black is beautiful" asserted that race was a positive, not negative, attribute of people. So, you occasionally will affirm identity as the basis of thought and action.

This is *not* to say that you always will accept the lifestyle choices of others. There will be times when the lifestyle choices that others have made don't appeal to you. And, you may find it impossible to accept appeals for cultural consistency—appeals to male bonding or sisterhood, to color, to your youth or status as an elderly person. Some questions will transcend cultural practices in your mind and you'll be forced to reject them, as happens for example when most Americans are confronted by white supremacists. Even then, however, it's vitally important that you understand all you can about culture as lived, thought, and performed so that you can select successful communication strategies.

Throughout much of this book, you'll find us returning to questions of cultural life, multiculturalism, and the search for unity. We do not approach these questions of social life for political reasons. While multiculturalism assuredly has strongly political dimensions, our focus on it is cultural, not political. As a speaker, you'll have great difficulty speaking to any but your own close circle of culturemates if you don't understand that speakers must adapt to their listeners' cultures. Social life—and hence communication—is rooted in cultural practices.[15] It becomes your job to understand and adapt your public speaking strategies to those practices.

ASSESSING YOUR PROGRESS

Chapter Summary

1. Culture is a social group's system of meanings.
2. Culture as lived puts an emphasis on demographic or social categories for classifying people into groups.

3. Multiculturalism recognizes the co-cultures that interpenetrate yet are separate from each other.

4. Culture as thought depends upon ideology and hegemony.

5. An ideology is a system of thought that embodies social values and perceptual orientations to the world.

6. Hegemony refers to the power that defines social relationships.

7. Culture is performed through embodiment whereby ideas, attitudes, values, and social character are incorporated in communication actions.

8. Enactment is a communication process whereby a person behaves in a manner consonant with a society's cultural rules.

9. At least five primary strategies for communicating unity through diversity are available to public speakers: (a) recognizing diversity while calling for unity; (b) negotiating among diverse values; (c) accepting multiple paths to shared goals; (d) working through the lifestyle choices of others; and (e) maintaining self-identity in the face of cultural difference.

Key Terms

culture (p. 49)

culture as lived (p. 50)

culture as performed (p. 54)

culture as thought (p. 53)

embodiment (p. 53)

enactment (p. 53)

hegemony (p. 53)

ideology (p. 52)

multiculturalism (p. 51)

Assessment Activities

1. Do a demographic profile of your speech classroom. Have everyone anonymously record their sex, age, the economic status of their family, place of birth or home state, and ethnic background. Your instructor will tabulate the results and then distribute them to everyone. Write down the central idea or claim for your next speech, and ask yourself: In what ways should the cultural backgrounds of my listeners as seen in the demographic profile affect the ways I handle this idea or claim? Turn it in for your instructor's comments.

2. Choose one of the following topics and identify several positions that might be held by ideologically liberal, conservative, and middle-of-the-road people. Then, suggest at least two shared goals you think might be acceptable to all three groups. Work with one of the following topics:

   undocumented (illegal) aliens

   control and financing of public education

   health care reform

   juvenile crime

   environmental protection

Surfing the Web

1. Locate a Web site for your school, company, or friend. Does the Web site convey cultural meaning? Does it imply a sense of authority? What language or code is assumed? Now, randomly locate a Web site for a university, an institution, or a person completely unknown to you. What differences can you identify between this unfamiliar site and the more familiar one? How can culture be conveyed through media such as the Internet?

2. There is much useful information on the general dimensions of culture as well as specific cultures on the Internet. Begin your search generally with culture. What did you locate? Next, investigate a specific culture such as Native American, Asian American, African American, and so on. Share your discoveries with your classmates.

References

1. The classic essays on speaking and class membership are Gerry Philipsen, "Speaking 'Like a Man' in Teamsterville: Culture Patterns of Role Enactment in an Urban Neighborhood," *Quarterly Journal of Speech*, 61 (1975): 13–22; and his "Places for Speaking in Teamsterville," *Quarterly Journal of Speech*, 62 (1976): 16–25. Cf. D. N. Maltz and R. A. Borker, "A Cultural Approach to Male-Female Miscommunication," in *Language and Social Identity*, edited by J. J. Gumperz (Cambridge, England: Cambridge University Press, 1982), 196–216.

2. For a discussion of co-cultures, see the introduction and essays in Alberto Gonzalez, Marsha Houston, and Victoria Chen, eds., *Our Voices. Essays on Culture Ethnicity and Communication*, 2nd ed. (Los Angeles: Roxbury Press, 1996).

3. For discussions of relationships between thought/speech and culture, see Donal Carbaugh, "'Soul' and 'Self': Soviet and American Cultures in Conversation," *Quarterly Journal of Speech*, 79 (1993): 182–200; Randall A. Lake, "Between Myth and History: Enacting Time in Native American Protest Rhetoric," *Quarterly Journal of Speech*, 77 (1991): 123–51; and Alberto Gonzalez, "'Participation' at WMFX-FM: Interventional Rhetoric of Ohio Mexican Americans," *Western Journal of Speech Communication*, 53 (1989): 398–410.

4. On the naturalization of myths and ideologies in our lives, see the classic work by French cultural theorist Roland Barthes, *Mythologies* (London: Paladin, 1973).

5. For a summary of much work on ideology and hegemony, see the writings of John Fiske, for example, *Television Culture* (New York: Methuen, 1987) and *Media Matters: Everyday Culture and Political Change* (Minneapolis: University of Minnesota Press, 1994).

6. For a study of a communication practice (graffiti) as a kind of embodiment, see Dwight Conquergood, "Homeboys and Hoods: Gang Communication and Cultural Space," in *Group Communication in Context: Studies of Natural Groups*, edited by Lawrence R. Frey (Hillsdale, NJ: Lawrence Earlbaum Associates, 1994), 23–55.

7. For an interesting study of enactment, see Y. Griefat and Tamar Katriel, "Life Demands Musayara: Communication and Culture Among Arabs in Israel," in *Language, Communication, and Culture*, edited by Stella Ting-Toomey and Filipe Korzenny (Newbury Park, CA: Sage, 1989), 121–137.

8. For example, the Western linear approach to idea development is quite different from the emotion- or pathos-centered approach in classical Chinese rhetorical practice. See Mary M. Garrett, "Pathos Reconsidered from the Perspective of Classical Chinese Rhetorics," *Quarterly Journal of Speech,* 79 (1993): 19–39. African Americans likewise draw from different cultural resources. See Patricia A. Sullivan, "Signification and African-American Rhetoric: A Case Study of Jesse Jackson's 'Common Ground and Common Sense' Speech," *Communication Quarterly,* 42 (1993): 1–15.

9. Jesse Jackson, "Common Ground and Common Sense," *Vital Speeches of the Day,* 54 (August 15, 1988). See note 8 for a discussion of the style of this speech. This is not to say that Jackson never got into trouble himself over an ethnic comment. For an analysis of his remarks about New York as "Hymietown," see William L. Starosta and L. Coleman, "Jesse Jackson's 'Hymietown' Apology—A Case Study of Interethnic Rhetorical Analysis," in *Interethnic Communication,* edited by Y. Y. Kim (Beverly Hills: Sage, 1986), 117–135.

10. Adapted from "How to Define 'Family Values,'" *USA Weekend,* August 9–11, 1996, 4–5.

11. Henri Mann Morton, "Strength Through Cultural Diversity," keynote address at the Northwest's Colville and Okanogan National Forest conference on cultural diversity, March 23, 1989, reprinted in Bruce E. Gronbeck et al., *Principles and Types of Speech Communication,* 12th ed. (New York: Longman, 1994), 327.

12. On lifestyle choices, see Victoria Chen, "Mien Tze at the Chinese Dinner Table: A Study of the Interactional Accomplishment of Face," *Research on Language and Social Interaction,* 24 (1990/91): 109–140, and Shohana Blum-Kulka and Tamar Katriel, "Nicknaming Practices in Families: A Cross-Cultural Perspective," in *Cross-Cultural Interpersonal Communication,* edited by Stella Ting-Toomey and Filipe Korzenny (Newbury Park, CA: Sage, 1991), 58–78.

13. Clarence Thomas, "I Am a Man, a Black Man, an American," (July 29, 1998). Text available on-line at http://douglass.speech.nwu.edu.thom.b30.htm

14. Mary Fisher, address to the Republican National Convention, August 12, 1996, transcription of the C-SPAN broadcast.

15. This point is driven home in John C. Hammerback and Richard J. Jensen, "Ethnic Heritage as Rhetorical Legacy. The Plan of Delano," *Quarterly Journal of Speech,* 80 (1994): 53–70.

Chapter 5

Understanding Your Audience

Every time a salesperson gets ready to call on a client, every time a lawyer prepares to address a jury, every time a teacher plans a lecture, and every time you get ready to give a speech, audience analysis comes into play. Successful salespeople, lawyers, teachers, and speakers know that effective public speaking is audience-centered. You improve your chances of getting the desired response by tailoring your communication to your listeners—whether a client, a jury, a classroom, or an audience. People understand things in terms of their own experiences. To be most effective, you must analyze your listeners and select experiences common to them.

As you know by now, you need to interact with the people you are addressing. Because of the richness and diversity of the American population, you can't assume everyone thinks and acts exactly as you do.

Think about your listeners as you select your speech topic, establish your purpose, and narrow your subject. Each of the remaining steps in speech preparation—selecting supporting materials, arranging the sequence of ideas, and developing introductions and conclusions—also requires that you keep your audience in mind. Your effectiveness as a speaker depends on how you adapt to your audience.

Obviously you can't address your speech to each person individually. But you can identify common features among your listeners. Think of your audience as an onion. You peel away one layer and find others. The most effective way to understand your audience may be to peel away as many layers as possible. Identifying those layers or characteristics is the key to audience analysis. Once you have determined the primary features of your listeners, you can begin to adapt your ideas to them. This chapter will discuss the demographic and psychological features of listeners, how to find out about your audience, and how to use what you learn. Let's first turn to demographic analysis.

ANALYZING YOUR AUDIENCE DEMOGRAPHICALLY

Web Exploration
For more demographic analysis go to
http://awl.com/german

Demographic analysis is the study of observable characteristics in groups of people. In any audience, you will notice traits that group members share. You should determine your listeners' general age, gender, education, group membership, and cultural and ethnic background. Let's examine each of these factors individually.

Age

Are your listeners primarily young, middle-aged, or older? Does one age group seem to dominate a mixed audience? Is there a special relationship between age groups—parents and their children, for instance? Are your listeners your peers, or are you much younger or older?

Watch a nursery school teacher talk to preschool children and you'll see how age gaps of twenty years or more can be overcome. Nursery school teachers know that they must adapt to their young listeners or risk chaos. They adapt partly by simplifying their vocabulary and shortening their sentences. If you've ever read a story to a child, you know another secret to engaging youngsters. You can command their attention through animation. If you talk like a wizard or a teapot or a mouse, you can see children's eyes widen. The point is this: even if your listeners are much different than you are, you can still engage them by recognizing what captures their attention. In this way, you are using audience analysis to make your message more effective.

Gender

Is your audience predominantly male or female, or is the group made up of both genders? Do your listeners maintain traditional gender roles, or do they assume different roles? Ted chose date rape as the topic for a classroom speech. He was concerned about the lack of information about date rape on his campus and wanted to provide his classmates with the facts. But two things bothered Ted. First, one of his friends asked him why he was giving a speech on this topic. To the friend, it seemed that date rape was an inappropriate topic for a male speaker. Ted was surprised at his friend's reaction but also wondered if others in his class would have the same thought. In addition, Ted realized that both men and women were members of his class. He wondered how he could interest everyone in the subject.

After some thought, Ted decided to handle the problem of gender by convincing his listeners that date rape is not an issue that affects just women. Everyone should be concerned. To reveal the extent of the problem, Ted planned to present statistics showing the rising number of date rapes. Ted would tell his listeners that he hadn't realized the extent of the problem until a good friend confided that she'd been raped by another student who offered to walk her back to her apartment after a party. By using a personal example, he tackled the stereotype of the rapist as an unknown midnight assailant lurking in a dark alley. In this way, Ted was able to convince his classmates that date rape affected both men and women. Because he was legitimately concerned about the problem and engaged everyone in his audience, Ted stimulated their concern about date rape. Ted's awareness of gender as a demographic variable allowed him to deal with his audience effectively.

Education

How much do your listeners already know about your subject? Does their experience allow them to learn about this subject easily and quickly? Obviously, people who have worked with a computer word-processing program, for example, will learn its new features more quickly than people who have not.

Knowing the educational background of your audience can guide you in your choice of language, kinds of supporting material, and organizational pattern. Assume that you are addressing the faculty senate as a student advocate of expanded student parking on campus. This audience will demand strong support for your arguments. You can express complex arguments in technical language. The general educational level of your listeners requires that you adapt your ideas and their development. However, when you are invited to speak to a local citizens' group about the proposal for expanded student parking, you will have to broaden your language, supporting material, and organization for a more diverse audience.

Group Membership

Do your listeners belong to groups that represent special attitudes or identifiable values? Are they part of a formal organization such as a church, chamber of commerce, or scouting group, or have they spontaneously come together? Can you pick out common traditions or practices within the organization? What is the cultural climate of the organization?

In some ways, Americans are joiners. We form churches, fan clubs, support groups, hobby organizations, chat rooms—the list seems endless. You can find a group to join for almost any purpose. We come together to share common experiences, to solidify common values, and to express feelings. Often group members share demographic characteristics. For example, doctors, lawyers, and dentists join professional societies based on occupational similarities. Consumer advocacy groups and support groups are united by purpose. Members of labor unions hold jobs and economic welfare in common. Homeowners' groups share geographic features. Political parties and religious groups attract people who share common values. Tee ball clubs, high school reunions, and associations of retired persons unite people who are similar in age. Groups share similar interests and goals that can be identified readily. Identifying these common interests is an important element of assessing your audience, as the following example illustrates.

The city council in Abby's hometown wanted to build an incinerator for disposal of solid waste to save money. Abby was against the incinerator project and, after voicing her opinions at a backyard barbecue, she found herself representing a grassroots group of local homeowners. Abby attended the next city council meeting to express the views of the neighborhood. She told the city council that more money could be saved by recycling household plastics, selling aluminum cans, and mulching grass clippings. Those simple steps would reduce the waste significantly and make a new incinerator unnecessary. Abby's clinching argument was to remind council members that several of them were up for reelection. Her arguments hit a nerve; the incinerator project was canceled. As members of a group, the city council was dependent on homeowners' approval for their jobs.

Cultural and Ethnic Background

Are members of your audience predominantly from particular cultural groups? Do your listeners share a special heritage? Can you identify common origins among listeners? More and more, the United States is becoming a multiracial, multicultural society. Currently, over twenty-five percent of all Americans identify themselves as nonwhite. The number of nonwhites in this country is expected to grow rapidly in the next ten years. Many Americans celebrate their roots in other countries or cultures, and those strong cultural heritages may bear on your speechmaking experience. It is important to recognize the cultural and ethnic diversity of your listeners, as the following example shows.

Ed, a student in mass communication, was invited to talk about American media to a group of visiting students sponsored by the Japanese Youth Exchange Program. He realized that some of his examples would be familiar to his listeners. Many Japanese are avid sports fans, follow *The Simpsons,* and have fan clubs for American celebrities. The Japanese also enjoy their own programs. Considering this, Ed decided to investigate Japanese television more fully. He found many examples of high-quality programs. After reading some particularly interesting research on Japanese soap operas, Ed discovered *Oshin,* the daily serial drama rated highest among television programs in Japan. He read about the series, which dramatizes the life of an early-twentieth-century heroine. The struggle of new ideas with traditional values is featured in most episodes, and Ed realized how conflict characterizes both Japanese and American soap operas. This recognition of the similarity in television programming gave Ed an idea for his speech. He decided to focus on conflict in soap opera programming and to use both American and Japanese programs as examples. The speech was a hit. Like Ed, you should recognize when the background of your audience influences the speech topic and its development.

Using Demographic Information

The importance of demographic analysis does not lie in simply recognizing the variables present in an audience. This is just the first step. The key is to decide which of these demographic factors will affect your listeners' reception of your message. In other words, you must shape your message with your audience in mind.

Sometimes several factors may affect your message. For example, if you've been asked to talk to a local kindergarten class about your baseball card collection, you must take age and education into consideration. You should adapt to your young listeners by using simplified concepts—talking about the number of hits rather than ERAs. You should also keep your talk brief to accommodate shorter attention spans. And, most importantly, you should involve children by using visual aids. Bring several cards for them to hold and examine.

If you were to talk about your baseball card collection to a group of local business owners, on the other hand, your message would be very different. The age and education of your listeners would still influence your message development, but since those demographic factors would be different, your message should be adapted to the changes. Since your listeners are older and better educated, they can understand more complex ideas. For example, you might focus on the investment potential of baseball card collections. As owners of businesses, their group membership suggests that they would be interested in the commercial aspects of your collection.

Demographic analysis helps you adapt your message to your listeners more effectively. Demographic analysis can assist you in understanding your listeners by pinpointing the factors that are common among them. You can better select and develop your key ideas if you know who is listening to your speech.

ANALYZING YOUR AUDIENCE PSYCHOLOGICALLY

Careful psychological analysis of your audience may provide clues about how they think. This is especially important if you intend to influence your listeners. Before you can hope to alter their thoughts or actions, you need to know what ideas they already hold.

To analyze your audience psychologically, you do **psychological profiling;** that is, you identify what your listeners think and feel much as you would specify their demographic characteristics. Beliefs, attitudes, and values are the key concepts in discussing the psychology of listeners. After we examine each of these concepts, we'll discuss ways you can use them to tailor your message to your listeners.

Speech Writer's Workshop
Use the Speech Handbook to learn more about analyzing your audience.

Beliefs

The first task of psychological profiling is understanding audiences' beliefs. **Beliefs** are convictions about what is true or false. They arise from first-hand experiences, from public opinion, from supporting evidence, from authorities, or even from blind faith. For example, you might believe "Calculus is a difficult course," based on your own experience. At the same time, you may also believe that calculus is important for your career because of what others have told you. And, you probably enrolled in college in the first place because your parents and high school teachers encouraged you to try college courses. Although each of these beliefs is held for different reasons, you consider each to be true.

Beliefs supported by strong external evidence are **facts.** When you say, "Research has proven that infant blue whales gain an average of ten pounds per day," you're very sure of that belief. While you may not know much about baby blue whales, you have confidence in the marine biologists who do. You hold facts with certainty because you have hard evidence to support them.

Other beliefs take the form of opinions. **Opinions** are personal beliefs that may not be supported by strong external evidence. You may think that all cats are nasty animals because you have been scratched by cats or because you are allergic to them. However, your experience is limited. Many people like cats. Normally, you signal to your listeners when your beliefs are opinions. You might say, "It's my opinion that cats are worthless creatures," or "In my opinion, cats are vicious." In this way, you are telling your listeners that your evidence to support your claims is limited. Thus, an opinion is a personal belief supported with less compelling external evidence than a fact.[1]

Web Exploration
For more on the occasional disparity between facts and opinions go to http://awl.com/german

Since both facts and opinions are matters of belief, sometimes the difference between them is blurred. In colonial America, for instance, many people knew "for a fact" that regular bathing caused disease, just as their ancestors knew that the best cure for mumps was to walk backwards three times around a pigsty wearing a donkey halter. If many people harbor similar opinions, those opinions may be taken for facts. It's important to recognize that opinions and facts are psychological constructs.

Beliefs are held with varying degrees of conviction. Some are relatively open to change, while others are fixed. Obviously, it is more difficult to change fixed beliefs than variable beliefs. **Fixed beliefs** are those that are highly resistant to change. They have been reinforced throughout a lifetime, making them central to one's thinking. Many early childhood beliefs, such as "Bad behavior will be punished," and "If you work hard, you'll succeed," are fixed. These beliefs have hardened in your mind and become resistant to change.

In contrast, **variable beliefs** are less well anchored in your mind. You might enter college thinking you want to be a chemist; however, after an instructor praises your abilities in a composition class, you may consider becoming a writer. Then, you take a marketing class and find out that you're good at planning advertising campaigns. This self-discovery goes on as you take additional classes. Your beliefs about your talents change with your personal experiences; since your beliefs are still not firmly fixed, they may change again as you encounter new experiences.

Once you have investigated your audience's beliefs, how can you use this information? You need to determine which beliefs will help you and which are obstacles to be overcome. Imagine that you oppose granting rights to gay personnel in the military. You want to convince your classmates to accept your point of view. Immediately you recognize the controversy centering on this subject, about which people hold many different facts and opinions. First, consider what your listeners believe to be true. If they accept that gays already serve in the military and have served with distinction, then you may have to convince them that the presence of gays is disruptive.

On the other hand, if they think that the number of gays in the armed forces is negligible or that gay personnel do not make good soldiers, your job is much easier. Thus, determining your audience's beliefs will help you to focus your ideas.

Before you speak, it's also important to know which of your audience's beliefs are *fixed* (difficult to change) and which are *variable* (more easily altered). You can set more realistic expectations if you know that your listeners are unlikely to change their fixed beliefs, and you can concentrate on changing variable beliefs before you attack fixed beliefs. For example, consider trying to convince your classmates that education is a waste of time. Most likely, their belief that education is valuable is fixed and you'll have trouble changing it. On the other hand, you might have more luck getting them to change majors or take a class outside their majors. Their beliefs about which classes to take probably are variable.

Attitudes

The second goal of psychological profiling is to identify audience attitudes. **Attitudes** are tendencies to respond positively or negatively to people, objects, or ideas. Attitudes express our individual preferences and feelings such as, "I like my public speaking class," "Classical music is better than rap music," and "Prague is a beautiful city." In other words, they are emotionally weighted.

SPEAKING OF . . . *Ethics*
Using Audience Analysis Ethically

Marketers can often determine the underlying emotions and values that drive consumer choices using a process called "psychographics." This ability to understand consumer behavior based on demographic and psychological profiling gives marketers an impressive tool. It also gives rise to some ethical concerns. Consider the following uses of audience analysis:

1. Research suggests that many people who suffer from alcoholism feel deep social inadequacy and alienation. Advertisers often associate alcohol with social situations such as parties. Is this attempt to target alcoholics by tapping their need for companionship an ethical use of audience analysis?
2. Some fixed beliefs are **stereotypes,** the perception that all individuals in a group are the same. Is it appropriate for speakers to use stereotypes? For example, a speaker might say, "We all know the rich cheat on their taxes. Let's raise the tax rates in the higher income brackets to compensate." Or, "You can't trust him—he's a politician!"
3. Should advertisers of security devices such as pepper sprays, alarm systems, and handguns play on women's fears of rape and assault?
4. Tobacco companies target young people by offering inducements to purchase cigarettes, such as free gifts. Is this ethical?

For more information on psychographics, see: Rebecca Piirto, *Beyond Mind Games: The Marketing Power of Psychographics* (Ithaca, NY: American Demographics Books, 1991).

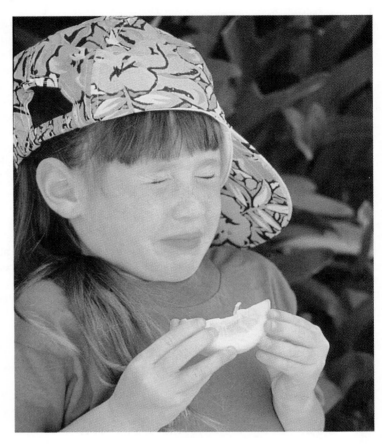

People's attitudes can vary dramatically. Powerful attitudes often come into play in our everyday lives.

Attitudes often influence our behavior. One dramatic example of the strength of attitudes occurred when the Coca-Cola Corporation introduced new Coke, a refigured formula, with disastrous results. Although extensive blind taste tests indicated that people preferred new Coke's flavor, consumers reacted negatively because of their loyalty to the classic formula. Their attitudes influenced their purchasing behavior, and the corporation wisely "reintroduced" Coca-Cola Classic.

As a speaker, you should consider the dominant attitudes of your listeners. Audiences may have attitudes toward you, your speech subject, and your speech purpose. Your listeners may think you know a lot about your topic, and they may be interested in learning more. This is an ideal situation. However, if they think you're not very credible and they resist learning more, you must deal with their attitudes. For example, if a speaker tells you that you can earn extra money in your spare time by selling magazine subscriptions, you may have several reactions. The thought of extra income from a part-time job is enticing. At the same time, you suspect that it might be a scam and you feel uncomfortable because you don't know the speaker well. These attitudes toward the speech topic, purpose, and speaker will undoubtedly influence your final decision about selling subscriptions.

Web Exploration

For examples of highly opinionated editorials go to
http://awl.com/german

TABLE 5.1   Beliefs and Attitudes

Beliefs and attitudes are psychological constructs held by individuals or by groups.

Beliefs	Attitudes
Seat belts save lives.	Fastening my seat belt takes too much time.
Vegetables contain important minerals and vitamins.	Broccoli tastes good.
My grandparents came from Mexico City.	I love my grandfather.

Values

The third component of psychological profiling is understanding audience values. **Values** are the basic concepts organizing one's orientation to life. They underlie an individual's particular attitudes and beliefs. For many Americans, life, freedom, family, and honesty are basic values. These are deeply ingrained and enduring; as a result, they are very resistant to change. Imagine trying to convince a friend to renounce American citizenship. No matter how noble your cause, you will probably meet powerful resistance because you are attacking fundamental values.

Values are more basic than beliefs or attitudes. They serve as the foundations from which beliefs and attitudes may spring (see Figure 5.1). For example, a person

Values serve to motivate people to action. Political change is often based upon shared value orientations.

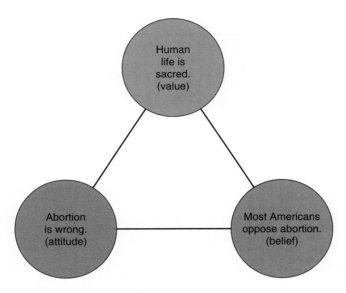

FIGURE 5.1   Belief, Attitude, and Value Cluster

Beliefs, attitudes, and values are interdependent. They often form clusters that reinforce each other.

may hold the value "Human life is sacred." That value can be expressed in multiple attitudes: "Abortion is wrong" or "Mercy killing is immoral." That value may also be expressed in beliefs such as, "A fetus should be treated as a human being," "Most Americans are opposed to abortion rights legislation," or "Religious authority ought to be respected on questions of morality."

Values, then, underlie an individual's particular attitudes and beliefs. Former Representative Barbara Jordan, the first African American woman to give the keynote address at the Democratic National Convention, identified basic values that her audience shared. Among them, she listed "equality for all and privileges for none."[2] Her speech is highly regarded because she highlighted common ground—shared values that organized and influenced the beliefs and attitudes of her listeners.

DISCOVERING DEMOGRAPHIC AND PSYCHOLOGICAL FACTORS

Speech Writer's Workshop
Use the Speech Workshop to practice demographic and psychological analysis.

Now that you understand which demographic and psychological factors are important to consider when developing a speech, you should think about how you're going to discover this information. You may already know the answer: you can ask your listeners for their opinions and you can observe them and draw inferences from your observations. Let's look at each option.

Surveying Your Listeners

Often the best source of information about your audience is your listeners themselves. Ask them. You may not have the services of a professional pollster, but you can conduct informal interviews with members of the group or develop a more formal survey to assess their beliefs, attitudes, and values.

Suppose you are concerned about the rapidly rising number of sexually transmitted diseases among local teenagers. As the parent of a teenager, you are convinced that every effort should be made in the schools to halt this trend, including making condoms available to all students. If you intend to convince the school board to take action on this issue, you need to know how the members of the board currently feel about the issue. Your plan is clear: you talk to the members of the board individually and find out.

However, you may also have to convince the local Parent-Teacher Association to support your plan. This presents an entirely different problem since there are thousands of parents in your school district. Even if you spent hours on the phone, you still probably couldn't interview every parent in the district. Your alternative is to talk to parents active in the organization or call a representative sample to get an accurate profile of their views.

In each case, the questions you will ask are basic. You want action, so it's clear that you will ask how they would vote on the issue. It's also important to know whether they'll vote at all, so you will need to find out whether they regularly attend meetings. Finally, you need to understand why they feel the way they do about the issue. By asking this question, you'll be able to identify the basic points of conflict.

Observing Your Listeners

Sometimes you don't have direct access to members of your audience. If this is the case, then you must rely on indirect observation and inference for your audience analysis. Occasionally you'll have public statements, earlier conversations, voting behaviors, purchasing decisions, and other information on which to base your analysis. At other times, you will have to rely on indirect information from others.

If you aren't closely tied to the group you will address, you'll want to (1) think through your personal experiences with members of the group; (2) talk with program chairpersons and others who can tell you who is in the audience and something about their interests, and (3) ask speakers who have addressed this or similar audiences what you can expect. Keep in mind that these strategies provide limited information. You can supplement this information by attending a few meetings of the group yourself or reading the constitution of or other literature about the group. Don't forget to check the Internet. Many groups maintain home pages and you can gain information from them. In combination, these observations will help you adjust your speech to your listeners.

Finally, you can consult published sources that provide demographic and survey information on broad segments of our society. Opinion polls, market surveys, political profiles, and demographic shifts are all available in your library or on the Internet in sources such as *Statistical Abstract of the United States, Survey of Current Business, Business Conditions Digest, Bureau of Labor Statistics News, Statistics of Income Bulletin,* and *Facts on File.*

Using Your Psychological Profile

After you have developed a profile of your audience's beliefs, attitudes, and values, how can you use this information? Understanding your audience's beliefs, attitudes, and values will help you make decisions about three aspects of your speech: your ideas, your supporting materials, and your phrasing. Your psychological profile can help you:

1. *Frame your ideas.* For example, if your listeners believe childhood is a critical time of development, you can move from this belief to recruit volunteers for a day care co-op. If they value family life, you can touch on this theme to solidify their commitment. On the other hand, if your listeners are apathetic about childhood development, you must establish the critical nature of the early years of child development before you can hope to persuade them to support a co-op.

2. *Choose your supporting materials.* If your audience analysis shows that your listeners consider statistics to be reliable, you should use scientific studies or numerical data in your speech. On the other hand, if your audience believes in the divine inspiration of the Bible, you can cite biblical testimony to sway them.

3. *Phrase your ideas.* You can choose your words to reflect the intensity of your audience's convictions. If your listeners are ready to picket a local video rental store, then your language should show the urgency of immediate action. Demand action now. On the other hand, if they are reluctant to take up placards, then you should use less forceful words.

USING AUDIENCE ANALYSIS IN SPEECH PREPARATION

Audience analysis helps you search for clues to the way your listeners think and act. Identifying the demographic and psychological characteristics of your listeners is an important step toward good communication. Using these characteristics helps you discover what might affect the audience's acceptance of your ideas. Let's focus on how audience analysis helps you prepare to speak through audience targeting and audience segmentation.

As you consider your reasons for speaking, you need to determine what you can realistically expect to accomplish with your particular audience in the time you have available. Analysis of your audience helps you develop your speaking purposes, your goals, and the appeals you will use.

Developing Your Purposes

Suppose you have a part-time job with your college's Career Planning and Placement Office; you know enough about its operations and have enough personal interest in it to want to speak about career planning and placement to a variety of listeners. What you've discovered about different audiences should help you determine appropriate, specific purposes for each. If you were to talk to a group of incoming students, for example, you would know that they probably:

✓ Know little about the functions of a career planning and placement office (have few beliefs in this area, none of which are fixed).

✓ Are predisposed to look favorably on career planning and placement (have a positive attitude toward the subject).

✓ Are more concerned with such short-term issues as getting an adviser, registering, and learning about basic degree requirements than they are with long-range matters such as finding jobs (are motivated by practical values).

✓ See you as an authoritative speaker and, consequently, are willing to listen to you (have a positive attitude toward the speaker).

Given these audience considerations, you would probably provide basic rather than detailed information about career planning and placement. You might phrase your specific purpose as follows: "To brief incoming students on the range of services offered by the Career Planning and Placement Office." This orientation will include a brief description of each service and a general appeal to your audience to use these services to make some curricular decisions.

If you spoke to a group of graduating college seniors on the same subject, you would address your listeners differently. You would discover that they:

✓ Are familiar with the Career Planning and Placement Office through personal use or through roommates and friends who have used it (have beliefs that are fixed).

✓ Have strong positive feelings about career planning and placement because they are hoping to use such services to find jobs when they graduate (have a positive attitude toward the subject).

✓ Tend to think education has prepared them to "earn a decent living" (have a practical perspective on the topic).

✓ May view you as an unqualified speaker on this subject, especially if you aren't a senior or aren't a full-time employee of the office (have a negative attitude toward the speaker).

Given these factors, you should offer more specific details in some areas. Because your listeners are probably aware that they will soon need career placement help, you might describe the special features of the office rather than simply outlining its general duties. You could reassure them that the office successfully places many students and point out that the process is more successful when students allow ample time for resume development, job searching, and interviewing. You could demonstrate your expertise by talking about career possibilities across a variety of fields—especially if you know what fields are represented in the group you are addressing. You might phrase your specific purpose as follows: "To inform graduating seniors about ways that the office can help students find employment, and about specific types of information and assistance that the office provides to students." Audience analysis will help you shape your specific purposes and determine which are most appropriate to your listeners.

Developing Your Goals

As a speaker, ask your listeners to accomplish only what is within their capacity. You can often discover your listeners' potential for action through audience analysis. Demographic factors will tell you about the channels of action available to your listeners. Voters can cast their ballots in elections, parents can teach their children, consumers can boycott products, and many people can contribute money. You can use the psychological factors that you discover through audience analysis to stimulate listeners' motivations to act.

You can also determine ranges of authority through audience analysis, especially through analysis of demographic factors. For example, in speaking with a local school's Parent-Teacher Association about instituting an after-school program of foreign language and culture instruction, you're addressing an audience made up of school administrators, teachers, and parents. Each of these groups has certain powers to act. School administrators can seek funding from the school board; teachers can offer instructional time; and parents can petition the school board, enroll their children, and volunteer to help with the program. Your speech could include these specific goals for each group of listeners.

Be realistic about the degree of change you can expect from your listeners. How intensely can you motivate an audience to react to a topic? If your listeners are strongly opposed to downtown renovation, a single speech—no matter how eloquent—will probably not reverse their opinions. One attempt may only neutralize some of their objections. This is a more realistic goal for a single speech than completely reversing opinions.

How much action can you expect after your speech? If your prespeech analysis indicates that your listeners vehemently oppose nuclear power plants in your area, you may be able to recruit many of them to work long hours picketing, lobbying, and participating in telephone marathons. However, if they moderately oppose nuclear facilities, you might ask for a small monetary donation rather than an actual time commitment. Audience analysis should help you set more realistic communication goals.

Developing Your Appeals

So far, we've focused on how audience analysis helps you to target your audience as a group. Keep in mind that no matter how close together people are seated in the room, they are still individuals. Sometimes you can approach each listener individually. However, such communication is time-consuming and inefficient when you're dealing with matters of broad public concern.

Using an approach called **audience segmentation** you can divide your listeners into a series of subgroups or "target populations." A typical college audience, for example, might be segmented by academic standing (incoming students through seniors), by academic major (art through zoology), by classroom performance (A+ to F), or even by extracurricular activity (ROTC, SADD, Young Republicans, Pi Kappa Delta). You can direct main ideas to each of these subgroups.

Suppose you were to give a speech to members of a local community club, urging them to fund a scholarship. Through audience analysis you discover that the

SPEAKING OF . . . *Skills*
Handling Hostile Audiences

How do you gain a positive response from people who disagree with you? While it is unreasonable to expect to convert every member of a hostile audience, you can improve your chances of getting them to listen with the following strategies:

1. *Establish goodwill.* Let them know you are concerned about the issues or problems you're discussing.
2. *Start with areas of agreement.* Develop some common ground before you launch into controversial territory.
3. *Offer principles of judgment.* Determine the basis on which you and your listeners can evaluate ideas.
4. *Develop positive credibility.* If your listeners respect you, they are less likely to reject your ideas.
5. *Use experts and supporting material to which your audience will respond.* Choose your supporting material with your audience in mind.
6. *Disarm your listeners with humor.* Mutual laughter establishes positive rapport.
7. *Use a multisided presentation.* Recognize more than one perspective on the issues.

Above all, be realistic when addressing a hostile audience. Remember that the more strongly an audience opposes your position, the less change you can reasonably expect to occur.

For more information, see: Herbert Simons, *Persuasion* (New York: Random House, 1986), pp. 150–160.

club is composed of social service personnel, educators, and business people. By thinking of the club as segmented into these subgroups, you are in a position to offer each subgroup some reasons to support your proposal. For example, you might appeal to social service workers by saying: "The social-team concept means educating others who will contribute to the improvement of the community." For the educators in your audience, you could state: "By denying education to capable students, we neglect to tap into one of the most important resources of our community—young people." Finally, for business people, you might declare: "Well-educated citizens contribute more to the financial resources of the community as investors, property owners, and heads of households."

You can see how each statement is directed to segments of your audience. These main ideas implicitly refer to the commitment of social services to helping people from all strata of life, to educators' beliefs and attitudes that youth are a national resource, and to business leaders' commitment to financial responsibility and success.

Understanding your audience is a key step in speech preparation. To become a competent speaker, you must make many decisions about your topic, specific purposes, and phrasing for central ideas and main ideas. Demographic and psychological analyses of audience members will help you make these decisions. If you learn all you can about your listeners and use relevant information to plan your speech, you'll improve your chances for success.

A SAMPLE AUDIENCE ANALYSIS

In this chapter we have surveyed various factors that you will consider as you analyze your audience and occasion. If you work systematically, these choices will become clearer. Suppose you want your local city council to adopt a program in which drug addicts can exchange used hypodermic needles for clean ones. You think such a program will help prevent the spread of AIDS (acquired immunodeficiency syndrome) among drug addicts. You might prepare the following analysis of your audience as you plan your speech:

I. *General Description of the Audience:* The city council comprises 15 members elected to office by local districts. The city manager and mayor also attend council meetings. Citizens sometimes attend and speak at council meetings.

II. *Demographic Analysis*

A. *Age:* Most of the council members are between 45 and 65.

B. *Gender:* The council is composed of 12 men and 3 women. The mayor and city manager are men.

C. *Education:* All but four of the council members have finished high school; several completed B.A. degrees in various fields, including political science, pharmacy, nursing, home economics, and accounting. Two health professionals on the council are familiar with disease history and control.

D. *Group Membership:* All listeners are politically active and registered voters. Although they do not necessarily share party affiliation, they all value participation in the democratic process.

E. *Cultural and Ethnic Background:* Ethnic background is mixed, but predominantly African American, European, and Hispanic.

III. *Psychological Profile*

A. *Factual Beliefs:* Anyone who contracts AIDS will die of it. In spite of promising new research, there is no cure for AIDS.

B. *Opinions:* Most consider AIDS to be a problem associated with particular groups, including homosexual males, hemophiliacs, and intravenous-drug users.

C. *Attitudes:* Members of the council probably were surprised by the recent news of the AIDS death of a prominent community resident. They probably do not consider themselves likely victims.

D. *Values:* They are committed to the democratic process and take pride in political involvement at the community and state levels. They see themselves as common people—"the heart of America"—fulfilling the American dream. Council members often point to community progress in civil rights issues, general educational reforms, and high voter turnout during elections.

With this prespeech audience analysis completed, you have a better idea of how to frame your speech. From your analysis you conclude that the council may initially resist your needle exchange proposal because they think that AIDS affects only a small number of people who engage in high-risk behaviors. They may believe that most citizens are not at risk. Realizing this, you can choose among several approaches:

1. Stress the listeners' commitment to the welfare of the community and nation, their belief in the democratic process, and their belief in the rights of citizens in minority groups. Encourage their feelings of pride in previous civic accomplishments and challenge them to face the AIDS crisis. In other words, show them that it is in their best interests to confront and discuss unpopular issues for the well-being of the entire community.

2. Make it clear that the needle exchange program is not simply a moral issue. While recognizing the importance of traditional national values, also stress the practical importance of treating disease, regardless of moral issues. Use projections of future infection rates to emphasize that everyone's health may be affected if AIDS is allowed, through ignorance or neglect, to spread unchecked.

3. Identify other communities that have used needle exchange programs with success. Overcome audience apathy and hostility by encouraging members to discuss the disease further.

4. Ask the council to sponsor an open forum for continued attention to the issue, rather than demanding immediate commitments or political action.

5. Praise the group's excellent record in community projects. Stress the far-sightedness of the council on other difficult issues. Point out that, in a democracy, fair play requires that each side be given equal time and consideration before anyone reaches a final decision. Aim the bulk of the speech at gaining approval for open-minded discussions.

As you can see, when you understand your listeners it's much easier to tailor a specific message for them. You are more likely to develop an effective speech when you first consider the demographic and psychological characteristics of your listeners.

ASSESSING YOUR PROGRESS

Chapter Summary

1. Public speaking is audience-centered.

2. The primary goal of audience analysis is to discover the demographic and psychological characteristics of your listeners that are relevant to your speech purposes and ideas.

3. Demographic analysis is the study of audience characteristics such as age, gender, education, group membership, and cultural and ethnic backgrounds.

4. Psychological profiling seeks to identify the beliefs, attitudes, and values of audience members.

5. Beliefs are convictions about what is true or false.

6. Beliefs may be facts or opinions, fixed or variable.

7. Attitudes are tendencies to respond positively or negatively to people, objects, or ideas.

8. Values are basic concepts organizing one's orientation to life.

9. Audience analysis allows you to identify audience subgroups for more effective selection of main ideas.

Key Terms

attitudes (p. 75)

audience segmentation (p. 82)

beliefs (p. 73)

demographic analysis (p. 70)

facts (p. 74)

fixed beliefs (p. 74)

opinions (p. 74)

psychological profiling (p. 73)

stereotypes (p. 75)

values (p. 77)

variable beliefs (p. 74)

Assessment Activities

1. Choose the text of a speech from this textbook, from *Vital Speeches of the Day* (or another anthology of speeches), or from a newspaper, such as the *New York Times*. Identify statements of fact and opinion in the speech. Determine the speaker's attitudes and values from statements in the speech. Develop a profile of the audience and assess the effectiveness of the speech for this group of listeners.

2. Gather some magazine advertisements and bring them to class. As a class or in groups, share your advertisements. Speculate about the audiences for which they were intended. To what attitudes are the advertisers trying to appeal? Are they trying to create beliefs? What tactics do they use? How effective do you think these tactics are?

3. Imagine that you are the chief speechwriter for each of the individuals listed below. Decide which audience subgroups you will need to address. What values, attitudes, and beliefs are they likely to hold? What can you say in your speech to engage their attention and support?

   a. The president of the United States, addressing the nation on primetime television concerning the latest international diplomatic development.

   b. The president of your student government, welcoming first-year students to campus at the beginning of the academic year.

   c. A defense lawyer, conducting closing arguments in a murder trial.

   d. A ninth-grade teacher, cautioning a class about the use of illegal drugs.

Surfing the Web

1. Locate a home page for an organization. What insight does the page give you into the nature of the organization? From the material provided, determine who is likely to belong to the group. Speculate about age, gender, education, and cultural or ethnic background. What attitudes, beliefs, and values do you think members of this organization might hold in common? Explain your conclusions.

2. Make a list of your primary interests and hobbies. Search the Internet for clubs, chat rooms, and resource groups for each of the items on your list. Compare your results with other class members.

References

1.   For more discussion, see: David L. Bender (ed.), *American Values* (San Diego, CA: Greenhaven Press, 1989); Milton M. Rokeach, *Beliefs, Attitudes, and Values: A Theory of Organization and Change* (San Francisco: Jossey-Bass, 1968); and Rokeach, *The Nature of Human Values* (New York: Collier-Macmillan, Free Press, 1973).

2.   See Wayne Thompson, "Barbara Jordan's Keynote Address: Fulfilling Dual and Conflicting Purposes," *Central States Speech Journal,* 30 (1979): 272–277.

Finding Supporting Materials

You have just come out of the twentieth century, called by many the **Communications Century.** You have at your disposal the miracles that have resulted from putting electricity to work in the arenas of human communication: from the telegraph, telephone, and film to television, the computer chip, satellites, fax machines, electronic mail, cell phones, and digital sound reproduction. Electronically, you can access and experience wildly diverse people, places, and events all over the world. You can now retrieve more data than at any other time in history. In a few minutes through the Internet alone, you can find a weather forecast for Mongolia, a map of Ankara, and the latest headline news from American, British, French, or Russian international broadcasters.

You have access to staggering amounts of information. To conquer this glut of data, you need to

89

know where to look for the information that you need. This chapter explores the challenge of finding and assembling the materials relevant to your speeches, your audiences, and the speech occasions. *Your challenge, ultimately, is to turn information into knowledge—an entity usable by human beings in meeting their needs and desires.*

Finding supporting materials should be a purposeful, targeted search, not an aimless bibliographical spree in the library or on the Internet. You must develop some sense of the supporting materials you will need, of the location of those materials, and of efficient ways to record the information you find. You will also need to know how to use supporting materials ethically. In this chapter we won't deal with these matters exhaustively, because your own libraries will have their own particular ways of organizing and handling materials. However, we do hope to get you off to a good start.

DETERMINING THE KINDS OF SUPPORTING MATERIALS YOU'LL NEED

To guide your choice of supporting materials, you need to consider your main topic, your audience, and the ideas you intend to discuss. Thinking about these elements should help you decide what kind of supporting materials you will need. Consider the following critical questions to guide the selection of supporting materials before you begin your search process.

1. *What support does your topic require?* Specific topics require certain sorts of supporting materials. It's obvious that you wouldn't use the same kind of supporting material to describe your experience biking in Maui as you would to report your international relation club's financial status. The rational requirements of your speech topic should suggest the appropriate forms of supporting material.

   Consider another example: if you tell your listeners that tuition has increased, you need to show how much. This topic demands statistics that show a trend of rising tuition. The statistics provide a general picture and develop the scope of the problem. You might add testimony, examples, and comparisons and contrasts to depict details and to develop audience interest.

2. *What does your audience need to know?* No matter what forms of support you choose, merely citing the findings of research is clearly not enough. You also need to think about what your audience already knows and what they need to know. Your search for supporting materials should reflect your listeners' needs.

   If you give a speech on skin cancer, your audience is probably most interested in knowing their chances of getting it. They may be unaware that certain practices, like the use of tanning beds, increase the risk of getting skin cancer, and they probably don't know about the latest treatment methods. These are certainly things you will want to find out as you search for supporting material on this topic.

3. *Which form of support will be most effective for your topic?* As you conduct your research, you should realize that you will discover many forms of support.

SPEAKING OF . . . *Skills*
How Much Is Enough?

Have you ever found yourself wondering, "How much supporting material should I use in my speech?" While there's no absolute rule governing the number or kind of supporting materials, you need enough support to establish your points. This varies according to the quality and kind of supporting materials. Here are some guidelines:

1. *Complex or abstract ideas are enhanced by concrete supporting materials such as visual aids and specific examples.* A graph or example from daily life would clarify a speech on chaos theory.
2. *Controversial points require a lot of authoritative evidence.* This means that a speech for raising income taxes would benefit from statistics, budget trend information, and well-respected testimony.
3. *Speakers with low credibility need more supporting material than speakers with high credibility.* If you plan to speak on educational reform for the next century but your only experience has been as a student, you should use a lot of supporting material.
4. *If your topic is abstract or distant from your listeners' experiences, use concrete supporting material to establish identification with listeners.* A speech on life in a space station doesn't come alive until you insert specific details and concrete examples.
5. *If your audience's attention or comprehension is low, use more examples.* Enliven a speech on accounting procedures with a story or a specific instance.

However, different forms of supporting material accomplish different results. Explanations, comparisons, and statistics will help you develop the topic so your listeners can better understand it. Examples and testimony will lend interest to the topic. In an introduction to a speech on fire alarms, you might use an example of a local house fire to stimulate audience interest and then, in the body of the speech, use statistics to establish the importance of installing fire alarms.

4. *How objective is your supporting material?* To read and think critically, you must be able to distinguish among sources of information. One way to differentiate is to distinguish between what historians call **primary sources** (eyewitness/first-hand accounts) and **secondary sources** (accounts based on other sources of information). The diary of a woman who survived the 1950 massacre of South Korean civilians under the bridge near No Gun Ri would be a primary source; a *New York Times* story about the event in the fall of 1999 would be a secondary source. Obviously, the South Korean woman may not have had a "typical" experience, or her own personal prejudices may have influenced what she recorded. The same may be true of the historian. Furthermore, sometimes the sources a historian works from color the resulting history.

This initial thinking about your topic (a) helps you decide what supporting materials your topic requires, (b) guides your selection of supporting materials in light of your audience demands, (c) determines which forms of supporting material are most effective for your topic, and (d) indicates what supporting material will be most objective.

SOURCES OF SUPPORTING MATERIALS

So, where do you find the materials you'll need for your speeches? You'll find those materials exactly where you find all ideas in this world: in electronic networks and storage technologies, in print, in interaction with others with special knowledge, and in information-gathering instruments you construct.

The Electronic World

You've seen the ads: AT&T promising you access to information from anywhere, the Pentium III chip bringing you sounds and images from every imaginable source, and your own college or university promising to link you internationally with other institutions of learning and with new ideas. But how? To survive, you must learn to surf the 'Net, download information from the increasingly large stack of CD-ROMs of data in your libraries, and even search your own library electronically with a click of a mouse.

The Electronic Card Catalog   Most colleges and universities either have or will soon install a computerized search system for their holdings. If you have access to such a system, it should be your first stop. For example, the University of Iowa uses the Oasis system, popular among larger research libraries. It allows you to search Iowa's card catalog and holdings of consortium libraries, the Humanities and Social Sciences Indexes, and Psychological Abstracts.

Suppose you want to do a speech on the financing of home health care for the terminally ill through hospice organizations. In early 1999, if you entered "death" at the University of Iowa, you'd pull up 1,521 hits—far, far too many. If you entered "hospice," you'd still have 78 items—overpowering. But, if you then dropped to the subcategory "hospice-costs," you'd come down to 4 books. That much you can handle.

Learning to narrow through precise specification of topic or through subcategorization will make your searches less frustrating. Most systems offer you **Boolean searches,** where you use such words as "and," "or," and "not" to control the subject matter. So, "medieval *or* architecture" gets you all references with either word; "medieval *and* architecture" pulls up references to all works with both words in them; and "medieval *and* architecture *not* England" will highlight medieval architecture everywhere except England. Also knowing authors, titles, and the like will help even more. Take time to look at the pamphlet or online help menu to make sure that you can use your local electronic catalog with maximum efficiency.

Finally, find out what databases you can access through your library system. ERIC (Educational Resources Information Center) will help you locate scholarly papers in the humanities; MEDLINE will get you into psychosocial and physiological studies of disease and associated medical problems; LEXIS-NEXIS will give you access to a staggering number of public and commercial information sources—news, politics, economic matters, polling, and the like in newspapers, magazines, organizational newsletters, and other data sources.

CD-ROM Searches   We're living through a great explosion in the use of the CD-ROM—a technological device that uses the compact disk (CD) as a storage vehicle for computer data. CDs hold much more information than computer disks and so are used to store and to retrieve data from multiple volumes. Check the holdings of your local library. Many offer on CD-ROMs sources like the *New York Times Index, The Oxford English Dictionary, The Modern Language Association Indexes, Encyclopaedia Britannica,* perhaps even the *Table of Contents to Communication Journals,* which will include as databases all articles published in National Communication Association journals since 1990. As more and more databases become available on CD-ROM, you'll be able to link electronically with the actual articles you want.

The World Wide Web   The **Information Superhighway** was the first great metaphor of the 1980s and early 1990s—a system allowing everyone to access information electronically from around the globe. With the coming of hypertext abilities, however, the metaphor changed to the **World Wide Web,** because now you not only travel (telnet) to information sources, but you merely have to click on a word in one source to jump to another. The Highway is transportation; the Web is a way of raiding many sources at once. The Web is an access protocol that allows you to enter the maze of computerized languages, pictures, and sounds from any point in that maze, and then to move from site to site by a simple click. A little vocabulary might also help you work through the Web:

- ✓ Telnet: a command taking you to remote sites.
- ✓ http: HyperText Transport Protocol is a command to your computer to take you to some site.
- ✓ FTP: a file transfer protocol that lets you retrieve information.
- ✓ Usenets: interactive accounts that link you to newsgroups—that is, to interactive discussions.
- ✓ Archie, Gopher, Veronica, WAIS (Wide Area Information Servers): multiple tools for accessing information sites in useful ways.
- ✓ HTML: HyperText Markup Language, which is a script used to create the main or home page of a Web site (other languages also are used).
- ✓ FAQ: computerese for Frequently Asked Questions—check it when you're unsure.
- ✓ Hypertext: highlighted words that, when clicked, transport you to other texts if you're on the Web (also known as "links").
- ✓ URL: Uniform Resource Locator, that is, the address of a site. Addresses include endings that give information about the owner of the page: .com = commercial

company; .edu = an educational institution; .net = a company that connects you to the Internet; .gov = a governmental site; .org = a non-profit organization; .mil = a military group; .us = someone in the United States who doesn't fit into another category; and then specific codes for other countries (e.g., .uk for United Kingdom, .se for Sweden, .jp for Japan).

✓ World Wide Web: the network of servers (computers online) that provides hypertext searches on the Internet, usually with the abbreviation "www" in them.[1]

Speech Research on the Web By now, you probably cannot tune into a sports broadcast, news hour, or even primetime television show without being told that you can use a "www" command to get to its home page: ESPNET's sports scores for the day, CNN International's informational background on big stories, *USA Today* online, or National Public Radio's discussion group. You soon discover that you can go to Mississippi State University for the Internet Movie Database, to SCREENsite for links between the Library of Congress and directories on film and television resources, to the Harvard-MIT-Tufts consortium on negotiation and conflict resolution, to the University of Maryland's site full of resources and simulations for high school students, to the University of Iowa's Communication Studies site for Desktop Resources (sources of information on social-political issues), to state and federal government sources through ".gov" locations. Here is a sample of useful sites for speech resources:

Web Exploration
To practice using different types of URLs go to
http://awl.com/german

Subject	Site
Genealogy	http://www.genealogy.org/~ngs
Health (disease control)	http://www.cdc.gov/cdc.htm
Health (advice)	http://www.drkoop.com
Electronic newspapers	http://www.enews.com
USA Today	http://www.usatoday.com
Automobiles	http://www.edmunds.com
City networks	http://www.city.net
Outer space	http://www.space.com
Maps	http://www.mapquest.com
Links to people	http://www.bigfoot.com
Sports	http://www.wwcd.com/hp/sports.html
White House	http://www.whitehouse.gov
House of Representatives	http://www.house.gov
U.S. Senate	http://www.senate.gov
Subject guide to the WWW	http://gateway.lib.uiowa.edu/index.htm

When telneting to sites on the Web around the world, you'll discover utterly amazing places: the places where the Aryan (white power) women hang out; individuals' home pages paying homage to Marilyn Monroe or Nostradamus; full texts of song lyrics; places where you can watch the election returns live from many countries; sites with sound bites and video clips; and, of course, sites where you can shop

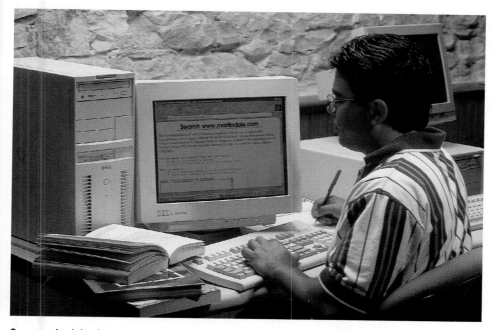

Computerized database searches can yield volumes of information rapidly and efficiently.

for John Deere tractors or find parts for your 1950 9N Ford tractors. Because almost anyone can put up a site on the Web for modest cost, you must learn to evaluate sites for quality of information and importance of opinion. Here are some of the tests outlined by Esther Grassian of the UCLA College Library:[2]

Content and Evaluation

1. How complete and accurate are the information and the links provided by this source?
2. How good is this site vis-à-vis other sites or print sources? (A librarian can help you answer this question.)
3. What are the dates on the site and its materials?
4. How comprehensive is it? Is the site-builder interested only in certain aspects of a topic (e.g., the Arab side of the Arab-Israeli conflict)? Does it attempt to cover everything available—and if so, how? Are evaluations of links to other sources provided?

Sources and Dates

1. Who produced the site? Why? What authority or knowledge does the producer have? Is there a sponsoring organization that has a vested interest in what results from people using the site?
2. Is there an evident bias in the materials that you find?

3. When was the site mounted and when was it last revised? How up-to-date is it?
4. Is it easy to contact the producer with questions?

Structure

1. Does the site follow good graphics principles? Is the use of art purposive or just decorative?
2. Do the icons clearly represent what is intended?
3. Does the text follow basic tenets of good grammar, spelling, and composition?
4. Can the text be used by both line-mode (text-only) and multimedia (words/sound/pictures) users?
5. Are links provided to Web subject-trees in directories—lists of Web sources arranged by subject?
6. How usable is the site? Can you get through it in a reasonable time?

Other

1. Is appropriate interactivity available?
2. Can you transfer secure information to and from the site?
3. Are links to search engines provided?

Search Help   Grassian's last point also is ours: You need to be able to use **search engines** to help you through the maze of material available electronically. A search engine is an online database that allows you to explore broad subjects and find specific information by being directed to a source. It's like the bibliographies in your library's reference area, and some—the super engines—are like the bibliographies of bibliographies. They come with different virtues: *Large databases* include Yahoo!, All the Web, AltaVista, HotBot, Northern Light, Excite, InfoSeek, and Lycos. *Advanced search features* allow you to search in special ways—Ask Jeeves asks you questions in natural language, Simpli.com has pull-down menus to help you focus, and both InfoSeek and AltaVista help you refine questions. *Annotated directories* tell you how to get into the search process—AlphaSearch or the University of Iowa's Gateway center noted above are examples of such directories, as are the Britannica Internet Guide, LookSmart, Snap.com, and The Mining Company. Included among *business directories* are Livelink Pinstripe, Dow Jones Business Directory, SearchZ, and Northern Light Industry Search. A nice online guide to search engines, *Guide to Meta-Search Engines* by Jian Liu, will help you even further as you make your way through these and other tools.[3] See Table 6.1 for advice on which search engines to use for which approaches to information finding and retrieving.

Web Exploration
For more on Internet content evaluation go to
http://awl.com/german

The Print World

Most teachers and experts will tell you, however, to be careful of what you use from the Web and to do your final research, when possible, in the print world. There simply are more controls on print than electronic sources, generally speaking. The

TABLE 6.1   Internet Search Engines

Information Needed	Characteristics of the Search Engine
Overview of topic	Yahoo! And LookSmart organize information in "trees" from general to specific topics.
Relevant hits only	Excite has excellent summaries, and you can ask for "more documents like this one"; Simpli.com asks questions about which meanings of a word you're interested in (e.g. "java" as a programming language or as a drink).
Review of what's available on the Internet	MetaCrawler works across engines; Inference Find searches engines, merges the results, and removes redundancies.
Pinpoint research	AltaVista is massive yet has a fast indexer of full texts; MSN and Ask Jeeves work well on subcategories.
Common words	HotBot is fast and powerful, and ranks results as well other options for searches; Excite, Yahoo!, and Lycos are tailored to less-experienced searchers.
Have a date	HotBot Super Search limits by date.
Scientific information	AltaVista has the best rating among general engines.
Proper names	AltaVista and InfoSeek are sensitive to capital letters; HotBot can search names in regular or reversed order (Sam Jones; Jones, Sam); Real Names lets you search "Ford Explorer" directly without going through the general Ford Motor Co. site first.
Images, sounds, media types (Java, VRML), extensions (e.g., .gif)	Try Lycos Media; HotBot Super Search; The Amazing Picture Machine; Yahoo! Computers and Internet; Multimedia:Pictures, ditto.com.
E-mail discussion groups	LISZT is a directory of listservs and those (majordomos) who run them.
Quotations	Go to The Quotations Page; Bartlett; Land of Quotes.

Information taken from material prepared by Debbie Abilock (1996), updated 6/13/98, at http://nuevaschool.org/~debbie/library/research/adviceengine.html and Jennifer Tanaka, "The Perfect Search," *Newsweek*, September 27, 1999, pp. 71–72. See also commentary by Danny Sullivan at SearchEngineWatch.com.

trick for using traditional print competently is to look for different kinds and qualities of information in different places.

Newspapers   Newspapers are obviously a useful source of information about events of current interest. Moreover, their feature stories and accounts of unusual happenings provide a storehouse of interesting illustrations and examples. You must be careful, of course, not to accept as true everything printed in a newspaper, since the haste with which news must be gathered sometimes makes complete accuracy difficult. Your school or city library undoubtedly keeps on file copies of one or two highly reliable papers, such as the *New York Times, The Observer,* the *Wall Street Journal,* or the *Christian Science Monitor,* as well as the leading newspapers of your state or region. Through the *New York Times Index,* you can locate the paper's accounts of people and events from 1913 to the present. Another useful and well-indexed source of information on current happenings is *Facts on File,* issued weekly since 1940. Almost all major newspapers will run their own Web sites as well, and Lexis-Nexis gives you electronic access to more than 200 major and local newspapers.

Magazines   The average university library subscribes to hundreds of magazines and journals. Some, such as *Time, Newsweek,* and *U.S. News & World Report,* summarize weekly events. *The Atlantic* and *Harper's* are representative of monthly publications that cover a wide range of subjects of both passing and lasting importance. *The Nation, Vital Speeches of the Day, Fortune, Washington Monthly,* and *The New Republic,* among other magazines, contain comment on current political, social, and economic questions. More specialized magazines include *Popular Science, Scientific American, Ebony, Sports Illustrated, Field and Stream, Ms., Better Homes and Gardens, Rolling Stone, Byte, Today's Health, National Geographic,* and *The Smithsonian.*

This list is, of course, just the beginning—there are hundreds of periodicals available covering thousands of subjects. To find a specific kind of information, use the *Readers' Guide to Periodical Literature,* which indexes most of the magazines you'll want to consult in preparing a speech. Or, if you'd like more sophisticated material, consult the *Social Sciences Index* and the *Humanities Index,* now computerized in most libraries. Similar indexes are available for publications from technical fields and professional societies; a reference librarian can show you how to use them.

Yearbooks and Encyclopedias   The most reliable source of comprehensive data is the *Statistical Abstracts of the United States,* which covers a wide variety of subjects ranging from weather records and birth rates to steel production and election results. Information on Academy Award winners, world records in various areas, and the "bests" and "worsts" of almost anything can be found in the *World Almanac, The People's Almanac, The Guinness Book of World Records, The Book of Lists,* and *Information Please.* Encyclopedias, such as the *Encyclopaedia Britannica* and *Encyclopedia Americana,* attempt to cover the entire field of human knowledge and are valuable chiefly as initial reference sources or for background reading. Refer to them for important scientific, geographical, literary, or historical facts; for bibliographies of authoritative books on a subject; and for supplemental information.

Documents and Reports   Various government agencies—state, national, and international—as well as many independent organizations publish reports on special subjects. The most frequently consulted governmental publications are the hearings and recommendations of congressional committees in the publications of the U.S. Department of Health and Human Services or Department of Commerce. Many state universities publish reports on issues related to agriculture, business, government, engineering, and scientific experimentation. Such endowed groups as the Carnegie, Rockefeller, and Ford Foundations and such special interest groups as the Foreign Policy Association, the Brookings Institution, the League of Women Voters, Common Cause, and the U.S. Chamber of Commerce also publish reports and pamphlets. Though by no means a complete list, *The Vertical File Index* serves as a guide to some of these materials.

Books   Most subjects suitable for a speech have been written about in books. As a guide to these books, use the subject-matter headings in the card catalog of local libraries. Generally, you will find authoritative books in your school library and more popularized treatments in your city's public library. You can now access the card catalog via computer in many libraries. This often makes your search more efficient and productive.

Biographies   The *Dictionary of National Biography,* the *Dictionary of American Biography, Who's Who, Who's Who in America, Current Biography,* and more specialized works organized by field contain biographical sketches especially useful in locating facts about famous people and in documenting the qualifications of authorities whose testimony you may quote.

The World of Broadcasting

Lectures, discussions, and the formal public addresses of leaders in government, business, education, and religion are frequently broadcast over radio or television. Many of these talks are later printed by the stations or organizations that sponsor them. Usually, as in the case of CBS's *Meet the Press* or National Public Radio's *All Things Considered,* copies of broadcasts may be obtained for a small fee. Other broadcast content, such as national news broadcasts, is indexed by Vanderbilt University; your library may subscribe to that index, which is helpful in reconstructing a series of events. There are also computer databases that track media programs.

If manuscripts or transcripts are not available, you may take careful notes from videotaped or audiotaped programs. Be exact! Just as you must quote printed sources accurately and honestly, so, too, you are ethically obligated to give a person full credit for their radio and television remarks.

Obviously, you won't have to investigate all of these sources of materials for every speech you make. The key concept is relevance: go to the sources that will yield materials relevant to your topic. You are more likely to find historical statistics in print materials than in a television program or to find a viewpoint on a local problem in an interview than in a computer search. Think as you select sources of materials to investigate and then carry out the search carefully. If you do, you'll find the materials to make your speech authoritative and interesting.

The Face-to-Face World

When looking for material, many of us forget the easiest and most logical way to start—by asking questions. The goal of an **informational interview** is to obtain answers to specific questions. In interviewing someone, you seek answers that can be woven into the text of your speech. Interviews increase your understanding of a topic so that you will avoid misinforming your audience, drawing incorrect inferences from information, and convoluting technical ideas. Your interviewee may be a content expert or someone who has had personal experience with the issues you wish to discuss. If you're addressing the topic of black holes, who is better qualified to help you than a physicist? If you're explaining the construction of a concrete boat, you might contact a local civil engineer for assistance. If you wish to discuss anorexia nervosa,

Speaking of ... *Skills*

Conducting an Interview

You need to observe these general guidelines in planning an informational interview:

1. *Decide on your specific purpose.* What do you hope to learn from the interview? Can the person you are interviewing provide precise information from a unique perspective? Determine what you would like to glean from the interview and communicate that purpose directly to the person you plan to interview.
2. *Structure the interview in advance.* Plan your questions in advance so that you have a clear idea of *what* to ask *when.* The interview may not follow your list exactly, so you'll need to remain flexible and free to deviate from your interview plan to clarify or elaborate on a previous response. Begin the interview by setting limits on what will be covered during the session. End the interview by recapping the main ideas and expressing your appreciation.
3. *Remember that interviews are interactive processes.* Adept interviewers should be good listeners. You should listen carefully to what is said and accurately interpret the significance of those comments. There is a definite pattern of "turn-taking" in interviews that allows plenty of opportunity to clarify remarks and opinions.
4. *A good interviewer builds a sense of mutual respect and trust.* Feelings of trust and respect are created by revealing your own motivation, by getting the person to talk, and by expressing sympathy and understanding. Good communication skills and a well-thought-out set of questions build rapport in interview situations. You should always follow up the interview with a note or letter expressing your appreciation for the person's shared time and expertise.

you might interview a person who has suffered through the disorder. Interviews can provide compelling illustrations of human experiences. (See the box above.)

The Snail-Mail World

Even as you improve your search skills through e-mail, hyperlinks, and CD-ROM searches, you should not neglect "snail mail"—the mail that travels in semis, little white Jeeps, and the leather bags that postal carriers bring to your front door. You probably get enough junk mail to realize that there's still profit to be made in writing people the old-fashioned way, through letters of inquiry and questionnaires.

Letters of inquiry are just that—short, easy-to-follow letters asking someone for some information or other help. You might write the U.S. Government Printing Office for their latest catalog on consumer protection pamphlets or a local beverage distributing company for some product posters that you can use as visual aids. In writing such letters, be clear, specific (which product posters?), and timely, letting them know the latest you can use whatever it is that you're asking for. Include a stamped, self-addressed envelope for a reply, or even just a postcard for quick action on their part.

Questionnaires will demand some of your best letter-writing skills, as many people hate them. But, if you explain the use you'll make of their opinions, write the questions clearly and specifically, and keep it short enough to be done in three to five minutes without asking them to disclose much personal information, people often are willing to help. Use closed questions (for example, "yes/no" or "strongly agree/agree/disagree/strongly disagree" responses) when you can. Test the questionnaire on people around you to make sure it's as clear and specific as it can be. Again, include a self-addressed, stamped envelope for its return.

RECORDING INFORMATION

When you find the information you've been looking for, you'll need a system for recording it. First, record the source citation completely. You'll need this information when you cite the source during your speech. Note the title of the book or article, author, and publication data including the place, publisher, and date of publication. Include the volume number if you're citing a journal article. It's helpful to record the call number or location of the source just in case you need to consult the information again.

Sometimes it's easiest to make photocopies of materials. However, if you take notes, you may find that notecards are more flexible than a notebook because they can be shuffled by topic area or type of support. If you do use a notebook, try to record each item on half of each page. There are two reasons to do this: First, since most of your information won't fill a page, you will save paper. Second, cutting the sheets in half will make it easier to sort your data or to adopt a classification scheme and record information in accordance with particular themes or subpoints of your speech. (See Figure 6.1)

Speech Writer's Workshop
Use the Documentor to record and format your sources.

GENERAL SUBJECT: IMPORTANCE OF ORAL COMMUNICATION

Specific information: Socrates' critique of writing

"Socrates' critique of writing thus is not just a flourish toward the end of an elaborate dialogue, but a logical outgrowth of the argument that good and just relations among people require a knowledge of and care for souls."

Source: John Durham Peters, Speaking into the Air: A History of the Idea of Communication (Chicago: University of Chicago Press, 1999), 47.

FIGURE 6.1 A Sample Notecard

You can use a notecard format like this to record information for later use.

USING SOURCE MATERIAL RESPONSIBLY

Web Exploration
For further explanation of plagiarism go to
http://awl.com/german

Now that we've discussed locating and generating material for your speeches, we come to a major ethical issue—plagiarism. **Plagiarism** is defined as "the unacknowledged inclusion of someone else's words, ideas, or data as one's own."[4] One of the saddest things an instructor has to do is cite a student for plagiarism. In speech classes, students occasionally take material from a source they've read and present it as their own. Many speech teachers and members of audiences habitually scan the library periodicals section. Even if listeners have not read the article, it soon becomes apparent that something is wrong: the wording differs from the way the person usually talks, the style is more typical of written than spoken English, or the speech is a patchwork of eloquent and awkward phrasing. In addition, the organizational pattern of the speech may lack a well-formulated introduction or conclusion or be one not normally used by speakers. Often, too, the person who plagiarizes an article reads it aloud badly—another sign that something is wrong.

Plagiarism is not, however, simply undocumented verbatim quotation. It also includes (a) undocumented paraphrases of others' ideas and (b) undocumented use of others' main ideas. For example, you are guilty of plagiarism if you paraphrase a movie review from *Newsweek* without acknowledging that staff critic David Ansen had those insights, or if you use economic predictions without giving credit to *Business Week*.

SPEAKING OF . . . *Ethics*
What Is the Ethical Response?

1. You can't find exactly the right testimony from an expert to prove a point you want to make in a speech. Is it okay to make up a quotation to use if you know it will result in a better grade on your speech?
2. Should you rip out a page from a magazine in the library if it contradicts something you plan to say in your speech? If the page is missing, nobody will know about the contradiction.
3. If you are a spokesperson for a company, is it okay to suppress facts about the side effects of a new fat-free product? What if side effects aren't fatal and the product will let thousands of people lose weight?
4. If you can sell more life insurance when you exaggerate the death benefits, should you do it? What if your job depends on increasing your monthly sales? Is it okay to distort facts to keep your job?
5. Should you post a message on the Internet that you know isn't supported by facts? What if it's just a joke?
6. Should you deliberately conceal the source of a fact because you know it's not credible? What about attributing the fact to another, more credible source?

Suppose you ran across the following idea while reading Neil Postman's *Amusing Ourselves to Death: Public Discourse in the Age of Show Business:*[5]

The television commercial is not at all about the character of products to be consumed. It is about the character of the consumers of products. Images of movie stars and famous athletes, of serene lakes and macho fishing trips, of elegant dinners and romantic interludes, of happy families packing their station wagons for a picnic in the country—these tell nothing about the products being sold. But they tell everything about the fears, fancies and dreams of those who might buy them. What the advertiser needs to know is not what is right about the product but what is wrong about the buyer. And so, the balance of business expenditures shifts from product research to market research. The television commercial has oriented business away from making products of value and toward making consumers feel valuable, which means that the business of business has now become pseudo-therapy. The consumer is a patient assured by psycho-dramas.

Imagine that you wanted to make this point in a speech on the changing role of electronic advertising. Of course, you want to avoid plagiarism. Here are some ways you could use the ideas ethically:

1. *Verbatim quotation of a passage.* Simply read the passage aloud word for word. To avoid plagiarism, say, "Neil Postman, in his 1985 book *Amusing Ourselves to Death: Public Discourse in the Age of Show Business,* said this about the nature of television advertisements: [then quote the paragraph]."

2. *Paraphrasing of the main ideas.* Summarize the author's ideas in your own words: "We've all grown up with television advertising, and most of the time we endure it without giving it much thought. In his book *Amusing Ourselves to Death: Public Discourse in the Age of Show Business,* Neil Postman makes the point that instead of selling us on the virtues of a product, advertisers sell us our own fears and dreams. Advertisements are more about us than about the products being sold."

3. *Partial quotation of phrases.* Quote a brief passage and summarize the rest of the author's ideas in your own words: "Postman suggests that the shift from product research to market research indicates a shift in emphasis away from the product being sold and toward the consumer. He says that business now focuses on making the consumer feel better through, quote 'pseudo-therapy. The consumer is a patient assured by psycho-dramas.'" Be sure to pause and say "quote" to indicate when you are quoting the author's words.

Plagiarism is easy to avoid if you take reasonable care. Moreover, by citing such authorities as Postman, who are well educated and experienced, you add their credibility to yours. Avoid plagiarism to keep from being expelled from the class or even from your school. Avoid it for positive reasons as well: to improve your ethos by associating your thinking with that of experts.

ASSESSING YOUR PROGRESS

Chapter Summary

1. Your search for supporting materials should be purposeful; you should attempt to assemble materials relevant to your speeches, your audiences, and the occasions on which you're speaking.

2. To plan your search, you should consider (a) the rational requirements of the topic, (b) the audience demands, (c) the power to prove generally associated with various kinds of supporting materials, and (d) the objectivity of your sources.

3. In executing your searches, learn to access the electronic world (electronic card catalogs, CD-ROMs, and the World Wide Web), the print world (newspapers, magazines, yearbooks and encyclopedias, documents and reports, books, and biographical dictionaries), the face-to-face world (interviews), and the snail-mail world (letters of inquiry and questionnaires).

4. You need to record information carefully and in a form you can use easily.

5. You must also remember to use source material ethically, avoiding plagiarism.

Key Terms

Boolean searches (p. 92)

Communications Century (p. 89)

informational interview (p. 99)

information superhighway (p. 93)

plagiarism (p. 102)

primary sources (p. 91)

search engines (p. 96)

secondary sources (p. 91)

World Wide Web (p. 93)

Assessment Activities

1. Select a major problem, incident, or celebration that has appeared in the news recently. Examine a story or article written about it in several of the following: the *New York Times, Christian Science Monitor, USA Today, Time, Newsweek, The New Republic,* and either the *Wall Street Journal* or *Business Week.* In a column from each source, note specifically what major facts, people, incidents, and examples or illustrations are included and what conclusions are drawn. Evaluate the differences among the sources you consulted. How are their differences related to their readership? What does this exercise teach you about the biases or viewpoints of sources?

2. Your instructor will divide your class into groups of two to four people, trying to make sure that at least one person in each group has access to the Internet. Work in pairs, with each pair assigned four items to find—one student working in print resources, the other, electronically. Look for the following material, recording the source with a careful citation of where the information was found:

   a. Weekly or daily summary of current national news

   b. Daily summary of stock market information

c. Text of Bill Clinton's grand jury testimony of August 17, 1998

d. A mission statement for the National Education Association

e. Current status of California legislation on social services for illegal immigrants

f. A list of CDs put out by John Pizzarelli

g. Brief sketch of the Big Ten conference's basketball schedules

h. At least three different definitions of the word "wit" and dates when those meanings came into use

3. Plan an interview of a celebrity or famous person. First, find out about the person by conducting a library search. Then, develop your interview questions. You might consider interviewing political leaders such as Tony Blair, Jesse Ventura, or Nelson Mandela. Or, you could choose controversial social figures like Dr. Jack Kevorkian, Howard Stern, or Camile Paglia. What questions will you ask? Why? What is the best method for recording answers during the interview?

4. Consider the following sources for a speech on breast cancer. Which are primary and which are secondary sources? When would you use each?

a. A summary of breast cancer research from 1983 to 1993 in an American medical journal

b. Your aunt's account of her mastectomy

c. A local newspaper article on the seven warning signs of cancer

d. A book titled *Surviving Cancer Surgery*

e. The meeting notes of a local cancer support group

f. A radio commentary on the importance of annual mammograms

g. A journal written by a cancer specialist who underwent breast cancer treatment

h. A U.S. government study evaluating the success of various treatments for breast cancer

References

1. For a larger vocabulary, find a good basic book on the Web or check out *Kathy Schrock's Guide for Educators* at http://www.capecod.net/schrockguide/yp/iyprch.htm.

2. Esther Grassian, "Thinking Critically About World Wide Web Resources," http://www.library.ucla.edu/libraries/college/instruct/web/critical.htm, 1997.

3. Found at http://www.indiana.edu/~librcsd/search/sla.html. Because IBM helped Indiana University puts its library online, it has become a most important research source.

4. Louisiana State University, "Academic Honesty and Dishonesty," adapted from LSU's Code of Student Conduct, 1981.

5. Neil Postman, *Amusing Ourselves to Death: Public Discourse in the Age of Show Business* (New York: Viking Penguin, 1985), 128.

Chapter 7

Using Supporting Materials

As you put your speeches together, you will need to consider the information you've assembled. The functions of supporting materials are to clarify, amplify, or strengthen the ideas that you're offering to your listeners. Just as a plant needs sun, water, and soil to bring it to life and sustain its growth, the ideas in a speech need supporting materials to thrive. If you're telling your classmates about local career opportunities, you'll need examples of those jobs and information about how to apply for them. If you're arguing that "The Olympic Games have become too commercialized," you must authoritatively define "commercialized" and provide statistical and illustrative materials to support your contention. If you don't provide such materials, you're wasting your time as well as that of your listeners.

Devoting careful thought to how you will use your supporting materials before you assemble your speech will pay off in efficient use of your preparation time, in confidence that your ideas are well supported, and in self-assurance when you approach the audience. This chapter seeks to provide some of the critical thinking skills you need to use supporting materials to earn audience acceptance of your ideas. First, we'll examine the functions and forms of supporting materials. Then, we'll suggest some ways of using these materials.

FUNCTIONS OF SUPPORTING MATERIALS

As you choose supporting materials for your speech, or as you listen to others speak, you should be conscious of how the supporting material clarifies, amplifies, and strengthens the ideas. Examples and statistics are especially helpful in clarifying ideas. These materials allow you to present information that simplifies an idea for an audience. Such simplification is especially useful when your listeners have little background or knowledge about the topic or when the subject matter is complex.

When your audience has only minimal knowledge of a concept, you should use comparisons, illustrations, and statistical magnitudes and trends to help you amplify the idea. These forms of support expand on your idea so that your audience can more easily comprehend and examine the concept.

To strengthen or lend credibility to a point, you can use factual illustrations, specific instances, statistics, and testimony. These forms strengthen the idea by making it vivid and believable.

While there is no absolute rule about how each kind of supporting material functions, there is general agreement about what supporting materials accomplish in your speech. Here are some guidelines for choosing your supporting materials:

1. *Complex and abstract ideas benefit from the use of specific information.* Use examples (illustrations, narratives, or specific instances) to clarify complex or abstract ideas. Compare the relationship of subatomic particles to balls on a billiard table, for instance. Specific examples (illustrations, narratives, or specific instances) provide more vivid details and make ideas more immediate. Thus, they can stimulate your listeners' enthusiasm for complex or abstract material.

2. *If your idea is controversial or if members of your audience are hostile, use supporting material such as statistics and testimony.* These forms of supporting material are generally regarded as highly rational and credible, so they work well with controversial topics or hostile listeners. If you are trying to get management to accept a union, for example, you will certainly need credible supporting material. When there is disagreement among experts on the issue, you will need an abundance of supporting material.

3. *Supporting materials can enhance your credibility as a speaker.* While your listeners may question your ability to understand the complex nature of the International Monetary Fund, they will respect authorities on the subject. They

will also probably be reluctant to question supporting material such as statistical information. You should always use supporting materials when you are not an expert or when your status is lower than that of your listeners.

4. *Supporting materials provide audience members with ammunition for later discussions.* When you ask for a raise, you are more likely to get it by providing information about your job performance. Your supervisor can use this information in defending your raise to others. If you are asking your listeners to make sacrifices or to accept ideas that are unfamiliar to them, use plenty of supporting material. It provides the reassurance they need to take a risk and embrace a new thought.

5. *Generally, examples create human interest, while statistics provide reasonable proof.* Listeners tend to respond subjectively to narratives. On the other hand, their response to statistics is often more detached and objective. In a speech on street children in Brasilia, you would establish the significance of the problem by providing statistics. But, you would involve your listeners by telling them about the danger and hunger suffered by Emilio, who lives on the streets.

Web Exploration
For an example of how to use supporting materials go to
http://awl.com/german

FORMS OF SUPPORTING MATERIALS

The supporting materials used to clarify, amplify, or strengthen your ideas fall into four categories: (1) comparisons and contrasts, (2) examples, (3) statistics, and (4) testimony (see Figure 7.1).

SPEAKING OF . . . *Skills*
Choosing Supporting Materials

Recent research compared qualitative and quantitative supporting material. Qualitative supporting material includes examples, anecdotes, and analogies such as "a friend of mine was in a car crash and a seatbelt saved her." Quantitative supporting materials are statistical or numerical information such as "a recent investigation found that people are 50% more likely to be injured if they are not wearing a seatbelt."

The research found that both qualitative and quantitative supporting material are equally effective in changing attitudes initially. However, qualitative supporting materials worked much better over time. There are two reasons that qualitative supporting materials strengthen long-term attitude change:

1. Qualitative supporting materials are more vivid and the impact of vivid images is greater than that of numbers.
2. We can more easily remember qualitative supporting materials than numerical information.

See: Dean C. Kozoleas, "A Comparison of the Persuasive Effectiveness of Qualitative versus Quantitative Evidence," *Communication Quarterly*, 41 (1993): 40–50.

FIGURE 7.1 The Forms of Supporting Materials

The supporting materials used to clarify, amplify, or justify your central ideas or claims are comparison and contrast, examples, statistics, and testimony. What should you consider as you choose supporting material?

Comparisons and Contrasts

Comparisons and contrasts are useful verbal devices to clarify ideas—to make them distinctive and focused. Pointing out similarities and differences helps listeners comprehend your ideas and opinions.

Comparisons **Comparisons** connect something already known or believed with ideas a speaker wishes to have understood or accepted. Comparisons, therefore, stress similarities; they create analogies. During the darkest days of the Civil War, when critics attacked his administration's policies, President Lincoln answered them by comparing the plight of the government with that of the famous tightrope walker, Blondin, attempting to cross Niagara Falls:

> *Gentlemen, I want you to suppose a case for a moment. Suppose that all the property you were worth was in gold, and you had put it in the hands of Blondin, the famous ropewalker, to carry across the Niagara Falls on a tightrope. Would you shake the rope while he was passing over it, or keep shouting to him, "Blondin, stoop a little more! Go a little faster!"? No, I am sure you would not. You would hold your breath as well as your tongue, and keep your hands off until he was safely over. Now the government is in the same situation. It is carrying an immense weight across a stormy ocean. Untold treasures are in its hands. It is doing the best it can. Don't badger it! Just keep still, and it will get you safely over.*

With this example, Lincoln created an analogy between the U.S. government and the tightrope walker Blondin. The similarities developed in the story made it easier for Lincoln's listeners to understand how critics were endangering the nation while it was at war.

Contrasts **Contrasts** help clarify complex situations and processes by focusing on differences. A speaker explaining arena football would want to contrast it with the more familiar rules governing interscholastic football. To clarify the severity of the 1999 drought in the East, the news networks contrasted average rainfall for normal summers with the current rainfall.

Contrasts can be used not only to clarify unfamiliar or complex problems, but also to strengthen the arguments that you wish to advance. A student speaker argued that regulations governing ocean vessels should be strictly enforced. Explaining the reasons for the huge federal fine against Royal Caribbean Cruise Lines in July 1999, she said: "While crew members wore 'Save the Whales' buttons, ships discharged hazardous chemicals into their ocean wakes." This speaker brought the issue of enforcement into sharp focus by stressing the contradictions in an actual instance. Contrasts can cut to the heart of issues quickly and dramatically.

In another case, H. Ross Perot spoke at the Reform Party Nominating Convention in 1996. He used this contrast to show why private enterprise works better than government: "In business, you can promote people based on their performance. In politics, you get promoted based on your acting ability."[1]

Perot's contrast is startling, but serves as clear support for his central idea that a business leader should be the next president of the United States. Helping your listeners reason along with you by visualizing differences is an excellent strategy for getting them to accept your ideas.

Comparisons and Contrasts Used in Combination   You can use comparisons and contrasts together to double their impact on your audience. For example, a student speaker focused on the messages in cartoons. To help his listeners understand how cartoons provide commentary, he compared and contrasted *Rocky and Bullwinkle* with *Beavis and Butthead*. He said:

> *Both cartoons have stirred up considerable public controversy. In the 1960s, some people boycotted* Rocky and Bullwinkle *just as some refuse to watch* Beavis and Butthead *today. There are major differences, however.* Rocky and Bullwinkle *episodes pitted the pair against Boris and Natasha, mimicking the Cold War conflict between the United States and the Soviet Union.* Beavis and Butthead, *on the other hand, avoid political commentary while focusing on the struggle of the main characters with adolescence.*

Whenever using comparisons and contrasts, try to make sure that at least one of the items is familiar to listeners. Comparing arena football and interscholastic football will make no sense to an Irish fan, who probably doesn't know anything about either one. You'd have to compare and contrast arena football and European soccer to clarify the arena game for her.

Examples

Examples can be powerful ways to involve an audience in your topic because they make abstract or general ideas easier to comprehend. If the example describes a concept, condition, or circumstance, it's called an **illustration;** if it's in story form, it's a **narrative.** A list of undeveloped illustrations are **specific instances.**

Hypothetical examples are made up. **Factual examples** (or real examples) are recitations of events that actually happened or persons, places, and things that actually exist. If you were giving a speech on why homeowners should move into apartments, you might narrate a "typical" homeowner's day: a leaky faucet to fix, a lawn to mow, real estate taxes to pay, and a neighbor's dog to chase out of the flower garden. Although not all of these events occurred in the same day, asking listeners to imagine what life would be like if they did would help you convey the carefree life of an apartment dweller.

For many audiences, fact-based examples are more potent. President Ronald Reagan was famous for his reliance on homey little narratives. Many other speakers have been equally successful with this type of supporting material. For instance, Sue Suter used her own life experiences as a woman with a disability to argue for changing the lives of women. To other examples she added this one to clinch her case: "It was not so long ago that stories filtered from our own Illinois School for the Deaf about a young deaf girl who asked a hearing dorm counselor if she was going to die soon. She was nearing graduation, and she had only seen a few deaf adults. What happened to the others?"[2] Suter continued her speech, pointing to the importance of offering women with disabilities the same chances as their non-disabled sisters, even if doing so meant rocking the boat.

While some speakers glean examples from their own lives, others illustrate ideas with the lives of others. Minnesota Governor Jesse Ventura advocated extending rights to gay partners with this example: "I have two friends who have been together for forty-one years. If one of them becomes sick, the other one is not even allowed to be at the bedside. I don't believe government should be so hostile, so mean-spirited. . . . Love is bigger than government."[3] Notice how Ventura drew his conclusion immediately after the example. This helps listeners to grasp the point of the example, strengthening your argument.

Specific instances are undeveloped illustrations or examples. Usually they are grouped together or listed one after another to drive the speaker's point home. They're undeveloped because their power comes from cumulative effect rather than vivid detail. You can use a single specific instance if you only need a quick example, for instance: "You're all familiar with the windows in this classroom, but you might not have noticed their actual construction. I want to talk about those windows— those double-glazed, low-emissivity, gas-filled windows—and how the use of such windows contributes to reduced energy consumption on campus and in your life."

More often, though, speakers pile up specific instances to help establish a point. In the famous passage in his declaration of war, President Franklin Delano Roosevelt listed the nations attacked by the Japanese Imperial forces. More recently, Mary Fisher spoke at the 1996 Republican National Convention about AIDS. She said to the delegates: "[T]he AIDS virus is not a political creature. It does not care whether you are Democrat or Republican, it does not ask whether you are Black or White, male or female, gay or straight, young or old." She continued by adding details to the series of specific instances:

> *Tonight, I represent an AIDS community whose members have been reluctantly drawn from every segment of American society. Though I am White, and a mother, I am one with a Black infant struggling with tubes in a Philadelphia hospital. Though I am female, and contracted this disease in marriage, and enjoy the warm support of my family, I am one with the lonely gay man sheltering a flickering candle from the cold wind of his family's rejection.*[4]

With these accumulated instances, Fisher demonstrated to her listeners the impact of the disease on all Americans.

Web Exploration

For the full text of this speech go to http://awl.com/german

Choosing Examples When selecting illustrations, narratives, and specific instances, whether hypothetical or factual, you should keep three considerations in mind:

1. *Is the example relevant?* If the connection is vague, it won't accomplish its goal. If your hypothetical story about a spring break road trip is fun to listen to but not related to your speech on saving the Florida everglades, you're in trouble!

2. *Is it a fair example?* An audience can be quick to notice unusual circumstances in an illustration or story; exceptional cases are seldom convincing. Having parachutists landing in the Wal-Mart parking lot to change a flat tire in your story, for example, would stretch the credulity of your listeners.

3. *Is it vivid and impressive in detail?* Be sure your extended examples are pointed and visual. When a student argued for more humane treatment of slaughter animals, he described the procedures at a local auction barn, traced typical routes to processing plants, and detailed the handling of animals in the holding pens. This example was specific and detailed enough to convince listeners that there was cause for change.

Statistics

Statistics are numbers that show relationships between or among phenomena—relationships that can emphasize size or magnitude, describe subclasses or parts (segments), or establish trends. By reducing large masses of information into generalized categories, statistics clarify situations, substantiate potentially disputable central ideas, and make complex aspects of the world clear to your listeners.

Magnitudes We often use statistics to describe a situation or to sketch its scope or seriousness; that is, its size or **magnitude.** The effect on listeners can be especially strong if one statistical description of the size of a problem is piled up on others. Notice how former U.S. Surgeon General Antonia Novello used multiple statistical descriptions of magnitude while urging citizens to think of violence as a community health problem:

Violence is a legitimate public health concern. It is your challenge—and mine. My friends, it is no small problem that: homicidal violence is now the leading cause of death among our youth; and that, in fact, every 14 hours a child younger than 5 is murdered. Firearms are now involved in one in every four deaths among 15- to 24-year-olds. And it is no small problem that domestic violence— along with child abuse and the abuse of the elderly—is found in every community and one-fourth of all American families; and [among] up to six often-married couples. Domestic violence today is the second most common cause of injury to women overall, and the leading cause of injuries to women ages 15 to 44. It is more common than automobile accidents, muggings, and rapes combined.[5]

Not all uses of magnitudes, of course, need such piling up of instances. Simple, hard-hitting magnitudes sometimes work even better. For example, Brenda Theriault of the University of Maine, arguing that there is "very little nutritional value in a hamburger, chocolate shake, and fries," simply noted that "of the 1,123 calories in this meal, there are 15 calories of carbohydrates, 35 calories of protein, and 1,073 calories of fat."[6] These were all the numbers the listeners needed in order to understand the nutrition in a typical fast-food meal.

Segments Statistics used to isolate the parts of a problem or to show aspects of a problem caused by separate factors, parts, or aspects are statistical **segments.** In discussing the sources of income for a college or university, for example, you'd probably segment the income by percentages coming from tuition and fees, state and federal money, gifts and contributions, special fees such as tickets, and miscellaneous sources. Then you'd be in a position to talk reasonably about next year's proposed tuition hike. A student speaker used survey results in this fashion to show how people shop on the World Wide Web:

> *In 1996, people spent a total of $518 million dollars on products and services they found via the Web. Computer products sales comprised 27 percent of this total and travel another 24.3 percent, making up over half of all Web sales. The remainder of the sales is divided almost equally among adult entertainment, general entertainment, food/drink, gifts/flowers, and apparel. This year Web sales are expected to set new records.[7]*

As this example illustrates, the most important value of statistics doesn't lie in the numbers themselves but in how you interpret and use them. In using statistical data, always answer the question, "What do these numbers mean or demonstrate?" In this case, it's clear that computer products and travel dominate Web site sales.

Web Exploration
For examples of how to use magnitudes, segments, and trends go to
http://awl.com/german

Trends Statistics often are used to point out **trends,** or indicators that tell us about the past, the present, and the future. The comparison of statistical data across time allows you to say that a particular phenomenon is increasing or decreasing (see Table 7.1). If you were arguing for stricter controls on chewing tobacco, you might cite Federal Trade Commission statistics revealing that chewing tobacco sales have increased steadily. Over the ten-year period from 1985 to 1995, revenues grew by more than $100 million annually, exceeding $1.7 billion in 1995.[8] This upward trend suggests that something should be done to control smokeless tobacco. You could

TABLE 7.1 Types of Statistics

In a speech to inform, a speaker might use three types of statistics to describe students at Central University. What other forms of supporting material could complement these numbers?

Magnitudes	Segments	Trends
"Three fourths of all Central University students come from the state."	"Sixty percent of all Central University students major in business: 25 percent are humanities majors; the remaining 15 percent are in fine arts."	"Since 1975, enrollment at Central University has increased by 90 percent every five years."

SPEAKING OF . . . *Ethics*
The Numbers Game

The rise of science in this century has been accompanied by the rise of numerical data—and its public exhibition. By now you've been told by one poll that the public favors a liberalization of abortion laws two-to-one but by another poll that the public favors tightening abortion laws by an equal percentage. You know that four out of five dentists surveyed recommend a particular brand of toothpaste. You've heard that a brand of cigarettes has the lowest level of tar and nicotine—from more than one manufacturer. As both listener and speaker, you have to make some ethical calls when encountering such data:

1. Contradictory polls such as the ones on abortion often result when questions are asked in slanted ways. "Do parents have the right to know when their underaged kids seek a dangerous abortion?" tends to encourage a positive answer, while "Ought women have the right to control their own bodies without external interference from others?" also encourages a positive answer—but one in favor of a very different public policy than the first. Questions can be loaded in favor of opposing public policies. You're wise to consider the actual questions when evaluating poll results.
2. Who were those "four out of five dentists surveyed"? Is it moral to cite statistics without reviewing how they were gathered and calculated?
3. If your favorite brand of cigarettes is one of five brands that all have the same low tar and nicotine content, technically, of course, yours has the lowest—and so do the other four brands. Is it moral, however, to claim your brand is "the lowest" or must you say that it is "one of the lowest"?

It's easy to fiddle with numbers: to round up or down, to compare only parts rather than wholes, to ignore key details that would properly contextualize information for listeners. It's easy, but if you play fast and loose with numbers, you might get caught. Learn to play the numbers game honestly so as to protect your reputation.

make your case even stronger by citing a corresponding upward trend in cancers of the lips, gums, and tongue.

An interesting use of a trend argument is found in testimony given to the U.S. House Subcommittee on Human Resources by Hortense Hunn, Executive Director of the California Preschool Services Department in San Bernardino County. She laid out what she considered to be a trend in spending on the Head Start program:

> There are numerous official fact sheets documenting Head Start's growth and development since its inception in 1965. I do not intend to reiterate the litany of glowing statistics which are readily available; suffice it to say that the National Head Start Program has grown from an "embryonic" program enrolling 561,000 children for about $96 million in the summer of 1965 to an "adolescent" program serving over 721,000 children and families for $1.7 billion in this year."[9]

Notice the cleverness with which Hunn framed her argument: she talked about "glowing statistics" in order to dispose her audience to see them favorably; she used metaphors of maturation ("embryonic," "adolescent") to subtly project the need for further growth in Head Start (to "adulthood"); and she emphasized Head Start's direct service to children rather than its general family-services orientation, given that appeals to children usually are successful with listeners.

Using Statistics When you use statistics to indicate magnitude, to split phenomena into segments, or to describe trends, you can help your listeners by softening the numbers. Four strategies you can use are:

1. *Translate difficult-to-comprehend numbers into more understandable terms.* In a speech on the mounting problem of solid waste, Carl Hall illustrated the immensity of 130 million tons of garbage by explaining that trucks loaded with that amount would extend from coast to coast three abreast.[10]

2. *Don't be afraid to round off complicated numbers.* "Nearly 400,000" is easier for listeners to comprehend than "396,456"; "just over 33 percent" or, better yet, "approximately one third" is preferable to "33.4 percent."

Statistical supporting material can be enhanced when it is represented visually. Your audience can see the relationships you are talking about.

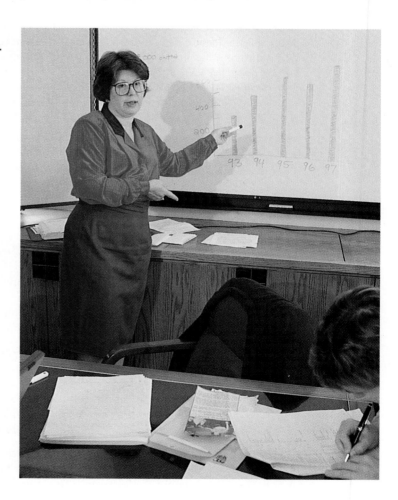

3. *Use visual materials to clarify statistics whenever possible.* Use a computer-generated graph; hand out a photocopied sheet of numbers; prepare a chart in advance. Such aids will allow you to concentrate on explaining the significance of the numbers rather than on making sure the audience hears and remembers them.

4. *Use statistics fairly.* Arguing that professional women's salaries increased 12.4 percent last year may sound impressive to listeners until they realize that women are still paid less than men for equivalent work. In other words, provide fair contexts for your numerical data and comparisons.

Testimony

When you cite the opinions or conclusions of others, you're using **testimony.** Sometimes testimony merely adds weight or impressiveness to an idea, as when you quote Mahatma Gandhi or Mother Teresa. At other times, it lends credibility to an assertion, especially when it comes from expert witnesses. When Janice Payan addressed the Adelante Mujer Conference, she used testimony in another way. She cited her favorite poem as a source of inspiration for her listeners. She urged them to seek success as she quoted the poet: "I wish someone had taught me long ago, How to touch mountains."[11]

Testimony should relate to the ideas you are discussing and should strengthen them. When you use quotations in your speech, they should accomplish more than simply amplifying or illustrating an idea.

Testimony also should satisfy four more specific criteria:

1. *The person quoted should be qualified, by training and experience, to speak on the topic being discussed.* Athletes are more credible talking about sports equipment or exercise programs than they are endorsing breakfast food or local furniture stores.

2. *Whenever possible, the authority's statement should be based on firsthand knowledge.* A Florida farmer is not an authority on an Idaho drought unless he or she has personally observed the conditions. Veterinarians aren't usually experts on human diseases and Hollywood stars may not know much about scriptwriting.

3. *The judgment expressed shouldn't be unduly influenced by personal interest.* Asking a political opponent to comment on the current president's performance will likely yield a self-interested answer.

4. *Your listeners should perceive the person quoted to be an actual authority.* An archbishop may be accepted as an authority by a Roman Catholic audience but perhaps not by Protestant or Hindu listeners. When citing testimony, don't use big names simply because they're well known. The best testimony comes from subject-matter experts whose qualifications your listeners recognize.

Finally, always acknowledge the source of an idea or particular phrasing. Avoid **plagiarism**—claiming someone else's ideas, information, or phraseology as your own. Plagiarism is stealing. Give your source credit for the material, and give yourself credit for having taken the time to do the research. (See "Using Source Material Responsibly" in Chapter 6.)

CRITICAL THINKING AND THE USE OF SUPPORTING MATERIALS

Most of us, with some effort, can gather supporting materials. The hard part is using those materials well. The effective use of supporting materials is an exercise in **critical thinking**—assessing the reasonableness of the connections between your assertions and your supporting materials. As you prepare your speeches, or when you listen to the speeches of others, you should practice critical thinking. You can start by asking yourself questions such as:

1. *Is the speaker providing supporting material or is the idea simply asserted?* An **assertion** is a statement made without corroborating support. For example, you could assert that "Americans are now more dependent than ever before on

TABLE 7.2   Checklist for Supporting Materials

You should evaluate your supporting materials when you plan your speeches. Answer the questions on this checklist as you plan your supporting materials.

Comparisons and Contrasts

_____ 1. Is at least one of the items in a comparison or contrast familiar to my listeners?

_____ 2. Is the basis of the comparison clear?

_____ 3. Is the contrast distinct enough?

Examples

_____ 1. Is the illustration or narrative clearly related to the idea it's intended to support?

_____ 2. Is the example fair?

_____ 3. Is the illustration or narrative vivid and adequately detailed?

Statistics

_____ 1. Are my statistics easy to understand?

_____ 2. Have I rounded off complicated numbers?

_____ 3. Should I use visual materials to clarify complicated numbers?

_____ 4. Am I using statistics fairly?

Testimony

_____ 1. Is the authority qualified to speak on the topic being discussed?

_____ 2. Is the authority's statement based on firsthand knowledge?

_____ 3. Is the authority's opinion subject to personal influence or bias?

_____ 4. Will my listeners accept this person as an authority?

foreign sources of oil." A careful listener, however, will want to know why you made this statement. Do you have statistics to show a trend of increasing dependence on foreign oil? Did an expert reach this conclusion?

2. *Is a qualified source of the supporting material cited?* Some speakers will provide statistics and examples but fail to tell you whether they obtained those facts from a reliable source. Listen for sources. A speaker who lists *Webster's Dictionary* as the source of a definition of *habeas corpus* probably hasn't done enough research. *Black's Law Dictionary* is a more credible source.

3. *Is the supporting material offered adequate?* Has the speaker given enough support for the main idea? Perhaps the speaker has found an isolated fact or statistic or opinion. Demand more than a single piece of supporting material, especially if the ideas are controversial or unusual. Scientists arguing for the existence of life on Mars provide analysis of mineral data and high-tech photography to reveal microfossils of once-living organisms. However, until additional supporting material is available, some skeptics aren't convinced that life once existed on Earth's next-door neighbor.

4. *Is the supporting material varied?* Strong use of supporting material includes variety. You may find an article that says everything you want, but you shouldn't stop there. Find more support for your ideas. In your speech, you will want to cite a variety of evidence such as testimony, examples, and statistics. Active listeners will concentrate on the kinds of supporting material you use. So ask yourself if you are offering enough varied supporting material for reasonable acceptance of your ideas.

5. *Does the material cited support the speaker's ideas?* Sometimes we get so caught up in a narrative that we forget to consider the point of it. Or, a rush of statistics will leave us gasping. Don't forget to question the link between the statistics and the ideas of the speech. For example, a speaker who cites a 10 percent increase in Ford truck sales and concludes that the auto industry is healthy may be gravely mistaken. Ford truck sales are only one segment of a much larger industry.

By asking yourself if the supporting materials are present, well qualified, adequate, varied, and relevant, you'll be thinking critically about ideas rather than just blindly accepting them. As a speaker, you should ask these questions as you prepare your speech. As a listener, you should concentrate on how the speaker is using supporting materials. Test supporting materials to be sure that they contribute to the development of ideas. The two outlines that follow illustrate how supporting materials can be used.

SAMPLE OUTLINE FOR AN INFORMATIVE SPEECH

In the outline, note how the speaker has combined verbal and visual material to establish and develop the central idea. In this speech, the supporting material is used to amplify the idea.

How We Breathe

The speaker establishes the comparison, an analogy, immediately upon starting the speech.

I. The human breathing mechanism may be likened to a bellows, which expands to admit air and contracts to expel it.
  A. When we inhale, two things happen.
    1. Muscles attached to the collarbone and shoulder bones pull upward and slightly outward.
    2. Muscles in the abdominal wall relax, allowing the diaphragm—a sheet of muscle and tendon lying immediately below the lungs—to fall.

The speaker might point to parts of the body as they're mentioned—collarbone, shoulder bones, abdominal wall, diaphragm.

  B. This permits the spongy, porous lungs to expand.
    1. A vacuum is created.
    2. Air rushes in.
  C. When we exhale, two things happen.
    1. Gravity causes the rib cage to move downward.
    2. Muscles in the abdominal wall contract, squeezing the diaphragm upward.

An explanation reveals the function of the muscles.

  D. The space available to the lungs is thus reduced.
    1. The lungs are squeezed.
    2. Air is emitted.
  E. The similarity between the breathing mechanism and a bellows is represented in this diagram:
    [Show "How We Breathe" diagram.]

Demonstrative movements also would be appreciated by the audience: a lifting of the shoulders and chest cavity when talking about inhalation, a dropping of the rib cage and abdominal wall when describing exhalation.

II. In summary, then, to remember how the human breathing mechanism works, think of a bellows.
  A. Just as increasing the size of the bellows bag allows air to rush in, so increasing the space available to the lungs allows them to admit air.
  B. Just as squeezing the bellows bag forces air out, so contracting the space the lungs can occupy forces air to be emitted.

The summary compares a bellows to how the lungs work.

SAMPLE OUTLINE FOR A PROBLEM-SOLUTION SPEECH

Study the following outline. Notice that a variety of supporting materials are used to strengthen each of the points in the speech. Although the proof of a single point may not require as many different supporting materials as are used in this outline, the variety of support shows how a number of different forms can be comined in a speech.

The Heartbreak of Childhood Obesity

I. Childhood obesity is an increasing problem in our society.
  A. Michelle is a typical American child—15% overweight.

This speech starts with an illustration and trend statistics.

B. U.S. Department of Health and Human Services survey reveals a 54% increase in childhood obesity between 1963 and 1993.

C. The prediction for the future is even more bleak.

D. After defining the nature of obesity, let's examine the causes of obesity in children, and investigate some solutions we can implement.

II. Obesity is defined as a positive energy balance.

A. This means that more energy is conserved than expended.

B. Over time, the excess energy is stored by the body in fat cells.

C. Approximately every 2500 extra calories become an extra pound of body weight.

III. There are three primary causes for childhood obesity.

A. Some children inherit the tendency to acquire extra weight.

1. Parents who are obese tend to have children who are also obese.

2. Experiments with mice have located genetic triggers for overeating.

3. The genetic predisposition to gain extra weight is a contributing factor in childhood obesity, according to experts.

B. Eating style also contributes to obesity.

1. Dr. Daniel A. Kirschenbaum, who specializes in childhood obesity, reports that obese children typically show a "high-density" eating style.

2. A "high-density" eating style refers to both the quantity and frequency of eating among children.

3. High-density eating is a behavior that contributes to obesity.

4. Emotional stress may trigger high-density eating style.

C. Television viewing is also a culprit among obese children.

1. Dr. Steven Gortmaker of Harvard University says that many children watch over 30 hours of television weekly.

2. Inactivity, including television watching, results in a positive energy balance and, over time, leads to obesity.

3. In addition, Dr. William Dietz of Tufts University notes that children's eating habits are influenced by television commercials for food high in sugar and fat.

IV. You can control weight gain in children with four steps.

A. Don't assume the child will grow out of it.

1. If your family has a history of weight problems, be alert for them in your children.

2. Four out of five children can be helped if the problem is dealt with immediately.

3. Dealing with weight gain immediately will prevent psychological and medical problems later.

An explanation clarifies what is meant by obesity.

The problem of obesity is developed as a three-part explanation.

To develop the problem, the speaker provides a comparison with lab mice, testimony of Dr. Kirschenbaum and Dr. Dietz, an explanation of high-density eating style, and magnitude statistics.

In the solution section, the speaker uses magnitude statistics, explanations, testimony, segment statistics, and examples.

B. Monitor mealtimes.
  1. To limit high-density eating style, do not permit between-meal snacks.
  2. Teaching children to consume food at a slower pace, according to Dr. William Johnson and Dr. Peter Stalonas, is also helpful.
  3. It is easier on the child if the entire family switches to a low-fat diet.
C. Substitute other activities for television viewing.
  1. Over 50% of obesity problems in children could be controlled more effectively if parents simply turned off the television set.
  2. Encourage activity in the child.
    a. Enroll the child in athletic activities like swimming or soccer.
    b. Encourage walking to and from school; just a half hour of walking per day can correct a positive energy balance.
D. Join a support group for the parents of obese children.
  1. Contact the World Service Office of Overeaters Anonymous.
  2. Speak to a representative of your local community service organization.
V. Now that you understand the causes of childhood obesity and some of the solutions, it's time to act.
A. Think about the consequences if you don't act now.
  1. Obesity in childhood predisposes a person to a lifetime of medical and psychological trouble.
  2. Obesity contributes to 90% of the cases of Type II diabetes in later life; over half of the cases of cardiovascular disease; and immeasurable emotional distress.
B. According to Pam Webber of Overeaters Anonymous: "It's better to risk hurting a child's feelings today, than let them live a lifetime of unhappiness."
C. Remember Michelle? If her parents begin now, they can spare Michelle the bleak future faced by too many of our overweight American children.

The conclusion to the speech offers segment statistics and testimony, plus a reference to the introductory illustration.

ASSESSING YOUR PROGRESS

Chapter Summary

1. Supporting materials clarify, amplify, or strengthen the speaker's ideas.
2. Comparisons and contrasts point out similarities and differences between things.

3. Examples are illustrations, narratives, or specific instances that provide specific details about ideas or statements you want listeners to accept.

4. Illustrations are detailed examples; narratives are examples in story form; and specific instances are clusters of undeveloped examples. They can be hypothetical (fictional) or factual (real).

5. Statistics are numbers that show relationships between or among phenomena. Some emphasize size or magnitude; some describe subclasses or segments; and some establish trends or directions over time.

6. Testimony comes from the opinions or conclusions of credible persons.

7. To effectively use forms of support, you must learn critical thinking skills to: (a) identify assertions; (b) listen for reliable sources; (c) demand adequate support for ideas; (d) offer varied supporting materials; and, (e) understand the relevance of supporting materials to ideas.

Key Terms

assertion (p. 118)

comparisons (p. 110)

contrasts (p. 110)

critical thinking (p. 118)

factual (real) examples (p. 111)

hypothetical examples (p. 111)

illustration (p. 111)

magnitudes (p. 113)

narrative (p. 111)

plagiarism (p. 117)

segments (p. 114)

specific instances (p. 111)

statistics (p. 113)

testimony (p. 117)

trends (p. 114)

Assessment Activities

1. Bring a local or national newspaper to class. Choose several articles and locate the kinds of supporting material used in each article. Share your results with class members. Ask the following questions about the supporting material you've discovered: Is it adequate? Does it reveal the reporter's biases? What additional support is required to convince you?

2. Amplify each of the following statements with a comparison/contrast, an example, statistics, and testimony. Share your results with your classmates. Evaluate the effectiveness of each form of supporting material. Which support is most involving for listeners? Which is most convincing? Which establishes the scope of the idea?

   a. Abraham Lincoln was our greatest president.

   b. Most Americans consume too much processed sugar.

   c. May is the best month for vacationing.

   d. The combustion engine changed human life more than any other invention in history.

   e. Without practical experience, education is unfinished.

 Surfing the Web

1. The federal government compiles data on hundreds of topics. Check the variety of statistical information you can obtain from government sources. Use your search engine to locate the GAO (Government Accounting Office) reports or consult http://lib-www.ucr.edu/govpub/ for a database of federal, state, and local government resources that can be accessed by subject, keyword, or title.

2. Spice up your speeches with quotations from experts and celebrities. Search for specific persons such as David Letterman, Maya Angelou, Groucho Marx, and Margaret Atwood. You can also search for compilations of quotations.

3. Archives for social science data are readily available online. Two excellent starting points are the Smithsonian Institution Research Information Web site and the Interuniversity Consortium for Political and Social Research at the University of Michigan.

References

1. H. Ross Perot, CNN Coverage of the Reform Party Nominating Convention, Long Beach, CA (August 11, 1996).

2. Sue Suter, "Women with Disabilities: How to Become a Boat Rocker in Life," Speech for Ethics in Rehabilitation Conference, Dunedin, New Zealand, 16 August 1993. Located at http://gos.sbc.edu/s/suter3.html.

3. Jesse Ventura with Jay Waler, Jessica Allen, and Bill Adler, *The Wit and Wisdom of Jesse 'the Body' ('the Mind') Ventura* (New York: Quill Books, 1999).

4. Mary Fisher, "A Whisper of AIDS," reprinted in *Women's Voices in Our Time,* edited by Victoria L. DeFrancisco and Marvin D. Jensen (Prospect Heights, IL: Waveland Press, 1994).

5. Antonia Novello, "Your Parents, Your Community—Without Caring There Is No Hope," *Vital Speeches of the Day,* 59 (15 July 1993): 591.

6. Brenda Theriault, "Fast Foods," Speech given at the University of Maine, Spring 1992.

7. John Simons, "The Web's Dirty Secret," *U.S. News & World Report,* 121 (19 August 1996): 51.

8. Federal Trade Commission, *1997 Smokeless Tobacco Report.* Available at: http://www.ftc.gov/bcp/reports/smokeless97.htm.

9. Hortense Hunn, "Testimony Before House," 8 April 1993. *Oversight Hearing Regarding the Head Start Program,* House of Representatives Hearing, 103rd Congress (Washington, D.C.: U.S. Government Printing Office, 1993), 88.

10. Carl Hall, "A Heap of Trouble," *Winning Orations,* 1977.

11. Janice Payan, "Opportunities for Hispanic Women: It's Up to Us," *Vital Speeches of the Day,* 56 (1 September 1990): 591.

Organizing and Outlining Your Speech

DEVELOPING YOUR SPEECH PLAN

SPEECH-CENTERED PATTERNS OF
ORGANIZATION

AUDIENCE-CENTERED PATTERNS OF
ORGANIZATION

OUTLINING YOUR SPEECH

 SPEAKING OF . . . SKILLS: MEMORY AND
ORGANIZATION

ASSESSING YOUR PROGRESS

Think of the last shopping trip you made for groceries. How did you do it? Did you wander aimlessly around the store looking for something that you might need? If you shop this way, you probably get home and discover that you forgot something important. Giving a speech is somewhat like a shopping trip. If you don't plan and organize it, you're undoubtedly going to leave out something important. Like an efficient shopper, you can organize your speaking so that both you and your listener get the most out of it. We'll discuss how to choose the pattern of organization and outline your speech. Let's begin with developing a speech plan.

DEVELOPING YOUR SPEECH PLAN

Approaching your speech in an organized manner is important for several reasons. Just as you waste time wandering around a store if you don't have a shopping list, you appear to be confused if you give a disorganized speech. The result can be chaotic. There are five reasons to organize your speeches:

1. *Your listeners learn more from an organized speech because there is an obvious pattern for categorizing the new material you present.* When you arrange the information, it's easier for them to learn it. So good organization leads to better comprehension.

2. *An organized speech is easier for you to present.* The ideas fit together more logically and even if you forget a phrase or two, the speech will still flow naturally because the ideas hold it together.

3. *You will appear more credible when you give an organized speech.* Your listeners will realize that you have prepared well and will be more likely to accept your expertise.

4. *Some evidence suggests that well-organized speeches are more persuasive.* You can see why—if listeners trust your preparation and don't have to strain to understand the ideas, they are more likely to be impressed by your message.

5. *Good organization lowers the frustration level for everyone—you and your listeners.* This is reason enough to practice developing clear and effective organization in your speaking.

Developing Your Central Idea

The first step in planning your organization is determining your central idea. As you may recall from Chapter 2, your central idea is a statement of your speech goal, developed when you blend your general purpose to inform or to persuade with your topic.

Phrasing a central idea is especially critical, because the words you select limit the focus of your speech and control your relationship with your audience. Your central idea determines the way you develop your whole talk—your main points, the information you include, the organization you follow, and the ways you link your points. For example, each of the following central ideas expresses a different focus and relationship with listeners:

"You can conserve energy by recycling aluminum cans, walking to classes, and using lower-wattage light bulbs at home."

"The development of the computer chip began twenty years ago and continues today."

"If our city builds a new parking garage, it will dangerously strain city finances."

These three central ideas establish very different parameters for developing a speech. The first offers three tangible actions a listener can take to save energy. The scope of the speech is limited to practical solutions. It also establishes listener involvement and responsibility in implementing the solution. The second topic, on the other hand, suggests a historical perspective that provides information and less directly involves the audience. Finally, the speaker who proposes the third topic is preparing to develop an argument.

In each case, the phrasing of the central idea determines how the topic will be approached and what will be the role of the listener. This, in turn, should help you determine which organizational pattern is best for your speech.

Choosing Your Organizational Plan

To help you further, here are some clear general guidelines for organizing your speech. After you have identified your central idea, ask these questions to determine what you're looking for in an organizational pattern:

1. *What structure is best suited to the ideas in my speech?* Your speech topic may offer natural groupings among ideas that will be easy for your listeners to recognize. For example, if your speech traces the Battle of Gettysburg day by day, it is probably organized by time. If, on the other hand, you are detailing the causes, symptoms, and cures for Lyme disease, your ideas fall into a causal pattern. And, a speech on the layout of your campus is clearly spatial. You should identify the configuration suggested by the ideas of your speech as you think about organizing your speech.

2. *What structure is best adapted to my audience's needs?* Keep your listeners in mind—what they know, expect, and need. If your listeners have never heard of bioremediation, then you need to develop your speech on this topic in a very different way than if they are environmental scientists. You can't ignore your listeners' need to process information efficiently. That means beginning with what they already know.

3. *How can I make the speech move steadily forward toward a satisfying finish?* Listeners need a sense of forward motion—of moving through a series of main points toward a clear destination. Backtracking slows down the momentum of the speech, giving it a stop-and-start progression rather than a smooth forward flow. You'll also enhance the sense of forward motion with internal summaries and forecasts, as well as transitions and physical movement to indicate progression.

Once you've planned your central idea and answered basic questions about the plan of your speech, you're ready to choose the type of arrangement. Often, your topic will determine the type of organization needed. Some topics require chronological order, while other topics can be organized in topical, spatial, or causal patterns. However, the needs of your audience may require a special pattern of organization adapted to them. We will discuss first some speech-centered types of organization. Then we'll consider some audience-centered patterns of organization.

SPEECH-CENTERED PATTERNS OF ORGANIZATION

Web Exploration
To further analyze different types of organization go to
http://awl.com/german

As we use the term here, **organization** is the order or sequence of ideas in a pattern that suggests their relationship to each other. There are four general categories of organization for speeches that arise from the demands of the topic: chronological, spatial, causal, and topical.

Chronological Patterns

Chronological patterns arrange ideas in a time sequence. When using a chronological sequence, you might relate events in the order they occurred or describe a process as it should be completed. You begin at one point in time and move forward or backward to some concluding point. For example, you might describe how to prepare an elegant cinnamon pear tart beginning with preparation of the crust and ending with baking instructions. The results wouldn't be the same if you presented the instructions in another order.

Where you begin and end will depend on your central idea. Suppose you wanted to trace the evolution of modern flight. You could start in 1903 with the Wright brothers or from Russia's launching of *Sputnik* in 1957. The beginning of the chronology depends on your goal. Are you trying to tell the whole story of aviation or the more specific story of space flight? Similarly, suppose you wanted to argue that children acquire vital language skills in the first months of their lives. You would need to begin tracing language acquisition even before the child's first vocalizations.

The following example traces the history of experts' advice to parents over the past century. Notice how time organizes the ideas in the speech:

I. Early in the twentieth century, experts began to focus on childhood as an important period of individual development.
   A. In 1914, books advised mothers to thwart bad habits like thumb sucking by pinning an infant's sleeves to the bed.
   B. During the Great Depression of the 1930s, the federal government developed welfare plans to aid children.

II. The baby boom years from 1940–1960 saw the rise of behaviorism.
   A. Behaviorist models using stimulus-response training were popular.
   B. In 1946, pediatrician Dr. Benjamin Spock published one of the most popular manuals for raising children, offering an alternative to behaviorist models.
   C. In 1952, French psychologist Jean Piaget identified distinct stages in the intellectual maturation of children.

III. More recently, advice to parents focuses on nurturing children to strengthen their emotional development.
   A. In 1969, English psychiatrist Dr. John Bowlby proved that babies seek out specific adults for protection.

B. In 1997, the Conference on Early Childhood Development and Learning drew attention to the crucial first years in a child's life.

Spatial Patterns

In **spatial patterns,** the major points of the speech are organized by their position, that is, their location or direction from each other. A speech on the movement of weather systems from the north to the south across the United States would fit such a pattern. If you conduct a tour of your campus or describe the constellations in the Southern Hemisphere, you would probably use a spatial pattern. Spatial patterns can trace ideas from east to west, top to bottom, left to right, or even from inside to outside. Consider how this example circles the globe:

    I. Volcanoes are one of the natural forces constantly at work changing the face of the earth.

   II. The sheer power and beauty of nature evident in volcanoes should motivate you to see them. Suppose you wanted to take trip to view volcanoes:

     A. Start at Mt. St. Helens in the state of Washington (1991 eruption).

     B. Journey to the Aleutian Islands off the Alaskan coast to Mt. Akutan (1990 eruption).

     C. Cross the Pacific to Japan to Mt. Asama (1991 eruption).

     D. Drop down to Sumatra to find Mt. Kerinci (1987 eruption).

     E. Head west to Zaire in Africa to Mt. Nyamuragira (1988 eruption).

     F. Then to Italy's Etna (1990 eruption), Iceland's Hekla (1991 eruption), and home again.

  III. A visit to any of these active volcanoes could be the trip of a lifetime.[1]

Causal Patterns

Causal patterns of speech organization show a relationship between causes and effects. Causal patterns assume that one event results from or causes another. This pattern of organization gives listeners a sense of coherence because ideas are developed in relationship to each other. Causal patterns may move in two directions: (a) from present causes to future effects or (b) from present conditions to their apparent causes.

When using a *cause-effect pattern,* you might point to the increasing cost of attending college, and then argue that one of the effects of increased costs is reduced enrollments. Or, using an *effect-cause pattern,* you could note that dropping college enrollments resulted, at least in part, from increasing costs. Compare the following two outlines:

    I. Colleges and universities across the United States are raising tuition.

   II. The effect of these tuition increases is to limit enrollments.

     A. Middle-income students are squeezed by tuition increases.

     B. Financially disadvantaged students often must drop out.

    I. Enrollments in U.S. colleges and universities have been steadily dropping since 1990.

   II. Tuition increases have caused limited access to higher education.

     A. Middle-income students are not able to afford additional tuition increases.

     B. Financially disadvantaged students are forced to choose employment over education.

Notice that the first outline uses a cause-effect pattern; the second uses an effect-cause pattern. Adapt your speech to the situation by beginning with ideas that are better known to audience members; then proceed to the lesser-known facets of the problem. Use cause-effect if listeners are better acquainted with the cause; use effect-cause if the opposite is true.

Topical Patterns

Some speeches on familiar topics are best organized in terms of subject-matter divisions that are easily recognized. Sports strategy is divided into offense and defense; kinds of courts into municipal, county, state, and federal jurisdictions; and types of trees into deciduous and evergreen categories. When you use a **topical pattern** of organization, you list aspects of persons, places, things, or processes. Occasionally, a speaker tries to list all aspects of the topic. More often, however, a partial listing of the primary or most interesting aspects is sufficient. For example, suppose you wanted to give a speech to a general audience about stress. The following outline shows how you could organize the speech topically:

    I. Symptoms of stress

     A. Recognizing stress

     B. Reacting to stress

   II. Types of stress inducers

     A. Physical stress

     B. Emotional stress

  III. Methods of stress reduction

     A. Relaxation techniques

     B. Meditation

     C. Exercise

Topical patterns are among the most popular and easiest to use. If you plan to list only certain aspects of the topic, take care to explain your choices early in your speech. If you don't talk about biofeedback as a means of reducing stress, you should tell your listeners. You might say, "I will focus on the three most common approaches to stress reduction and will present simple techniques that everyone can apply immediately."

The patterns of speech organization discussed so far—chronological, spatial, causal, and topical—are determined principally by the subject matter. While these patterns do not ignore the audience, it's the subject that usually suggests the pattern of organization.

AUDIENCE-CENTERED PATTERNS OF ORGANIZATION

At times, audience-oriented patterns of organization will more effectively arrange your material. These patterns often work well because they're based on the listeners' needs. You can ask several questions to determine if an audience-oriented pattern of organization will work for you:

✓ Can I introduce a new idea by comparing it to something my listeners already know?

✓ How would a person approach this idea for the first time?

✓ What are common, recurring questions about this topic?

✓ Am I presenting a solution to a problem?

✓ Can I eliminate all but one alternative solution to a question or problem?

If you've answered "yes" to any of these questions, you might consider organizing your speech based on your listener's needs.

We'll examine five audience-centered patterns of organization: familiarity-acceptance order, inquiry order, question-answer order, problem-solution order, and elimination order.

Familiarity-Acceptance Order

Familiarity-acceptance order begins with what the audience knows or believes (the familiar) and moves on to new or challenging ideas (the unfamiliar). In an informative speech on quarks, you can begin with what the audience already knows about molecules and then introduce the new information on the subatomic particles called quarks.

Familiarity-acceptance order is very well suited to persuasive speeches, especially if your listeners are skeptical or hostile. You can begin your speech by acknowledging values or ideas that are accepted by your listeners and then proceed to more controversial issues. When your reasoning is valid and your conclusions sound, your listeners will have difficulty rejecting your claim without denying the underlying facts or values that they already accept.

Here are the main points from a persuasive speech outline using familiarity-acceptance order:

I. How many of us here are married or plan on getting married sometime in the future?

II. Marriage is an important social institution because it publicly expresses the love and commitment of two people for each other.

III. Homosexual marriages should be allowed.

A. Public recognition would discourage discrimination and violence directed toward homosexuals.

B. Homosexuals would be allowed to participate in employee benefit plans now reserved for heterosexual married partners.

C. Legal sanctions involving spouses, such as property inheritance and hospital visitation, would become inclusive.

Even if you don't agree with the conclusions of this speaker, it is more difficult to reject the central idea of the speech because the speaker began with something you probably accept and then moved to the more controversial part of the speech.

Inquiry Order

Inquiry order provides a step-by-step explanation of how you acquired information or reached a conclusion. Often, scientists use this pattern as they carefully describe their research procedures in order to demonstrate the reliability of their findings. Similarly, if you want to persuade your neighbors to plant a new variety of oak tree, you could recount how you studied the varieties that seemed to be dying in your neighborhood, investigated possible choices, and searched for new varieties until the kind you now advocate emerged as the best.

Inquiry order has a double advantage. First, it displays all facts and possibilities for the audience. Second, it enables listeners to judge for themselves the worth of the information or policy being presented as it unfolds.

Question-Answer Order

Question-answer order raises and answers listeners' questions. First, you must determine which questions are most likely to arise in your listeners' minds. Then you need to develop your speech to answer each key question in a way that favors your conclusion. For example, when you buy a new car, you want to know about its principal features, the available options, its gas mileage, and its cost. When first learning about a new bond issue, listeners wonder how it will affect their taxes or government services. By structuring your speech to address these questions, you can maintain audience interest and involvement.

Problem-Solution Order

When you advocate changes in action or thought, your main points may fall naturally into a **problem-solution order.** First, you establish the existence of the problem. If your listeners are already aware of the problem, you can remind them of the primary issues. For example, if your listeners walk or ride bicycles to classes, they'll be unaware that there aren't enough parking spaces on campus; but if they drive automobiles, they'll be quite familiar with the parking shortage. You also need to depict the problem in a way that will help your listeners perceive it in the same way that you do. For example, your listeners may tolerate the parking shortage as a simple inconvenience of college life. You will need to show them that there is no reason to accept a parking shortage.

Once you've established that a problem exists, you must propose a solution to it. Your solution should be workable and practical. It would be silly to suggest that a multimillion-dollar parking complex be built if financing isn't available or if the parking complex still wouldn't accommodate enough automobiles. However, a car-pooling or busing system would be less expensive and limit the number of cars on campus.

Elimination Order

When your cassette player doesn't work, you probably systematically search for what's wrong: Are the batteries fresh? Is the pause switch off? Does the pickup spool turn? Is the tape jammed? Just so, with **elimination order,** you first survey all the available solutions and courses of action that can reasonably be pursued. Then, proceeding systematically, you eliminate each of the possibilities until only one remains.

Elimination order is well suited to persuasive speeches. If you want student government to bring a special performer to campus, you might show that all other suggested entertainers are booked up, too expensive, or lack widespread appeal. In this way, you lead the members of student government to agree with the choice you advocate.

To use elimination order effectively, you first must make an inclusive survey of options. If you overlook obvious choices, your listeners won't be convinced by your analysis. Second, you must make the options mutually exclusive; otherwise, your listeners may choose more than one. Consider this example in which the speaker makes only one alternative seem the best:

I. Three options have been proposed.
   A. Jeep Grand Cherokee is a mid-priced vehicle.
   B. Ford Explorer is more expensive than the Jeep.
   C. Isuzu Trooper is least expensive of the three options.
II. The first two options should be eliminated.
   A. The Jeep Grand Cherokee is so popular that you get less for your money than you do with the others.
   B. The Ford Explorer is the newest of the three, and, feature for feature, the most expensive.
III. The Trooper is therefore the best way to go.
   A. It has the same features as the others for less money.
   B. It's been around long enough to have a solid history of customer care and good repair.

Of course, the elimination order works best if listeners agree with the criteria you've suggested for judgment. If cost is no object, the Grand Cherokee or Explorer still will be considered. Or, someone might object that while the Explorer is a comparatively new model, Ford Motor Company has a long history in the United States. Study your listeners to make sure the criteria for elimination are acceptable to them.

Web Exploration

For some examples of clearly organized speeches go to
http://awl.com/german

OUTLINING YOUR SPEECH

Once you have determined the type of organization you will use to arrange your ideas, you should record the ideas in an outline. Outlining is an important tool for a speaker for two reasons:

1. *Testing.* A rough outline allows you to see your ideas. When you outline a speech, you can discover which ideas you've overemphasized to the exclusion or underdevelopment of others. Your outline is a testing device.

2. *Guiding.* When you're actually delivering a speech, a speaking outline is the preferred form of notes for many, perhaps even most, speakers. A good speaking outline shows you where you've been, where you are, and where you want to get before you sit down. You even can include in your speaking outline special directions to yourself ("show map here"; "emphasize this idea").

To profit from both the testing and guiding aspects of outlines, you must learn to build complete, solid structures. Two types of outlines are most helpful for speakers. You can benefit from a rough outline as you plan your speech. And you need to develop a speaking outline to help you present your speech. So, we'll discuss some strategies for developing the rough outline (a testing device) and a speaking outline (a guiding device).

Types of Outlines

You should develop your outline, as well as the speech it represents, gradually through a series of stages. Your outline will become increasingly complex as the ideas in your speech evolve and as you move the speech closer to its final form. But then, once you're ready to speak, the outline becomes simplified again. For the purposes of the public speaker, the rough outline and the speaking outlines are most important because they govern the discovery of ideas and the presentation of them. So, we'll concentrate on these.

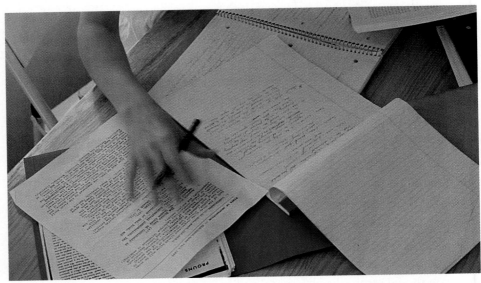

You identify a reasonable number of topics, arrange them, and amplify the ideas of your speech as you construct your rough outline.

Developing a Rough Outline   A **rough outline** establishes the topic of your speech, clarifies your purpose, and identifies a reasonable number of subtopics. Suppose your instructor has assigned an informative speech on a subject that interests you. You decide to talk about drunk driving because a close friend was recently injured by an intoxicated driver. Your broad topic area, then, is drunk driving.

In the six to eight minutes you have to speak, you obviously can't cover such a broad topic adequately. After considering your audience and your time limit, you decide to focus your presentation on two organizations, Mothers Against Drunk Driving (MADD) and Students Against Driving Drunk (SADD).

As you think about narrowing your topic further, you jot down some possible ideas. You continue to narrow your list until your final ideas include the following:

Founders of MADD and SADD.

Accomplishments of the two organizations.

Reasons the organizations were deemed necessary.

Goals of MADD and SADD.

Action steps taken by MADD and SADD.

Ways your listeners can get involved.

Then, help your listeners follow your thinking by clustering similar ideas. Experiment with several possible clusters before you decide on the best way to arrange your ideas.

Your next step is to consider the best pattern of organization for these topics. A chronological pattern would enable you to organize the history of MADD and SADD, but it would not allow you to discuss ways your listeners could help. Either cause-effect or effect-cause would work well if your primary purpose were to persuade. However, this is an informative speech, and you don't want to talk about the organizations only as the causes of reducing alcohol-related accidents.

In considering the audience-centered patterns, you decide that an inquiry order might work. You discard it, however, when you realize that you don't know enough about audience members' questions to use this organizational pattern effectively. After examining the alternatives, you finally settle on a topical pattern. A topical pattern allows you to present three clusters of information:

1. Background of MADD and SADD: information about the founders, why the organizations were founded.

2. Description of MADD and SADD: goals, steps in action plans, results.

3. Local work of MADD and SADD: the ways in which parents work with their teenagers and with local media to accomplish MADD and SADD goals.

As you subdivide your three clusters of information, you develop the following rough outline:

I. Background of MADD and SADD

  A. Information about the founders

  B. Reasons the organizations were founded

Speech Writer's Workshop
Use the Speech Workshop to generate and develop your outline.

II. Description of the organizations
   A. Their goals
   B. The action steps they take
   C. Their accomplishments so far
III. Applications of their work on a local level
   A. "Project Graduation"
   B. Parent-student contracts
   C. Local public service announcements

A rough outline identifies your topic, provides a reasonable number of subtopics, and reveals a method for organizing and developing your speech. Notice that you've arranged both the main points and subpoints topically. A word of warning: You should make sure that the speech doesn't turn into a "string of beads" that fails to differentiate between one topic and the next. With topical outlines, always figure out a way to make the topics cohere, hold together. Doing so will help you develop effective transitions as you practice your speech.

The next step in preparing an outline is phrasing your main headings as precisely as possible. Then you can begin to develop each heading by adding subordinate ideas. As you develop your outline, you'll begin to see what kinds of information and supporting materials you need to find.

Developing a Speaking Outline   Your rough outline would be maddening to use when you're actually delivering your speech. It would be too detailed to manage from a lectern; you'd probably be tempted to read to your listeners because it would include so many details. If you did that, you'd lose your conversational tone. Therefore, you need to compress your rough outline into a more useful form. A **speaking outline** uses key words or phrases to jog your memory when you deliver your speech. It is a short, practical form to use while delivering your speech (see Figure 8.1 on p. 140). The actual method you use to create your speaking outline will depend on your personal preference; some people like to work with small pieces of paper, others with notecards. Whatever your choice, however, your speaking outline should be unobtrusive. Large notebook pages will distract your listeners from what you have to say. There are five things to keep in mind as you prepare your speaking outline:

1. *Note most points with only a key word or phrase.* A word or two should be enough to trigger your memory, especially if you've practiced the speech adequately.
2. *Write out fully the ideas that must be stated precisely.* You don't want to make mistakes with people's names or statistical information or exact quotations.
3. *Include directions for delivery such as "SHOW POSTER."*
4. *Find methods of emphasis that will easily catch your eye, show the relationship of ideas, and jog your memory during your speech delivery.* You might use capital letters, white spaces, underlining, indentation, dashes, and highlighting with colored markers to emphasize important ideas.

SPEAKING OF . . . *Skills*
Memory and Organization

Research on organization and memory has shown that taking some specific outlining steps will help you and your listeners remember what you're talking about:

1. *The magic numbers.* In a classic study, psychologist George Miller concluded that there is a limit to the number of items a person can easily recall—seven, plus or minus two. More recent research has suggested that a more manageable number of items is five, plus or minus two. Limit the number of points you make to from three to seven (preferably in the three-to-five range).

2. *Chunking.* But what if you want to include a lot more information? The answer: "chunk it." Divide the information into chunks or groups. Listeners are much more likely to remember 5 chunks of information than 17 separate points.

3. *Map your movement.* As we've suggested throughout this chapter, mapping your ideas helps your listeners follow your speech. Listeners can't read your speaking outline so you have to give them a verbal map of your ideas. You can signal your most important ideas ("I have three main points.") and subordinate ideas ("There are two advantages of my first argument."). Letting an audience see, by means of your language, the coordinated or equal relationships among your main ideas will help keep listeners from getting lost.

4. *Mnemonics.* Mnemonics help you remember ideas. When you learned "Thirty days hath September, April, June, and November. . . ," you learned an easily recalled ditty that in turn helped you remember which months had 30 and which had 31 days. Speakers, too, can sometimes find a mnemonic to help listeners remember: for example, the three R's of conserving resources ("Recycle," "Reduce," and "Re-use") or the ABC sequence ("airwaves," "breathing," "compression") for cardiopulmonary resuscitation taught in CPR classes.

For Further Reading: G. Mandler, "Organization and Memory," in *Human Memory: Basic Principles,* edited by Gordon Bower (New York: Academic Press, 1977), 310–354. See also Mandler's articles in C. R. Puff, ed., *Memory Organization and Structure* (New York: Academic Press, 1979), 303–319. G. A. Miller, "The Magic Number Seven, Plus or Minus Two: Some Limits on Our Capacity for Processing Information," *Psychological Review,* 63 (1956): 81–97.

5. *Use your speaking outline during your practice sessions so that you are familiar with it when you give your speech.*

Guidelines for Preparing Outlines

The amount of detail that you include in an outline will depend on your subject, on the speaking situation, and on your previous experience in speech preparation. New subject matter, unique speaking contexts, and limited prior speaking experience all indicate the need for a detailed outline. Your instructor may even require a full-sentence outline to help you develop the content of your speech. Under any circumstances, a good outline should meet these basic requirements:

1. *Each unit in the outline should contain one main idea.* If two or three ideas merge under one subpoint, your audience will lose direction and become confused. Suppose you are outlining a speech advocating that Athens, Greece,

Web Exploration

To view some sample outlines go to

http://awl.com/german

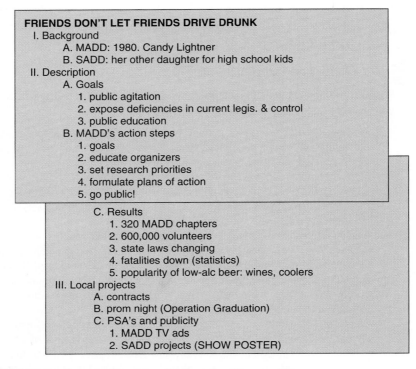

FRIENDS DON'T LET FRIENDS DRIVE DRUNK
I. Background
   A. MADD: 1980. Candy Lightner
   B. SADD: her other daughter for high school kids
II. Description
   A. Goals
      1. public agitation
      2. expose deficiencies in current legis. & control
      3. public education
   B. MADD's action steps
      1. goals
      2. educate organizers
      3. set research priorities
      4. formulate plans of action
      5. go public!
   C. Results
      1. 320 MADD chapters
      2. 600,000 volunteers
      3. state laws changing
      4. fatalities down (statistics)
      5. popularity of low-alc beer: wines, coolers
III. Local projects
   A. contracts
   B. prom night (Operation Graduation)
   C. PSA's and publicity
      1. MADD TV ads
      2. SADD projects (SHOW POSTER)

FIGURE 8.1 Sample Speaking Outline (on Notecards)

should be the permanent site for the Olympic Games. You include the following subpoint: "Also, the costs are prohibitive, and returning the games to their homeland would place renewed emphasis on their original purpose." Notice that this point combines two separate ideas about costs and the games' purpose. It would be more effective to separate the ideas and develop them as individual points. You could do it this way:

a. Costs for building new sites in new locations every four years are becoming prohibitive.

b. Returning the games to their homeland would place renewed emphasis on their original purpose.

2. *Less important ideas in the outline should be subordinate to more important ones.* Subordinate ideas are indented in an outline, and they are marked with subordinate symbols. Doing a good job with subordination helps you know what to emphasize when you're speaking. Proper subordination lets the main arguments stand out and the evidence clearly relate to those arguments. Consider the following example:

I. The cost of medical care has skyrocketed.

A. Hospital charges are high.

1. A private room may cost more than $1,500 a day.
2. Operating room fees may amount to tens of thousands of dollars.
3. X-rays and laboratory tests are expensive.

B. Doctors' charges constantly go up.
1. Complicated operations cost thousands.
2. Office calls usually cost between $35 and $100.

C. Drugs are expensive.
1. Most antibiotics cost $4 to $7 per dose.
2. The cost of nonprescription drugs has mounted.

3. *Phrase your main points effectively.* You can help your listeners understand your message better if you are concise, choose vivid language, and use parallel structure.

Be concise. Choose your words carefully. State your main points as briefly as you can without distorting their meaning. Crisp, clear, straightforward statements are easier to grasp than rambling, vague, complex declarations. Say, "Get regular exercise," not "Regular exercise, considering age and physical conditioning, lends itself to improved physiological functioning."

Use vivid language. Whenever possible, state your main points in evocative words and phrases. Drab, colorless statements are easily forgotten; punchy lines grab attention. Phrase your main points so they'll appeal directly to the concerns of your listeners. Instead of saying, "We should take immediate action to reduce the costs of higher education," say, "Cut tuition now!"

Use parallel structure. In a speech, your listeners have only one chance to catch what you're saying; parallelism in sentence structure helps them do so. The repetition of a key phrase aids the listener in remembering this series: "Cope with cold and flu season by washing your hands, getting enough sleep, and taking vitamin C. Wash your hands to destroy the viruses. Get enough sleep to reduce physical stress. Take vitamin C to fortify your body." Notice in this series that the most important phrases are repeated. Such parallelism will help your listeners grasp and remember the major ideas in your speech.

ASSESSING YOUR PROGRESS

Chapter Summary

1. An organized speech is: (a) easier for listeners to comprehend, (b) easier to present, (c) perceived as more credible, (d) often more persuasive, and (e) lowers both speaker and listener frustration.

2. A well-developed central idea helps determine the best organizational pattern for a speech.

3. Organization is the sequence of ideas in a pattern that suggests their relationship to each other.

4. Four speech-centered types of organization are: chronological, spatial, causal (effect-cause and cause-effect), and topical.

5. Audience-centered organizational patterns include familiarity-acceptance, inquiry, question-answer, problem-solution, and elimination order.

6. Speakers use outlines for testing their ideas and guiding their oral presentation of those ideas.

7. Rough outlines test ideas; speaking outlines guide ideas.

8. Guidelines for outlining include: (a) each unit should contain only one idea; (b) less important ideas should be subordinate to more important ones; (c) main ideas should be phrased effectively.

9. When phrasing main points, be concise, use vivid language, and use parallel structure.

Key Terms

causal pattern (p. 131)

chronological pattern (p. 130)

elimination order (p. 135)

familiarity-acceptance order (p. 133)

inquiry order (p. 134)

organization (p. 130)

problem-solution order (p. 134)

question-answer order (p. 134)

rough outline (p. 137)

spatial pattern (p. 131)

speaking outline (p. 138)

topical pattern (p. 132)

Assessment Activities

1. For each of the following topics, suggest two ways that materials might be organized. Consider which organizational pattern would be more effective:

   a. Directions for driving in snow.

   b. The evolution of stereophonic sound.

   c. A rationale for including women in combat.

   d. The effect that the influx of tourists from the West will have on Russia.

   e. A description of the proposed route for a highway bypass.

2. Bring a short magazine or newspaper article and a photocopy of it to class. Cut the photocopy into separate paragraphs or sentences. Ask a classmate to assemble the separated paragraphs or sentences into a coherent story. Compare your classmate's results to the original article.

3. For a speech entitled "The Investigator as a Resource," discussing why a lawyer may want to hire a private investigator on a case-by-case basis, rearrange the following points and subpoints in proper outline form:

   a. Investigative services can save the lawyer time.

   b. Investigative reports indicate areas the lawyer should concentrate on to build a case.

c. It is advantageous for a lawyer to employ an investigator on a case-by-case basis.

d. The investigator performs two basic services.

e. Known witnesses must be interviewed and other witnesses identified.

f. The investigator examines reports from the FBI and other governmental and private agencies and evaluates them for reliability and to determine what must be done.

g. The investigator examines, collects, preserves, and analyzes physical evidence.

h. The investigator compiles information in an effort to reconstruct an incident.

i. Lawyers may need detective assistance only occasionally, on especially critical cases.

j. Investigative reports can be used in out-of-court settlements.

 ## Surfing the Web

1. Many online tutorials are available to help you develop outlining skills. You might do a general search under the key word "outlining." Or, check out sites maintained by colleges and universities, such as Purdue University (http://owl. english.purdue.edu).

2. Visit two sites on the Internet that cover similar information but organize it differently. For example, you could visit two college Web sites, two automotive Web sites, two newspaper Web sites, etc. How did each Web site organize its information? Which organizational pattern did each site use? Was one site more visual than the other? Was one clearer and easier to use? Why? Was information quickly obtained or did you have to hunt for data?

References

1. The data in this outline were taken from *The World Almanac and Book of Facts 1992* (New York: World Almanac, 1991), 529–530.

Chapter

Beginning and Ending Your Speech

CAPTURING AND HOLDING ATTENTION

BEGINNING YOUR SPEECH

 SPEAKING OF . . . ETHICS: REVEALING RESPONSIBLE INTENTIONS

 SPEAKING OF . . . SKILLS: HOW LONG SHOULD IT BE?

ENDING YOUR SPEECH

SAMPLE OUTLINE FOR AN INTRODUCTION AND CONCLUSION

FRIENDS DON'T LET FRIENDS DRIVE DRUNK

ASSESSING YOUR PROGRESS

Just as aerobics instructors begin with warm-ups and end with cool-downs, so must you systematically prepare your audience to encounter new ideas and then take them back to their own worlds at the end of your speech. Your success in getting a listener's attention is partly due to how well you frame your speech ideas with a powerful introduction and conclusion. Well-prepared introductions and conclusions allow you to develop two kinds of relationships with audiences: (1) between you as a thinking, acting human being and them as fellow human beings and (2) between your ideas and theirs. And, too, the introduction and conclusion signal clearly when your speech starts and ends so as to prevent confusion among your listeners and to structure that speech as a kind of formalized association between you and them.

145

Introductions and conclusions are not trivial aspects of public speaking. Introductions form first impressions that can affect your listeners' perceptions of the remainder of the speech. Conclusions give you one last opportunity to reinforce your main ideas, leave a lasting impression, and cement the relationship with them that you're seeking. In fact, people most often remember what they first hear or see (the **primacy effect**) and what they most recently have seen or heard (the **recency effect**). That is why introductions and conclusions require special effort when you prepare your speeches.

In this chapter, we'll review ways to capture and sustain listeners' attention, examine the purposes of introductions and conclusions, and suggest various strategies for beginning and ending speeches.

CAPTURING AND HOLDING ATTENTION

When you engage a favorite Web site, you can block out the rest of the world. Sometimes you can pay attention so completely that it seems like only minutes instead of hours have passed. **Attention** is the ability to focus on one element in a given perceptual field. When attention is secured, competing elements in the perceptual field fade and, for all practical purposes, cease to exist. That explains why everything else disappears when you are hooked up to a Web site.

In contrast, watch an audience and you'll quickly realize that listeners' attention can drift away from the message. Their attention ebbs and flows as listeners think about last night, the cold room, the lawn mower out the window, or paying the rent on time. Unless you capture listeners' attention in your introduction and maintain it throughout your speech, a complete message will not be transmitted.

How can you capture and hold the attention of your listeners when giving a speech? Your ideas can be accompanied by nine appeals that have high attention value. These factors of attention can be used anywhere in your speech. You can exploit them in your introduction or conclusion, or at any important point in mid-speech. The **factors of attention** are: activity, reality, proximity, familiarity, novelty, suspense, conflict, humor, and the vital (see Figure 9.1).

Web Exploration
For some examples of how the factors of attention can be utilized go to
http://awl.com/german

Activity

Suppose you've got two TV sets side by side. On one set, two journalists discuss American foreign policy options in the Mideast, while on the other, you're seeing fiery Arab and Israeli stump speakers getting crowds to go wild. Which set are you likely to watch? You, too, can create a sense of pure activity by seeking to:

Choose active verbs. Raced, tore, shot through, slammed, ripped, slashed, catapulted, flew, flashed—most of these are simple verbs, but they depict activity.

Select dynamic stories. Use illustrations that depict action, that tell fast-moving stories. Propel your story forward, and your audience will stay with you.

Use short segments. Keep your speech moving—it will seem to drag if one point is expanded while other points are skimmed over.

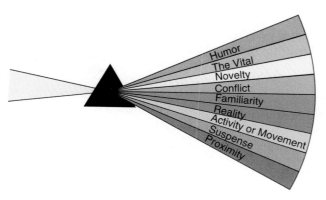

FIGURE 9.1   The Factors of Attention

You can use the factors of attention to capture and hold the interest of your listeners.

Reality

The earliest words you learned were names for tangible objects such as *mommy, cookie,* and *toy.* While the ability to abstract—to generalize—is one of the marks of human intelligence, don't lose your audience by becoming too abstract. Refer to specific events, persons, and places. For example, when we referred to "tangible objects," an abstract phrase, we gave you three real examples: *mommy, cookie,* and *toy.* Concrete words have more force than general references.

Proximity

Proximity means *nearness;* we usually notice things that closely surround us. A direct reference to a person in the audience, a nearby object or place, an incident that has just occurred, or the immediate occasion helps you to command attention. The following introduction uses proximity to engage the listeners:

> *Do you realize how much beer is available within three blocks of this classroom? Think about it—the Airport, Gene's, the Green Bottle, Tippler's, the Sports Page, Deadhead's, Bo Madison's, the Irish Tradition, Mondora's, the Lynn Street Café, the Underground, Mac's, the Taco Grande, Vince's, the Piazza, Gin Alley. And that doesn't include every restaurant that serves beer and wine with meals. Should we start wondering what our zoning laws are encouraging, especially involving potential damage to our bodies and our minds?*

Familiarity

References to the familiar are attention-sustaining, especially in the face of new or strange ideas. The familiar is comfortable. People drive the same route to work, children sing the same songs over and over, and you've probably watched your favorite movie more than once. Stories about Cap Anson, Shoeless Joe Jackson, Babe Ruth, Dizzy Dean, and Joe DiMaggio get repeated on occasions when cultural memories are used to support the primacy of baseball as America's great sport. How many times have you heard speakers repeat Martin Luther King, Jr.'s famous phrase, "I have a dream"? We like the reassurance that such familiarity provides.

Novelty

Novel happenings, dramatic incidents, or unusual developments attract attention. Look at the tabloid newspaper headlines next time you're in the grocery checkout line: "Grandmother Gives Birth to Quadruplets," "Madonna to Marry Martian Citizen," "Elvis Sighted at County Fair." These bizarre stories catch our attention. References to size and contrast work well to create novelty.

When using novelty, blending the familiar and the novel, the old and the new, often yields the best results. Otherwise you risk stretching the credulity of your listeners, as do those supermarket tabloids. To stimulate interest in the evolving nature of the self-defense plea in criminal courts, you might cite recent highly publicized trials in which alleged victims claim self-defense in response to years of physical or mental abuse. Citing specific cases, such as the Menendez brothers' murder of their parents, provokes interest through novelty.

Suspense

Much of the appeal in mystery stories arises because we don't know how they will end. Films such as *Pulp Fiction* and *American Beauty* have enough unusual twists to hold audiences spellbound. You, too, can use uncertainty in your speeches by pointing to puzzling relationships or unpredictable forces. Introduce suspense into the stories you tell, building up to a surprising climax. Hint that you'll divulge valuable information later: "Stay with me through this speech, because by the end you'll learn how to cut your book bill in half every semester."

Conflict

Controversy grabs attention. Soap operas are fraught with love, hate, violence, passion, and power struggles. Conflict, like suspense, suggests uncertainty; like activity, it's dynamic. The next time you hear the news, listen for conflict. Newscasters often portray shipwreck survivors as "battling nature." Sportscasters describe athletes as "overcoming adversity." And even weather forecasters talk about "fighting off Arctic blasts of frigid air." The concept of struggle brings the sense of urgency to the day's events.

In your speeches, you can create conflict among ideas, such as the competing theories about the aggressiveness of young boys: are males genetically programmed to be aggressive, or are they made that way by environmental influences such as combative fathers, taunting older boys, and the portrayal of fighting in films and television shows? Put these competing theories in conflict with each other, depicting what aspects of male aggressiveness each accounts for. When your ideas are cast as pugilists, they become dramatic and engaging.

Humor

Listeners usually pay attention when they're enjoying themselves. Humor can unite you and your audience by relaxing everyone and providing a change of pace. When using humor to capture and hold attention, remember to stick close to your central idea by choosing humor that is relevant. Be sure to use only humorous stories that are in good taste, and so avoid offending members of your audience. Comedian Bill Cosby met both of these requirements when he poked fun at a University of South Carolina graduating class. In his commencement speech, Cosby reminded his listeners:

> *All across the United States of America, people are graduating. And they are hearing so many guest speakers tell them that they are going forth. As a parent I am concerned as to whether or not you know where "Forth" is. Let me put it to you this way: We have paved a road—the one to the house was already paved. "Forth" is not back home.[1]*

The Vital

The phrase *the vital* was coined by Alan Monroe, the original author of this textbook, to reflect our tendency to be concerned with things that immediately benefit us. We pay attention to matters that affect our health, reputation, property, or employment. When a speaker says, "Students who take internships while in college find jobs after graduation three times as fast as those who don't," you're likely to pay attention—getting a job is vital to you. Appealing to *the vital,* therefore, is a matter of personalizing the speech for a particular audience—making it as relevant to their concrete circumstances as possible.

There are nine different ways to stimulate attention: activity, reality, proximity, familiarity, novelty, suspense, conflict, humor, and the vital. Use these attention-getters to grab and maintain your listeners' attention throughout your speech. They give your speech sparkle and spunk, they reach out to your listeners, and they help your listeners follow and remember your speech.

BEGINNING YOUR SPEECH

The beginning of a speech must gain the listeners' attention, secure goodwill and respect for the speaker, and prepare the audience for the discussion to follow. As noted already, you can use the factors of attention to engage your listeners during the beginning moments of your speech. But attention is not enough. In many situations, your own reputation or the chairperson's introduction will help to generate goodwill. You can also refer to your own experience with the topic to boost your credibility. You gain additional respect from your listeners when you share your background research with them.

However, there may be times when your audience is opposed to you or your topic. In these instances, it's important to deal with opposition openly so that you will receive a fair hearing. By commenting on the differences between your views and those of your listeners, you can let them know that you're aware of disagreements but are seeking areas of consensus. And, when confronted by indifference, distrust, or skepticism, you must take steps early in the speech to change these attitudes so that your position will be received openly. Even if your listeners don't agree, you can often secure their respect for your honesty and integrity by dealing directly with them.

Finally, you can prepare your listeners for your speech by stating your purpose early: let them engage the subject matter clearly and openly. Audiences that are

SPEAKING OF . . . *Ethics*
Revealing Responsible Intentions

Consider this scenario: You are planning a speech in which you hope to persuade your listeners to donate money to your political caucus. Should you reveal your intention in your introduction?

While we generally are unaffected by the awareness that persuasion is intended, we strongly react to deception. Research suggests the worst effect on listeners will occur if you disguise your intent but it is discovered as you speak.

Other factors such as your listeners' initial attitudes also influence how they will respond to your intention. If your listeners are highly involved or strongly committed to an opposing view, they will be less inclined to listen to you if they know your goal is to persuade.

In every case, avoid the appearance of direct manipulation. You should say, "Let's investigate the options together," rather than "Today I'm going to persuade you to. . . ." Most of us like to think that we have free choice.

For further information, see: Richard Petty and John Cacioppo, "Effects of Forewarning, Cognitive Responding, and Resistance to Persuasion," *Journal of Personality and Social Psychology,* 35 (1970): 645-655.

forced to guess the purpose of a speech soon lose interest. A preview of your ideas and speech structure will help your audience follow along.

An introduction that secures your audience's attention and goodwill and prepares them to listen lays a solid foundation for acceptance of the central idea of your speech. You can establish attention by presenting your ideas in ways that create interest. We will examine a number of established means for tailoring your introduction to achieve the best results.

Referring to the Subject or Occasion

If your audience already has a vital interest in your subject, you need only to state that subject before presenting your first main point: "I'm glad to see how many of you came to learn more about finding summer internships. As the poster around campus indicated, I'm here tonight to talk about how you let people in your hometown know about this college's requirements for an acceptable summer internship relationship between a local business and student spending that summer back home."

Although such brevity and forthrightness may strike exactly the right note on some occasions, you should not begin all speeches this way. Some audiences aren't so directly tied to you and the occasion. Sometimes you need to discuss what brought you and your audience together. Notice how Eugene Zeltmann, president of the New York Power Authority, worked to find a connection between himself and an audience of engineers at Cornell University:

> *In looking at the conference program, I noticed that just about all the other speakers had a Cornell connection. So I'm grateful to my son—who's a freshman*

here—for getting in the door. And, in case you're wondering, that "PA" next to my name on the program stands for parent—not Power Authority.

It's fitting that we're spending some time talking about the role of the consumer in electricity deregulation. Because all that we're doing—no matter how complex and far-reaching it may seem—is ultimately directed at providing lower rates and continued reliable service for the people who use our electricity. If we fail in that, nothing else will matter.[2]

Notice how Zeltmann ties in his relationship to the place personally before moving on to mention the importance of the topic to the occasion—a conference on the electric power industry. He gains a personal connection first, then a topical one, in just a few sentences.

Using a Personal Reference or Greeting

At times, a warm, personal greeting from a speaker or the remembrance of a previous visit to an audience or scene should be made even more important. This often is the case when someone representing an organization or political unit in a visit to another organization or political unit is going to speak. Official ties are one thing, but if they can be personalized, then the audience may be even more open to developing a relationship with the speaker.

When Donald Bishop, deputy counselor for press and cultural affairs in the American embassy, delivered an address to American scholars about to teach in China as Fulbright lecturers, he looked for ways to personalize a relationship between himself as a government employee and those scholars:

It's an honor for me to speak to you at this gathering of Americans who have come to China as professors under the Fulbright Program, along with Chinese colleagues from the institutions that host you. I bring the greetings of Ambassador Sasser and U.S. Information Service director Paul Blackburn. Both had to remain in Beijing because Secretary Albright is due in China this weekend. Let me extend one more warm welcome on their behalf.

It's also a pleasure to join this conference, allowing me to set aside the hassles of embassy work to join, for a few hours, the fellowship of scholars, where I spent some happy years before I joined the foreign service. I was teaching history at the Air Force Academy when I took the foreign service examination. We wore our blues in class, but anyone could spot me walking through Fairchild Hall by the chalk dust covering my uniform.

They haven't given me chalk and a blackboard today, but I'm sure you'll soon recognize I still have some of the historian inside me.[3]

The way a personal reference introduction can be used to gain the attention of a hostile or skeptical audience is illustrated by a speech presented by Anson Mount, manager of public affairs for *Playboy,* to the Christian Life Commission of the Southern Baptist Convention:

I am sure we are all aware of the seeming incongruity of a representative of Playboy *magazine speaking to an assemblage of representatives of the Southern*

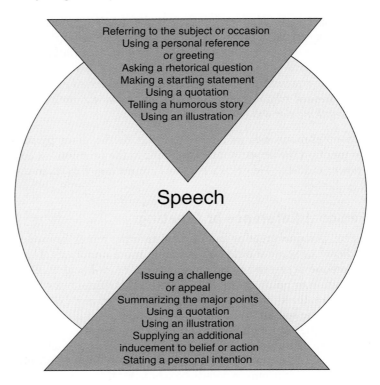

FIGURE 9.2 Types of Introductions and Conclusions

You can choose among different types of introductions and conclusions for your speeches. As you choose your introduction, ask yourself if it orients your audience to your purposes and ideas. When choosing a conclusion, ask if it summarizes your ideas and achieves closure.

Baptist Convention. I was intrigued by the invitation when it came last fall, though I was not surprised. I am grateful for your genuine and warm hospitality, and I am flattered (though again not surprised) by the implication that I would have something to say that could have meaning to you people. Both Playboy *and the Baptists have indeed been considering many of the same issues and ethical problems; and even if we have not arrived at the same conclusions, I am impressed and gratified by your openness and willingness to listen to our views.*[4]

If a personal reference is sincere and appropriate, it will establish goodwill as well as gain attention. Avoid extravagant, emotional statements, however, because listeners are quick to sense a lack of genuineness. At the other extreme, avoid apologizing. Don't say, "I don't know why I was picked to talk when others could have done it so much better" or, "Unaccustomed as I am to public speaking. . . ." Apologetic beginnings suggest that your audience needn't waste time listening. Be cordial, sincere, and modest, but establish your authority and maintain control of the situation.

Asking a Question

Another way to open a speech is to ask a question or series of questions to spark thinking about your subject. For example, Nicholas Fynn of Ohio University opened a speech about free-burning of timberland by saying: "How many of you in this room have visited a national park at one point in your life? Well, the majority of you are in good company."[5] Such a question introduces a topic gently and, with its direct reference to the audience, tends to engage the listeners.

Rhetorical questions, i.e., those for which you do not expect direct audience response, are often used to forecast the development of the speech. After thanking the Charlotte, North Carolina, business community for the invitation to address them about the euro, the new European monetary unit (EMU), Lawrence Summers, the U.S. deputy secretary of the treasury, introduced the body of his speech with rhetorical questions: "Three questions arise in thinking about EMU: what its effect will be on the economies of Europe; what implications the euro might have for the dollar; and how EMU will affect Europe's role in the world and its relations with the United States."[6] Such questions most often are used with topical organizations, when other types of forecasts are more difficult to use.

Making a Startling Statement

On certain occasions, you may choose to open a speech with what is known as the *shock technique,* making a startling statement of fact or opinion. This approach is especially useful when listeners are distracted, apathetic, or smug. It rivets their attention on your topic. For example, the executive director of the American Association of Retired Persons (AARP), after asking some rhetorical questions about health care, caught his listeners' attention with a series startling statements:

> *Given what we're spending on health care, we should have the best system in the world. But the reality is that we don't. Thirty-seven million Americans have no health insurance protection whatsoever, and millions more are underinsured. We are twentieth—that's right, twentieth—among the nations of the world in infant mortality. The death rate for our black newborn children rivals that of Third World countries. And poor children in America, like their brothers and sisters in Third World nations, receive neither immunizations nor basic dental care.*
>
> *Those statistics give us a sense of the scope of the problem. What they don't adequately portray is the human factor—the pain and the suffering. While terminally ill patients may have their lives extended in intensive care units—at tremendous cost—middle-age minority women die of preventable and treatable cancer, hypertension and diabetes.[7]*

Avoid overusing shock techniques. The technique can backfire if your listeners become angry when you threaten or disgust them.

Using a Quotation

A quotation may be an excellent means of introducing a speech, because it can prod listeners to think about something important and it often captures an appropriate emotional tone. Nigel Atkin, director of communications in British Columbia's

Department of Assessment, opened a speech by saying, "Thank you. I am pleased to be here tonight to provide context as you focus on values. John Ralston Saul in *The Doubter's Companion: A Dictionary of Aggressive Common Sense* (1994) defined ethics as: 'A matter of daily practical concern described glowingly in universal terms by those who intend to ignore them.'"[8] That quotation signaled to the audience that: (1) the speaker was fully aware of how the topic of ethics was ignored by governmental officials and (2) he was going to work especially hard to make it practical and relevant to them.

Quotations can be used seriously, as well, to capture the theme of a speech. Harlan Cleveland, president of the World Academy of Art and Science, opened a speech to business executives concerned with human services in this manner:

> *From my very first moments at Silver Bay [home of the conference], I found your company wonderfully congenial. Truth usually comes in small paradoxical packages, and one of them greeted me at our opening session. Our experience together, said Adrienne Riley, would be "very intense and totally relaxed." On both counts, her paradox quickly became true.*
>
> *I was especially glad to encounter in our program folder a quote from Mary Parker Follett, one of my favorite authors in my one-time field of public administration: "All polishing is done by friction," she wrote long ago. "The music of the violin we get by friction. We left the savage style when we discovered fire by friction. So we talk of the friction of mind on mind as a good thing."*
>
> *That's a hard sell to young students. I used to tell graduate students in public administration that the executive's task is not to get staff members to agree with each other. That's much too easy. The hard thing, the important thing. . . .*[9]

We need not finish his thought—you can. The quotation from Follett set a theme—friction—that obviously now would become the theme of a speech on how to create an imaginative business organization. Quotations are more than decoration: they can set the mood and direct the flow of thought in positive directions.

Telling a Humorous Story

You can begin a speech by telling a funny story or relating a humorous experience. When doing so, however, observe the following three rules of communication:

1. Be sure that the story is at least amusing, if not funny; test it out on others before you actually deliver the speech. Be sure that you practice sufficiently so you can present the story naturally. And use the story to make a point instead of making it the center of your remarks. In other words, brevity is crucial.

2. Be sure that the story is relevant to your speech; if its subject matter or punch line is not directly related to you, your topic, or at least your next couple of sentences, the story will appear to be a mere gimmick.

3. Be sure that your story is in good taste; in a public gathering, an off-color or doubtful story violates accepted standards of social behavior and can under-

mine an audience's respect for you. You should avoid sexual, racist, antireligious, ageist, homophobic, and sexist humor.

Professor Emeritus William Peterson observed all three of these rules when talking to a company's sales engineering meeting. He opened with put-downs about his own fields of expertise:

> *Welcome to the Dismal Science of Economics and that classic oxymoron, Political Science. Political Science? A definition of politics can be sensed from its derivation, from its Greek roots. "Poli" means of course many, and "ticks" means bloodsucking parasites.*
>
> *Economics can be sensed from a story told by President Harry S. Truman who had reported to him the nation's first Council of Economic Advisers. He explained that a one-armed economist would never do, for how could that economist say, "On the other hand . . ."?[10]*

After relating his anecdote, Peterson was ready to talk about the politics of free trade.

Web Exploration

For an overview of the different types of introductions go to http://awl.com/german

Using an Illustration

A real-life incident, a passage from a novel or short story, or a hypothetical illustration can also get a speech off to a good start. An illustration should be not only interesting to the audience but also relevant to your central idea. Deanna Sellnow, then a student at North Dakota State University, used this technique to introduce a speech on private credit-reporting bureaus:

> *John Pontier, of Boise, Idaho, was turned down for insurance because a reporting agency informed the company that he and his wife were addicted to narcotics, and his Taco Bell franchise had been closed down by the health board when dog food had been found mixed in with the tacos. There was only one small problem. The information was made up. His wife was a practicing Mormon who didn't touch a drink, much less drugs, and the restaurant had never been cited for a health violation.[11]*

The existence of a problem with private credit-reporting bureaus is clear from this introduction. If the illustration is humorous instead of serious, the effect is different but the introduction can be equally useful, as was the case when the chancellor of California State University, Charles Reed, opened the body of a lecture in this manner:

> *As I mentioned, I want to talk today about a K–12 education continuum. But I first want to share with you a story about education as a lifelong continuum.*
>
> *When the renowned Justice Oliver Wendell Holmes Jr. was hospitalized at age 92, he received a visit from President Franklin D. Roosevelt. The president was surprised to see Justice Holmes reading a Greek primer.*
>
> *"What are you doing?" President Roosevelt asked him.*

"I am reading," replied Justice Holmes.

"I can see that," said the president. "But why a Greek primer?"

The justice looked at him and said, "Why, to improve my mind, of course."

This story serves as a good illustration of the fact that the education of the human mind never stops. It does not stop at grade 8, grade 12, or after four years of college.[12]

Completing Your Introduction

You can use one of the approaches that we've discussed alone or you can combine two or more. You might open with a startling illustration or a humorous reference to the occasion, for example. No matter what type of introduction you use, you should have three purposes in mind: arousing the attention, winning the goodwill and respect of your listeners, and setting a tone and direction for the substance of your talk. Your introduction should be relevant to the purpose of your speech and should lead smoothly into the first of the major ideas that you wish to present; that is, your introduction should be an integral part of the speech.

Your introduction should also forecast the speech's development by means of a preview. The preview establishes your listeners' confidence in your organization, thus enhancing your credibility. It creates listener receptivity by providing a structure for you and your listeners to follow during the speech. Here are some examples of types of previews:

1. *Announce the organizational pattern.* You might say, "I'll develop the effects of the problem of spousal abuse and then examine its causes" (causal pattern). "In demonstrating how to check basic problems with your computer, I'll consider three topics. I'll be talking about the hard drive, the ancillary drive systems, and the word processing program" (topical order).

SPEAKING OF . . . *Skills*

How Long Should It Be?

According to a classic study, the average speaker spends about 10 percent of the total speech on the introduction and 5 percent on the conclusion. The introduction may increase to 13 percent in speeches designed to stimulate or inspire, such as sermons, dedications, or memorials. In practical terms, this means that you will probably take one minute to introduce a ten-minute speech and thirty seconds to conclude it.

Can you think of circumstances when you'd spend more time introducing or concluding your remarks? Less time?

For the original study, see: N. Edd Miller, "Speech Introductions and Conclusions," *Quarterly Journal of Speech,* 32 (1946): 181–183.

2. *Use mnemonic devices.* Acronyms aid memory; for example, "I'm going to discuss the ABCs of jogging: **A**lways wear good shoes. **B**aby your feet. **C**all a podiatrist if problems develop."

3. *Employ alliteration.* Rely on sound similarities to create interest. For example: "My advice for finding someone to marry? Use the three A's—availability, attitude, and *amour.*"

4. *Use repetition.* Reinforce your message by repeating the main phrases. You can say, "We need to examine how a lack of extensive night street lights creates a problem on campus, a problem on nearby streets, a problem on downtown streets, and, ultimately, even a problem on the seemingly quiet, wooded streets of suburbia."

When effective, your introductory remarks will both establish a common ground of interest and understanding and provide a structure to guide your audience toward the conclusion that you intend to reach.

ENDING YOUR SPEECH

Just as the introduction to your speech accomplishes specific purposes, so too does the conclusion. An effective conclusion does two things well: (1) it rounds off the message of the speech, letting listeners understand one more time the importance and significance of what you're saying, and (2) it completes the relationship you've constructed between you and them. If your speech has one dominant idea, you should restate it in a clear and forceful manner. If your speech is more complex, you may summarize the key points, or you may spell out the action or belief that these points suggest. And always say something that signals, even if indirectly, the end for now of your relationship—say 'bye—whether it's been personalized or is just based on shared information. This needn't be too formal. You might say, "Thanks for listening to what I've been thinking about as I plan for next year's study-abroad experience. If any of you want to talk with me more about this topic, see me after class." At other times, for example when you're trying to get a significant number of people to attend a meeting to unionize cafeteria workers, you'll want to say more because you're trying to construct a continuing relationship with them.

In addition to reinforcing the central idea, your conclusion should leave the audience in the proper mood. If you want your listeners to express vigorous enthusiasm, stimulate that feeling with your closing words. Decide whether the response you seek is a mood of seriousness or good humor, of warm sympathy or utter disgust, of thoughtfulness or action. Then end your speech in a way that will create that mood.

Finally, a good ending should convey a sense of completeness and finality. Listeners grow restless and annoyed when they think the speech is finished, only to hear the speaker ramble on. Tie the threads of thought together so that the pattern of your speech is brought clearly to completion.

Speakers employ many strategies to convey a sense of closure to their speeches. We will examine the conclusion techniques that are used regularly.

Issuing a Challenge

You may conclude your speech by issuing a challenge to your listeners, requesting support or action, or reminding them of their responsibilities. That challenge can be as simple as the one used by Kofi Annan when addressing the U.N. Security Council on promoting peace in the new millennium: "This is the core challenge of the Security Council and the United Nations as a whole in the next century: to unite behind the principle that massive and systematic violations of human rights conducted against an entire people cannot be allowed to stand."[13] At other times, especially when aiming to create a mood of inspiration and determination, the challenge is expanded, as Harvard research associate Peter Gibbon did when talking to journalists about the need to become more self-critical:

> *In the Age of Information, journalists and citizens face the same challenges. We need to study the past so as not to become arrogant, to remember the good so as not to become cynical, and to recognize America's strengths so as not to dwell on her weaknesses. We need to be honest and realistic without losing our capacity for admiration—and to be able to embrace complexity without losing our faith in the heroic.[14]*

Notice Gibbon's use of parallel structure—to study, to remember, to recognize, and then "to be honest . . . without" and "to be able to embrace . . . without." Such attention to style elevates the challenge, giving it a seriousness that makes it harder for listeners to avoid it.

Summarizing the Major Points or Ideas

In an informative speech, a summary allows the audience to pull together the main strands of information and to evaluate the significance of the speech. In a persuasive speech, a summary gives you a final opportunity to present, in brief form, the major points of your argument. For example, a student presented this summary of an informative speech on tornadoes:

> *You've seen the swirling funnel clouds on the six o'clock news. They hit sometimes without much warning, leaving in their paths death and destruction. Now you should understand the formation of funnel clouds, the classification of tornadoes on the Fujita scale, and the high cost of tornadoes worldwide in lives and property. Once you understand the savage fury of tornadoes, you can better appreciate them. Tornadoes are one of nature's temper tantrums.*

If the student's purpose had been to persuade listeners to take certain precautions during a tornado alert, the summary of the speech might have sounded like this:

> *The devastation left in the path of a tornado can be tremendous. To prevent you and your loved ones from becoming statistics on the six o'clock news, remember what I told you this afternoon. Seek shelter in basements, ditches, or other low areas. Stay away from glass and electric lines. And, remember the lesson of the*

Xenia, Ohio, disaster. Tornadoes often hit in clusters. Be sure the coast is clear before you leave your shelter. Don't be a statistic.

In each case, summarizing the main ideas of the speech gives the speaker another opportunity to reinforce the message. Information can be reiterated in the summary of an informative speech, or the major arguments or actions can be strengthened in the summary of a persuasive speech.

Using a Quotation

You can cite others' words to capture the spirit of your ideas in the conclusion of your speech. Quotations are often used to end speeches. Quoted prose, if the author is credible, may gather additional support for your central idea. So in a speech on the need to reformulate this country's system of managed care, Howard Veit said: "I believe all the dynamics are in place for this transformation [of care systems] to take place. Dwight Eisenhower once said: 'Neither a wise man nor a brave man lies down on the tracks of history to wait for the train of the future to run over him.' Well, the train is coming. Fortunately, you have a choice about how you'll react."[15]

Poetry, too, may distill the essence of your message in uplifting language. Bishop Leontine Kelly concluded her speech celebrating the diversity of human talents with the words of a well-known Christian hymn: "How firm a foundation ye saints of the Lord, Is laid for your faith in God's excellent word."[16] The recognition of these familiar words probably inspired members of her audience.

Using an Illustration

Illustrations engage your listeners emotionally. If you use a concluding illustration, it can set the tone and direction of your final words. Your illustration should be both inclusive and conclusive—inclusive of the main focus or thrust of your speech and conclusive in tone and impact. Capturing the message and the way a speaker wanted an audience to feel about the message is nicely illustrated in American Medical Association president Nancy Dickey's description of a new AMA plan for health reform:

Web Exploration
For an overview of the different types of conclusions go to
http://awl.com/german

There is an old painting that hangs in many medical museums that depicts this relationship [between patient and doctor] better than any words I can offer here. Perhaps some of you have even seen it. It shows a physician at a child's bedside. The physician is pensive, maybe even a bit prayerful. The child's parents are all but faded into the background. And there sits the physician—with none of today's tools or technologies to call upon—but nonetheless clearly connected to his patient.

I want to be sure, that as we craft this new health system, that I am again allowed—even encouraged—to connect in that way to my patients . . . to listen, to hear, and to respond to their concerns.

Yes, I want to keep all of the glories of modern medicine and technology, but I also want to combine them with the caring of a human heart. And I believe that working together, this imaginative, intellectual, and committed country can do that—if we put our minds to it, and give it the proper priority. I look forward to your help.[17]

Supplying an Additional Inducement to Belief or Action

Sometimes you may conclude a speech by quickly reviewing the principal ideas presented in the body and then supplying one or more additional reasons for endorsing the belief or taking the proposed action. So, in a student speech, Michael Twitchell spoke at length about the devastating effects of depression. After proposing numerous reasons for people to get involved in the battle, he offered in the conclusion to his speech an additional inducement:

> *Why should you really care? Why is it important? The depressed person may be someone you know—it could be you. If you know what is happening, you can always help. I wish I had known what depression was in March of 1978. You see, when I said David Twitchell could be my father, I was making a statement of fact. David is my father. I am his son. My family wasn't saved; perhaps now yours can be.[18]*

Stating a Personal Intention

Stating your own intention to adopt the action or attitude you recommend in your speech is particularly effective when your prestige with the audience is high or when you have presented a concrete proposal requiring immediate action. By professing

Speakers sometimes indicate their personal intentions to take action. This is especially effective when the speaker is highly regarded by listeners or when immediate actions are urged.

your intention to take immediate action, you and your ideas gain credibility. In the following example, a speaker sets himself up as a model for the actions he wants his listeners to take:

Today I have illustrated how important healthy blood is to human survival and how blood banks work to ensure the possibility and availability of blood for each of us. It is not a coincidence that I speak on this vital topic on the same day that the local Red Cross Bloodmobile is visiting campus. I want to urge each of you to ensure your future and mine by stopping at the Student Center today or tomorrow to make your donation. The few minutes that it takes may add up to a lifetime for a person in need. To illustrate how firmly I believe in this opportunity to help, I'm going to the Student Center to give my donation as soon as this class is over. I invite any of you who feel this strongly to join me.

Regardless of the means you choose for closing your speech, remember that your conclusion should focus the attention of your listeners on the central theme you've developed. In addition, a good conclusion should be consistent with the mood or tenor of your speech and should convey a sense of completeness and finality.

SAMPLE OUTLINE FOR AN INTRODUCTION AND CONCLUSION

An introduction and conclusion for a classroom speech on MADD and SADD might take the following form. Notice that the speaker uses suspense in combination with startling statements to lead the audience into the subject. The conclusion combines a summary with a final illustration and a statement of personal intention.

Friends Don't Let Friends Drive Drunk

INTRODUCTION

I. Many of you have seen the "Black Gash," the Vietnam War Memorial in Washington, D.C.
   A. It contains the names of more than 40,000 Americans who gave their lives in Southeast Asia between 1961 and 1973.
   B. We averaged over 3000 war dead a year during that painful period.
II. Today, another enemy stalks Americans.
   A. The enemy kills, not 3000, but over 20,000 citizens every 12 months.
   B. The enemy is not hiding in jungles but can be found in every community in the country.

    C. The enemy kills, not with bayonets and bullets, but with bottles and bumpers.

III. Two organizations are trying to contain and finally destroy the killer.

    A. Every TV station in this town carries a public service ad that says "Friends Don't Let Friends Drive Drunk."

    B. In response to the menace of the drunk driver, two national organizations—Mothers Against Drunk Driving and Students Against Driving Drunk—have been formed and are working even in this community to make the streets safe for you and me.

    C. [Central idea] MADD and SADD are achieving their goals with your help.

    D. To help you understand what these familiar organizations do, first I'll tell you something about the founders of MADD and SADD; then, I'll describe their operations; finally, I'll mention some of the ways community members get involved with them.

[Body]

CONCLUSION

I. Today, I've talked briefly about the Lightners and their goals for MADD and SADD, their organizational techniques, and ways in which you can get involved.

II. The work of MADD and SADD volunteers—even on our campus, where I'm sure you've seen their posters in the Student Center—is being carried out to keep you alive.

    A. You may not think you need to be involved; but remember: After midnight, one in every five or fewer drivers on the road is probably drunk. You could be involved whether you want to be or not.

    B. That certainly was the case with Julie Smeiser, a member of our sophomore class, who just last Friday was hit by a drunk driver when going home for the weekend.

III. If people don't take action, we could build a new "Black Gash"—this time for victims of drunks—every two years, and soon fill Washington, D.C., with monuments to needless suffering.

    A. Such monuments would be grim reminders of our unwillingness to respond to enemies at home with the same intensity with which we attacked enemies abroad.

    B. A better response would be to support actively groups such as MADD and SADD, who are attacking the enemy on several fronts at once in a war on motorized murder.

IV. If you're interested in learning more about SADD and MADD, stop by Room 324 in the Student Center tonight at 7:30 to hear the president of the local chapter of SADD talk about this year's activities. I'll be there; please join me.

ASSESSING YOUR PROGRESS

Chapter Summary

1. You can capture and sustain your listeners' attention by using one or more of the nine factors of attention: activity, reality, proximity, familiarity, novelty, suspense, conflict, humor, and the vital.

2. Introductions should seize attention, secure goodwill, and prepare an audience for what you will be saying.

3. Types of introductions include referring to the subject or occasion, using a personal reference or greeting, asking a rhetorical question, making a startling statement of fact or opinion, using a quotation, telling a humorous story, and using an illustration.

4. In concluding your speech, you should attempt to focus the thoughts of your audience on your central theme, maintain the tenor of your speech, close off (or extend) the relationship built between speaker and listeners, and convey a sense of finality.

5. Techniques for ending a speech include issuing a challenge or appeal, summarizing the major points or ideas, using a quotation, using an illustration, supplying an additional inducement to belief or action, and stating a personal intention.

Key Terms

attention (p. 146)

factors of attention (p. 146)

primacy effect (p. 146)

recency effect (p. 146)

Assessment Activities

1. You've been asked to speak on a controversial issue. Assume that the setting for three versions of the speech will include three different occasions: a classroom at your school, where audience members are mixed in their support; a favorable ("pro") audience, highly sympathetic to you and your position; and an unfavorable ("anti") audience, hostile to you and your position. Write three introductions, one for each setting. Include a brief paragraph explaining your rhetorical strategies. Either turn these in or read them aloud as parts of a class discussion.

2. Consult the Internet or an almanac to find out what famous events occurred on this date in history. Then, write an introduction for an informative speech to your classmates referring to the occasion. Ask your listeners if you secured their interest.

3. Participate in a chain of introductions and conclusions. One student will begin by suggesting a topic for a speech. A second student will suggest an appropriate introduction and conclusion and justify those choices. A third student will challenge those selections and propose alternative introductions and/or conclusions. Continue this discussion until everyone has participated. Which examples were most effective? Determine why they were effective.

References

1. Bill Cosby, "University of South Carolina Commencement Address," 1990, unpublished manuscript available from the author.

2. Eugene W. Zeltmann, "Empowering the Electricity Consumer," *Vital Speeches of the Day,* 65 (15 June 1999).

3. Donald M. Bishop, "Closing the Understanding Gap," *Vital Speeches of the Day,* 65 (1 June 1999).

4. Anson Mount, Manager of Public Affairs for *Playboy* magazine, from a speech presented to the Christian Life Commission, in *Contemporary American Speeches,* 5th ed., edited by Wil A. Linkugel et al. (Dubuque, IA: Kendall/Hunt, 1982).

5. Nicholas Fynn, "The Free Burn Fallacy," *Winning Orations 1989.* Reprinted by permission of Larry Schnoor, Executive Secretary, Interstate Oratorical Association, Mankato, MN.

6. Lawrence H. Summers, "Transatlantic Implications of the Euro," *Vital Speeches of the Day,* 65 (15 January 1999).

7. Horace B. Deets, "Health Care for a Caring America: We Must Develop a Better System," *Vital Speeches of the Day,* 55 (1 August 1989).

8. Nigel Atkin, "Communication and Politics," *Vital Speeches of the Day,* 65 (15 March 1999).

9. Harlan Cleveland, "Imagination and Creativity," *Vital Speeches of the Day,* 65 (1 February 1999).

10. William H. Peterson, "Free Trade and Capitalism," *Vital Speeches of the Day,* 65 (1 April 1999).

11. Deanna Sellnow, "Have You Checked Lately?" *Winning Orations.* Reprinted by permission of Larry Schnoor, Executive Secretary, Interstate Oratorical Association, Mankato, MN.

12. Charles B. Reed, "Collaborating for Excellence: Building a Seamless K–12 System for California," *Vital Speeches of the Day,* 65 (1 June 1999).

13. Kofi Annan, "Relevance of the U.N. Security Council: Promoting International Peace in the Next Century," *Vital Speeches of the Day,* 65 (15 June 1999).

14. Peter H. Gibbon, "The End of Admiration: The Media and the Loss of Heroes," *Vital Speeches of the Day,* 65 (15 June 1999).

15. Howard Veit, "The Next Generation of Managed Care: The Age of Consumerism," *Vital Speeches of the Day,* 65 (15 April 1999).

16. Bishop Leontine Kelly, "Celebrating the Diversity of Our Gifts," reprinted in *Women's Voices in Our Time,* edited by Victoria L. DeFrancisco and Marvin D. Jensen (Prospect Heights, IL: Waveland Press, 1994), 115.

17. Nancy W. Dickey, "Health Care for the New Millennium: The AMA Plan for Health System Reform," *Vital Speeches of the Day,* 65 (15 April 1999).

18. Michael A. Twitchell, "The Flood Gates of the Mind," *Winning Orations.* Reprinted by permission of Larry Schnoor, Executive Secretary, Interstate Oratorical Association, Mankato, MN.

Chapter 10

Wording Your Speech

Language functions on multiple levels. It is a referential, relational, and symbolic medium of communication. As language refers to things, it is *referential*. When you label or name things like "dog," "tree," "cupcake," you are employing the referential nature of language. As you probably realize, young children learn the power of language as a referential tool early.

Language also has *relational powers*; it suggests associations between people. "Give me that cupcake" not only points to the cupcake, but also indicates that one person has the power or authority to command another person. Some groups even use their own special languages that exclude others. Technical language is used most often by professionals. Slang doesn't sound right when spoken by an outsider. It might sound odd, for example, to hear your grandmother say, "That's a gnarly set of wheels, man."

167

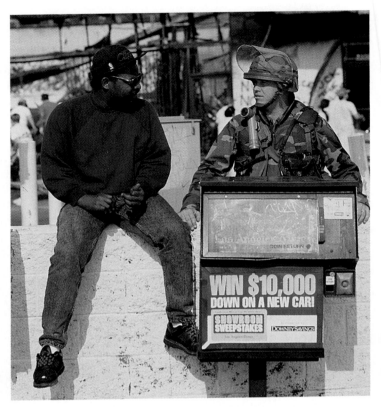

Getting someone to see your point of view often depends on strategic rhetorical decisions.

And, language is *symbolic*, by which we mean that it can be disconnected from the concrete world. We can talk about unreal things like unicorns and gremlins or abstract constructs like democracy and love. Whole empires of thought can be constructed out of language. When you speak, it's not enough to know the words; you must also understand how language reflects human relationships and shared senses of reality—your culture and thinking.

In the next three chapters, we'll turn our attention to the encoding of messages. **Encoding** occurs when you put ideas into words and actions. Encoding includes your choice of language, use of visual aids, and even bodily and vocal behaviors. In this chapter, we'll focus on selecting your speaking style, creating a speaking atmosphere, and using language strategically.

SELECTING YOUR STYLE

Generally, spoken language is uncomplicated; it has to be since we use it every day—at the grocery store, over the back fence, around the supper table, and in the street. Usually public speakers adopt the conversational quality of everyday language because listeners prefer it. Most of the time when you speak, you will choose this oral style.

Oral style is informal, similar to conversation. Occasionally, spoken language assumes a more complicated and formal style. This is the type of language more closely resembling written work and naturally referred to as **written style.** It usually indicates a formal occasion or weighty topic. Consider the following examples of written and oral style:

Written Style	Oral Style
Remit the requested amount forthwith.	Pay your bill.
Will you be having anything else?	Whutkinahgitcha?
To avoid injury, keep hands away from the cutting surface.	Don't touch the blade!
Contact a service representative to register your dissatisfaction with the product.	Call to complain.

If you write out your whole speech before giving it, the result is likely to be stilted and stiff. It may sound more like an essay than a speech. For example, consider the following introduction:

I am most pleased that you could come this morning. I would like to use this opportunity to discuss with you a subject of inestimable importance to us all— the impact of inflationary spirals on students enrolled in institutions of higher education.

Translated into an oral style, a speaker would say

Thanks for coming. I'd like to talk today about a problem for all of us—the rising cost of going to college.

SPEAKING OF . . . *Skills*
Oral Versus Written Style

How do you instantly recognize that a speaker has written out a speech? Inherently it sounds like it's been written. The speaker uses written rather than oral style. Here are some ways that oral style differs from written style:

1. The average sentence is shorter in oral communication.
2. You use fewer different words when you speak.
3. You also use a larger number of short words such as "it" and "the." In fact, fifty simple words constitute almost half of your speaking vocabulary.
4. You refer to people more often with words like "I," "you," "me," "our," and "us."
5. You use more qualifying words such as "much," "many," "a lot," and "most."
6. Your language choices are more informal and you use more contractions.

Notice how much more natural the second version sounds. The first is wordy—filled with prepositional phrases, complex words, and formal sentences. The second contains shorter sentences and simpler vocabulary, and it addresses the audience directly.

For most speech occasions, you should cultivate an oral style. On rare, highly ceremonial occasions, you may decide to read from a prepared text. However, even then, you should strive for an oral style.[1] There are four qualities that will help you develop a clear and effective oral style. Let's consider accuracy, simplicity, restatement, and coherence.

Accuracy

Careful word choice is an essential ingredient to effectively transmitting your meaning to an audience. Oral language is usually concrete and specific. If you tell a hardware store clerk, "I broke the doohickey on my whichamicallit and I need a thingamajig to fix it," you'd better have the whichamicallit in your hand or the clerk won't understand. When you speak, your goal is precision. You should leave no doubt about your meaning.

Since words are symbols that represent concepts or objects, your listeners may attach a meaning to your words that's quite different from the one you intended. This misinterpretation becomes more likely as your words become more abstract. Democracy, for example, doesn't mean the same thing to a citizen in the suburbs as it does to a citizen in the ghetto. Democracy will elicit different meanings from Americans who belong to the Moral Majority than it will from those who belong to the American Socialist Party.

Students of general semantics, the study of words or symbols and their relationships to reality, warn us that many errors in thinking and communication arise from treating words as if they were actual conditions, processes, or objects. Words are not fixed and timeless in meaning, nor does everyone use them in exactly the same way.

To avoid vagueness, choose words that express the exact shade of meaning you wish to communicate. You might say that an object shines, but the object might also *glow, glitter, glisten, flare, gleam, glare, blaze, shimmer, glimmer, flicker, sparkle, flash,* and *beam.* Each word allows you to describe the object more precisely.

Simplicity

"Speak," said Abraham Lincoln, "so that the most lowly can understand you, and the rest will have no difficulty." Because electronic media reach audiences and cultures more varied than Lincoln could have imagined, you have even more reason to follow his advice today. Say *learn* rather than *ascertain, try* rather than *endeavor, use* rather than *utilize, help* rather than *facilitate.* Don't use a longer or less familiar word when a simple one is just as clear. Evangelist Billy Sunday illustrated the effectiveness of familiar words in this example:

If a man were to take a piece of meat and smell it and look disgusted, and his little boy were to say, "What's the matter with it, Pop?" and he were to say, "It is undergoing a process of decomposition in the formation of new chemical compounds," the boy would be all in. But if the father were to say, "It's rotten," then the boy would understand and hold his nose. "Rotten" is a good Anglo-Saxon word, and you do not have to go to the dictionary to find out what it means.[2]

Simplicity doesn't mean *simplistic*, if you talk down to your audience, they will be insulted. Instead, speak directly using words that convey precise, concrete meanings.

Restatement

If accuracy and simplicity were your only criteria as a speaker, your messages might resemble a famous World War II bulletin: "Sighted sub, sank same." But because words literally disappear into the atmosphere as soon as they're spoken, you don't have the writer's advantage when transmitting ideas to others. Instead, you must rely heavily on restatement.

Restatement is the repetition of words, phrases, and ideas so as to clarify and reinforce them. The key here is not simply to repeat yourself, but to rephrase in order to advance listeners' understanding or acceptance of an idea. Advertisers frequently depend on restatement to reinforce their point. For example, the jingle for a typical laundry soap might make the point this way: "Suds gets your clothes clean. Suds removes dirt, stains, and odors. Suds tackles the toughest cleaning jobs your kids bring home."

Restating an idea from a number of perspectives usually involves listing its components or redefining the basic concept. You can see this principle of reiteration at work in this speech that a student gave on urban sprawl:

If you're like most Americans, your dream home is somewhere in the suburbs—plenty of fresh air, close to your job and schools, all on a wooded lot. But, more and more of us are discovering that we're the victims of urban sprawl, the unplanned growth of housing developments that contribute to air pollution, traffic congestion, and visual blight. If you live in Las Vegas, your view of the mountains will be obscured by smog. If you live in Atlanta, you'll experience the longest average commute of any city in the country. And, if you make Akron or Austin or Denver your home, population density increases yearly. The effects of urban sprawl can be seen across our nation. Every day, many Americans drive between 20 and 30 miles to work, more than 50 acres of farmland and woods are plowed under, and many of our cities can't meet federal clean air standards.[3]

This student speaker realized that her audience probably was uncertain about the meaning of the phrase "urban sprawl." She listed three effects of unchecked urban growth—air pollution, traffic congestion, and visual blight. Then she restated them in several ways so that her listeners could easily understand the focus of her speech.

Restatement can help your listeners remember your ideas more readily. However, be careful of mindless repetition; too many restatements, especially of simple ideas, can be boring.

Coherence

Just as you must use restatement because your audience doesn't have the luxury of reviewing the points, you must also signal where you're at in your speech because your listeners aren't able to perceive punctuation marks that might help them distinguish one idea from another as you speak. In order to be understood, oral communication requires **coherence,** or the logical connection of ideas. To achieve coherence you should use forecasts or previews, summaries, and signposts.

Forecasts or *previews* precede the development of the body of the speech, usually forming part of the introduction. They provide clues to the overall speech structure. Previews are especially helpful in outlining the major topics of the speech. Consider the following examples:

Today I am going to talk about three aspects of family life—trust, love, and commitment.

There are four major elements in developing a winning resume. We'll look at establishing your strengths, forming a positive impression, including sufficient detail, and developing an edge.

The history of the Vietnam War can be divided into two periods—the French involvement and the commitment of American troops.

Each of these forecasts provides a link between the introduction to the speech and the development of ideas in the body of the speech. A listener knows what to expect from each forecast. In a sense, you are providing a road map when you signal your speech structure in a forecast.

Summaries provide coherence in your speech by recapping ideas you've covered. You can summarize ideas at interim points before you move on to another topic, such as "Trust is an important ingredient in promoting a strong family life for the two reasons we just examined. It increases self-disclosure and promotes a sense of well-being. Now, let's examine a second element—love."

It is especially important to summarize your main ideas at the end of your speech. It is your last chance to remind listeners of your main topics and leave them with a final impression of your speech. A final summary usually forms part of the conclusion and often parallels the forecasts. For example, a final summary might look like this:

Today we talked about what constitutes a strong family life. Experts agree that there are three things that all families need—trust, love, and commitment.

When you sit down to apply for your first job, remember the four major elements in developing a winning resume. Think about establishing your strengths, forming a positive impression, including sufficient detail, and developing an edge.

The history of the Vietnam War has been divided into two periods—the French involvement and the commitment of American troops.

Notice that all three examples of final summaries parallel the forecast for the speech. They are direct, clear, and remind the listener of the primary structure of the speech.

In addition to forecasts and summaries, you must use **signposts** or *transitions*—linking phrases that move an audience from one idea to another. Signposts or transitions are words or phrases—such as *first, next,* or *as a result*—that help listeners follow the movement of your ideas. Signposts such as "the history of this invention begins in . . ." also provide clues to the overall message structure. The following are useful signposts:

✔ In the first place . . . The second point is . . .

✔ In addition to . . . notice that . . .

✔ Now look at it from a different angle . . .

✔ You must keep these three things in mind in order to understand the importance of the fourth . . .

✔ What was the result? . . .

✔ Turning now to . . .

The preceding signposts are neutral: they tell an audience that another idea is coming but don't indicate whether it's similar, different, or more important. You can improve the coherence of your speeches by indicating the precise relationships among ideas. Those relationships include parallel/hierarchical, similar/different, and coordinate/subordinate relationships. Here are some examples:

Parallel: Not only . . . but also . . .

Hierarchical: More important than these . . .

Different: In contrast . . .

Similar: Similar to this . . .

Coordinated: One must consider X, Y, and Z . . .

Subordinated: On the next level is . . .

Forecasts, summaries, and signposts are important to your audience. Forecasts and summaries give listeners an overall sense of your entire message; if listeners can easily see the structure, they'll better understand and remember your speech. The signposts lead your listeners step by step through the speech, signaling specific relationships between and among ideas.

CREATING AN ATMOSPHERE

You cultivate the atmosphere of the speaking occasion largely through your speaking style. In a graduation speech or an awards banquet address, you want to encourage the personal reflection of your listeners; but at a fraternity gathering or holiday celebration, you want to create a social, interactive atmosphere.

Sometimes the atmosphere of the occasion dictates what speaking style should be used. You don't expect a light, humorous speaking style during a funeral. Even so, sometimes a eulogist will tell a funny or amusing story about the deceased. Yet the overall tone of a speech at a funeral should be solemn. In contrast, a speech after a football victory, election win, or successful fund drive is seldom somber. Victory speeches are times for celebration and unity.

The speaking **atmosphere** is the mind-set or mental attitude that you attempt to create in your audience. A serious speaker urging graduating seniors to remember the most important things in life might say, "Rank your values and live by them." That same idea expressed by actor Alan Alda sounded more humorous:

> We live in a time that seems to be split about its values. In fact it seems to be schizophrenic.
> For instance, if you pick up a magazine like Psychology Today, you're liable to see an article like "White Collar Crime: It's More Widespread than You Think." Then in the back of the magazine they'll print an advertisement that says, "We'll write your doctoral thesis for 25 bucks." You see how values are eroding? I mean, a doctoral thesis ought to go for at least a C-note.[4]

How do you generate an atmosphere or mood in your listeners? The answer depends on the speaking situation, your speech purpose, and your listeners' expectations. You can adjust the intensity of your speech and manage the appropriateness of your language to communicate a relationship with your listeners.

Intensity

You can communicate your feelings about ideas and objects through word choices. You can communicate your attitude toward your subject by choosing words that show how you feel. This, in turn, suggests how you expect your listeners to react to the subject. In one way, you are demonstrating their response through your language choices. For example, consider these attitudinally weighted terms:

Highly Positive	Relatively Neutral	Highly Negative
Savior	G.I.	Enemy
Patriot	Soldier	Baby-killer
Freedom fighter	Combatant	Foreign devil

These nine terms are organized by their intensity, ranging from the highly positive "savior" to the highly negative "foreign devil." Notice the religious connotations present in the extreme examples of language intensity. Such terms have obviously potent associations with deeply held beliefs.

How intense should your language be? Communication scholar John Waite Bowers suggested a useful rule of thumb: let your language be, roughly, one step more intense than the position or attitude held by your audience.[5] For example, if your audience is already committed to your negative position on tax reform, then you can choose intensely negative words, such as *regressive* and *stifling*. If your audience is uncommitted, you should opt for comparatively neutral words, such as *burdensome*. And, if your listeners are in favor of tax changes, you can use still less negative words, such as *unfair*, to encourage them to keep an open mind and avoid having them tune you out. Intense language can generate intense reactions, but only if you match your word choices to your listeners' attitudes.

SPEAKING OF . . . *Ethics*
Doublespeak

Advertisers and politicians are often accused of using words that deceive or mislead. Think of any recent advertising or political campaign. *Liberal,* for instance, was once a positive label. In recent campaigns, the word became associated with negative attributes. It has come to connote the big spender—someone who wastes public energy and tax dollars on unrealistic schemes.

You can probably identify hundreds of words or phrases used to disguise facts. The Reagan and Clinton administrations didn't want to raise taxes but pursued *revenue enhancement* through *user fees.* People below the poverty line are *fiscal underachievers.* Nuclear weapons are labeled *radiation enhancement devices* and *peacekeepers.* And the 1984 invasion of Grenada was officially a *predawn vertical insertion.* Some language usage makes the unpleasant seem good and the positive appear negative. Language can shield us from the reality it represents.

Such name calling is by no means limited to politicians. Advertisers market *new and improved* products. We're tantalized with *real faux pearls* and *genuine imitation leather.* Advertisers exploit our health consciousness with *low-cholesterol* and *high-fiber* ingredients. Take a few moments to think about the following uses of language:

1. Suppose that you notice biased language in an article you're reading to research a speech topic. Should you cite the article as supporting material in your speech?
2. You genuinely believe in your recommendations for solving the problems you outline in a speech and you want to convince your listeners to sign a petition for change. Is it fair to use scare tactics or to tell them that they've got only one day left to act when in fact there's more time?
3. Should you ever use racy, obscene, or questionable language during a speech? Does it affect the relationship you establish with your listeners?
4. Is it ever fair to call people who aren't present crooks or attach similar labels to them?
5. Do you think language can obscure our understanding of reality? Under what circumstances do you think this happens? Should anything be done to make language more honest? What can you do to accomplish this?

Appropriateness

Your language should be appropriate to the speech topic and situation. Solemn occasions call for restrained and dignified language; joyful occasions call for informal and lively word choices. The language used for a marriage ceremony wouldn't work at a pep rally, and vice versa. Suit your language to the atmosphere of the occasion.

Informal Language   Make sure that your language is appropriate to your audience. Before you use informal language, check to see who's listening. Informal language, including slang, quickly goes out of style. *Gee whiz, wow, good grief, hip, cool, far out, homeboy, awesome, radical,* and *gnarly* became popular at different times. *Far out* would sound silly in a speech to your peers, and *gnarly* would sound ridiculous to an audience of senior citizens. As you work through your speech, consider your language choices as inherent elements in developing the tone of your speech.

Gender-Neutral Language Words can communicate values or attitudes to your listeners. As we suggested in the introduction to this chapter, they also suggest relationships between you and your audience. Gender-linked words, particularly nouns and pronouns, require special attention. **Gender-linked words** are those that directly or indirectly identify males or females—*policeman, washerwoman, poet,* and *poetess.* Pronouns such as *he* and *she* and adjectives such as *his* and *her* are obviously gender-linked words. **Gender-neutral words** do not directly or indirectly denote males or females—*chairperson, police officer,* or *firefighter.*

Since the 1960s and the advent of the women's movement, consciousness of gendered language has gradually surfaced. The question of whether language use affects culture and socialization still is being debated. However, as a speaker you must be careful not to alienate your audience or to propagate stereotypes unconsciously through your use of language. In addition to avoiding most gender-linked words, you've got to handle two more problems:

1. *Inaccurately excluding members of one sex.* Some uses of gendered pronouns inaccurately reflect social-occupational conditions in the world: "A nurse sees her patients eight hours a day, but a doctor sees his for only ten minutes." Many women are doctors, just as many men are nurses. Most audience members are aware of this and may be displeased if they feel that you're stereotyping roles in the medical profession.

2. *Stereotyping male and female psychological or social characteristics.* "Real men never cry." "A woman's place is in the home." "The Marines are looking for a few good men." "Sugar 'n spice 'n everything nice—that's what little girls are made of." Falling back on these stereotypes gets speakers into trouble with listeners, both male and female. In these days of raised consciousness, audiences are insulted to hear such misinformed assertions. In addition, these stereotypes conceal the potential in individuals whose talents are not limited by their gender.

These problem areas demand your attention. A speaker who habitually uses sexist language is guilty of ignoring important speaking conventions that have taken shape over the past several decades. How can you avoid sexist language? Here are four easy ways:

1. *Speak in the plural.* Say "Bankers are often . . . They face . . ." This tactic is often sufficient to make your language gender-neutral.

2. *Say "he or she" when you must use a singular subject.* Say "A student majoring in business is required to sign up for an internship. He or she can . . ." This strategy works well as long as you don't overdo it. If you find yourself cluttering sentences with "he or she," switch to the plural.

3. *Remove gender inflections.* It's painless to say "firefighter" instead of "fireman," "chair" or "chairperson" instead of "chairman," and "tailor" instead of "seamstress." Gender inflections can usually be removed without affecting your speech.

4. *Use gender-specific pronouns for gender-specific processes, people, or activities.* It is acceptable to talk about a mother as *her* or a current or former president of the

United States as *him*. Men do not naturally bear children, and a woman has not yet been elected to the White House.

Ultimately, the search for gender-neutral idioms is an affirmation of mutual respect and a recognition of equal worth and the essential dignity of individuals. Gender differences are important in many aspects of life, but when they dominate public talk, they're ideologically oppressive. Be gender neutral in public talk to remove barriers to effective communications.[6]

Selecting an appropriate style is a matter of assessing yourself, your audience, the situation or context, and your speaking purposes. A thorough assessment of these variables will help you select an appropriate style.

In summary, wording your speech demands careful thought about the clarity of your language use, the persuasive force lying behind words, and the overall sense of tone or style that results from choosing language with particular characteristics. In the world of international diplomacy, a wrong word can cause a breakdown in negotiations. In your world, it can produce confusion, misunderstanding, or even disgust. Take time to shape your oral language as carefully as you shape your ideas.

USING LANGUAGE STRATEGICALLY

Developing an effective oral speaking style is important. You will also, however, want to tap more directly into the powers of language—the powers to alter people's minds and move them to action. To accomplish those goals, you need to use oral language strategically. We will focus on three of the most common language strategies: definitions, imagery, and metaphor.

Speech Writer's Workshop
Use the Speech Workshop to refine your Language Strategy.

Definitions

Audience members need to understand the fundamental concepts of your speech. You can't expect them to understand your ideas if your language is unfamiliar. As a speaker, you have several options when working to define unfamiliar or difficult concepts.

You're most familiar with a **dictionary definition,** which categorizes an object or concept and specifies its characteristics: "An orange is a fruit (category) that is round, orange in color, and a member of the citrus family (characteristics)." Dictionary definitions sometimes help you learn unfamiliar words, but they don't help an audience very much. If you do use dictionary definitions, go to specialized dictionaries. You certainly wouldn't depend on *Webster's Third International Dictionary* to define foreclosure or liability for a presentation on real estate law. For this technical application, sources such as *Black's Law Dictionary* and *Guide to American Law* are more highly respected.

Occasionally, a word has so many meanings that you have to choose one. If that's the case, use a stipulative definition to orient your listeners to your subject matter. A **stipulative definition** designates the way a word will be used in a certain context. You might say, "By rich I mean, . . ." or you might use an expert's stipulative definition such as this one from former President Jimmy Carter:

Who is rich? I'm not talking about bank accounts. . . . A rich person is someone with a home and a modicum of education and a chance for at least a job and who believes that if you make a decision that it'll have some effect at least in your own life, and who believes that the police and the judges are on your side. These are the rich people.[7]

Web Exploration

To compare dictionary definitions with stipulative and other types of definitions go to

http://awl.com/german

You can further clarify a term or concept by telling your audience how you are not going to use the concept—by using a **negative definition.** So, Chicago police Sergeant Bruce Talbot defined "gateway drug" in this manner:

[F]or adolescents, cigarette smoking is a gateway drug to illicit drugs such as marijuana and crack cocaine. By gateway drug I do not mean just that cigarettes are the first drug young people encounter, alcohol is. But unlike alcohol, which is first experienced in a social ritual such as church or an important family event, cigarettes are the first drug minors buy themselves and use secretly outside the family and social institutions.[8]

Defining negatively can clear away possible misconceptions. Using a negative definition along with a stipulative definition, as did Sergeant Talbot, allows you to treat a commonplace phenomenon in a different way.

Sometimes you can reinforce an idea by telling your listeners where a word came from. One way to do this is by using an etymological definition. An **etymological definition** is the derivation of a single word; an example of this would be tracing the word *communication* back to its Latin origins.

One of the best ways to define is by an exemplar definition, especially if the concept is unfamiliar or technical. **Exemplar definitions** are familiar examples. You

Definitions help you to grasp concepts. Contextual definitions are used in specific contexts.

might tell your listeners, "Each day, most of you stroll past the Old Capitol on your way to classes. That building is a perfect example of what I want to talk about today—Georgian architecture." Be careful to use in your definition only those examples that are familiar to your audience members.

A **contextual definition** tells listeners how a word is used in a specific situation. For example, a driving instructor tells her student, "You're going to learn defensive driving. That means you'll be watching out for the other guy. It's not enough just to know the rules of the road. You need to be a proactive driver—watching out for danger spots and other drivers who aren't as careful as you are."

Still another means of making technical or abstract notions easier to understand is the **analogical definition.** An analogy compares a process or event that is unknown with known ones, as in, "Hospitals and labs use cryogenic tanks, which work much like large thermos bottles, to freeze tissue samples, blood, and other organic matter." By referring to what is familiar, the analogical definition can make the unfamiliar much easier to grasp. But the speaker must be sure that the analogy fits.

The points here are simple but important: (1) You have many different kinds of definitions to choose from when working with unfamiliar or difficult concepts. (2) Select definitional strategies that make sense for your subject matter, your audience, and your purposes.

Imagery

People grasp their world through the senses of sight, smell, hearing, taste, and touch. To intensify listeners' experiences, you can appeal to these senses. The senses through which you reach your listeners directly are the visual and the auditory. Listeners can see you, your facial expressions, your movements, and your visual aids, and they can hear what you say (see Figure 10.1).

You can stimulate your listeners' senses indirectly by using language to recall images they have previously experienced. **Imagery** consists of sets of sensory pictures evoked in the imagination through language. The language of imagery is divided into seven types, each related to the particular sensation that it seeks to evoke: visual (sight), auditory (hearing), gustatory (taste), olfactory (smell), tactile (touch), kinesthetic (muscle strain), and organic (internal sensations).

Visual Imagery   Visual imagery describes optical stimuli. Try to make your audience see the objects or situations that you're describing. Mention size, shape, color, and movement. Recount events in vivid visual language. Consider the conclusion from a speech by former Federal Communications Commissioner Newton N. Minow to the Gannett Foundation Media Center in 1991. He envisioned a past event, a look at primitive TV in 1938, to reintroduce some timeless problems:

> *I commend some extraordinary words to the new generation. E. B. White sat in a darkened room in 1938 to see the beginning of television, an experimental electronic box that projected images in the room. Once he saw it, Mr. White wrote: "We shall stand or fall by television, of that I am sure. I believe television is going to be the test of the modern world, and that in this new opportunity to see beyond the range of our vision, we shall discover either a new and unbearable disturbance to the general peace, or a saving radiance in the sky."*

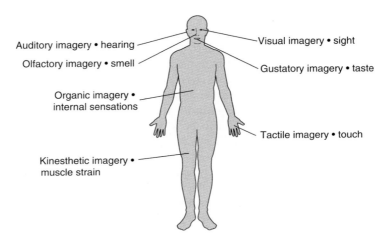

Auditory imagery • hearing
Olfactory imagery • smell
Organic imagery •
internal sensations
Kinesthetic imagery •
muscle strain
Visual imagery • sight
Gustatory imagery • taste
Tactile imagery • touch

FIGURE 10.1   The Types of Imagery

Speakers can stimulate their listeners' senses indirectly through language which triggers sensations.

> *That radiance falls unevenly today. It is still a dim light in education. It has not fulfilled its potential for children. It has neglected the needs of public television. And in the electoral process it has cast a dark shadow.*
>
> *This year, television has enabled us to see Patriot missiles destroy Scud missiles above the Persian Gulf. Will television in the next thirty years be a Scud or a Patriot? A new generation now has the chance to put the vision back into television, to travel from the wasteland to the promised land, and to make television a saving radiance in the sky.*[9]

In this example, Minow played off the "vision" of television as well as the imagery of light (or dark, in the case of the Gulf War of 1991). Vision became a wonderfully ambiguous word referring both to light and to what we learn to see in the world.

Auditory Imagery   To create auditory imagery, use words that describe sounds. Auditory imagery can project your listeners into a scene by helping them hear noises. Author Tom Wolfe described a demolition derby by recounting the chant of the crowd as it joined in the countdown, the explosion of sound as two dozen cars started off in second gear, and finally "the unmistakable tympany of automobiles colliding and cheap-gauge sheet metal buckling."[10] During a fictional conversation in his novel *Hannibal,* Thomas Harris allows the reader to "hear" the voice of a character by writing: "Margot, her voice rough and low, tough-mouthed as a livery pony and resentful of the bit."[11]

Gustatory Imagery   Gustatory imagery depicts sensations of taste. Sometimes you may even be able to help your audience taste what you're describing. Mention its saltiness, sweetness, sourness, or spiciness. Remember that foods have texture as well as taste. While demonstrating how to make popcorn, you might mention the crispness of the kernels, the oily sweetness of melted butter, and the grittiness of salt. Such descriptions allow your listeners to participate in the experience through their imaginations.

Olfactory Imagery Olfactory imagery describes sensations of smell. Help your audience smell the odors connected with the situation you describe. Smell is a powerful sense because it normally triggers a flood of associated images. You can stimulate this process by describing the odor or by comparing the odor with more familiar ones. Elspeth Huxley remembered her childhood trek to Kenya at the turn of the century by recalling its smells:

> *It was the smell of travel in those days, in fact the smell of Africa—dry, peppery yet rich and deep, with an undertone of native body smeared with fat and red ochre and giving out a ripe, partly rancid odour which nauseated some Europeans when they first encountered it but which I, for one, grew to enjoy. This was the smell of the Kikuyu, who were mainly vegetarian. The smell of tribes from the Victoria Nyanza basin, who were meat-eaters and sometimes cannibals, was quite different; much stronger and more musky, almost acrid, and, to me, much less pleasant. No doubt we smelt just as strong and odd to Africans, but of course we were fewer in numbers, and more spread out.*[12]

Like Huxley, Margaret Atwood relies on olfactory imagery when she describes the night sky. However, Atwood makes an unusual link between scent and feeling: "The alcohol smell is on my fingers, cold and remote, piercing, like a steel pin going in. It smells like white enamel basins. When I look up at the stars in the nighttime, cold and white and sharp, I think they must smell like that."[13]

Tactile Imagery Tactile imagery is based on the sensations that come to us through physical contact with external objects. In particular, tactile imagery gives sensations of texture and shape, pressure, and heat or cold. Let your audience feel how rough or smooth, dry or wet, or slimy or sticky modeling clay is (texture and shape). Let them sense the pressure of physical force on their bodies, the weight of a heavy laundry bag, the pinch of jogging shoes, the blast of a high wind on their faces (pressure).

Sensations of heat or cold are aroused by thermal imagery. General Douglas MacArthur's great speech to the cadets of West Point on "duty, honor, and country" used vivid examples of tactile imagery as he described soldiers of the past,

> *bending under soggy pack on many a weary march, from dripping dusk to drizzly dawn, slogging ankle deep through mire of shell-pocked roads; to form grimly for the attack, blue-lipped, covered with sludge and mud, chilled by the wind and rain, driving home to their objective, and for many, to the judgment seat of God.*[14]

Kinesthetic Imagery   Kinesthetic imagery describes the sensations associated with muscle strain and neuromuscular movement. Let your listeners experience for themselves the agonies and joys of marathon racing—the muscle cramps, the constricted chest, the struggle for air—and the magical serenity of getting a second wind and gliding effortlessly toward the finish line.

Organic Imagery   Hunger, dizziness, nausea—these are organic images. Organic imagery captures internal feelings or sensations. There are times when an experience is not complete without the description of inner feelings. The sensation of dizziness as a mountain climber struggles through the rarefied mountain air to reach the summit is one example. Another is the way the bottom drops out of your stomach when a small plane tips sharply, then rights itself. Since such imagery is powerful, you shouldn't offend your audience by overdoing it. Develop the rhetorical sensitivity required to create vividness without making the resultant image gruesome, disgusting, or grotesque.

The seven types of imagery we have considered—visual, auditory, gustatory, olfactory, tactile, kinesthetic, and organic—open new levels of awareness that help listeners experience your message. Different people respond to different kinds of imagery, so you should insert several types of imagery in your speeches. In the following example, note how the speaker combines various sensory appeals to arouse listener interest and reaction:

Image-evoking language can recreate experiences for others.

The strangler struck in Donora, Pennsylvania, in October of 1948. A thick fog billowed through the streets enveloping everything in thick sheets of dirty moisture and a greasy black coating. As Tuesday faded into Saturday, the fumes from the big steel mills shrouded the outlines of the landscape. One could barely see across the narrow streets. Traffic stopped. Men lost their way returning from the mills. Walking through the streets, even for a few moments, caused eyes to water and burn. The thick fumes grabbed at the throat and created a choking sensation. The air acquired a sickening bittersweet smell, nearly a taste. Death was in the air.[15]

In this example, college student Charles Schaillol uses vivid, descriptive phrases to affect the senses of his listeners—visual: "thick sheets of dirty moisture"; organic: "eyes to water and burn"; and olfactory, gustatory: "sickening bittersweet smell, nearly a taste."

To be effective, such illustrations must appear plausible. The language must convey a realistic impression that the situation described could happen. The speaker who describes the strangler that struck Donora offers a plausible account of the event. More important, he does so in a fashion that arouses feelings. His listeners wouldn't have shared the experience if he had simply said, "Air pollution was the cause of death in Donora."

Metaphor

Images created by appealing to the senses are often the result of metaphors. A **metaphor** is the comparison of two dissimilar things. Charles Schaillol's description of fog as "thick sheets of dirty moisture" is one example. Scholar Michael Osborn notes that the metaphor should "result in an intuitive flash of recognition that surprises or fascinates the hearer."[16] Furthermore, good metaphors extend our knowledge or increase our awareness of a person, object, or event. When they're fresh or vivid, they can be powerful aids in evoking feelings. For example, referring to a table's "legs" is a metaphor, but it's boring. It's much more interesting to say, "Balanced on four toothpicks, the antique table swayed under its heavy burden."

Web Exploration

To explore the use of metaphor in speeches go to

http://awl.com/german

Metaphors drawn from everyday experiences provide wide audience appeal. In the following speech, Martin Luther King, Jr., relied on our experiences of light and darkness:

With this faith in the future, with this determined struggle, we will be able to emerge from the bleak and desolate midnight of man's inhumanity to man, into the bright and glittering daybreak of freedom and justice.[17]

This basic light-dark metaphor allowed King to suggest (a) sharp contrasts between inhumanity and freedom and (b) the inevitability of social progress as "daybreak" follows "midnight." The metaphor communicated King's beliefs about justice and injustice and urged others to action. Words are not neutral pipelines for thought. Words not only reflect the world outside your mind, but also, as critic Kenneth Burke suggests, help shape our perceptions of people, events, and social contexts. Language has a potent effect on people's willingness to believe, to feel, and to act.

SAMPLE SPEECH

William Faulkner (1897–1962) presented the following speech on December 10, 1950, as he accepted the Nobel Prize for literature. His listeners might have expected a speech filled with the kind of pessimism so characteristic of his novels. Instead, he greeted them with a stirring challenge to improve humankind.

Notice in particular Faulkner's use of language. Although known for the tortured sentences in his novels, he expresses his ideas clearly and simply in his speech. His style suggests a written speech, yet his use of organic imagery and powerful metaphors keeps the speech alive. The atmosphere is generally serious, befitting the occasion. You might expect a Nobel Prize winner to talk about himself, but Faulkner did just the opposite. He stressed his craft, writing, and the commitment necessary to practice that craft; this material emphasis led naturally to an essentially propositional rather than narrative form. More than 50 years ago, William Faulkner offered a speech that is as relevant today as it was in 1950.

Faulkner establishes a series of contrasts built around a "not this . . . but this" construction to deflect attention from himself to his work. The contrasts sharpen the points he'll make throughout the speech; it's the art, not the artist, that counts; creating art is extraordinarily hard work; we can't write out of fear but out of the need to elevate the soul and spirit of humanity.

He frames his whole speech as an address to young writers.

When he addresses the issue of the bomb and our fear of it, he attacks that fear immediately. First, he suggests the presence of the fear and then via restatement comes back to it in the next three sentences. Second, he continues the linguistic contrasts between fear and spirit, human heart in conflict and the agony and the sweat.

On Accepting the Nobel Prize for Literature William Faulkner[18]

I feel that this award was not made to me as a man, but to my work—a life's work in the agony and sweat of the human spirit, not for glory and least of all for profit, but to create out of the materials of the human spirit something which did not exist before. So this award is only mine in trust. It will not be difficult to find a dedication for the money part of it commensurate with the purpose and significance of its origin. But I would like to do the same with the acclaim too, by using this moment as a pinnacle from which I might be listened to by the young men and women already dedicated to the same anguish and travail, among whom is already that one who will some day stand here where I am standing./1

Our tragedy today is a general and universal physical fear so long sustained by now that we can even bear it. There are no longer problems of the spirit. There is only the question: When will I be blown up? Because of this, the young man or woman writing today has forgotten the problems of the human heart in conflict with itself which alone can make good writing because only that is worth writing about, worth the agony and the sweat./2

He must learn them again. He must teach himself that the basest of all things is to be afraid; and, teaching himself that, forget it forever, leaving no room in his workshop for anything but the old verities and truths of the heart, the old universal truths lacking which any story is ephemeral and doomed—love and honor and pity and pride and compassion and sacrifice. Until he does so, he labors under a curse. He writes not of love but of lust, of defeats in which nobody loses anything of value, of victories without hope and, worst of all, without pity or compassion. His griefs grieve on no universal bones, leaving no scars. He writes not of the heart but of the glands./3

Until he relearns these things, he will write as though he stood among and watched the end of man. I decline to accept the end of man. It is easy enough to say that man is immortal simply because he will endure: that when the last ding-dong of doom has clanged and faded from the last worthless rock hanging tideless in the last red and drying evening, that even then there will still be one more sound: that of his puny inexhaustible voice, still talking. I refuse to accept this. I believe that man will not merely endure: he will prevail. He is immortal, not because he alone among creatures has an inexhaustible voice, but because he has a soul, a spirit capable of compassion and sacrifice and endurance. The poet's, the writer's, duty is to write about these things. It is his privilege to help man endure by lifting his heart, by reminding him of the courage and honor and hope and pride and compassion and pity and sacrifice which have been the glory of his past. The poet's voice need not merely be the record of man, it can be one of the props, the pillars to help him endure and prevail./4

Faulkner expands this central idea via a series of literal and metaphorical contrasts. Read these sentences aloud to capture the pounding rhythm that guides them. Body metaphors complete the paragraph.

Faulkner concludes with a flood of imagery: images are auditory, visual, tactile, and organic ("lifting his heart").

The restatement of vocabulary, the images, the affirmation of life, and, of course, the sheer presence of Faulkner himself combine to make this one of the two or three greatest Nobel Prize speeches ever given.

ASSESSING YOUR PROGRESS

Chapter Summary

1. Language functions on referential, relational, and symbolic levels.

2. Encoding occurs when you put ideas into words and actions.

3. Successful speeches generally follow oral style that is typical of conversations.

4. You can cultivate oral style through accurate word choice, simple phrasing, restatement, and the coherent connection of ideas.

5. The intensity and appropriateness of language can be altered to contribute to the atmosphere or mental attitude created in your audience.

6. Rhetorical strategies are word and phrase choices intended to control the impact of the speech. Three of the most common rhetorical strategies are definition, imagery, and metaphor.

7. Speakers can define unfamiliar or difficult concepts in many ways including dictionary, stipulative, negative, etymological, contextual, and analogical definitions.

8. Imagery consists of word pictures that intensify listeners' experiences through their senses. There are seven types of images: visual, auditory, gustatory, olfactory, tactile, kinesthetic, and organic sensations.

9. Metaphor is the comparison of two dissimilar things.

Key Terms

analogical definition (p. 179)

atmosphere (p. 174)

coherence (p. 172)

contextual definition (p. 179)

dictionary definition (p. 177)

encoding (p. 168)

etymological definition (p. 178)

exemplar definition (p. 178)

forecast (p. 172)

gender-linked words (p. 176)

gender-neutral words (p. 176)

imagery (p. 179)

metaphor (p. 183)

negative definition (p. 178)

oral style (p. 169)

restatement (p. 171)

signposts (p. 173)

stipulative definition (p. 177)

summary (p. 172)

written style (p. 169)

Assessment Activities

1. Choose one of the items listed below and describe it, using the seven kinds of imagery to create an involving portrait for your listeners. How many kinds of imagery did you use? Which was most effective for your listeners?

   A scene from your favorite movie.

   Your favorite cologne.

   A tropical plant.

   A breakfast food.

   A roller coaster ride.

   A complicated machine.

   The oldest building on campus.

   A walk through the park.

2. Find a complicated message (e.g., an insurance policy, an agreement for a credit card, income tax instructions, or a difficult passage from a book). Rewrite it in simple, yet accurate language. Bring copies of both messages to class and present them to your classmates. Which was most effective? Why?

Surfing the Web

1. Begin an Internet search with the general term *dictionary*. What results did you find? Compare the kinds of general dictionaries available online. Next, refine your search by looking for medical, legal, architecture, slang, engineering, and philosophy dictionaries. What other specialized dictionaries can you find online?

2. There are multiple resources for writers and speakers available online. Check out handbooks for writers and speakers. If you're looking for another word to capture your thought, try searching for a thesaurus.

References

1. For a summary of several technical studies distinguishing between oral and written styles, and for a discussion of sixteen characteristics of oral style, see John F. Wilson and Carroll C. Arnold, *Public Speaking as a Liberal Art,* 5th ed. (Boston: Allyn and Bacon, 1983), 227–229.

2. Quoted in John R. Pelsma, *Essentials of Speech* (New York: Crowell, Collier, and Macmillan, 1934), 193.

3. Information for this example was taken from an article by Daniel Pedersen, Vern E. Smith, and Jerry Adler, "Sprawling, Sprawling," *Newsweek,* (19 July 1999), pp. 23–27.

4. Alan Alda, "A Reel Doctor's Advice to Some Real Doctors," in Stephen E. Lucas, *The Art of Public Speaking* (New York: Random House, 1983), 364.

5. John Waite Bowers, "Language and Argument," in *Perspectives on Argumentation,* edited by G. R. Miller and T. R. Nilsen (Glenview, IL: Scott, Foresman, 1966), 168–172.

6. There are many studies of gender and communication. For overviews, see Barbara Bate, *Communication and the Sexes* (New York: Harper & Row, 1987); Judith C. Pearson, *Gender and Communication* (Dubuque, IA: Wm. C. Brown, 1985); and Lea P. Stewart, Pamela J. Cooper, and Sheryl A. Friedly, *Communication Between the Sexes: Sex Differences and Sex-Role Stereotypes* (Scottsdale, AZ: Gorsuch Scaribrick, 1986).

7. James E. Carter, "Excellence Comes from a Repository That Doesn't Change," *Vital Speeches of the Day,* 59 (1 July 1993), 548.

8. Bruce Talbot, "Statement," Hearings before Senate Committee on Commerce, Science, and Transportation, *Tobacco Product Education and Health Promotion Act of 1991, S. 1088,* 14 November 1991, 102nd Congress (Washington, D.C.: U.S. Government Printing Office, 1991), 77.

9. Newton N. Minow, "How Vast the Wasteland Now?" *Representative American Speeches, 1990–1991,* edited by Owen Peterson (New York: H. W. Wilson Co., 1992), 169.

10. A selection from Tom Wolfe, *The Kandy-Kolored Tangerine-Flake Streamline Baby* (Thomas K. Wolfe, Jr., 1965). Reprinted by permission of Farrar, Straus and Giroux, Inc. and International Creative Management.

11. Thomas Harris, *Hannibal* (New York: Random House, 1999), 269.

12. Elspeth Huxley, *The Flame Trees of Thika: Memories of an African Childhood* (London: Chatto & Windes, 1959), 4.

13. Margaret Atwood, *Cat's Eye* (New York: Doubleday, 1989), 24.

14. Excerpt from Douglas MacArthur, "Duty, Honor and Country," *The Dolphin Books of Speeches,* edited by George W. Hibbit (George W. Hibbit, 1965). Reprinted by permission of Doubleday & Company, Inc.

15. From Charles Schaillol, "The Strangler," *Winning Orations.* Reprinted by permission of Larry Schnoor, Executive Secretary, Interstate Oratorical Association, Concordia College, Moorhead, MN. Published by The Interstate Oratorical Association.

16. Michael Osborn, *Orientations to Rhetorical Style* (Chicago: Science Research Associates, 1976), 10.

17. From Martin Luther King, Jr., "Love, Law and Civil Disobedience" (Martin Luther King, Jr., 1963). Reprinted by permission of Joan Daves.

18. William Faulkner, "On Accepting the Nobel Prize for Literature," *The Faulkner Reader* (New York: Random House, 1954).

Delivering Your Speech

Chapter 11

If you're struggling with the physical aspects of delivering your speeches, you're in good company. Many famous speakers have had to overcome severe delivery problems before becoming effective speakers. Abraham Lincoln suffered from extreme speech fright; Eleanor Roosevelt was awkward and clumsy; John F. Kennedy had a strong dialect and repetitive gestures; Helen Keller was blind and deaf. These speakers realized that success depends not only on careful planning before the speech but also on effective presentation. They each worked hard to develop the oral delivery skills that heightened the impact of their ideas.

You must be aware that you communicate with your entire body—your face, your gestures, your voice, and your posture. Your voice and bodily movements help transmit your feelings and attitudes about

189

yourself, your audience, and your topic. You may see speakers who approach the lectern dragging their feet and fussing with their notes. Their attitudes are abundantly clear even before they utter their first words. Unwittingly, these speakers establish audience predispositions that work against them. Even if their ideas are important, those ideas are overshadowed by distracting nonverbal communication.

If you've heard a recording or seen a video of Martin Luther King, Jr., giving his "I Have a Dream" speech, you can appreciate the dramatic difference between hearing him speak and merely reading a copy of the speech. The same is true of Jesse Jackson, Camille Paglia, Rush Limbaugh, Colin Powell, Ann Richards, and Susan Molinari. Oral presentation can add fire to the message. Orality's great strength—its edge—comes from the personal presence established by your voice and your physical presence.

Your speech will gain strength and vitality if it's presented well. To help you achieve this objective, we'll discuss three important aspects of presentation: selecting the method of presentation, using your voice to communicate, and using your body to communicate.

SELECTING THE METHOD OF PRESENTATION

How should you present your speech? Your choice will be based on several criteria, including the type of speaking occasion, the purpose of your speech, your audience analysis, and your own strengths and weaknesses as a speaker. Attention to these considerations will help you decide whether your method of presentation should be impromptu, memorized, read from a manuscript, or extemporized.

The Impromptu Speech

An **impromptu speech** is delivered on the spur of the moment, without preparation. The ability to speak off the cuff is useful in an emergency, but impromptu speeches produce unpredictable outcomes. It's certainly not a good idea to rely on impromptu speaking in place of solid preparation. Whenever possible, you should carefully prepare and practice your speeches.

In an impromptu speech, you must rely entirely on previous knowledge and skill. You might be asked in the middle of a sorority meeting, for example, to give a progress report on your pledge committee. Or, you might be called on in class to summarize the ideas in a paper you turned in last week.

For best results when speaking on an impromptu basis, try to focus on a single idea, carefully relating all details connected to that idea. If you relay the main theme for the annual March-of-Dimes fund drive or the central thesis of your paper, you'll be more likely to stay on track. Sticking with a single idea will keep you from rambling incoherently.

The Memorized Speech

On rare occasions, you may write out your speech and commit it to memory. When notecards or a TelePrompTer cannot be used, it may be acceptable for you to give a **memorized speech.** When making a toast at your parents' twenty-fifth wedding anniversary, for example, you probably wouldn't want to speak from notecards. Some speakers, such as comedians, deliver their remarks from memory to free their hands to mimic the movements of the character they are playing.

Speakers who use memorized presentations are usually most effective when they write their speeches to sound like informal and conversational speech rather than formal, written essays. Remember that with a memorized speech, you'll have difficulty responding to audience feedback. Since the words of the speech are predetermined, you can't easily adjust them as the speech progresses.

The Manuscript Speech

A **manuscript speech** is written out beforehand and then read from a manuscript or TelePrompTer. By using TelePrompTers, speakers can appear to be looking at their listeners while they're really reading their manuscripts projected onto clear sheets of Plexiglas. When extremely careful wording is required, the manuscript speech is appropriate. When the president addresses Congress, for example, a slip of the tongue could misdirect domestic or foreign policies. Many radio and television speeches are read from manuscripts because of the strict time limits imposed by broadcasting schedules.

The Extemporaneous Speech

Most speeches that you'll deliver will be extemporaneous. An **extemporaneous speech** is one that is prepared in advance and presented from abbreviated notes. Most of the advice in this textbook pertains to extemporaneous speaking. Extemporaneous speeches are nearly as polished as memorized ones, but they are more vigorous, flexible, and spontaneous.

Before giving an extemporaneous speech, you must plan and prepare a detailed outline and speaking notecards. Then, working from the notecards, you practice the speech aloud, using your own words to communicate the ideas. Your expressions differ somewhat each time you deliver the speech. Your notes, however, regulate the order of ideas. With this approach, you gain control of the material and also preserve your spontaneity of expression. Good preparation is the key to extemporaneous speaking. Otherwise, your speech may resemble an impromptu speech; in fact, the terms impromptu and extemporaneous are often confused.

While you may use all four types of speech presentation for different occasions during your lifetime, extemporaneous speaking is the most important. Extemporaneous speaking displays your enthusiasm for speaking and the sincerity of your ideas. In order to develop your skills as an extemporaneous speaker, you will need to learn to use both your voice and your body to communicate with your listeners.

USING YOUR VOICE TO COMMUNICATE

Your voice is an instrument that helps convey the meaning of language. Since preliterate times, when all cultures were oral, voice has been the primary connector between people. Sounds flow among people, integrating them, creating a sense of identification, of community.[1] Although you've been speaking for years, you've probably not tapped the full potential of your voice—its power to connect you with others. You'll need to take time to practice in order to achieve your vocal potential, just as you would to master any instrument. The suggestions in this section will help you to get started.

You communicate your enthusiasm to your listeners through your voice. By learning about the characteristics of vocal quality, you can make your ideas more interesting. Listen to a stock market reporter rattle off the daily industrial averages. Every word might be intelligible, but the reporter's vocal expression may be so repetitive and monotonous that the ideas seem unexciting. Then, listen to Al Michaels doing a play-by-play of a football game or Dick Vitale covering a basketball game. The excitement of their broadcasts depends largely on their voices.

Our society prizes one essential vocal quality above all others—a sense of "conversationality."[2] The conversational speaker creates a sense of two-way, interpersonal relationship, even when behind a lectern. The best hosts of afternoon talk shows or evening newscasts speak as though they're engaging each listener in a personal conversation. Speakers who've developed a conversational quality—Oprah Winfrey, Peter Jennings, Barbara Walters, and Jay Leno, for example—have recognized that they're talking with, not at, an audience.

Web Exploration
For some examples of vocal exercises go to
http://awl.com/german

The Effective Speaking Voice

Successful speakers use their voices to shape their ideas and emotionally color their messages. A flexible speaking voice possesses intelligibility, variety, and understandable stress patterns.

Intelligibility **Intelligibility** refers to the ease with which a listener can understand what you're saying. It depends on volume, rate, enunciation, and pronunciation. Most of the time, slurred enunciation, a rapid speaking rate, or soft volume is acceptable because you know the people you're talking with and because you're probably only three to five feet from them. In public speaking, however, you may be addressing people you don't know, often from twenty-five feet or more away. When speaking in public, you have to work on making yourself intelligible:

1. *Adjust your volume.* Probably the most important single factor in intelligibility is how loudly you speak. **Volume**—how loudly or softly you speak—is related to the distance between you and your listeners and the amount of noise that is present. You must realize that your own voice sounds louder to you than it does to your listeners. Obviously, if you're speaking in an auditorium filled with several hundred people, you need to project your voice by increasing your volume. However, you shouldn't forget that a corresponding reduction in volume is required when your listeners are only a few feet away. The amount of surrounding noise with which you must compete also has an effect on your volume. (See Figure 11.1.) Increase your volume to counter a distraction.

2. *Control your rate.* **Rate** is the number of words spoken per minute. In animated conversation, you may jabber along at 200 to 250 words per minute. This rate is typical of people raised in the northern, midwestern, or western United States. As words tumble out of your mouth in informal conversations, they're usually intelligible because they don't have to travel far. In large auditoriums or out-

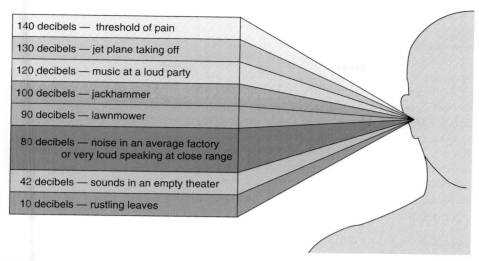

140 decibels — threshold of pain

130 decibels — jet plane taking off

120 decibels — music at a loud party

100 decibels — jackhammer

90 decibels — lawnmower

80 decibels — noise in an average factory
or very loud speaking at close range

42 decibels — sounds in an empty theater

10 decibels — rustling leaves

FIGURE 11.1   Loudness Levels

As you can see, noise varies considerably. You should adjust your volume when you speak to a "quiet" audience as well as if you are competing with a lawnmower outside the building.

doors, though, rapid delivery can impede intelligibility. Echoes sometimes distort or destroy sounds in rooms; ventilation fans interfere with sound. Outdoors, words seem to vanish into the open air. When addressing larger audiences, cut your rate by a third or more. Obviously you don't go around timing your speaking rate, but you can remind yourself of potential rate problems as you prepare to speak. Get feedback from your instructors and classmates regarding your speaking rate.

3. *Enunciate clearly.* **Enunciation** refers to the crispness and precision with which you form words. Good enunciation is the clear and distinct utterance of syllables and words. Most of us are "lip lazy" in normal conversation. We slur sounds, drop syllables, and skip over the beginnings and endings of words. This laziness may not inhibit communication between friends, but it can seriously undermine a speaker's intelligibility.

When speaking publicly, force yourself to say "going" instead of "go-in," "just" instead of "jist," and "government" instead of "guvment." You will need to open your mouth wider and force your lips and tongue to form the consonants firmly. If you're having trouble enunciating clearly, ask your instructor for some exercises to improve your performance. (See "Speaking of . . . Skills: Vocal Exercises.")

4. *Meet standards of pronunciation.* To be intelligible, you must meet audience expectations regarding acceptable pronunciation. Any peculiarity of pronunciation is sure to be noticed by some listeners. For example, the "t" in "often" is silent although some speakers pronounce it. Your different pronunciation may distract your listeners and undermine your credibility as a speaker.

Web Exploration
To learn more about different dialects go to
http://awl.com/german

A **dialect** is language use—including vocabulary, grammar, and pronunciation—unique to a particular group or region. Your pronunciation and grammatical or syntactical arrangement of words determine your dialect. You may have a foreign accent, a southern or northern dialect, a Vietnamese pitch pattern, a New England twang, or a Hispanic trill. A clash of dialects can result in confusion and frustration for both speaker and listener. Audiences can make negative judgments about the speaker's credibility—that is, the speaker's education, reliability, responsibility, and capacity for leadership—based solely on dialect.[3] Researchers call these judgments *vocal stereotypes*.[4] Wary of vocal stereotypes, many news anchors have adopted a midwestern American dialect, a manner of speaking that is widely accepted across the country. Many speakers become bilingual, using their own dialects when facing local audiences but switching to midwestern American when addressing more varied audiences. When you speak, you'll have to decide whether you should use the grammar, vocabulary, and vocal patterns of middle America.

Variety   As you move from conversations with friends to the larger arena of public speaking, you may discover that listeners accuse you of monotony of pitch or rate. When speaking in a large public setting, you should compensate for the greater distance that sounds have to travel by varying certain characteristics of your voice. Variety is produced by changes in rate, pitch, stress, and pauses.

1. *Vary your rate.* Earlier, we discussed the rate at which we normally speak. Alter your speaking rate to match your ideas. Slow down to emphasize your own thoughtfulness or quicken the pace when your ideas are emotionally charged. Observe, for example, how Larry King varies his speaking rate from caller to caller or how an evangelist changes pace regularly. A varied rate keeps an audience's attention riveted to the speech.

2. *Change your pitch.* **Pitch** is the frequency of sound waves in a particular sound. Three aspects of pitch—level, range, and variation—are relevant to effective vocal communication. Your everyday pitch level—whether it is habitually in the soprano, alto, tenor, baritone, or bass range—is adequate for most of your daily communication needs.

The key to successful control of pitch depends on understanding the importance of *pitch variation*. As a general rule, use higher pitches to communicate excitement and lower pitches to create a sense of control or solemnity. Adjust the pitch to fit the emotion.

Stress   A third aspect of vocal behavior is stress. **Stress** is the way in which sounds, syllables, and words are accented. Without vocal stress, you'd sound like a computer. Vocal stress is achieved in two ways—through vocal emphasis and through the judicious use of pauses.

Use Vocal Emphasis   **Emphasis** is the way that you accent or attack words. You create emphasis principally through increased volume, changes in pitch, or variations in rate. Emphasis can affect the meanings of your sentences. Notice how the meaning of "Jane's taking Tom out for pizza tonight" varies with changes in word emphasis:

✓ "JANE's taking Tom out for pizza tonight." (Jane, not Alyshia or Shani, is taking Tom out.)

✓ "Jane's taking TOM out for pizza tonight." (She's not taking out Olan or Christopher.)

✓ "Jane's taking Tom OUT for pizza tonight." (They're not staying home as usual.)

✓ "Jane's taking Tom out for PIZZA tonight." (They're not having hamburgers or tacos.)

✓ "Jane's taking Tom out for pizza TONIGHT." (They're going out tonight, not tomorrow or next weekend.)

A lack of vocal stress not only gives the impression that you are bored but also causes misunderstandings of your meaning. Changes in rate can also be used to add emphasis. Relatively simple changes can emphasize where you are in an outline: "My s-e-c-o-n-d point is. . . ." Several changes in rate can indicate the relationship among ideas. Consider the following example:

We are a country faced with [moderate rate] . . . financial deficits, racial tensions, an energy crunch, a crisis of morality, environmental depletion, government waste [fast rate], . . . and - a - stif - ling - na - tion - al - debt [slow rate].

The ideas pick up speed through the accelerating list of problems but then come to an emphatic halt with the speaker's main concern, the national debt. Such variations in rate emphasize for an audience what is and what isn't especially important to the speech. If you want to emphasize the many demands on their time faced by parents, you could relate a list of daily activities at increasingly rapid rate. By the end of the list, your listeners would probably feel some of the stress facing parents.

Use Helpful Pauses   Pauses are the intervals of silence between or within words, phrases, or sentences. When placed immediately before a key idea or before the climax of a story, they can create suspense: "And the winner is [pause]!" When placed after a major point, pauses can add emphasis, as in: "And who on this campus earns more than the president of the university? The football coach [pause]!" Inserted at the proper moment, a dramatic pause can express feelings more forcefully than words. Clearly, silence can be a highly effective communicative tool if used sparingly and if not embarrassingly prolonged. Too many pauses and those that seem artificial will make you appear to be manipulative or overrehearsed.

Sometimes speakers fill silences in their discourse with sounds: um, ah, er, well-uh, you know, and other meaningless fillers. Undoubtedly, you've heard speakers say, "Today, ah, er, I would like, you know, to speak to you, um, about a pressing, well-uh, like, a pressing problem facing this, uh, campus." Such vocal intrusions convey feelings of hesitancy and a lack of confidence. You can make a concerted effort to remove these intrusions from your speech by being completely familiar with your notecards and the ideas of your speech. Practice your speech until the sentences flow naturally.

On the other hand, don't be afraid of silences. Pauses allow you to stress important ideas, such as the punch line in a story or argument. Pauses also intensify the involvement of listeners in emotional situations, such as when Cokie Roberts or William F. Buckley, Jr. pauses for reflection during an interview.

Practicing Vocal Control

Your vocal qualities are of prime importance in determining the impression you make on an audience. While you can't completely control your vocal qualities, you can be alert to their effects on your listeners. Keep your repertoire of vocal qualities in mind as you decide how to express key ideas for an audience.

Don't assume that you'll be able to master all of the vocal skills we have described in one day. Take your time to review and digest the ideas presented. Above all, practice aloud. Record yourself on tape and then listen to the way you're conveying ideas. Ask your instructor to provide exercises designed to make your vocal instrument more flexible. When you're able to control your voice and make it respond to your desires, you'll have a great deal more control over your effect on listeners. Before any vocal skill can sound natural and be effective with listeners, it must become so auto-

SPEAKING OF . . . *Skills*
Vocal Exercises

If you are concerned about improving your vocal control, these exercises can be helpful. Here's a sample of what you can do:

1. *Breath control.* Say the entire alphabet, using only one breath. As you practice, try saying it more and more slowly so as to improve your control of exhalation.
2. *Control of pitch.* Sing "low, low, low, low," dropping one note of the musical scale each time you sing the word until you reach the lowest tone you can produce. Then sing your way back up the scale. Now sing "high, high, high, high," going up the scale to the highest note you can reach. Sing your way back down. Go up and down, trying to sense the notes you're most comfortable with—your so-called optimum pitch. Give most of your speeches around your optimum pitch.
3. *Articulatory control.* Pronounce each of the following word groups, making sure that each word can be distinguished from the others. Have someone check your accuracy: jest, gist, just; thin, think, thing; roost, roosts, ghost, ghosts; began, begun, begin; wish, which, witch; affect, effect; twin, twain, twine. Or try the following tongue twisters:

   The sixth sheik's sixth sheep's sick.

   Three gray geese in the green grass grazing; gray were the geese and green was the grazing.

   Barry, the baby bunny's born by the blue box beating rubber baby buggy bumpers.

matic that it will work with little conscious effort. Once your voice responds flexibly in the enlarged context of public speaking, you'll be able to achieve the sense of conversationality so highly valued in our society.

USING YOUR BODY TO COMMUNICATE

Just as your voice can add dimension to your message, your physical behavior carries messages through the visual channel. You can use both your voice and your body to create a better understanding of your presentation. To help you explore the ways of enhancing your use of the visual channel, we'll examine the speaker's physical behavior.

Dimensions of Nonverbal Communication

While some use the phrase *nonverbal communication* to refer to all aspects of interpersonal interaction that are nonlinguistic, we'll focus the discussion here on physical behavior in communication settings. In recent years, research has reemphasized the important role of physical behavior in effective oral communication.[5] Basically, three generalizations about nonverbal communication should guide your speechmaking:

1. *Speakers disclose their emotional states through their nonverbal behaviors.* Your listeners read your feelings toward yourself, your topic, and your audience from your facial expressions. Consider the contrast between a speaker who walks briskly to the front of the room, head held high, and one who shuffles, head bowed and arms hanging limply. Communication scholar Dale G. Leathers summarized a good deal of research on nonverbal communication processes: "Feelings and emotions are more accurately exchanged by nonverbal than verbal means. . . . The nonverbal portion of communication conveys meanings and intentions that are relatively free from deception, distortion, and confusion."[6]

2. *The speaker's nonverbal cues enrich the message that comes through words.* You can use physical movement to reinforce the ideas of your speech. The words "We must do either this or that" can be illustrated with appropriate arm-and-hand gestures. Taking a few steps to one side tells an audience that you're moving from one argument to another. A smile enhances your comment on how happy you are to be there, just as a solemn face reinforces the dignity of a wedding.

3. *Nonverbal messages form a reciprocal interaction between speaker and listener.* Listeners frown, smile, shift nervously in their seats, and engage in many types of nonverbal behavior. The physical presence of listeners and the natural tendency of human beings to mirror each other when they're close together mean that nonverbal behavior is a social bonding mechanism.

For this chapter, we'll concentrate on the speaker's control of physical behavior in four areas: proxemics, movement and stance, facial expressions, and gestures.

Proxemics   **Proxemics** is the use of space by human beings. Two components of proxemics, physical arrangement and distance, are especially relevant to public speakers. Physical arrangements include the layout of the room in which you're speaking, the presence or absence of a lectern, the seating plan, the location of chalkboards and similar aids, and any physical barriers between you and your audience. Distance refers to the extent or degree of separation between you and your audience.[7]

Both of these components affect the message you communicate publicly. Typical speaking situations involve a speaker facing a seated audience. Objects in the physical space—the lectern, a table, several flags—tend to set the speaker apart from the listeners. This setting apart is both physical and psychological. Literally as well as figuratively, objects can stand in the way of open communication. If you're trying to create a more informal atmosphere, you should reduce the physical barriers in the setting. You might stand beside or in front of the lectern instead of behind it. In very informal settings, you might even sit on the front edge of a table while talking.

So, what influences your use of physical space?

1. *The formality of the occasion.* The more solemn or formal the occasion, the more barriers will be used; on highly formal occasions, speakers may even speak from an elevated platform or stage.

2. *The nature of the material.* Extensive quoted material or statistical evidence may require you to use a lectern; the use of visual aids often demands such equipment as an easel, computer-aided projection equipment, a VCR, or an overhead projector.

3. *Your personal preference.* You may feel more at ease speaking from behind rather than in front of the lectern.

Elizabeth Dole used physical space in an unusual way in her speech to the 1996 Republican National Convention. Normally, convention-goers are separated from speakers by the raised stage. But Dole chose to move down among her listeners, captivating them and television audiences. Dole told her audience, "Tradition is that speakers at National Republican Conventions remain at this imposing podium. I'd like to break with tradition for two reasons. I'm going to be speaking to friends and secondly I am going to be speaking about the man I love. Just a lot more comfortable for me to do that down here with you."[8] Her explanation of her use of physical space addresses the three factors we've just discussed.

The distance component of proxemics adds a second set of considerations. In most situations, you'll be talking at what anthropologist Edward T. Hall has termed a "public distance"—twelve feet or more from your listeners.[9] (See Figure 11.2.) To communicate with people at that distance, you obviously can't rely on your normal speaking voice or subtle changes in posture or movement. Instead, you must compensate for the distance by using larger gestures, broader shifts of your body, and increased vocal energy. By contrast, you should lower your vocal volume and restrict the breadth of your gestures when addressing a few individuals at a closer distance. If you don't, you'll probably notice them backing away from you.

Movement and Stance   The ways you move and stand provide a second set of bodily cues for your audience. **Movement** includes physical shifts from place to place; **posture** refers to the relative relaxation or rigidity and vertical position of the body. Movements and posture can communicate ideas about yourself to an audience. The

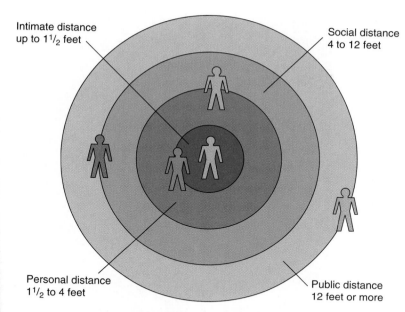

Intimate distance
up to 1½ feet

Social distance
4 to 12 feet

Personal distance
1½ to 4 feet

Public distance
12 feet or more

FIGURE 11.2   Classification of Interhuman Distance

Anthropologist Edward T. Hall has indentified typical distances for various human interactions. Typically, public speaking occurs within social distance and public distance.

speaker who stands stiffly and erectly may, without uttering a word, be saying, "This is a formal occasion" or "I'm tense, even afraid, of this audience." The speaker who leans forward, physically reaching out to the audience, often is saying silently, "I'm interested in you. I want you to understand and accept my ideas." The speaker who sits casually on the front edge of a table and assumes a relaxed posture may suggest informality and readiness to engage in a dialogue with listeners.

Movements and postural adjustments regulate communication. As a public speaker, you can, for instance, move from one end of a table to the other to indicate a change in topic; or you can accomplish the same purpose by changing your posture. At other times, you can move toward your audience when making an especially important point. In each case, you're using your body to reinforce transitions in your subject or to emphasize a matter of special concern.

But keep in mind that your posture and movements can also work against you. Aimless and continuous pacing is distracting. Nervous bouncing or swaying makes listeners seasick, and an excessively erect stance increases tension in listeners. Your movements should be purposeful and enhance the meaning of your words. Stance and movement can help your communicative effort and produce the impressions of self-assurance and control that you want to exhibit.

Facial Expressions   When you speak, your facial expressions function in a number of ways. First, they express your feelings. What researchers Paul Ekman and

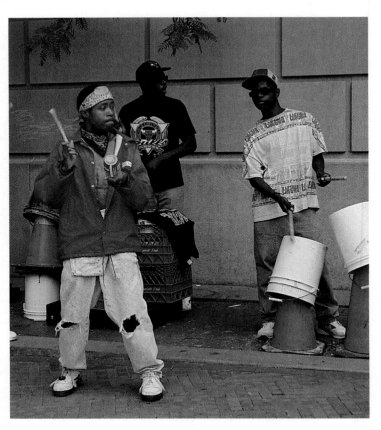

**Movement and stance can communicate
ideas about you to others around you.**

Wallace V. Friesen call "affect displays" are communicated to an audience through the face. **Affect displays** are facial signals of emotion that an audience perceives when scanning your face to see how you feel about yourself and how you feel about them.[10]

Second, facial changes provide listeners with cues that help them interpret the contents of your message. Are you being ironic or satirical? Are you sure of your conclusions? Is this a harsh or pleasant message? Researchers tell us that a high percentage of the information conveyed in a typical message is communicated nonverbally. Psychologist Albert Mehrabian has devised a formula to account for the emotional impact of the different components of a speaker's message. Words, he says, contribute 7 percent, vocal elements 38 percent, and facial expression 55 percent.[11] From this formula, you can see how important the dimensions of delivery are in communication, particularly your voice and facial expressions. In fact, some Internet users have devised a set of symbols called "emoticons" such as LOL meaning "laugh out loud" to give expression to their computer messages.

Third, the "display" elements of your face—your eyes, especially—establish a visual bond between you and your listeners. Our culture values eye contact. The speaker who looks people square in the eye is likely to be perceived as earnest, sincere, forthright, and self-assured. In other words, regular eye contact with your listeners helps establish your credibility. Speakers who look at the floor, who read from notes, or who deliver speeches to the back wall sever the visual bond with their audiences and lose credibility.

Of course, you can't control your face completely, which is probably why listeners search it so carefully for clues to your feelings. You can, however, make sure that your facial messages don't contradict your verbal ones: when you're uttering angry words, your face should be communicating anger; when you're pleading with your listeners, your eyes should be engaging them intently. In short, let your face mirror your feelings. That's one of the reasons it's there!

Gestures   Gestures are purposeful movements of the head, shoulders, arms, hands, and other areas of the body that support and illustrate the ideas you're expressing. Fidgeting with your clothing and notecards and playing with your hair aren't purposeful gestures. They distract from the ideas you're communicating. The effective public speaker commonly uses three kinds of purposeful gestures:

1. *Conventional gestures* are physical movements that are symbols with specific meanings assigned by custom or convention, such as the circle formed by placing the thumb on the index finger to signal "Okay." These gestures condense ideas: they are shorthand expressions of things or ideas that would require many words to describe fully. A speaker can use the raised-hand "stop" gesture to interrupt listeners who are drawing premature conclusions or the "thumbs up" sign when congratulating them for jobs well done. Since culture determines the meanings of conventional gestures, you should understand how your audience views the gestures you'll use. Misunderstandings can be embarrassing or disastrous.

Many of the gestures we use can have culturally defined meanings. These are called conventional gestures.

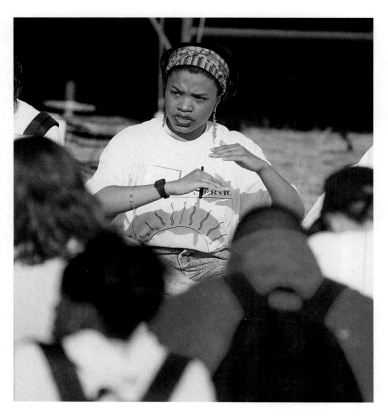

Descriptive gestures depict size, shape, or location.

2. *Descriptive gestures* are physical movements that describe the idea to be communicated. Speakers often depict the size, shape, or location of an object by movements of the hands and arms; that is, they draw pictures for listeners. You might demonstrate the size of a box by drawing it in the air with a finger or raise an arm to show someone's height.

3. *Indicators* are movements of the hands, arms, or other parts of the body that express feelings. Speakers throw up their arms when disgusted, pound the lectern when angry, shrug their shoulders when puzzled, or point a threatening finger when issuing a warning. Such gestures communicate emotions to your listeners and encourage similar responses in them. Your facial expressions and other body cues usually reinforce such gestures.[12]

You can improve your gestures through practice. As you practice, you'll obtain better results by keeping in mind that relaxation, vigor and definiteness, and proper timing affect the effectiveness of gestures.

1. *If your muscles are tense, your movements will be stiff and your gestures awkward.* You should make a conscious effort to relax your muscles before you start to

speak. You might warm up by taking a few steps, shrugging your shoulders, flexing your muscles, or breathing deeply.

2. *Good gestures are natural and animated.* They communicate the dynamism associated with speaker credibility. You should put enough force into your gestures to show your conviction and enthusiasm. Avoid exaggerated or repetitive gestures such as pounding the table or chopping the air to emphasize minor ideas in your speech. Vary the nature of your gestures as the ideas in your speech demand.

3. *Timing is crucial to effective gestures.* The *stroke* of a gesture—that is, the shake of a fist or the movement of a finger—should fall on or slightly before the point the gesture emphasizes. Just try making a gesture after the word or phrase it was intended to reinforce has already been spoken. It appears ridiculous. Practice making gestures until they're habitual, and then use them spontaneously as the impulse arises.

Adapting Nonverbal Behavior to Your Presentations

You can gain more effective control of your physical behavior by learning how to orchestrate your gestures and other movements. You can make some conscious decisions about how you will use your body together with the other channels of communication to communicate effectively.

1. *Signal your relationship with your audience through proxemics.* If you're comfortable behind a lectern, use it; however, keep in mind that it's a potential barrier between you and your listeners. If you want your whole body to be visible to the audience but you feel the need to have your notes at eye level, stand beside the lectern and arrange your notecards on it. If you want to relax your

SPEAKING OF . . . *Apprehension*

Breathe Through Your Fears

You can adapt some of the breathing techniques from yoga and meditation to help you control the physical stress that inhibits movement and vocal quality. Here's a simple, but effective exercise to try:

1. Breathe in slowly, counting to 6 (one-one thousand, two one-thousand, etc.).
2. Hold your breath for a count of 3.
3. Exhale slowly counting to 6.

Repeat this exercise before you practice your speech. Then, use it again to prepare for the delivery of your speech.

body, sit behind a table or desk; but compensate for the resulting loss of action by increasing your volume. If you feel relaxed and want to be open to your audience, stand in front of a table or desk. Learn to use the space around you while speaking publicly.

Consider your listeners' needs as well. The farther you are from them, the more important it is for them to have a clear view of you, the harder you must work to project your words, and the broader your physical movements must be. The speaker who crouches behind a lectern in an auditorium of 300 people soon loses their interest. Think of large lecture classes you've attended or outdoor rallies you've witnessed. Recall the delivery patterns that worked effectively in such situations. Put them to work for you.

2. *Adapt the physical setting to your communicative needs.* If you're going to use visual aids—such as a chalkboard, flipchart, or working model—remove the tables, chairs, and other objects that might obstruct your audience's view. Increase intimacy by arranging chairs in a small circle or stress formality by using a lectern.

3. *Adapt your gestures and movement to the size of the audience.* Keeping in mind what Hall noted about public distance in communication, you should realize that subtle changes of facial expression or small hand movements can't be seen clearly in large rooms or auditoriums. Although many auditoriums have a raised platform and a slanted floor to make you more visible, you should adjust to the distance between yourself and your audience by making your movements and gestures larger.

4. *Establish eye contact with your audience, looking specific individuals in the eye.* Your head should not be in constant motion, scanning the audience with rhythmic, nonstop machine-gun movement. Rather, take all your listeners into your field of vision periodically; establish firm visual bonds with individuals occasionally. Such bonds enhance your credibility and keep your auditors' attention riveted to you.

Some speakers identify three audience members—one to the left, one in the middle, and one to the right—and make sure they regularly move from one to the other of them. For those who don't have trouble moving from side to side, another technique is to do the same thing from front to back, especially if the audience isn't too big. Making sure that you are achieving even momentary eye contact with specific listeners in different parts of the audience creates the sense of visual bonding that you want.

5. *Use your body to communicate your feelings.* When you're angry, don't be afraid to gesture vigorously. When you're expressing tenderness, let that message come across your relaxed face. In other words, when you communicate publicly, use the same emotional indicators as you do when you talk to individuals on a one-to-one basis.

6. *Regulate the pace of your presentation with bodily movement.* Shift your weight as your speech moves from one idea to another. Move more when you're speaking more rapidly. Reduce bodily action and gestures accordingly when you're slowing down to emphasize particular ideas.

7. *Finally, use your full repertoire of gestures.* You probably do this in everyday conversation without even thinking about it; recreate that behavior when addressing an audience. Physical readiness is the key. Keep your hands and arms free and loose so that you can call them into action easily, quickly, and naturally. Let your hands rest comfortably at your sides, relaxed but ready. Then, as you unfold the ideas of your speech, use descriptive gestures to indicate size, shape, or relationships, making sure the movements are large enough to be seen in the back row. Use conventional gestures also to give visual dimension to your spoken ideas. Keep in mind that there is no right number of gestures to use. However, as you practice, think of the kinds of body movements and gestures that complement your message and purpose.

Selecting the appropriate method of presentation and using your voice and body productively will enhance your chances of gaining support for your ideas. Practice is the key to the effective use of these nonverbal elements. Through practice, you'll have an opportunity to see how your voice and body complement or detract from your ideas. The more you prepare and practice, the more confident you'll feel about presenting the speech and the more comfortable you'll be. Remember that the nonverbal channel of communication creates meaning for your audience.

ASSESSING YOUR PROGRESS

Chapter Summary

1. Every speaker should effectively use both body and voice to convey meaning.

2. Choose an appropriate method of presentation—impromptu, memorized, manuscript, or extemporaneous delivery.

3. Several factors will determine your choice of presentation method: the type of speaking occasion, the seriousness and purpose of your speech, your audience analysis, and your own strengths and weaknesses as a speaker.

4. A flexible speaking voice has intelligibility, variety, and understandable stress patterns.

5. Volume, rate, enunciation, and pronunciation interact to affect intelligibility.

6. Different standards of pronunciation create regional differences known as dialects.

7. Changes in rate, pitch, and stress and pauses create variety in presentation and help eliminate monotonous delivery.

8. Three generalizations about nonverbal communication are significant: (a) speakers reveal and reflect their emotional states through their nonverbal behaviors; (b) nonverbal cues enrich or elaborate the speaker's message; and (c) nonverbal messages form an interaction between speaker and listener.

9. Speakers can use proxemics or space to create physical and psychological intimacy or distance. A speaker's movement and posture regulate communication.

10. Facial expressions communicate feelings, provide important cues to meaning, establish a visual bond with listeners, and establish speaker credibility.

11. Relaxed, definite, and properly timed gestures can enhance the meaning of a message.

12. Speakers commonly use conventional gestures, descriptive gestures, and indicators.

Key Terms

affect displays (p. 200)

dialect (p. 194)

emphasis (p. 194)

enunciation (p. 193)

extemporaneous speech (p. 191)

gesture (p. 201)

impromptu speech (p. 190)

intelligibility (p. 192)

manuscript speech (p. 191)

memorized speech (p. 190)

movement (p. 198)

pitch (p. 194)

posture (p. 198)

proxemics (p. 197)

rate (p. 192)

stress (p. 194)

volume (p. 192)

Assessment Activities

1. Divide the class into teams and play charades. For rules, see David Jauner, "Charades as a Teaching Device," *Speech Teacher*, 20 (1971), 302. A game of charades will help you focus on the nonverbal elements of communication. Identify conventional gestures, facial expressions, and movements that clarify messages during the game.

2. Form small task groups. Appoint a member of the group to record ideas and then think of as many situations as possible in which each of the four methods of presentation would be used. Choose a reporter to convey the group's examples to the class. How many of the situations do you think you will encounter? Which situations are tied to success in a career?

3. Choose a selection from a poetry anthology and practice reading it aloud. As you read, vary your volume, rate, pitch and emphasis, and use pauses. Practice reading the poem in several ways to heighten different emotions or to emphasize different interpretations. Record your reading of the poem on tape and play it back to evaluate it, or ask a friend to listen and offer suggestions.

Surfing the Web

1. You can download software that will allow you to take advantage of sound-supported Internet sites. Use your browser to locate the Real Audio Web site to get you started.

2. Many Web sites as well as encyclopedias and other resources now accompany speech texts with segments of audio and video. Locate a famous speech such as Martin Luther King's "I Have a Dream" speech or John F. Kennedy's inaugural address. View the video and listen to the words of these speakers.

References

1. For a fascinating discussion of oral speech's communal powers—of its "psychodynamics"—see Chapter 3 of Walter J. Ong, *Orality and Literacy: The Technologizing of the Word* (London: Methuen, 1982).

2. Thomas Frentz, "Rhetorical Conversation, Time, and Moral Action," *Quarterly Journal of Speech,* 71 (1985): 1–18.

3. Mark Knapp, *Essentials of Nonverbal Communication* (New York: Holt, Rinehart & Winston, 1980).

4. Klaus R. Scherer, H. London, and Garret Wolf, "The Voice of Competence: Paralinguistic Cues and Audience Evaluation," *Journal of Research in Personality,* 7 (1973): 31–44; Jitendra Thakerer and Howard Giles, "They Are—So They Spoke: Noncontent Speech Stereotypes," *Language and Communication,* 1 (1981): 255–261; Peter A. Andersen, Myron W. Lustig, and Janis F. Andersen, "Regional Patterns of Communication in the United States: A Theoretical Perspective," *Communication Monographs,* 54 (1987): 128–144.

5. Much of the foundational research is summarized in Mark L. Knapp and Judith Hall, *Nonverbal Communication in Human Interaction,* 3rd ed. (New York: Holt, Rinehart & Winston, 1982).

6. Dale G. Leathers, *Nonverbal Communication Systems* (Boston: Allyn & Bacon, 1975), 4–5.

7. For further discussion, see Leathers, 52–59.

8. Elizabeth Dole, "This is a Defining Moment in Our Nation's History: Speech to the 1996 Republican National Convention." (http://gos.sbc.edu/d/dole.html)

9. Hall divides interhuman communication distances into four segments: *intimate distance,* up to 1½ feet apart; *personal distance,* 1½ to 4 feet; *social distance,* 4 to 12 feet; and *public distance,* 12 feet or more. With these distinctions, he has carefully noted how people's eye contact, tone of voice, and ability to touch and observe change from one distance to another. See Edward T. Hall, *The Hidden Dimension* (New York: Doubleday, 1969), chap. 10.

10. Paul Ekman, *Emotion in the Human Face,* 2nd ed. (Cambridge: Cambridge University Press, 1982).

11. Albert Mehrabian, *Silent Messages* (Belmont, CA: Wadsworth, 1972); Robert Rivlin and Karen Gravelle, *Deciphering the Senses: The Expanding World of Human Perception* (New York: Simon & Schuster, 1984), 98. Such numbers, of course, are only formulaic estimates and are important only as proportions of each other.

12. For a complete system of classifying gestures, see Paul Ekman and Wallace V. Friesen, "Hand Movements," *Journal of Communication,* 22 (1972): 360.

Using Visual Aids

Chapter **12**

Television, film, videotape, videodiscs, CD-ROM and related digital technologies, overhead and opaque projectors, billboards, sidewalk posters—images from an amazing range of sources dominate our everyday world.[1] From the time you participated in "show and tell" in elementary school, you've used visual aids in your communication efforts. As you learn to speak in front of an audience, you'll continue to make use of visual aids as an essential part of the speech transaction. For these reasons, it's important for you to learn more about visual aids.

Research on visual media, learning, and attitude change has given us a lot of information about the impact of visual aids on audiences.[2] In this chapter, we'll combine what we've learned from social-scientific research with your needs as a speaker. First, we'll focus on the functions of visual aids; then we'll examine the various types of visual aids and explore ways to use them effectively.

THE FUNCTIONS OF VISUAL AIDS

Visual aids are illustrative and persuasive materials that rely primarily on sight. Visual materials enhance your presentation in two ways: (a) they aid listener comprehension and memory, and (b) they add persuasive impact to your message.

Comprehension and Memory

Remember the old saying "A picture's worth a thousand words"? This saying contains a great deal of truth. We understand ideas better and remember them longer if we see them as well as hear them. Research has demonstrated that bar graphs are especially effective at making statistical information more accessible to listeners. Charts and human-interest visuals, such as photographs, have proven to help listeners process and retain data.[3] Even simple pictures have significant effects on children's recall and comprehension during storytelling.[4] Visuals can be immensely valuable if your purpose is to inform or teach an audience. Visuals make information easier to understand, retain, and recall.

Persuasion

In addition to enhancing comprehension and memory, visuals can heighten the persuasive impact of your ideas because they engage listeners actively in the communicative exchange. Lawyers, for example, aware of the dramatic persuasive effects of visuals, often include visual evidence such as photographs of injuries or diagrams of crime scenes in their cases in order to sway the opinions of juries. Some lawyers even have experimented with the use of video technology to create dramatic portrayals of events in order to influence jury decisions; for example, by showing the dangerous traffic flow of an intersection in a vehicular homicide case.

Undeniably, good visuals enhance both your credibility and your persuasiveness.[5] By satisfying the "show-me" attitude prevalent among listeners, visual materials provide a crucial means of meeting listener expectations.[6]

Web Exploration
To analyze research on the impacts of visual aids on audiences go to
http://awl.com/german

TYPES OF VISUAL SUPPORT

There are many different types of visual materials. Depending on your speech topic and purpose, you may choose one or several types of visual support. We will discuss each type and examine specific approaches to using it to supplement your oral presentations.

Actual Objects

You can often bring to a presentation the actual objects you're discussing. Live animals or plants can, under some circumstances, be used to enhance your speeches. If your speech explores the care and feeding of iguanas, you can reinforce your ideas by bringing to the speech an iguana in a properly equipped cage. Describing the differences between two varieties of soybeans may be easier if you demonstrate the differences with real plants. Discretion and common sense will help make such visuals work for you rather than against you. You might be stretching your luck, for example, by bringing a real mule into the classroom to demonstrate saddling techniques or by bringing an untrained cat to show off the virtues of clumping litter.

Using the actual object should focus audience attention on your speech, not serve as a distraction. A speech about boogie board skiing is enhanced by a display of the essential equipment. A speech about how to repair holes in a plaster wall is clarified by showing pieces of plasterboard at the various stages. Cooking demonstrations are enlivened with samples prepared before the presentation, since you usually don't have time to perform the actual work during the speech.

You can use your own body to add concreteness and vitality to your presentation. You might, for example, demonstrate yo-yo tricks, warm-up exercises, swing dance steps, sign language, or tennis strokes during your speech. Remember to control the experience. Make sure that everyone, even people in the back rows, can see you. Demonstrate stretching exercises on a sturdy tabletop rather than on the floor. Slow the tempo of a tennis stroke so that the audience can see any intricate action and subtle movements. One advantage of properly controlled visual action is that with it you can control the audience's attention to your demonstration. You also should dress appropriately. A physical therapy major might add credibility by wearing a uniform when demonstrating CPR, and an aerobics instructor can wear a leotard and tights. Of course, the clothing should not substitute for a clearly visible demonstration of CPR or aerobics.

If you decide to ask another person to demonstrate a technique while you describe it, plan ahead. Instead of hoping for someone to volunteer from the audience, contact one of your classmates and practice the demonstration before you give your speech. In this way, you'll avoid the embarrassing silence that can accompany a request for a volunteer and you'll be certain that your partner can adequately demonstrate the process as you relate it.

Photographs and Slides

Photographs can often be a good substitute for the real thing. Photographs can give the audience a visual sense of your topic. For example, photos can illustrate fire damage to ravaged homes or show the beauty of a woods threatened by a new shopping mall. Make sure that your audience is able to see details from a distance. You can enlarge photos or use slides so that people can see them more easily. Avoid passing small photos through the audience, because such activity is disruptive. The purpose of a visual aid is to draw the attention of all members of the audience simultaneously.

Like photographs, slides (35-mm transparencies) allow you to depict color, shape, texture, and relationships. It is also easier to show many slides than many photographs. If you're describing the Padre Islands as a good place to vacation, you may use slides to show your audience the buildings and landscape of both islands. If you're giving a speech on the history of locomotives, you can use slides to show various types. If you're speaking against the construction of a river reservoir, you can enhance your persuasiveness by showing slides of the whitewater that will be disrupted by the dam.

Representations convey information in various ways. For instance, a photograph of an inline skate *(top)* gives an audience a realistic but complicated view of the object, whereas an abstract representation, such as a diagram *(bottom left)*, strips away unnecessary details to illustrate the parts of the object more clearly. Also abstract yet highly visible, an action shot *(bottom right)* provides a feeling of a three-dimensional image of the object, allowing a speaker to point out its parts and discuss its functions.

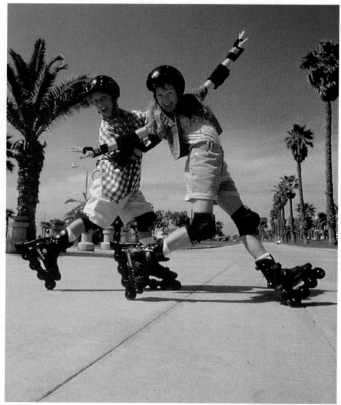

If you're discussing stylistic differences among famous artists, you may wish to show slides of art works from the neoclassical and baroque periods.

Using slides requires sure practice in handling equipment. It also requires some forethought about the setup of the presentation. Will the correct equipment be available? Have you loaded the slides in the cartridge correctly? Will you speak from the front of the room or from next to the projector? Will your voice carry over the noise of the projector? Do you know how to change the projection lamp? Did you bring along a spare bulb just in case? Will you need an extension cord? Do you know how to remove a jammed slide? Attention to small, seemingly inconsequential details like these will make a major difference in how smoothly the presentation goes. If you operate on the assumption that whatever can go wrong will, you'll be prepared to solve most problems.

Videotapes and Films

Videotapes and films let you put action into pictures. Videotaped segments from several current sitcoms can dramatically reinforce your claim that minorities are underrepresented in comedy-centered television. Two or three videotaped political ads can help you illustrate methods for savaging opponents. As with all projection equipment, familiarity with the operation of a videocassette recorder or film projector ensures a smooth presentation. Make sure that you can operate the equipment properly and quickly. Forward to the segment you wish to use. Delays increase your nervousness and detract from your presentation.

SPEAKING OF . . . *Ethics*

Can Pictures Lie?

Can pictures lie? Aren't they each worth a thousand words? Isn't seeing believing? Isn't showing better than telling? Not necessarily—especially in today's visually centered world. Consider:

- Hopes of finding American soldiers missing in action in Vietnam (MIAs) were briefly inspired by photos that seemed to show the Americans holding signs that displayed current dates. Those pictures turned out to have been faked.
- During the 1992 presidential campaign, political action committees (PACs) ran ads that showed Bill Clinton holding hands in victory with Ted Kennedy on the Democratic Convention stage. What the PAC had done was morphed a picture of Kennedy's head on Vice President Al Gore's body.

Thanks to digital editing, you now can easily add to or subtract from pictures, printing the altered photos so cleanly that the forgery is almost impossible to detect. Pictures can be altered to "say" something that isn't true. Or, images that transform the meanings of words can be added. The visual dimension can be helpful to both speaker and audience when it is used in morally defensible ways. It can be destructive of the truth when it's not.

Chalkboard Drawings

Chalkboard drawings are especially valuable when you need a quick illustration or want to show something step by step. By drawing each step as you discuss it, you can center the audience's attention on your major points. Coaches often use this approach when showing players how to execute particular plays. Time sequences also can be sketched on a chalkboard. To visually represent the history of the civil rights movement in the United States, you can create a timeline that illustrates key events, such as the arrival of the first slaves in Jamestown, the signing of the Emancipation Proclamation, and the passage of the 1965 Voting Rights Act.

Whether you use drawings will depend on the formality of the situation. If you're brainstorming ideas for building renovation with a prospective client, quick sketches may suffice. However, if you're meeting with the client's board of directors, the same rough drawings will be inadequate. The board will expect a polished presentation, complete with a professionally prepared prospectus. Similarly, chalkboard drawings may be sufficient to explain the photovoltaics of solar power to a group of classmates, but when presenting those data as part of a science fair project, you need refined visual support materials. Most of the time, the care with which you prepare these visuals will convey to your audience an attitude of either indifference or concern. Consider chalkboard drawings for informal presentations.

Overhead Projections

You can use an overhead projector just as you would use a chalkboard, to illustrate points as you talk. However, an overhead projector offers some advantages over a chalkboard: you can turn it off when you've made your point, thus removing a competing image that might distract listeners. Another advantage is that you can uncover one part of the overhead screen at a time, keeping the remainder covered so as to control the flow of information. Finally, you can prepare overheads including computer-generated graphics before the speech, giving them a more professional appearance than chalkboard drawings; hence, they dominate corporate talks.

When you're using an overhead projector, be aware of your technique. First, make your illustrations large enough so that the audience can see them. If you are using computer-generated visual materials, you should probably enlarge them. Second, talk to the audience rather than to the screen or the light source. Otherwise, your listeners' attention may drift away from you and your message. Third, be sure to stand so that you don't block the audience's view of your visuals. Fourth, when you're through talking about the illustration, turn off the projector to eliminate the competing message source.

Graphs

Graphs show relationships among various parts of a whole or between variables across time. Graphs are especially effective for representing numerical data. There are several types of graphs:

Web Exploration
To practice using and understanding graphs go to
http://awl.com/german

1. **Bar graphs** show the relationships between two or more sets of figures (see Figure 12.1). Research has demonstrated that plain bar graphs are the most effective method for displaying statistical comparisons, perhaps because bar

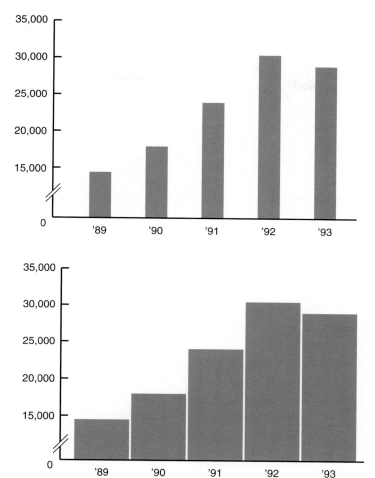

FIGURE 12.1 Bar Graph

Bar graphs illustrate relationships. Changing the space and size of bars can affect the visual message.

graphs represent numbers in a visual form.[7] If you were illustrating the difference among male and female incomes in various fields, you'd probably use a bar graph.

2. **Line graphs** show relationships between two or more variables, usually over time (see Figure 12.2). If you were interested in showing popular support for GOP presidential hopefuls Elizabeth Dole, George W. Bush, and John McCain, from July through December 1999, you'd use a line graph.

3. **Pie graphs** show percentages by dividing a circle into the proportions being represented (see Figure 12.3). A speaker raising funds for a local hospice could use a

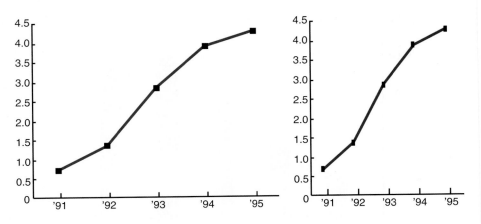

FIGURE 12.2 Line Graph

Line graphs can reveal relationships, but they can also deceive the unwary. These graphs show the same data but use different spacing along the axes to change the visual image, with the second version making the increase in hotel prices seem much greater. *Source:* Smith Travel Research, as reported in *USA Today,* October 27, 1995, B1.

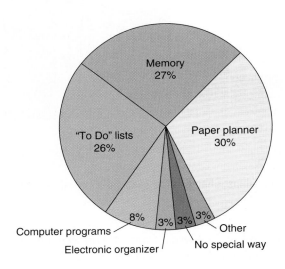

FIGURE 12.3 Pie Graph

Pie graphs dramatize relationships along a limited number of segments. Ideally, a pie graph should have from two to five segments, never more than eight. This one compares seven different methods people use as organizational reminders. *Source:* Opinion Research Corporation for Fuji Computer Products, as reported in *USA Today,* October 27, 1995, B1.

pie graph to show how much of its income was spent on administration, nursing care, drugs, and equipment for terminally ill patients. City managers use pie graphs to show citizens what proportion of their tax dollars go to municipal services, administration, education, recreation, and law enforcement.

4. **Pictographs** function like bar graphs but use symbols instead of bars to represent size and numbers (see Figure 12.4). A representation of U.S., Canadian and Russian grain exports might use a miniature drawing of a wheat shock or an ear of corn to represent 100,000 bushels; this representation would allow a viewer to see at a glance the disparity among the exports of the three countries. You can easily create pictographs with computer clip art.

Your choice of bar, line, pie, or pictorial graphs will depend on the subject and the nature of the relationship you wish to convey. A pie graph, for example, can neither easily illustrate discrepancies between two groups nor show change over time. Bar and line graphs don't easily show the total amount being represented.

Regardless of the type of graph you choose, when you're preparing these visual aids, you must be very careful not to distort your information. A bar graph can create a misleading impression of the difference between two items if one bar is short and wide while the other is long and narrow. Line graphs can portray very different trends if the units of measurement are not the same for each time period. You can avoid misrepresenting information by using consistent measurements in your graphs and by using a computer to generate your graphs.

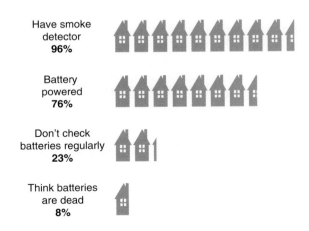

Have smoke
detector
96%

Battery
powered
76%

Don't check
batteries regularly
23%

Think batteries
are dead
8%

FIGURE 12.4   Pictograph

Speakers with artistic skills can create interesting visual aids, such as the graphic representation of the status of battery-powered smoke detectors. The pictures enhance the argument that people need to do more than merely install smoke detectors. *Source:* Angus Reid Group for American Sensors, as reported in *USA Today,* October 27, 1995, A1.

Charts and Tables

Charts and tables condense large blocks of information into a single picture. **Tables** present information in parallel columns, as in the tax tables in the U.S. 1040 tax form. **Charts** can present data in a number of varied forms. The periodic table of elements is a common chart you've probably seen. If not too complicated, charts and tables work well in technical speeches. So, if you discuss various contributions to the operation of the United Nations, you can break down the contributions of, say, ten countries to five of the major agencies of the UN. If you want to show why the United States has such trouble establishing a consistent energy policy, your presentation will be much easier to follow if you can show your listeners an organizational chart for the federal government.

There are two special types of charts: **flipcharts** unveil ideas one at a time on separate sheets; **flowcharts** show relationships among ideas or facts on a single sheet. Both flipcharts and flowcharts may include drawings or photos. If you present successive ideas with a flipchart, you'll focus audience attention on specific parts of your speech. In a speech on fighting in the Persian Gulf War of 1991, you could use a separate chart for each week of the engagement. If you presented the entire six weeks on one chart, the chart would become cluttered and your audience might stray from your explanation to read the entire chart. You could also use separate charts to focus on specific assaults by different countries.

You can use a flowchart to indicate the chronological stages of a process; for example, a flowchart will allow audiences to visualize the stages of a presidential campaign or the process of making cheese. You can also use a flowchart to show relationships among ideas or interdependent actions, such as the competition between conservative and liberal views of "family values." And, of course, you're familiar with organizational flowcharts used by groups to show the relationships among members of the group. In a speech on the passage of a legislative bill, a flowchart would clarify each step of the process. As long as the information is not too complex or lengthy, tables and charts may be used to indicate changes over time and to rank or list items and their costs, frequency of use, or relative importance.

Tables and charts should be designed so that they can be seen and so that they convey data simply and clearly. Too much information will force the audience to concentrate more on the visual support than on your oral explanation. For example, a dense chart, showing all the major and minor offices of your college, may simply overwhelm listeners as they try to follow your explanation. If the organization is too complex, you may want to develop several charts, each one focusing on a smaller unit of information.

Models

Models can be very attractive to listeners. **Models** are reduced or enlarged scale replicas of real objects. Architects construct models of new projects to show clients. You can use models of genes to accompany your explanation of the genome project. As with other visual aids, models need to be manageable and visible to the audience. You can increase listener interest if you use a model that comes apart so that different pieces can be examined. Be sure to practice removing and replacing the parts before your speech.

STRATEGIES FOR SELECTING AND USING VISUAL AIDS

Your decision about which visual aids will work best for you should be based on three considerations: (a) the characteristics of the audience and occasion, (b) your ability to integrate verbal and visual materials effectively, and (c) the potential of computer-generated visual materials.

Consider the Audience and Occasion

Think about the folks you're talking to when deciding on visuals. Do you need to bring a map of the United States to an audience of college students when discussing the spread of contagious diseases in this country? If you're going to discuss a volley-ball team's offensive and defensive formations, should you provide diagrams for your listeners? Can you expect an audience to understand the administrative structure of the federal bureaucracy without providing an organizational chart?

SPEAKING OF . . . *Skills*
Using Visual Aids in Business

It's wise to use visual aids when developing a professional presentation for a client or business meeting. Research has shown that visual aids are effective tools for three reasons. First, visual aids can make your presentation more persuasive. Second, they enhance your audience's estimate of your credibility and appearance of professionalism. Third, presenters using visual aids require less meeting time to achieve their results. Overall, it makes good sense to incorporate visual aids in your presentations. Observe some simple rules:

1. *Prepare a professional look.* The business world by now absolutely expects professional-looking visuals: desktop computer-generated overheads, high-quality slides, folders with eye-catching paper, PowerPoint computer projections, and so on. Sloppy work will kill you.
2. *Always make something to take away.* Large businesses, especially, run on team meetings and project presentation sessions—often, more than one a day. Give the folks coming to your presentation something to take away, so that they can remember your work. Summarize the main dimensions of the problem and your proposed solutions; hand out your business card with phone, fax, and e-mail numbers; popular these days is a computer disk with images and important materials on it, given how cheap disks are now.
3. Know the equipment before you start. Know how to run the particular VCR or computer projector in the room you're using. Try out the slide projector. Make sure you know where the switch for the power screen is. Fumbling because you don't know which remote runs the VCR and which the sound system will make you look less than professional.

These rules apply, with varying degrees of harshness, to your presentations in any other setting as well.

How can you answer those questions? It may be quite difficult, for example, to decide what your classmates know about governmental structures or what Rotary Club members know about football plays. Probably the best thing you can do is to do a little first-hand interviewing by speaking with several of your potential listeners ahead of time. In other words, before making any final decisions about visual supporting materials, do as much audience research as you possibly can.

You should also consider the response you'd like to achieve with your visual materials. In general, pictorial or photographic visuals can make an audience *feel* the way you do. For example, you can use slides, movies, sketches, or photographs of your travels in western Colorado to accompany your speech on high plateaus. Such visual aids stimulate your audience to share in the awe and tortured beauty that you experienced. If you show slides of civilian victims in Kosovo, you are likely to gain an emotional response. Such a response can maximize your efforts to persuade your listeners.

Visuals containing descriptive or written materials, on the other hand, can help an audience *think* the way you do. For example, models, diagrams, charts, and graphs about the population and economy of the Mediterranean area may persuade your listeners to conclude that the United States should send more foreign aid to Turkey. A timeline representing ethnic conflicts in the Balkans can help your listeners understand the historical context of contemporary fighting in the region. Such visual aids encourage understanding and thought rather than emotional responses.

As part of your preparation for using visuals, take into account the speaking occasion. Certain occasions demand certain types of visual support materials. The district manager who presents a report of projected future profits to the central office without a printed handout or diagram will probably find his or her credibility questioned. The military adviser who calls for governmental expenditures for new weapons without offering pictures or drawings of the proposed weapons and printed technical data on their operation is not likely to be a convincing advocate. A basketball coach without a chalkboard may succeed only in confusing team members at half time.

Plan ahead to supply the visual media demanded by the situation. If the speaking occasion doesn't appear to require certain visual supports, analyze the occasion further for different visual possibilities. Use your imagination. Be innovative. Don't overlook opportunities to make your speech more meaningful, more exciting, and more interesting for your listeners.

Integrate Verbal and Visual Materials Effectively

Web Exploration
To learn more about how to integrate verbal and visual materials effectively go to
http://awl.com/german

To be effective, your visual aids should complement your spoken message. Visuals should save time, enhance the impact of your speech, clarify complex relations, and generally enliven your presentation. Consider the following suggestions for getting the maximum benefit from your visuals:

1. *Use color to create interest.* Use contrasting colors (red on white, black on yellow) to highlight information in an organizational chart or to differentiate segments of a pie graph or bars in a bar graph. As a rule, color commands attention better than black and white.

SPEAKING OF . . . *Skills*

Using Visual Aids Effectively

Here are some tips and reminders to assist you in preparing and using visual aids in your presentation:

Good visuals reinforce the spoken message. They do not convey the entire message.

Have a presentation plan. Begin with an introduction, and end with a summary or set of conclusions. Identify several major points you want to cover; supporting points reinforce the main points but can be sacrificed if you're running out of time.

Words and graphics on visual aids should be kept simple.

- Complex ideas belong in a handout or paper.
- Tables generally are not effective. Schematic drawings often are too detailed, but you can modify and simplify the drawing to illustrate only the point you are making, leaving out unnecessary details.
- Organizational charts cannot be read. Simplify the chart to show only the segments you are discussing.
- Equations, by themselves, are not an effective visual aid. You can make an equation more visually appealing, however, by adding pictorial elements.
- Bar, pie, and line charts that are too busy can confuse the audience.

Design visuals to maximize their effectiveness.

- The type size of text or characters should be 18 to 24 points.
- Use bullets and dash lines, but avoid too many subtopics.
- Use a ragged right margin.
- Bold text is preferable to underlined text.
- Avoid overcrowding.

Use—but don't abuse—available technology to produce visuals.

- Use your spill check (spell), and then proofread.
- TEXT IN ALL CAPITALS IS HARD TO READ.
- Use color carefully: Black backgrounds cause problems. Dark blue works best, but red and blue appear to "jump" when used together.

Source: Adapted from http://omar.llnl.gov/EFCOG/tips.html.

2. *Keep visual aids clear and simple.* This advice is especially important for charts and other graphic devices. Make essential information stand out clearly from the background. Let simplicity guide your preparation. Many experts recommend that you use 18- to 24-point type for text (36-point type for headings) with no more than two fonts for an effective visual aid.[8]

3. *Make your visuals large enough to be seen easily.* Listeners get frustrated when they must lean forward and squint in order to see detail in a visual aid. Make your figures and lettering large enough so that everyone can see them. Follow

the example of John Hancock, who, when signing the Declaration of Independence in 1776, wrote his name large enough to "be seen by the King of England without his glasses."

4. *Make your visuals neat.* Draw neatly, spell correctly, make lines proportional, and make letters symmetrical. Such advice may seem unnecessary, but too often beginning speakers throw together visual materials at the last minute. They forget that their visual aids contribute to audiences' assessment of their credibility. Misspelled words and sloppy graphs will lower listeners' estimation of your competence.

5. *Decide in advance how to handle your visual aids.* Prepare and practice with your visual aids well in advance, especially for demonstration speeches. Suppose you want to show your listeners that anyone can change a tube even on the rear wheel of a bicycle without screwing up the chain and gear-shifting mechanisms. Do you bring in a whole bike? (Probably.) Do you actually change a tube on that bike? (Probably not—takes too long for the assigned length of the speech.) So, do you bring another wheel and change a tube on that? (Yup.) Do you demonstrate how to put the wheel back on the bike? (In part. Unlock the rear wheel on the bike you brought along, take the chain off the sprocket, slacken the cables, then put the chain back on and show your listeners how to adjust the cables. Then show them a chart recording the process step by step.) In thinking through how much of the process you can demonstrate in the available time, you can figure out how to handle actual objects and other visuals.

6. *Compensate orally for any distraction your visual aid may create.* Remember that you're always competing with other message sources for your listeners' attention. Listeners may find the visual aid so intriguing that they miss part of your message. You can partially compensate for any potential distraction by building repetition into your speech. By repeating your main ideas you give your listeners several chances to follow your thoughts. As added insurance, you also might keep your visual aid out of sight until you need to use it.

7. *Coordinate visual and verbal messages.* Mechanical or electronic messages from slides, films, overhead projections, and videotapes can easily distract your listeners. You need to talk louder and move vigorously when using a machine to communicate, or you need to show the film or slides either before or after you comment on their content. Whatever strategy you choose, make sure that your visual materials are well integrated into your oral presentation. That is, use transitions that integrate your visual aids with the speech. If you are using a chart, you might say, "This chart shows you what I've been saying about the growing season for different varieties of tomatoes." Also indicate where you obtained the information represented on the chart and summarize the information before you go on to your next idea.

8. *Hand your listeners a copy of the materials you wish them to reflect on after your speech.* If you're making recommendations to the tenant's association office, provide copies of your proposal for their subsequent action. Or if you're reporting the results of a survey, your listeners will better digest the key statistics if you give

each audience member a copy of them. Few people can recall the seven warning signs of cancer, but they might keep a wallet-sized list handy if you order enough for all your listeners from the American Cancer Society. Of course, don't duplicate your entire speech. Select only those items with lasting value.

These suggestions should enable you to take advantage of visual communication. Good visual aids illustrate and empower your ideas, taking advantage of the visual dimension that your listeners will respond to naturally as they process their feelings and ideas.

Evaluate Computer-Generated Visual Materials

You can tap into the digital world of computer graphics when you prepare your visual aids. While you may not be able to produce visuals similar to the action shots that accompany a televised football game, you can still use readily available computer-generated visual materials. Computers are very effective for processing numerical data and converting them into bar, line, and pie graphs; you can scan in images and even morph them for humorous effects; with a modem and a phone line, you can put a class online to a Web site halfway across the globe. As with other types of visual aids, you should choose the computer graphics that fit your purpose, physical setting, and audience needs. Here are some suggestions for ways to use such materials:

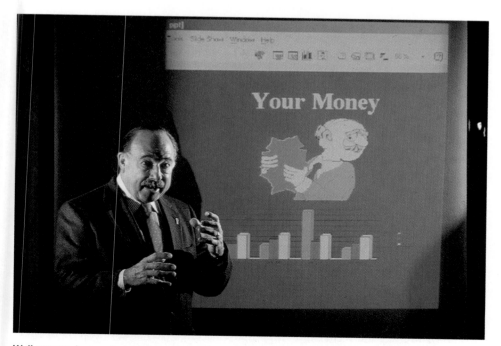

Well-executed computer graphics can be photographed and converted into a transparency (slide) or directly projected from a table designed for that purpose.

1. *Use computer graphics to create an atmosphere.* It's easy to make computer banners with block lettering and pictures. Hang a banner in the front of the room to set a mood or establish a theme. For example, a student urging her classmates to get involved in a United Way fund-raising drive created a banner with the campaign slogan, "Thanks to you, it works for all of us." Initially, the banner captured attention; during the speech the banner reinforced the theme. Or, if you're going to talk about negative political advertising and can get online, go to www.dnc.org to see what the Democratic National Committee is saying about Republican leaders and policies. That certainly will draw your listeners into your topic.

2. *Enlarge small computer-generated diagrams.* Most computer diagrams are too small to be seen easily by an audience. You can shoot a 35-mm slide right off your screen so that you can project it. Or, if you have access to a computer-projection table, images you've stored on a disk can be projected directly.

3. *Enhance the computer-generated image in other ways.* Suppose you print off some images or tables on the usual black-and-white printer. Use markers to color pie graphs or to darken the lines of a line graph. Use press-on letters to make headings for your graphs. Mixing media in such ways can give your presentations a professional look even if you're not working with color printers or computer projectors. If you have access to the right technology, you can create three-dimensional images of buildings, machines, or the human body.

The world of electrified sight and sound offers exciting possibilities for the public speaker. If you learn to integrate personal talk and audiovisual presentation, you'll find that your ability to reach audiences will be enhanced. Working an audience across channels—verbal, visual, acoustic—allows you to complicate your messages and yet give them a powerful presence that informs and persuades listeners who've been raised on sight and sound.

ASSESSING YOUR PROGRESS

Chapter Summary

1. Visual aids can boost listener comprehension and memory and add persuasive impact to a speech.
2. There are many types of visual aids: actual objects, photographs and slides, videotapes and films, chalkboard drawings, graphs, charts, and models.
3. Types of graphs include bar, line, pie, and pictographs.
4. Flipcharts unveil ideas one at a time; flowcharts show the entire process on a single sheet.
5. In selecting and using visual aids, consider the audience and the occasion, find ways to integrate verbal and visual materials effectively, and find ways to effectively use computer graphics.

Key Terms

bar graphs (p. 214)

charts (p. 218)

flipcharts (p. 218)

flowcharts (p. 218)

graphs (p. 214)

line graphs (p. 215)

models (p. 218)

pictographs (p. 217)

pie graphs (p. 215)

tables (p. 218)

visual aids (p. 210)

Assessment Activities

1. Work in small groups to develop at least three different types of visual aids for the following topics. Appoint a representative from each group to report to the class as a whole, telling about or showing the proposed visual aids.

   a. The procedure for gene splicing.

   b. How to splint a broken arm or leg.

   c. How to build sand castles or snow sculptures.

   d. The layout of bird-feeding stations.

   e. The procedure for rotating automobile tires.

   f. How to replace a washer in a drippy faucet.

   g. A method for downloading Internet images onto a computer's hard drive.

2. Videotape a home shopping or a how-to-do-it show and play the videotape in class. Evaluate the use of visual aids in the show. Were they easily seen? Did they demand attention? Did the speaker use the visual aids effectively? What would have made visual aids more effective? Alternatively, write up a one-page description and evaluation for assessment by your class instructor.

3. Without using any visual aids, describe an unusual place you have visited—for example, a cathedral in a foreign city or a historical site. Deliver a four- or five-minute speech to the class in which you describe this place as accurately and vividly as possible. Then ask the class to take a moment to envision this place. Now show them a picture of what you have described. How accurately were your listeners able to picture the place? How might you have ensured a more accurate description? What restrictions did you feel without the use of visual aids?

Surfing the Web

1. There is a great deal of help available online for using PowerPoint in presentations. Use the search words "PowerPoint presentations" and "GreenStar Productions" to discover tips, workshops, and examples.

2. Several magazines offering up-to-date information regarding technological developments are currently online. You'll find them by searching for the name of the publication, such as *Presentation* magazine, or for audiovisual publications.

References

1. Our century has also been labeled "occularcentric": Ocular = eye; centric = centered. See Jacques Ellul, *The Humiliation of the Word,* translated by Joyce Main Hanks (Grand Rapids, MI: William B. Eerdmans, 1985); Chris Jenks, ed., *Visual Culture* (New York: Routledge, 1995).

2. A good summary of research into multiple aspects of visual discourse can be found in Paul Messaris, *Visual Literacy. Image, Mind, & Reality* (Boulder, CO: Westview Press, 1994). Cf. Larry Raymond, *Reinventing Communication: A Guide to Using Visual Language for Planning, Problem Solving, and Reengineering* (Milwaukee: ASQC Quality Press, 1994).

3. William J. Seiler, "The Effects of Visual Materials on Attitudes, Credibility, and Retention," *Communication Monographs,* 38 (1971): 331–334.

4. Joel R. Levin and Alan M. Lesgold, "On Pictures in Prose," *Educational Communication and Technology Journal,* 26 (1978): 233–244. Cf. Marilyn J. Haring and Maurine A. Fry, "Effect of Pictures on Children's Comprehension of Written Text," *Educational Communication and Technology Journal,* 27 (1979): 185–190.

5. For more specific conclusions regarding the effects of various kinds of visual materials, see James Benjamin and Raymie E. McKerrow, *Business and Professional Communication* (New York: Longman, 1994), 175–179.

6. The best statement on the rationale for visuals we know of is Edgar B. Wycoff, "Why Visuals?" *AV Communication,* 11 (1977): 39, 59.

7. See G. D. Feliciano, R. D. Powers, and B. E. Kearle, "The Presentation of Statistical Information," *AV Communication Review,* 11 (1963): 32–39; M. D. Vernon, "Presenting Information in Diagrams," *AV Communication Review,* 1 (1953): 147–158; and L. V. Peterson and Wilbur Schramm, "How Accurately Are Different Kinds of Graphs Read?" *AV Communication Review,* 2 (1955): 178–189.

8. For more information on designing visual material, see Alan Brown, *Power Pitches: How to Produce Winning Presentations Using Charts, Slides, Video & Multimedia* (New York: Irwin Professional Publications, 1997); Margaret Rabb, *The Presentation Design Book: Projecting a Good Image with Your Desktop Computer,* 2nd ed. (Chapel Hill, NC: Ventana Press, 1994); Claudyne Wilder, *The Presentations Kit: 10 Steps to Selling Your Ideas* (New York: John Wiley, 1994); and Gene Zelazny, *Say It with Charts: The Executive's Guide to Visual Communication,* 3rd ed. (Burr Ridge, IL: Irwin, 1996).

Speeches to Inform

From business executives to day care providers and parents, speaking to inform is an important part of communication. We are awash in bits and pieces of facts, in the drone of "information radio," in digitized data. As a public speaker, you must compete with the mountain of information available to your listeners. You've got to find ways to grab them by the scruff of their psychological necks and the seat of their psychological pants and get them to sit up and take notice. You can do this by packaging facts and ideas in ways that they can understand and remember. That's what informative speaking is all about.

One theme will be sounded again and again in this chapter: "mere information" is useless until you put it together in ways that make it clear and relevant to others. Informative speeches clarify facts and ideas for audiences. Without clarification or interpretation, information is meaningless. The informative speaker's job is to adapt data and ideas to human needs. In this chapter, we'll discuss various types of informative speeches, outline the essential features of informative talks, and then review some ways of structuring each type of informative speech.

FACTS, KNOWLEDGE, AND THE INFORMATION AGE

Web Exploration
To learn more about the difference between information and knowledge go to http://awl.com/german

Our society almost worships facts. A staggering amount of information is available to us, particularly because of such technological developments as electronic media, photostatic printing, miniaturized circuitry, fax machines, and computerized data storage and retrieval systems. Jumping onto the World Wide Web via America Online, CompuServe, MCIAccess, or your school's mainframe computer puts you on the information superhighway, which has more lanes than the Santa Monica Freeway. Entire libraries are available online, as are huge collections of words, pictures, and sounds from around the world. Detective Joe Friday from the old *Dragnet* TV series would never dare say "Just the facts, Ma'am" today, for he'd immediately drown in data.

By themselves, mere facts tell us nothing. **Information** is but a collection of factoids until human beings shape, interpret, and act on it. Public speakers often serve as interpreters of information. They are called on to assemble, package, and present information to other human beings—to turn information into knowledge. To actually create **knowledge**—information that has been given human significance—you have to relate it to people's interests, needs, curiosities, and orientations to the world.

TYPES OF INFORMATIVE SPEECHES

Informative speeches take many forms depending on the situation, the level of knowledge possessed by listeners, and your own abilities as a presenter of data. Three of these forms—explanations or lectures, demonstrations, and oral reports—occur so frequently, however, that they merit special attention. They represent three common ways in which people package information to meet the needs of others.

Explanations or Lectures

"Mommy, what's a 'nerd'?" "Professor Martinez, what's the difference between a 'Web site' and a 'home page'?" "Chantel, before I take you on as a realtor, I want to know what a 'joint agency' is." You've been asking questions like these all of your life. A speech of explanation doesn't just offer a dictionary definition. Rather, **explanations** define concepts or processes in ways that make them relevant to listeners. Once 5-year-old Sarah knows what a nerd is, she'll know she has a human relations problem; once you know what kind of Web site a home page is, you'll know whether you want to build one; and once you know that a joint agency can represent both you and the seller or buyer, you'll have the information you need to know whether that's good or bad for your situation.

Lectures, which usually involve more extended explanations and definitions, also increase an audience's understanding of a particular field of knowledge or activity. For instance, a business executive might define "total quality management" and go on to show how such a style can make the company work better; a historian might tell a group of students what sociocultural forces converged to create the American Revolution; and a social worker could lecture an audience of government officials on the local impact the 1996 federal welfare reform package.

Demonstrations

Throughout your life, you've heard classroom instructions, seen job demonstrations, and read instructions for the performance of special tasks. Not only have you gone through many "tell" sessions but you've also had people "show" you how to execute actions—how to sort various kinds of paper for recycling, how to manage a counter at a fast food shop, how to set corner posts for a picket fence. Generally, **demonstrations** explain processes or both explain and illustrate those processes. Demonstrations involve the serial presentation of information, usually in steps or phases, and require clarity because your listeners are expected to learn or reproduce these steps themselves.

Oral Reports

An **oral report** is a speech that arranges and interprets information gathered in response to a request made by a group. Academic reports, committee reports, and executive reports are examples of oral reports. Scientists and other scholars announce

Informative speaking can take many forms.

SPEAKING OF . . . *Skills*

Choosing a Topic

If you're searching for informative speech topics, you can develop possible topics by brainstorming (see Chapter 2) or you can develop your ideas from standard subject areas. Consider these subject areas as you generate your own informative speech topics:

1. *People.* We're all curious about the lives of others. Build on this curiosity by focusing on someone you know, someone you admire, or someone unique. You might investigate the lives of the Wright brothers or Blanche Scott, the first American woman to fly. Or what about famous people like Bill Cosby or Clara Barton? Perhaps villians like Rasputin or John Dillinger fascinate you.
2. *Places.* This might be an opportunity to talk about a place you've visited or would like to visit—a city, museum, park, or another country. Cities like Rome or your hometown, museums like the Louvre or the local football hall of fame, parks like the Everglades or your favorite state park, and countries like Tanzania or Argentina can be intriguing speech topics.
3. *Things.* The possibilities are endless. Begin with what you already know. You could talk about your baseball card collection, the architectural style of your neighbor's house, or your uncle's antique automobile.
4. *Events.* Famous occurrences make good speech topics. There are recent events like political elections, the bombing of the World Trade Center, the floods caused by the Mississippi River, or the conflict in Bosnia-Herzegovina. In addition, you might talk about historical events such as famous battles, unusual discoveries, natural disasters, or memorable celebrations.
5. *Ideas.* Theories, principles, concepts, theologies, and traditions can make excellent informative speeches. You could explain the traditions of Taoism, the theory of relativity, the principles of capitalism, the concept of aging, or the funereal doctrines of Catholicism.
6. *Procedures.* Descriptions of processes can be fascinating. Your listeners may have wondered how watches work, what enables microwave ovens to cook food, or how ballets are choreographed.

their research findings in oral reports at professional conventions. Committees in business, industry, and government carry out special tasks and then present oral reports to their parent organizations or constituencies. Board chairpersons present annual oral reports to the stockholders on the past year's activities. You may have been asked to present a report on possible spring trips for an organization.

ESSENTIAL QUALITIES OF INFORMATIVE SPEECHES

Your goal as an informative speaker is to make it easy for your listeners to retain new information. There are five things you can do to ensure that your listeners remember what you say. You should strive for clarity, associate new ideas with familiar ones, package or cluster ideas, construct strong visualization, and provide motivational appeal.

Striving for Clarity

Informative speeches achieve maximum clarity when listeners can follow and understand what the speaker is saying. Clarity is largely the result of two factors: effective organization and the careful selection of words.

Achieving Clarity Through Effective Organization   The ideas in your speech will be clearer if you limit your points, use effective transitions, and keep your speech moving forward.

1. *Limit your points.* Confine your speech to three or four principal ideas, grouping whatever facts or ideas you wish to consider under these main headings. Even if you know a tremendous amount about the sinking of the ocean liner *Titanic,* you can't make everyone an expert with a single speech. Stick to the basics—the sequence of events and the tragic aftermath. Leave out the discrepancies between the movie depiction and historical facts, the design of the main staircase, and the fate of other White Star ocean liners.

2. *Use transitions to show relationships among ideas.* Word your transitions carefully. Make sure to indicate the relationship of the upcoming point to the rest of your ideas. You might say, "Second, you must prepare the chair for caning by cleaning out the groove and cane holes"; "The introduction of color to television sports in 1964 was followed by an equally important technology, the

SPEAKING OF . . . *Apprehension*

Information Overload

You're in the library, getting together materials for a speech, when suddenly you're bombarded with supporting materials stacking up around you like urban garbage. What to do?
  Consider doing the following:

- *Sample it.* Even if you've found thirteen great examples, pick out only two or three of them. Use the ones you think are most relevant to the audience's needs and desires.
- *Rotate it.* Use some of the examples this time, and some other ones when talking to friends about the topic.
- *Table it.* If you have too much information to deliver orally, put some of it on a graph or table and either project it or hand it out to your listeners. That way, you won't have to recite all of the numbers, yet they won't go to waste.
- *Distribute it.* Lots of juicy quotations? Use them not only in the body of the speech as supporting materials, but also in the introduction to set the tone and in the conclusion to wrap up your ideas.

If you do a good job at finding supporting materials, you'll have much too much at your disposal. That's all right. Better than having too little. Be happy in the knowledge that the opposite problem is much, much worse.

slow-motion camera"; "To test these hypotheses, we set up the following experiment." Such transitions allow listeners to follow you from point to point.

Web Exploration
To view examples of informative speeches go to
http://awl.com/german

3. *Keep your speech moving forward.* Rather than jumping back and forth between ideas, charging ahead, and then backtracking, develop a positive forward direction. Move from basic ideas to more complex ones, from background data to current research, or from historical incidents to current events. If you are informing your listeners about the triumphs and tragedies of the Kennedy family, you will want to discuss the sinking of PT-109 before the assassination of John F. Kennedy and the death of Michael Kennedy before the airplane crash of John F. Kennedy, Jr.

Achieving Clarity Through Word Choice   The second factor in achieving clarity is being understood. You can develop understanding through careful selection of your words. Recall the discussion of the use of language in Chapter 10. For now, think about the following ways to achieve clarity.

1. *Keep your vocabulary precise, accurate—not too technical.* In telling someone how to finish off a basement room, you might be tempted to say, "Next, take one of these long sticks and cut it off in this funny looking gizmo with a saw in it and try to make the corners match." An accurate vocabulary will help your listeners remember what supplies and tools to get when they approach the same project: "This is a ceiling molding; it goes around the room between the wall and the ceiling to cover the seams between the paneling and the ceiling tiles. You make the comers of the molding match by using a miter box, which has grooves that allow you to cut 45-degree angles. Here's how you do it."

2. *Simplify when possible.* If your speech on the operation of a dimmer switch sounds like it came out of the documentation for computer software, then it's too technical. Listeners can become confused and bored if they are bogged down in unnecessary detail and complex vocabulary. Include only as much technical vocabulary as you need. For a speech on the Heimlich maneuver, you will want to exclude its history and a discussion of the breathing process. Stick to the key ideas—how to detect signs of choking, where to exert pressure, and what to expect if you've completed the procedure correctly.

3. *Use reiteration to clarify complex ideas.* Rephrasing helps solidify ideas for those who didn't get them the first time. You might say, for example, "Unlike a terrestrial telescope, a celestial telescope is used for looking at moons, planets, and stars; that is, its mirrors and lenses are ground and arranged in such a way that it focuses on objects thousands of miles—not hundreds of feet—away from the observer." In this case, the idea is rephrased; the words aren't simply repeated.

Associating New Ideas with Familiar Ones

Audiences grasp new facts and ideas more readily when they can associate them with what they already know. In a speech to inform, try to connect the new with the old. To do this, you need to know enough about your audience to choose relevant experiences, images, analogies, and metaphors to use in your speech.

Sometimes such associations are obvious. A college dean talking to an audience of manufacturers about the problems of higher education presented his ideas under the headings of raw material, casting, machining, polishing, and assembling. He translated his central ideas into an analogy that his listeners, given their vocations, would understand. If you cannot think of any obvious association, you might have to rely on common experiences or images. For instance, you might explain the operation of a department store's pneumatic tube system by comparing it to sucking through a straw, or you could explain a cryogenic storage tank by comparing it to a thermos bottle.

Clustering Ideas

You can help listeners make sense of your speech by providing them with a well-organized package of tightly clustered ideas. Research on memory and organization has demonstrated that the "magic number" of items we can remember is seven, plus or minus two; more recent research has suggested that the number is probably five, again plus or minus two.[1] This research suggests that you ought to group items of information under three, five, or seven headings or in three, five, or seven clusters. You might, for example, organize a lecture on the history of American television around developments in key decades—the 1950s, 1960s, 1970s, 1980s, and 1990s—rather than breaking it down year by year. College registration may be presented to freshmen as a five-step process: (a) secure registration materials, (b) review course offerings, (c) see an adviser, (d) fill out the registration materials, and (e) enter the

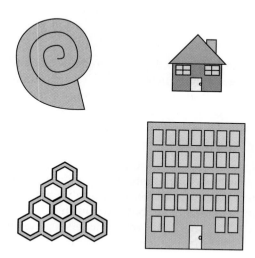

FIGURE 13.1   Association of New Ideas with Familiar Ones

Audiences grasp new concepts more quickly when those concepts are compared to things they already know. What familiar concepts could you use to explain molecules? Gene splicing? Inflation?

information into the computer. The American Cancer Society has organized the most common symptoms of cancer into seven categories to help you remember them.

Mnemonic devices in your outline also can provide memory triggers. CPR instructors teach the ABCs of cardiopulmonary resuscitation: (a) clear the *airways,* (b) check the *breathing* and (c) initiate chest *compressions.* A speaker giving a talk on the Great Lakes can show listeners how to remember the names of the lakes by thinking of HOMES: Huron, Ontario, Michigan, Erie, and Superior. These memory devices also help you remember the main points in your outline. Information forgotten is information lost; package your data and ideas in memorable clusters.

Constructing Relevant Visualizations

As we've been emphasizing, relevance is a key to speechmaking success. Using visualizations—recreations of events that people can "see"—can be a powerful technique for engaging listeners; if they can be made to see a process or event, they perhaps can be induced to project themselves mentally into it. So, for example, a student audience might know about the Vietnam War only through the mass media; that's where they had seen it, and thus references to movies and TV programs would be a good way for you to get into the topic. Word pictures help listeners into the world of your informative speech:

> *Picture this: You're walking down the Coleman Street in Collegeville, enjoying a sunny afternoon, when you come across a man who looks desperate, and says "Ca-oo-elp-mee-plee-plee-ahm-hafin', ahm-ahm-ahm-hafin'." What do you do? Is this person drunk? Crazy? Sick? In diabetic shock? Having a heart attack? Or maybe just someone participating in a psych experiment? How are you going to handle this situation? Well, in my speech today, I'm going to tell you how to handle it. Today, I want to talk to you about . . .*

Notice that the speaker tries to depict a familiar locale and a plausible event in that locale to set up a speech on the new kinds of first aid training currently offered to students at her school. If she's successful in conveying a sense of fear, uncertainty, and mistrust, then she's likely going to have her listeners following the rest of her talk.

Motivating Your Audience

Finally, and perhaps most important, you must be able to motivate your audience to listen. Unfortunately, many people ignore this essential feature of good informative speeches. Many of us blithely assume that because we are interested in something, our audience also will want to hear about it. You may be fascinated by collecting American commemorative stamps, but your listeners may yawn through your entire speech unless you motivate them. You need to give them a reason to listen. To make them enthusiastic, you might explain how stamps reflect our heritage or you might tell them how competitions are held for stamp art.

Keep in mind what we've said about attention in Chapter 9. You can use the factors of attention to engage the members of your audience and to draw them into your speech.

STRUCTURING INFORMATIVE SPEECHES

Now that we've described the various types of informative speeches and examined their essential features, it's time to examine ways to structure each type. Of course, it's possible to use any of the organizational patterns we described in Chapter 8, but some patterns are better suited to particular types of informative speeches than are others.

Explanations and Lectures

Because one of your primary jobs in explanations and lectures is to bring coherence and focus to information or concepts, structuring such speeches is a crucial activity.

Introduction   Because speeches of explanation and lectures treat either unfamiliar or familiar concepts in a new light, their introductions must accomplish two goals:

1. *Create curiosity.* Apathetic audiences are a special challenge in speeches on unfamiliar concepts since we're all tempted to say, "Well, if I've made it this far in life without knowing anything about quarks or double-entry bookkeeping or Library of Congress book coding, why should I bother with learning about these ideas now?" You need to make people wonder about the unknown. Use new information to attract attention and arouse curiosity.

2. *Adapt to audience needs.* Explanations and lectures must also be attentive to the needs or wants of the audience. In other words, their introductions should include explicit statements that indicate how the information can affect the listeners, such as, "Understanding the coding system used by the Library of Congress will help you find books you're looking for faster and, as an additional payoff, show you how to find other books like the one you're looking for."

You can also earn your listeners' attention by relating your topic to something they are familiar with or interested in—in the case of the Library of Congress, developing research skills that will result in higher grades. You should also include in your introduction a forecast of the structure of the explanation or lecture.

Body   Most explanations and lectures use a topical pattern because such speeches usually describe various aspects of an object or idea. It seems natural, for example, to use a topical pattern to structure a speech on careers in television around such topics as careers in broadcast TV, careers in cable TV, and careers in industrial TV.

There are occasions when other patterns may serve your specific purpose better than topical patterns. You might use an effect-cause pattern, for example, when preparing an informative speech on the laws of supply and demand. You could enumerate a series of effects with which people are already familiar—changing prices at the gas pumps—and then discuss the laws of supply and demand that account for such changes.

In many cases, there is competing information and conflicting conclusions about it. The key to packaging this information lies in the way in which the speaker constructs a *viewpoint* or *rationale*. Suppose that you wanted to explain the origins of

Speech Writer's Workshop
Use the Speech Workshop to structure your informative speech more effectively.

U.S. involvement in Vietnam in the 1950s. You could offer several explanations from varied viewpoints, depending on which story of that country and the war you wanted to tell. You might want to tell the French story, and the defense (with U.S. help) of its stronghold, Dien Bien Phu, in what was then called Indochina. Or, you could talk about allied support of the French, including $3 billion from the United States, and its impact on Euro-American foreign policy. You might prefer the cultural story of Indochina, its split between Western capitalism and Catholicism in the south and Chinese communism and Buddhism in the north, leading to a clash of lifestyles supported by superpowers on both sides. The military story itself also would make an interesting lecture: the French holding the fort at Dien Bien Phu, absolutely convinced that it was invulnerable to a peasant army, only to find themselves blown out in the siege of 1954. And, of course, the political story of Vietnam might also be told: the Cold War, the tension of Franco-American relations, SEATO (the South East Asia Treaty Organization), which committed the United States to defend east Asian countries against Communist aggressions.

All of these approaches are "correct," and each gives you a significant explanation about the importance of Vietnam to Western (including U.S.) interests as they were perceived at the time. If you tried to tell them all, you'd drive your audience crazy. A better strategy in most lectures, therefore, is to identify the viewpoint you'll take—"Let me tell you the story of American involvement in Vietnam from an economic (or cultural or military or political) point of view. If we look at Vietnam in this way, we'll see that. . . ." Such a statement signals your viewpoint, recognizes that you're not trying to be exhaustive, and tells your listeners what to listen for. Help them keep the story straight.

Conclusion Conclusions for explanations and lectures have two characteristics: (a) they usually include a summary of the main points, and (b) they often stress the ways in which people can apply the ideas that have been presented. For example, the speaker discussing diabetes could conclude by offering listeners the titles of books containing more information, the phone number of the American Diabetes Association, the address of a local clinic, or the meeting time and place of a diabetics support group.

A speech explaining diabetes could be outlined in a topical pattern as follows. Note several characteristics of this speech:

1. The speaker tries early on to engage listeners' curiosity and to review listeners' personal needs. The use of a personal example is particularly good for this kind of speech.

2. The speaker offers statistics on diabetes early so that the audience knows that the disease is widespread and serious.

3. Three topics are previewed, then developed in the body of the speech to engage three aspects of listeners' thinking.

4. After offering a summary of the central idea, the speaker returns to the personal example, adding closure to the speech.

SAMPLE OUTLINE FOR A SPEECH OF EXPLANATION

What Is Diabetes?[2]

INTRODUCTION

I. I never knew my grandmother. She was a talented artist; she raised six kids without all the modern conveniences like microwave ovens and electric clothes dryers; and my dad still talks about the time she foiled a would-be burglar by locking him in a broom closet until the police came. My grandmother had diabetes. It finally took her life. Now my sister has it. So do 16 million other Americans.

The speaker uses a vividly developed personal example to gain attention.

II. Diabetes threatens millions of lives, and it's one of nature's stealthiest diseases.

The scope of the problem is explained.

III. It's important to understand this disease because, more than likely, you or someone you know will eventually have to deal with it.

A motivation for listening is provided.

  A. Diabetes is the third leading cause of death behind heart disease and cancer, according to the American Diabetes Association.

Supporting testimony shows the severity of the disease.

  B. Over one third of those suffering from the disease don't even know they have it. That simple knowledge could make the difference between a happy productive life and an early death.

Listeners are warned that ignorance of the disease makes the problem worse.

  C. Furthermore, diabetes is implicated in many other medical problems: it contributes to coronary heart disease; it accounts for 40 percent of all amputations and most cases of new blindness.

The scope of the problem is expanded by pointing out that other medical conditions are complicated by diabetes.

  D. In the next few minutes, let's look at three things you should know about "the silent killer," diabetes—what it is, how it affects people, and how it can be controlled.

The three main ideas of the speech are previewed.

BODY

I. What diabetes is.

The first main point is stated.

  A. Diabetes is a chronic disease of the endocrine system that affects your body's ability to deliver glucose to its cells.

Diabetes is defined in medical terms.

  B. The symptoms of diabetes, according to Dr. Charles Kilo, are weight loss in spite of eating and drinking, constant hunger and thirst, frequent urination, and fatigue.

The symptoms of diabetes are explained.

II. How diabetes affects people.

The second main point is provided.

  A. Type I diabetes occurs when your body cannot produce insulin, a substance that delivers glucose to your cells.

Type I diabetes is operationally defined.

*Who is affected by
Type I is further
explained.*

1. Only 5 to 10 percent of all diabetics are Type I.
2. This type, also known as *juvenile diabetes,* usually shows up in the first 20 years of life.
3. Type I diabetes can be passed on genetically but is also thought to be triggered by environmental agents such as viruses.
4. Type I diabetics must take insulin injections to treat the disease.

*The treatment is
revealed.*

*Type II diabetes is
operationally defined.*

*Supporting statistics
show the scope of this
type.*
*Who is affected by
Type II is further
explained.*

B. Type II diabetes occurs when your body produces insulin but fails to use it effectively.
   1. Of all diabetics, 90 to 95 percent have Type II.
   2. This type usually shows up after a person turns 40.
   3. It often affects people who are overweight; more women are affected than men.
   4. Insulin injections are sometimes used to treat the disease, though exercise, proper diet, and oral medications often are enough.

*The treatment is
revealed.*

*The third main point is
provided.*

*The treatments for
Type I are explained.*

III. How to control diabetes.
   A. Type I diabetes cannot be cured, but it can be controlled.
      1. Patients must take insulin injections, usually several times a day.
      2. Patients need to monitor their blood sugar levels by pricking a finger and testing a drop of blood.

*Supporting testimony
is offered for new
treatments.*
*Near-infrared beams
determine blood sugar
levels.*

*New methods of
delivering insulin are
outlined.*

      3. According to *Science News,* several new treatments are available.
         a. One new device uses near-infrared beams to determine blood sugar level.
         b. Insulin can be taken through the nose or in pill form.
         c. Pancreatic transplants have been performed with limited success.

*The treatments for
Type II are explained.*

*Testimony supports the
value of weight loss.*

   B. Type II diabetes can be controlled through life-style modifications.
      1. Usually these diabetics are required to lose weight by exercising, according to Dr. JoAnn Manson.
      2. Changes in diet are also required.

*Insulin-stimulating
medications are
explained.*
*Insulin injections replace
unsuccessful behavior
modifications.*

      3. Some people take oral medications that stimulate the release of insulin, decrease glucose production in the liver, and foster insulin activity.
      4. If these modifications fail, Type II diabetics must take insulin injections.

CONCLUSION

*Listeners are reminded
of the definition of
diabetes.*

I. Diabetes is a serious disease in which the body can no longer produce or use insulin effectively.

II. The two types of diabetes occur at different stages in life and require different measures for control of the disease.

III. My grandmother lived with her diabetes for years but eventually lost her life to it. My sister has the advantages of new treatments and future research in her fight with diabetes.

IV. As we age, many of us will be among the 600,000 new diabetics each year. Through awareness, we can cope effectively with this silent killer.

The three main ideas of the speech are reiterated.

The speech reaches closure by referring to the introductory personal example.

Listeners are warned that diabetes could affect them.

Demonstrations

Flip through your television channels and you'll come across cooking demonstrations, home improvement shows, sewing instructions, home shopping demonstrations, and painting lessons. Each presents the steps required to complete a project. Like successful educational television shows, demonstrations should break down a process or procedure into a series of steps. Each step should be easy to understand and to visualize.

Introduction   In some speaking situations, such as presentations in speech communication classrooms, listener attendance may not be voluntary. On these occasions, you'll have to pay special attention to motivational matters. If your audience has invited you to speak or is attending your talk voluntarily, you can assume listener interest. When giving a demonstration, you'll usually need to spend only a little time generating curiosity or motivating people to listen. After all, if you're instructing listeners in a new office procedure or giving a workshop on how to build an iceboat, they already have the prerequisite interest and motivation; otherwise they wouldn't have come. When your audience is already motivated to listen, you can concentrate your introduction on two other tasks:

1. *Preview your speech.* If you're going to take your listeners through the steps involved in refinishing a bookcase, give them an overall picture of the process before you start detailing each operation.

2. *Encourage listeners to follow along.* Even though some of the steps may be difficult, urge everyone to listen. A process such as tombstone rubbing, for example, looks easier than it is: many people are tempted to quit listening and give up somewhere along the way. If, however, you forewarn them and promise them special help with the difficult techniques, they will be more likely to bear with you.

Body   As we suggested earlier, most speeches of demonstration follow a natural chronological or spatial pattern. Consequently, you usually will have little trouble organizing the body of a speech of demonstration. Your problems are more likely to be technical and may include the following:

1. *The problem of rate.* If you need to let a cream pie set and cool before building a top layer, what do you do? You can't just stand there and wait for cooling.

Instead, you also have a cooled pie, ready for the next step. You also need to plan some material for filling the time—perhaps additional background or a brief discussion of what problems can arise at this stage. Plan your remarks carefully for those junctures so you can maintain your audience's attention.

2. *The problem of scale.* How can you show various embroidery stitches to an audience of 25? When dealing with minute operations, you often must increase the scale of operation. In this example, you could use a large piece of poster board or even a 3- by 4-foot piece of cloth stretched over a wooden frame. By using an oversized needle, yarn instead of thread, and stitches measured in inches instead of millimeters, you could easily make your techniques visible to all audience members. At the other extreme, in a speech on how to make a homemade compost frame, you should work with a scaled-down model.

3. *The coordination of verbal and visual methods.* Demonstrations often demand that speakers "show" while "telling." To keep yourself from becoming flustered or confused, be sure to practice doing while talking—demonstrating your material while explaining aloud what you're doing. Decide where you'll stand when showing a slide so that the audience can see both you and the image; practice talking about your aerobic exercise positions while you're actually doing them; do a Web search for your speech in practice sessions so you'll be ready to do it for a real audience. If you don't, you'll inevitably get yourself into trouble in front of your listeners.

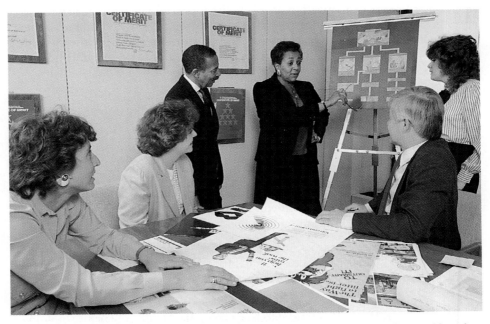

Practice coordinating verbal and visual materials while speaking so that you can do it smoothly and professionally.

Conclusion   Conclusions for demonstration speeches usually have three parts:

1. *Summary.* Most audiences need this review, which reminds them to question procedures or ideas they don't understand.

2. *Encouragement.* People trying new processes or procedures usually get in trouble the first few times and need to be reassured that such trouble is predictable and can be overcome.

3. *Offer of help.* What sounded so simple in your talk may be much more complicated in execution. If possible, make yourself available for assistance: "As you fill out your application form, just raise your hand if you're unsure of anything and I'll be happy to help you." Or point to other sources of further information and assistance: "Here's the address of the U.S. Government Printing Office, whose pamphlet X1234 is available for only three dollars; it will give you more details"; "If you run into a problem fetching computer files that I haven't covered in this short orientation, just go over to Maria McFerson's desk, right over here. Maria's experienced in these matters and is always willing to help." Such statements not only offer help but also assure your listeners that they won't be labeled as dimwitted if they actually have to ask for it.

Thinking through requirements of speeches of instruction and demonstration might result in a speaking outline like this one:

SAMPLE OUTLINE FOR A DEMONSTRATION SPEECH

Servicing Your Personal Computer

INTRODUCTION

I. It's 2 A.M. and you sit down at your PC, ready to write tomorrow's English composition. There's a flicker of light on the screen and nothing else. Has this ever happened to you?

A typical scenario catches listener attention.

II. With a little time and patience, you can make sure your personal computer is in tip-top shape, ready for those last minute assignments. Because these maintenance procedures are so easy to do, you can save costly repair bills by doing them yourself.

Motivation to listen is provided.

III. There are three basic services that you can complete easily and quickly—changing batteries, servicing keyboards, and cleaning the mouse. Let's get started with changing your battery:

Main topics are previewed.

BODY

I. Changing your battery.

A. Your computer relies on a replaceable battery to keep the date and time chips current when your computer is turned off.

The structure is repeated in each of the three sections of the speech.

First, listeners are given an overview.

Then, each step of the process is demonstrated.

1. You should replace this battery every two years.
2. Obtain a replacement at your local computer shop.

B. Here's how to replace the battery.

1. Unplug the power source.
2. Remove the cover from the system unit.
3. Locate the battery on the motherboard.
   a. In some computers, the battery is a cylindrical cell located at the edge of the motherboard and covered with a plastic cap.
   b. Another type of battery, found on older PCs, is held in place by wires that must also be removed.
   c. Occasionally, batteries are soldered in place and must be replaced at a service center.
4. Replace the battery.

II. Servicing your keyboard.

A. If your keys begin to stick or you've spilled a soda on your keyboard, it's time to clean it.

B. Here's how to clean your keyboard.

1. Disconnect the keyboard and turn it upside down.
2. Remove the assembly screws from the bottom.
3. Pry apart the keyboard housings.
4. There are three easy steps to cleaning the keyboard.
   a. Shake out the debris.
   b. Blow out the interior with canned air (don't do this near your computer!).
   c. Use electrical contact cleaner to flush out sticky residue or remove corrosion.
5. Put your keyboard back together.

III. Cleaning your mouse.

A. If your cursor moves erratically or if your mouse doesn't slide easily on its pad, it needs to be cleaned.

B. Here's how to service your mouse.

1. Turn the mouse over.
2. Remove the housing cover.
3. Remove the trackball.
4. Check for lint, dirt particles, or other debris.
5. Reassemble the mouse.

CONCLUSION

A final inducement is offered.

I. With a few simple tools and a little extra time, you can complete the routine maintenance steps to keep your computer running at its best.

II. You can change batteries, service your keyboard, and clean your mouse.

III. All it takes is a few minutes. Do it tonight, so you're ready for that next big English paper.

The main speech topics are summarized.

Final comments provide closure.

Oral Reports

Your principal strategy in an oral report must be to meet the audience's expectations with the information and the recommendations you present.

Introduction   An oral report is requested by a group, committee, or class; the audience, therefore, generally knows what it expects and why. As a result, in introducing oral reports, you need not spend much time motivating your listeners. Instead, you should concentrate on describing how you gathered and organized your information and pointing ahead to any action that your listeners are expected to take in light of your information. The key to a good introduction for an oral report is orientation—reviewing the past (your listeners' expectations and your preparations), the present (your goal now), and the future (your listeners' responsibilities once you are done). Remember that you're giving your report to your audience for a purpose.

Body   The principle for organizing the body of an oral report can be stated simply: select the organization pattern best suited to your audience's needs. Have you been asked to provide your listeners with a history of a group or a problem? Use a chronological pattern. Do they want to know how a particular state of affairs came to be? Try a cause-effect format. Have you been asked to discuss an organizational structure for the group? A topical pattern will allow you to review the constitutional responsibilities of each officer. Note the use of a topical pattern in this sample outline:

SAMPLE OUTLINE FOR AN ORAL REPORT

Report from the Massage Therapy Committee[3]

INTRODUCTION

I. Our committee was asked to investigate different kinds of massage therapy and then to recommend a therapy program for our exercise club.

A. We interviewed various kinds of massage therapists working in this area.

B. Different committee members had massages in each therapy done so that we can talk more specifically about each technique.

The charge of the committee is stated.

II. We examined five kinds of massage therapy:

A. Swedish massage is the most common in this area.
   1. Therapists use long strokes, kneading, and rubbing techniques on the outer layers of muscles on the surface of the whole body.
   2. This technique is especially useful for relaxation and improving circulation.

B. Deep-tissue massage is one alternative to Swedish massage.
   1. Here, slow strokes with harder pressure are used.
   2. This technique is used primarily to relieve muscle tension.

C. Neuromuscular or trigger-point therapy is practiced at several senior centers.
   1. Therapists use strong finger pressure at key trigger points, especially points of muscular tension.
   2. They are working on chronic pain, to break its cycles.

D. Sports massage is available at many fitness centers.
   1. Specific groups of muscles are worked on with pressure and heating ointments.
   2. It attacks muscles spasms, tendinitis, and tenderness.

E. Shiatsu (from Japan) and acupressure (from China) are growing in this area.
   1. Like acupuncture, shiatsu and acupressure rely on pressure to unblock energy (called "qi" ["chi"]) flowing along pathways in the body.
   2. These techniques are used for pain from headaches or chronic sources.

III. As we thought about the needs of our exercise group, we had the following thoughts:

A. The most common complaints from most of us are about tension and the chronic pain of growing older.

B. Some of you also wanted to learn some pain relief techniques that you could use by yourself at home.

C. Cost also is a consideration for many of you.

IV. Therefore, considering these factors, our committee recommends that two sorts of massage therapy be offered here.

A. A neuromuscular therapist should be asked in once a week to help those of us with chronic pain who want to learn some techniques we can use between visits to the therapist.

B. A Swedish masseur should be available at least every two weeks for rubdowns and relaxation from the cares of this world.

> C. We also agreed that a list of therapists in this area, by kind of therapy, should be distributed to everyone.
>
> D. I think we should thank the committee for its work, and its willingness to take your questions. Do you have any?

Conclusion   Most oral reports end with a conclusion that mirrors the introduction. Mention again your report's purpose; review its main points; publicly thank committee members; and then either offer a motion to accept the committee recommendations, or—in the case of informative reports—request questions from the audience. Conclusions to reports, when done well, are quick, firm, efficient, and pointed.

TABLE 13.1   Checklist for Introductions and Conclusions to Informative Speeches

Explanations or Lectures

_____ 1. Does my introduction raise listeners' curiosity?

_____ 2. Do I forecast my main topics in my introduction?

_____ 3. Does my conclusion suggest implications of the information listeners have received or call for listeners' action?

Demonstrations

_____ 1. Does my introduction encourage everyone to listen?

_____ 2. Does my introduction pique listener curiosity?

_____ 3. Do I preview my main points in my introduction?

_____ 4. Do I summarize my main points in my conclusion?

_____ 5. Do I encourage listeners to try new procedures even though they may experience initial difficulty?

_____ 6. Do I tell my listeners where they can find help or information in the future?

Oral Reports

_____ 1. Do I remind my listeners of their request for information?

_____ 2. Do I describe the procedures I used for gathering information for this report?

_____ 3. Does my introduction include a forecast of subtopics?

_____ 4. Does my introduction suggest the action that will be recommended in the report?

_____ 5. Does my conclusion mention the main purpose of the report?

_____ 6. Does my conclusion review the main points of the report?

_____ 7. Do I recognize and thank committee members for their contributions?

_____ 8. Do I call for action on a motion or questions from my listeners?

SAMPLE SPEECH

The following speech, "The Geisha," was delivered by Joyce Chapman when she was a freshman at Loop College, Chicago. It illustrates most of the virtues of a good informative speech: (1) it provides enough detail and explanations to be clear; (2) it works from familiar images of geishas, adding new ideas and information in such a way as to enlarge listeners' frames of reference; (3) its topical organization pattern is easy to follow; and, (4) it gives listeners reasons for listening.

The Geisha[4]   Joyce Chapman

A personal reference establishes an immediate tie between Ms. Chapman and her topic.

As you may have already noticed from my facial features, I have Oriental blood in me and, as such, I am greatly interested in my Japanese heritage. One aspect of my heritage that fascinates me the most is the beautiful and adoring Geisha./1

Ms. Chapman works hard to bring the listeners—with their stereotyped views of Geishas—into the speech through comments many might have made and references to familiar films.

I recently asked some of my friends what they thought a Geisha was, and the comments I received were quite astonishing. For example, one friend said, "She is a woman who walks around in a hut." A second friend was certain that a Geisha was, "A woman who massages men for money and it involves her in other physical activities." Finally, I received this response, "She gives baths to men and walks on their backs." Well, needless to say, I was rather surprised and offended by their comments. I soon discovered that the majority of my friends perceived the Geisha with similar attitudes. One of them argued, "It's not my fault, because that is the way I've seen them on TV." In many ways my friend was correct. His misconception of the Geisha was not his fault, for she is often portrayed by American film producers and directors as: a prostitute, as in the movie, *The Barbarian and the Geisha,* a streetwalker, as seen in the TV series, *Kung Fu,* or as a showgirl with a gimmick, as performed in the play, *Flower Drum Song.*/2

A Geisha is neither a prostitute, streetwalker, nor showgirl with a gimmick. She is a lovely Japanese woman who is a professional entertainer and hostess. She is cultivated with exquisite manners, truly a bird of a very different plumage./3

The central idea is stated clearly.

A transition moves the listeners easily from the introduction to the body of the speech via a forecast.

The first section of the body of the speech is devoted to an orienting history that cleverly wipes away most of the negative stereotypes of the Geisha.

I would like to provide you with some insight to the Geisha, and, in the process perhaps, correct any misconception you may have. I will do this by discussing her history, training, and development./4

The Geisha has been in existence since A.D. 600, during the archaic time of the Yakamoto period. At that time the Japanese ruling class was very powerful and economically rich. The impoverished majority, however, had to struggle to survive. Starving fathers and their families had to sell their young daughters to the teahouses in order to get a few yen. The families hoped that the girls would have a better life in the teahouse than they would have had in their own miserable homes./5

During ancient times only high society could utilize the Geisha's talents because she was regarded as a status symbol, exclusively for the elite. As the Geisha became more popular, the common people developed their own imitations. These imitations were often crude and base, lacking sophistication and taste. When American GIs came home from World War II, they related descriptive accounts of their wild escapades with the Japanese Geisha. In essence, the GIs were only soliciting with common prostitutes. These bizarre stories helped create the wrong image of the Geisha./6

Today, it is extremely difficult to become a Geisha. A Japanese woman couldn't wake up one morning and decide, "I think I'll become a Geisha today." It's not that simple. It takes sixteen years to qualify./7

At the age of six a young girl would enter the Geisha training school and become a Jo-chu, which means housekeeper. The Jo-chu does not have any specific type of clothing, hairstyle, or make-up. Her duties basically consist of keeping the teahouse immaculately clean (for cleanliness is like a religion to the Japanese). She would also be responsible for making certain that the more advanced women would have everything available at their fingertips. It is not until the girl is sixteen and enters the Maiko stage that she concentrates less on domestic duties and channels more of her energies on creative and artistic endeavors./8

The Maiko girl, for example, is taught the classical Japanese dance, Kabuki. At first, the dance consists of tiny, timid steps to the left, to the right, backward and forward. As the years progress, she is taught the more difficult steps requiring syncopated movements to a fan./9

The Maiko is also introduced to the highly regarded art of floral arrangement. The Japanese take full advantage of the simplicity and gracefulness that can be achieved with a few flowers in a vase, or with a single flowering twig. There are three main styles: Seika, Moribana, and Nagerie. It takes at least three years to master this beautiful art./10

During the same three years, the Maiko is taught the ceremonious art of serving tea. The roots of these rituals go back to the thirteenth century, when Zen Buddhist monks in China drank tea during their devotions. These rituals were raised to a fine art by the Japanese tea masters, who set the standards for patterns of behavior throughout Japanese society. The tea ceremony is so intricate that it often takes four hours to perform and requires the use of over seventeen different utensils. The tea ceremony is far more than the social occasion it appears to be. To the Japanese, it serves as an island of serenity where one can refresh the senses and nourish the soul./11

One of the most important arts taught to the Geisha is that of conversation. She must master an elegant circuitous vocabulary flavored

A nice transition moves Chapman to her second point on the rigors of Geisha training. She discusses the training in language technical enough to make listeners feel that they're learning interesting information but not so detailed as to be suffocating.

in Karyuki, the world of flowers and willows, of which she will be a part. Consequently, she must be capable of stimulating her client's mind as well as his esthetic pleasures./12

Having completed her sixteen years of thorough training, at the age of twenty-two, she becomes a full-fledged Geisha. She can now serve her clients with duty, loyalty, and most important, a sense of dignity./13

The Geisha would be dressed in the ceremonial kimono, made of brocade and silk thread. It would be fastened with an obi, which is a sash around the waist and hung down the back. The length of the obi would indicate the girl's degree of development. For instance, in the Maiko stage the obi is longer and is shortened when she becomes a Geisha. Unlike the Maiko, who wears a gay, bright, and cheerful kimono, the Geisha is dressed in more subdued colors. Her make-up is the traditional white base, which gives her the look of white porcelain. The hair is shortened and adorned with beautiful, delicate ornaments./14

As a full-fledged Geisha, she would probably acquire a rich patron who would assume her sizable debt to the Okiya, or training residence. This patron would help pay for her wardrobe, for each kimono can cost up to $12,000. The patron would generally provide her with financial security./15

The Geisha serves as a combination entertainer and companion. She may dance, sing, recite poetry, play musical instruments, or draw pictures for her guest. She might converse with them or listen sympathetically to their troubles. Amorous advances, however, are against the rules./16

So, as you can see the Geisha is a far cry from the back-rubbing, streetwalking, slick entertainer that was described by my friends. She is a beautiful, cultivated, sensitive, and refined woman./17

ASSESSING YOUR PROGRESS

Chapter Summary

1. Speeches to inform seek to package information or ideas so as to create knowledge in listeners.

2. Three types of informative speeches are explanations or lectures, demonstrations, and oral reports.

3. No matter what type of informative speech you're preparing, you should strive for five qualities: ensuring clarity; associating new ideas with familiar ones; clustering ideas to aid memory and comprehension; constructing relevant visualizations to aid in audience comprehension; and motivating your audience.

4. Carefully structuring the introduction, body, and conclusion of each type of informative speech can maximize your ability to reach your audiences.

Key Terms

demonstrations (p. 231)

explanations (p. 230)

information (p. 230)

knowledge (p. 230)

lectures (p. 231)

oral report (p. 231)

Assessment Activities

1. In a concise written report, indicate and defend the type of arrangement (chronological sequence, spatial sequence, cause-effect, and so on) you think would be most suitable for an informative speech on the following subjects:

   a. The status of minority studies on campus.

   b. Recent developments in genetic engineering.

   c. Mayan excavations in Central America.

   d. Tax-free savings for retirement.

   e. How a chat room works.

   f. Censorship of video games.

   g. Diet fads of the 1980s and 1990s.

   h. Residential colleges and universities.

   i. Buying your first house.

   j. What life will be like in the year 2500.

2. Ask each member of the class to reflect on an example from the past where they have had to demonstrate a procedure to another person. Share the experiences, commenting on the effectiveness of the demonstration. You might, for example, have shown a new employee how to assemble a hamburger or how to close out a cash register.

Surfing the Web

1. There are a wide range of reference materials available online, including encyclopedias, dictionaries, yearbooks, historical documents, biographies, magazines, and newspapers. Choose a topic and then conduct a search using online resources to discover facts about your topic. Conclude the exercise by discussing ways to organize and present the facts you've discovered.

2. Consult the Library of Congress Web page. It offers an in-depth discussion of how historians manage overwhelming mountains of data to develop coherent explanations of the past. Apply these strategies as you conduct research and uncover information for your next speech.

References

1. For background on information packaging, see G. Mandler, "Organization and Memory," in *Human Memory: Basic Processes,* edited by Gordon Bower (New York: Academic Press, 1977), 310–354; Mandler's articles in C. R. Puff, ed., *Memory Organization*

and Structure (New York: Academic Press, 1976); and the classic G. A. Miller, "The Magic Number Seven Plus or Minus Two: Some Limits on Our Capacity for Processing Information," *Psychological Review,* 63 (1956): 81–97.

2. Information for this outline is taken from Phyllis Barrier, "Diabetes: It Never Lets Up," *Nation's Business* (November 1992), 77; David Bradley, "Is a Pill on the Way for Diabetes?" *New Scientist* (27 June 1992), 17; C. Ezzell, "New Clues to Diabetes' Cause and Treatment," *Science News* (21 December 1991), 406; Charles Kilo and Joseph R. Williamson, *Diabetes* (New York: John Wiley & Sons, 1987); Mark Schapiro, "A Shock to the System," *Health* (July-August 1991), 75–82: Carrie Smith, "Exercise Reduces Risk of Diabetes," *The Physician and Sportsmedicine* (November 1992), 19; John Travis, "Helping Diabetics Shed Pins and Needles," *Science News* (6 July 1991), 4; Janice A. Drass and Ann Peterson, "Type II Diabetes: Exploring Treatment Options," *American Journal of Nursing,* 96 (November 1996): 45–49; personal experience of one of the authors.

3. Information for this review was taken from *Modern Maturity* (September-October 1996), 72.

4. Joyce Chapman, "The Geisha," in Roselyn Schiff et al., *Communication Strategy: A Guide to Speech Preparation* (Glenview, IL: Scott, Foresman and Co., 1981). Used with permission of Longman Publishers.

Chapter 14

Speeches to Persuade

You probably don't think about it, but you're bathed in persuasive appeals every day of your life. Billboards confront you on your way to school, posters call for your attention, teachers urge you to see their points of view, campus signs plead with you not to litter, and McDonald's tells you that "You deserve a break today"—as long as it involves a Big Mac®. Speaking publicly in order to persuade shares many features with other kinds of persuasion that we experience all the time.

The general purpose of persuasion is to change or reinforce attitudes or behaviors. The speaker who persuades makes a very different demand on the audience than does the speaker who informs. The informative speaker is satisfied when listeners understand what's been said. The persuader, however, attempts to influence the listener's thoughts or actions. The persuader

255

pleads with the audience to agree with or act on the speech. Occasionally, persuaders seek to reinforce ideas or actions that already exist in listeners. They may defend the status quo, urging rejection of proposed changes. Whatever the specific purpose, the general purpose of persuasion is to convince audiences in thought and deed.

To persuade audiences successfully, you must make them *want* to believe or act. When people feel forced to accept beliefs, as you might when studying for a test, they may soon abandon them. So, persuaders must always seek (a) to provide the audience with motives for believing, by appealing to their basic needs or desires, and (b) to convince them that recommended thoughts or actions will satisfy these desires. Consider the following story:

> *Spring break was still two months away, though time was getting short. Mora wanted to join some friends on South Padre Island, but how? She'd not only need her parents' permission, but she'd need a little cash as well. What appeals would reach them? "Everyone's doing it?" No, that didn't work last time. "I deserve a break after all of the hard work I've been doing this semester?" Not bad, but it wouldn't justify going to the Gulf of Mexico, exactly. Finally a thought occurred to Mora. She went to her adviser, who agreed to help. Then she headed to a supper with her parents, and started to talk: "You know I want a nice spring break to end my college career. But, I know I'm in college mainly to learn and improve my knowledge of my field. I know how I can do both. I want to go with some of my friends to South Padre Island. While I'm there, I can gather some plant samples, climatological data, and pictures of the terrain. Then when I'm back I can do an independent study with my adviser on relationships between flora and island geography. I'll have fun, but also earn academic credit and have an independent project I can put into a portfolio when I go job hunting. What do you think?"*

Mora worked hard to find the right motive and to convince her parents that a trip to the islands would satisfy their desires as well as her own. Mora's approach to fulfilling her desire for a great spring break was a classic exercise in audience analysis and verbal persuasion. She explored her experience in reaching this particular audience, considered its habitual grounds for granting her help and privilege, and kept on thinking about her parents until she figured out a way to satisfy both her desires and their expectations. Exchanges like this occur millions of times a day.

We'll begin this chapter with a discussion of motive needs and the motivational appeals that speakers can use to tap those needs. Then, we'll examine the motivated sequence, an organizational pattern that helps you to incorporate motivational appeals successfully into your speeches, reviewing actual persuasive speeches along the way.

CHANGING AUDIENCES' MINDS AND ACTIONS

We'll make a distinction in this chapter that may help you to focus more particularly on techniques for successfully persuading others to think and act in particular ways. A **persuasive speech** we'll identify as one that seeks to change an audience's beliefs,

Web Exploration
To view examples of persuasive appeals go to http://awl.com/german

We live in a world that runs on promotions and pitches—persuasion, in other words. What are some examples of persuasive advertising evident in this photo?

attitudes, or values—to reorient their thinking in some significant way. An **actuative speech,** on the other hand, we'll discuss as one that seeks to alter people's actual behavior. So, a speech that asks listeners to think of spouse abuse as a psychological disease rather than a social disgrace would be a persuasive speech; one that asks them to intervene in the lives of families with signs of abuse, to get them treatment, is an actuative speech. The distinction is not especially important except in one respect: you need to realize that it's one thing to convince people to change their minds, but quite another to get them to act upon that conviction.

✓ "Sure I believe in volunteer work, but, ah, well, like I'm over my head at work and school, OK?"

✓ "Sure I believe that physical plant workers like us are being ripped off, but, ah, support a union? I couldn't do that. I haven't got time for any more organizations/I'm too broke to pay union dues/they're just a bunch of outside agitators/I can't risk my job/etc."

The key to success in both persuasive and actuative speeches is motivation: Can you find ways to tap into the audience's motivations so as to change thought and behavior?

Analyzing the Needs and Desires of Listeners

Begin with the simple assumption that people's thoughts and actions are related to their needs (things that are missing and yet perceived as necessary to their lives) and desires (things that are hoped for as ends in themselves or means to new

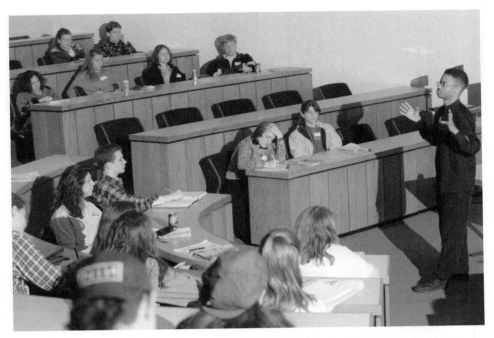

Society could not function were not citizens able to convince each other to take or avoid collective actions.

achievements). Generally speaking, therefore, a sense of **need** arises out of a perceived lack, and a sense of **desire,** from a hope to improve one's life. So, you need to eat (hunger being a sense of a lack of nourishment), but you desire a Thai chicken roll-up (a preferred kind of food, not necessary, but nonetheless hoped for).

The first step in constructing persuasive and actuative speeches thus begins with an attempt to assess needs and desires: (1) *What* do these people think they lack and *what* do they think would improve their lives in positive ways? (2) *How* can I use those needs and desires to construct a successful persuasive or actuative speech?

Turning Needs and Desires into Motivational Appeals

Needs and desires, of course, are psychological constructs—perceptions people have of themselves, their plight in life, their fantasies, their nightmares. Insofar as these perceptions drive people to think and act in particular ways, they are usefully thought of as motive needs. A **motive need** is an impulse to satisfy a psychological-social want or a biological urge. Such needs may arise from physiological considerations—pain, lack of food, or surroundings that are too hot or cold—or they may come about for sociocultural reasons, such as when you feel left out of a group. If you feel the need deeply, your feelings may compel you to do something about your situation. You might eat, adjust the thermostat, or join a group—you're motivated.

Once you recognize the power of motive needs to propel human action, you may ask, "How can I identify and satisfy these needs in a speech? How can I use these basic

SPEAKING OF . . . *Skills*
Persuading the Diverse Audience

As we noted in the opening to Chapter 4, one of the most difficult tasks a speaker faces is trying to convince a diversified audience to act together. How can you get racially diversified, bi-gendered, class-stratified audiences of young and old people to work in harmony?

The advice offered in that chapter bears repeating (and rereading if necessary):

- Recognize diversity even while calling for unity.
- Show that particular values are held in common even if they're operationalized differently by various groups of people.
- Encourage different paths to a goal they all can share.
- Exhort people to adjust some of their own lifestyle choices for the greater good of all.
- Assure people that they can maintain their self-identity even when working with people of different values, lifestyles, and cultures.

All of this is good advice, *but can you actually execute it? How?* Well, the bottom line is courage: the courage to recognize differences in explicit ways, to force people to confront and deal with their differences, and to make joint progress on problems caused by those very differences. If you are willing to tackle diversity problems in public speech, the following sorts of topics could be brought up:

1. *Gender differences:* Males as well as females should be talking about solutions to date rape.
2. *Racial differences:* Whites as well as blacks should be reading Malcolm X and Louis Farrakhan, and using them as authorities in speeches.
3. *Age differences:* The young as well as the old should be challenging the existence of deplorable living conditions in state mental institutions.
4. *Class issues:* Rich as well as poor need to know how ghetto-ization has developed across Europe and the United States, examining both its positive and negative cultural effects.

Without the courage to bridge cultural gaps in public talk, we'll remain divided from each other, eternally suspicious and uninformed, silently perpetuating divisions, incapable of working across our cultural gaps when the situation demands it.

needs, wants, and desires as the basis for effective public communication?" The answer to both of these questions is, "With the use of motivational appeals." A **motivational appeal** is either (a) a visualization of a desire and a method for satisfying it or (b) an assertion that an entity, idea, or course of action holds the key to fulfilling a particular motive need.

Suppose that you want to borrow a friend's DVD player for a weekend. How do you prepare to ask? Usually, you create scenarios in your mind. In these scenarios, you try out various motivation appeals: "Should I mention how I've got nothing that plays DVD movies? [*appeal to sympathy*] What about a reminder of the time I loaned my friend something? [*appeal to previous affiliation*] Should I ease my friend's fears by stressing my record in returning items I've borrowed before?" [*appeal to previous success*] By examining the alternatives, you assemble a group of motivational appeals and organize them into narratives that serve as prods to action.

At other times, you may create motivational appeals through verbal labeling or **attribution.**[1]

Suppose you have some strained muscles in your back, but avoid going to a massage therapy business because you think of massages as lascivious, immoral, a bad substitute for real medicine, and much too expensive for your college student budget. Finally, a friend convinces you to go for a Swedish massage. You discover that the massage has no sexual dimensions at all, that the therapist asks about the medical treatment you've been getting to make sure the massage is complementary to it, that you feel awfully good when it's over, and that it costs about half of what you expected. You decide that you've misconstrued massage therapy altogether. You set up a weekly massage schedule at least until your back is better.

What happened? You changed the attributes of *massage* in your mind. Instead of attributing negative terms, such as *debasing, immoral, nonscientific,* and *expensive* to *massage,* you began to attribute to it positive terms, such as *healing, beautiful, therapeutic,* and *valuable.* Your behavior eventually changed because you had begun to use different terms to label things. Motivational appeals may use language to activate desires in people.

Some Common Motivational Appeals

Web Exploration

To further analyze motive clusters go to http://awl.com/german

If you attempted to list the potential motivational appeals for every audience, you might never finish. The task is endless. Rather than trying to list each individual appeal, consider the general thrust of each motive cluster. A **motive cluster** is a group of individual appeals that are grounded in the same fundamental human motivation. Table 14.1 shows the three motive clusters—affiliation, achievement, and power—as

TABLE 14.1   Motive Clusters

Individual motivational appeals fall into clusters that share a common theme. Think of a current television advertisement and identify the motive clusters in it.

Affiliation	Achievement	Power
Companionship	Acquisition/saving	Aggression
Conformity	Success/display	Authority/dominance
Deference/dependence	Prestige	Defense
Sympathy/generosity	Pride	Fear
Loyalty	Adventure/change	Autonomy/independence
Tradition	Perseverance	
Reverence/worship	Creativity	
Sexual attraction	Curiosity	
	Personal enjoyment	

well as the motivational appeals within each cluster.[2] **Affiliation motives** include the desire to belong to a group or to be well liked or accepted. This cluster also includes love, conformity, dependence on others, sympathy toward others, and loyalty. **Achievement motives** are related to the intrinsic or extrinsic desire for success, adventure, creativity, and personal enjoyment. **Power motives** concern primarily the desire to exert influence over others.

If you begin with this list, you'll be in a better position to choose those motivational appeals with the greatest relevance to your topic and audience. Remember this guideline as you make your choices: *motivational appeals work best when they are associated with the needs and desires of your listeners.* Analyze your audience and then choose your motivation appeals based on what you've learned about it.

The Affiliation Cluster Affiliation motives are dominated by a desire for acceptance or approval. They're more focused on the social or interpersonal bonds attributed to people than with personal success or power over others.[3] A social desire to be part of a group is an affiliation motive. What follows are some examples of appeals to listeners' affiliation desires:

1. *Companionship and affiliation.* "A friend in need is a friend indeed." "Birds of a feather flock together." The fear of loneliness or separation from others is strong.

2. *Conformity.* "AARP—It's for People Like You." "To get along, you need to go along." Not only do we fear isolation but also being too different from others.

3. *Deference/dependence.* "Nine out of ten doctors recommend . . ." "America's deepest thinking president, Abraham Lincoln, has said . . ." You can be made to feel dependent on either majority-rule or extraordinary individuals.

4. *Sympathy/generosity.* "You could be the parent this child has never known for a dollar a day." "Give that others might live," and "Contribute today to help us 'Take Back the Night.'"

5. *Loyalty.* "The camaraderie becomes something that you carry the rest of your life with those individuals. Sometimes you never get a chance to see those individuals again, but in your heart you know you'd do anything for them because they did that for you in a situation which could have gotten them killed."[4] That's how Vietnam vet Ron Mitscher described loyalty in combat conditions.

6. *Tradition.* "It is through our sacred rituals and ceremonies that we are known as a people." The call to collective celebration or worship is a strong affiliative appeal especially in times of crisis and stress.

7. *Reverence or worship.* "But in a larger sense we cannot dedicate, we cannot consecrate, we cannot hallow this ground. The brave men, living and dead, who struggled here, have consecrated it far above our power to add or detract."[5]

8. *Sexual attraction.* "Don't Be Such a Good Boy" (Ad for the men's cologne Drakkar Noir). "Nothing gets between me and my Calvins" (Calvin Klein jeans).

The Achievement Cluster Achievement motives are focused on individual urges, desires, and goals—an explicit concern for self and for personal excellence, prestige, and success. The following appeals to achievement motives are aimed at audience members as individuals:

1. *Acquisition/saving.* "Earn good money now in our new Checking-Plus accounts!" "Buy U.S. savings bonds where you work—invest in America!" Both of these are blatant appeals to personal accumulation of wealth, but the second makes the act seem more generous by tying it to patriotic motives (see "Tradition" above).

2. *Success/display.* "Hear the Radio That Woke Up an Entire Industry [Bose— Better Sound through Research]." "Successful executives carry the Connerton electronic organizer." These ads play off two kinds of success—corporate (a kind of appeal to majority opinion) and personal (it will make you stand out from the rest).

3. *Prestige.* "L'Oreal—Because You're Worth It!" "The U.S. Marines—Looking for a Few Good Men." Prestige appeals can be focused on either self-reward (L'Oreal) or exceptionalness (the Marines).

4. *Pride.* "Be Proud of America. Support the Troops" (Gulf War slogan). "Lose weight through our diet plan and feel great about your body." Motivational appeals to pride can center on the collective (here, one's country) or on individual characteristics (here, your body, so often a source of anxiety, not pride).

5. *Adventure/change.* "The Polo Sport Arena: A place to test yourself and your environment." "Join the Navy and See the World." Again, appeals to adventure can be personal or collective—but are always centered on self-aggrandizement.

6. *Perseverance.* "It's not the size of the dog in the fight but the size of the fight in the dog." "If at first you don't succeed, try, try again." We want to believe that continual effort will be rewarded, so this appeal can be strong.

7. *Creativity.* "Dare to be different: design your own major." Appeals to creativity are almost always appeals to an inborn talent that separates you in a good way from everyone else—strongly related to pride.

8. *Curiosity.* "Will the Internet bring an end to business computing as we know it?" asks the Microsoft Corporation in one of its ads designed to engage corporate executives. "Curiosity killed the cat; satisfaction brought him back," says conventional wisdom, suggesting that curiosity is dangerous but rewarding.

9. *Personal enjoyment.* "Let the good times roll!" There's often a hedonistic element to this appeal.

The Power Cluster   All appeals in the power cluster focus on influence or control over others or the environment. All motives in this group feature appeals to one's place in the social hierarchy—a dominant place. People with power motives seek to manipulate or control others, but not all uses of power are negative. With power can (and should) come social responsibility, the demand that power be used in socially approved ways to benefit the group, community, and society. Appeals to power also depend heavily on appeals to affiliation, because power is most constructively used when people see it as being in their own best interest to grant it to others. So, motivational appeals from the power cluster are often accompanied by appeals to affiliation. We won't illustrate that in the examples that follow, but you should think how to do it in your speeches.

1. *Aggression.* "We must fight for our rights—if we are to be heard, we dare not let others silence us." Here, the appeal to power is specifically turned into an affiliative "we."

2. *Authority/dominance.* "If the FDA [Food and Drug Administration] will not protect us, we must protect ourselves." "By the power invested in me, I now pronounce you man and wife." Authority for oneself arises from the need for a leader; institutional authority usually comes from an external source, whether divine as in the marriage ceremony or secular, as when the president of the United States begins, "As commander-in-chief, I . . ."

3. *Defense.* "We fight not for our own glory and prestige, but to protect ourselves from ruthless enemies." If one's aggressive actions are viewed as defensive rather than offensive, they're usually thought to be more ethically justified.

4. *Fear.* "Friends don't let friends drive drunk." Here, the appeal to the fear of neglecting one's social responsibility is strong. Use fear appeals cautiously (see the "Speaking of . . . Ethics: Using Fear Appeals" box).

5. *Autonomy/independence.* "Just do it." For a decade, Nike has played on your sense of independent, autonomous action to sell you shoes.

You may have noticed that some of the appeals we've just described seem to contradict each other. For example, fear seems to oppose adventure; sympathy and conformity seem to work against independence. Remember that human beings are changeable creatures, who at different times may pursue quite different goals and

Advertisers change motivational appeals when aiming at different segments of society.

SPEAKING OF . . . *Ethics*

Using Fear Appeals

Among the most potent appeals to audiences are fear appeals. Research suggests fear appeals are so powerful that they actually can interfere with a listener's ability to process information critically. However, research indicates that fear appeals retain their effectiveness over extended periods of time.

Sometimes fear appeals are used for laudable goals, such as the Juvenile Awareness program at New Jersey's Rahway State Prison (the basis of the 1977 television special "Scared Straight"). In this program, delinquent youths are introduced to convicts who describe the horrors of prison life. Results suggest that the program helps deter young people from further delinquency activity. However, fear appeals are always accompanied by the potential for misuse. Think about the following applications of your classroom speaking. What would you do if you were the speaker? Why?

1. You are planning a persuasive speech to convince your audience that war is morally wrong. You are totally committed to peace and believe that anything you can do to maintain peace in this world is your moral obligation; therefore, you exaggerate some of the facts about recent world conflicts to frighten your audience about the results of war.
2. You give a speech on the increase of date rape on college campuses. In order to convince your audience that date rape is wrong and extremely common, you create scenarios that appeal to the fears of your listeners. Your scenarios are so vivid that several of your listeners, who are rape survivors, are visibly overcome with emotion. One of the listeners is so upset that she must leave the classroom during your speech. Everyone in the audience sees her leave.
3. You feel very strongly that the college president is wrong to continue investing college money in countries where torture and imprisonment without trial are legal. You present a persuasive speech in which you appeal to your audience's fears by suggesting that the college president is actually propagating torture and corrupting the values of U.S. citizens to the point that someday torture and imprisonment without trial might be legal in the United States. Your listeners become so incensed, as a result of your speech, that they march to the president's house and set his car on fire.
4. You are preparing to give a speech on hate crimes in the United States and you want to make sure that you have your audience's attention before you begin. Therefore, you decide to present the details of a series of grisly murders committed in your town by a psychopath—even though these murders were not motivated by hate but by mental illness and so they aren't examples of hate crimes.

thus who can be reached through many different kinds of verbalizations of their wants and desires. The clusters we've described aren't all-inclusive; but, this discussion is enough to get you started into your work on persuasion.

Using Motivational Appeals

In practice, motivational appeals are seldom used alone; speakers usually combine them. Suppose you were selecting a mountain bike. What factors would influence your decision? One would be price (*saving*); a second certainly would be performance (*adventure*); another might be comfort and appearance (*personal enjoyment*); a fourth probably would be the reputation of the manufacturer (*prestige*) or its uniqueness (*independence*). These factors combined would add up to *pride* of ownership. Some of these influences, of course, would be stronger than others; some might conflict. But all of them probably would affect your choice. You would base your decision to buy the bike on the strongest of the appeals.

Because motivational appeals are interdependent, it's a good idea to coordinate them. You should select three or four appeals that are related and that target segments of your audience. When you work from cluster appeals, you tap multiple dimensions of your listeners' lives. Consider the following appeal to your classmates to join in a demonstration against a proposed tuition hike when the Board of Regents meets next month. Most students are very unhappy about tuition increases, yet most think nothing can be done about them. So, can you reach them? You can try, perhaps through combining motivational appeals with visualization (see "Visualization" later in this chapter):

> *Just think of what we can accomplish. If we all* (affiliation) *gather in front of the administration building, we can show the regents that this is a serious matter. We can show the regents that we're as much a part of the decision-making process as they are* (authority) *and that our individual voices* (independence) *deserve to be heard as much as theirs. When we present our petition to the president of the Board, even after he's tried to ignore us* (perseverance), *he'll see that we're committed and standing on principle, and he'll have to admit that we've got a right to be heard* (success/display). *There's no need to be afraid* (fear) *when you're among friends* (companionship). *It's a cause that's right* (pride). *On that day we'll demonstrate our solidarity* (loyalty) *and force the Board of Regents* (aggression) *to listen to our side of the story!*

Notice the interweaving of affiliative and power motivational appeals, with even a couple of appeals to achievement (the prestige of independent action, success/display). Casting the appeals in a vision of success, the speaker hoped, would make them even more vivid and compelling to the listeners.

Review your appeals for their pertinence and consistency. After all, you don't want to describe the *adventure* of spelunking (cave exploration) so vividly that you terrify your audience *(fear)*, for raising the specter of fear is counterproductive in this case.

One final piece of general advice: inconspicuous appeals work best. Avoid saying, "I want you to *imitate* Jones, the successful honors student" or "If you give to the Russian democracy fund, we'll print your name in the newspapers so that your *reputation* as a caring person will be known to everybody." People rarely admit, even to themselves, that they act on the basis of self-centered motivations—greed, imitation, personal pride, and fear. Be subtle when using these appeals. For example, you might encourage listeners to imitate the actions of well-known people by saying, "Habitat for Humanity counts among its volunteers the former president and first lady, Jimmy and Rosalynn Carter."

Web Exploration
For examples of motivational appeals go to
http://awl.com/german

ORGANIZING PERSUASIVE SPEECHES: THE MOTIVATED SEQUENCE

Now it's time to think about organizing your appeals into a whole speech. As we've suggested, an important consideration in structuring appeals is your listeners' psychological tendencies—ways in which individuals' own motivations and circumstances favor certain ways of structuring ideas. You must learn to sequence supporting materials and motivational appeals to form a useful organizational pattern for speeches as a whole. Since 1935, the most popular such pattern has been called **Monroe's motivated sequence** (see Figure 14.1).[6] We will devote the rest of this chapter to it.

The motivated sequence ties problems and solutions to human motives. The motivated sequence for the presentation of verbal materials is composed of five basic steps:

1. *Attention.* Create interest and desire.
2. *Need.* Develop the problem by analyzing wrongs in the world and by relating them to the individual's interests, wants, or desires.
3. *Satisfaction.* Propose a plan of action that will alleviate the problem and satisfy the individual's interests, wants, or desires.
4. *Visualization.* Depict the world as it will look if the plan is put into action.
5. *Action.* Call for personal commitments and deeds.

Structuring Actuative Speeches

The motivated sequence provides an ideal blueprint for urging an audience to take action. That's what it was designed for—since it was used originally as the basis for sales presentations. Let's look first at some ways that you might use Monroe's sequence to structure actuative speeches.

Step 1: Getting Attention   You must wake up and engage your listeners at the very beginning of your speech if you hope to get them to move. Remember that startling statements, illustrations, questions, and other factors can focus attention on your message. You can't persuade an audience unless you have its attention.

Step 2: Showing the Need: Describing the Problem   Once you've captured the attention of your listeners, you're ready to explain why change is needed. To do this, you must show that a definite problem exists. You must point out, through facts and figures, just how bad the present situation is: "Last month our fund-raising drive to support the campus radio station fell $3,500 short of its goal. If we can't gain those dollars in this week's emergency drive, we'll have to close down two work-study positions. That will not only make it difficult for those students to stay in school but also we'll have to shut down our Friday night live coverage of local music."

In its full form, a need or problem step has four parts:

1. *Statement.* Give a definite, concise statement of the problem.
2. *Illustration.* Give one or more examples explaining and clarifying the problem.

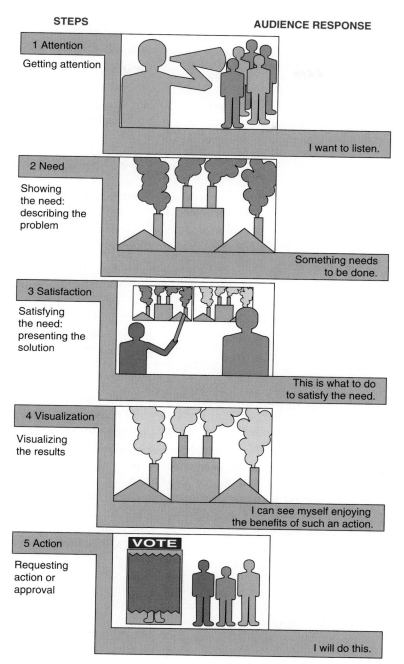

FIGURE 14.1   The Motivated Sequence

Notice how the audience should respond to each step of the motivated sequence.

3. *Ramification.* Offer additional examples, statistical data, testimony, and other forms of support showing the extent and seriousness of the problem.

4. *Pointing.* Offer an explanation of how the problem directly affects the listener.

Statement and *pointing* should always be present, but the inclusion of *illustration* and *ramification* will depend on the amount of detail required to convince the audience. Whether you use the complete development or only part of it, the *need* step is critical in your speech. Here your subject is first tied to the needs and desires of your listeners.

Step 3: Satisfying the Need: Presenting the Solution   The solution or satisfaction step urges the adoption of a policy. Its goal is to get your listeners to agree that the program you propose is the correct one. Therefore, this step consists of presenting your proposed solution to the problem and proving that this solution is practical and desirable.

Five items are usually contained in a fully developed satisfaction step:

1. *Statement.* State the attitude, belief, or action you wish the audience to adopt. This is a statement of action: "We need to adopt an incentive system for our Littleton carburetor plant."

2. *Explanation.* Make sure that your proposal is understood. Visual aids such as charts and diagrams can be very useful here. In our example, you would define the incentive system: "By *incentive system,* I mean that workers at the Littleton plant should be paid by the actual number of carburetors completed rather than the hours worked."

3. *Theoretical demonstration.* Show how your proposed solution meets the need. For example, you could say, "Worker productivity will rise because workers are paid not just for putting in time but for completing carburetors."

4. *Reference to practical experience.* Supply examples to prove that the proposal has worked effectively where it has been tried. Facts, figures, and the testimony of experts support your contention: "Production at our New Albany plant increased by 42 percent after we instituted this compensation schedule."

5. *Meeting objections.* Forestall opposition by answering any objections that might be raised against the proposal. You might counter the objections of the labor union by arguing, "Increased plant productivity will allow us to expand the medical benefits for plant workers."

Just as certain phases can sometimes be omitted from the need step, one or more of these phases can be left out of the satisfaction step. Also, the foregoing order does not always have to be followed exactly. Occasionally, you can best meet objections by answering them as they arise. In other situations, the theoretical demonstration and reference to practical experience can be combined. If the satisfaction step is developed properly, at its conclusion the audience will say, "Yes, you're right; this is a practical and desirable solution to the problem you identified."

Step 4: Visualizing the Results   The function of the visualization step is to intensify desire. It should picture for the audience future conditions if your proposal is or is not adopted. In the visualization step, you ask your listeners to project themselves into the future. This projection can be accomplished in one of three ways: by (1) the *positive method,* (2) the *negative method,* or (3) the *method of contrast.*

1. *The positive method.* Describe how conditions will improve under your proposal. Make such a description vivid and concrete. Select a situation that you are quite sure will arise. Then picture your listeners actually enjoying the conditions your proposal will produce. For example, if plant productivity allows better medical benefits, describe the advantages for everyone—lower deductibles, dental care, free eye examinations, and hospice services.

2. *The negative method.* Describe conditions as they will be in the future if your proposal is *not* carried out. Picture for your audience the evils that will arise from failure to follow your advice. Select the most undesirable conditions and show how they will be aggravated if your proposal is rejected. Describe plant employees being laid off, losing their pension plan, and experiencing the trauma of finding new jobs in a tight market.

3. *The method of contrast.* Combine the two preceding methods. Use the negative approach first and then use the positive approach. In this way, the benefits of the proposal are contrasted with the disadvantages of the present system. The following illustration shows how a speaker, urging an audience to get regular blood pressure checkups before problems are apparent, used visual contrasts:

> *So, what happens when you don't take that simple little step of getting your blood pressure checked regularly? You know what happens. Given how badly Americans eat, how little most of them exercise, and how tense the world of work becomes for too many of us, arteries begin a buildup of fatty deposits, openings narrow, blood flow becomes constricted, breathing becomes more difficult, and sooner or later—boom! You're on the ground in terrifying pain, hoping against hope that the person next to you can call 911 and knows some CPR well enough to sustain your life until professional help arrives.*
>
> *With proper and periodic blood pressure checks, however, you needn't face the prospect of open heart surgery. When Drs. Andrea Foote and John Erfurt established a worker health program, 92 percent of the hypertensive workers at four different industrial sites controlled their blood pressure. When the Hypertensive Education Program in Michigan and in Connecticut went into effect, insurance rates were cut in both states. Back in 1970, Savannah, Georgia, had the infamous title of "Stroke Capital of the World." But today, with fourteen permanent blood pressure reading stations and special clinics, its stroke rate's been cut in half. And, of course, if you take advantage of the blood pressure monitoring program at Student Health or even at the Walgreen's drug store downtown, you'll be secure in the knowledge that you're not one of America's 11 million people who have high blood pressure and don't even know it.[7]*

Whichever method you use—positive, negative, or contrast—remember that the visualization step must stand the test of reality. The conditions you picture must be vivid and reflective of the world as listeners know it. Let your listeners actually see themselves enjoying the advantages or suffering the evils you describe. The more realistically you depict the situation, the more strongly your listeners will react.

Step 5: Requesting Action   The function of the action step is to call for explicit action. You can do this by offering a challenge or appeal, a special inducement, or a statement of personal intention. For examples, review the conclusions discussed in Chapter 9. Your request for action should be short and intense enough to set your listeners' resolve to act. Finish your speech firmly and sit down.

The motivated sequence is flexible. You can adapt it to various situations once you are familiar with its basic pattern. Like cooks who alter good recipes to their personal tastes, you can adjust the formula for particular occasions—changing the number of main points from section to section, sometimes omitting restatement from the attention step, sometimes omitting the positive or negative projections from the visualization step. *Like any recipe, the motivated sequence is designed to give you a formula that fits many different situations.* It gives you an excellent pattern but does not remove the human element; you still must think about your choices. Consider the choices made in the following outline of an actuative speech using the motivated sequence.

SAMPLE ACTUATIVE SPEECHES

Following are two actuative speeches delivered during the dramatic U.S. House of Representatives debate over articles of impeachment focused on President Bill Clinton, December 18–19, 1998.[8] On Saturday the 19th, both Democrats and Republicans gave time to their best speakers to offer short, actuative speeches to justify votes for and against impeachment that were to occur in the afternoon. Among the best speakers that morning were Rep. Richard Gephardt (D-Missouri) and Rep. J. C. Watts (R-Oklahoma). Both sought to raise the vision of their colleagues through motivational appeals, arguing that the values embodied in those appeals should guide specific actions—votes for or against impeachment.

Rep. Watts spoke before Rep. Gephardt. His strategy was dual: appeal to our care and sympathy for children *[affiliation, companionship]* and to their clear, uncomplicated sense of honesty *[conformity, loyalty, tradition]*. Especially in paragraphs 2–5, the theme of "listening" to our children and their clear sense of rightness was sketched expertly. Rep. Watts contrasted their sense with adult attitudes, which he said we could see in public opinion polls (paragraphs 6–7). Having transcended the politics of impeachment with these appeals primarily to the affiliation cluster of motivational appeals, he then asked his listeners to apply those clear moral guidelines from children to the impeachment proceedings (paragraph 8). He concluded with a negative visualization: "In this moment, our children's future is more important than our future. If our country looks the other way, our country will lose its way" (paragraph 9).

Rep. Gephardt spoke later that morning, urging a motion of censure, not impeachment. He, too, went to affiliative motivational appeals when talking about the Founding Fathers *[tradition]* and "the altar of an unattainable morality" *[reverence]*. By paragraphs 7 and 8, he was contrasting "the death of representative democracy" *[fear]* from the power cluster with "healing" *[companionship]* from the affiliation cluster. Like Rep. Watts, therefore, he sought to transcend the political situation with communal appeals. He ended with negative and positive visualizations: The House now on "the brink of the abyss" in paragraph 10, contrasted with "a new politics of respect and fairness and decency" in paragraph 11. Such a new politics, he concluded, was possible only if Congress had "the wisdom and the courage and the goodness to save itself today" (paragraph 12). So, both Rep. Watts and Rep. Gephardt had warnings for their colleagues, though only Gephardt tried to turn the negative into a positive vision—and thereby, he hoped, to turn some votes for to votes against impeachment.

That there were Republican and Democratic votes both for and against impeachment—and that not all of the proposed articles of impeachment were passed—is testament to the power of actuative speech.

Speech for Impeachment   Rep. J. C. Watts

Mr. Speaker, there is no joy sometimes in upholding the law. It is so unpleasant sometimes that we hire other people to do it for us. Ask the police or judges. It is tiring and thankless. But we know it must be done, because if we do not point at lawlessness, our children cannot see it. If we do not label lawlessness, our children will not believe it./1

So if someone were to ask me, "J.C., why did you vote for the articles of impeachment?" I would say I did it for our children. How can we tell our children that honesty is the best policy if we do not demand honesty as a policy? How can we expect a Boy Scout to honor his oath if elected officials do not honor theirs? How can we expect a business executive to honor a promise when the chief executive abandons his or hers?/2

Whether it is a promise or a truth or a vow or an oath, a person's word is the firm footing our society stands upon, and the average kid understands that. They do not need a grand jury to enforce it. They say "cross your heart, hope to die"; "pinkie promise"; "king's X"; "blood brother." These are the childhood instincts that seek to draw a line between the honest and the dishonest, between the principled and the unprincipled./3

Ask the children. The kid who lies does not last and they do not bicker over what is and what is not a lie. They know. So do I. So do the American people./4

Time and again, we wanted the essence of truth and we got the edges of truth. We hear, "Let's get on with the business of our country." What business is more important than teaching our children right from wrong? Some say it is all about politics and party lines. If that were true, I would have given in to popular opinion. But what is popular is not always what is right./5

Some say polls are against this. Polls measure changing feelings, not steadfast principle. Polls would have rejected the Ten Commandments. Polls would have embraced slavery and ridiculed women's rights./6

Some say we must draw this to a close. I say we must draw a line between right and wrong; not with a tiny fine line of an executive fountain pen, but with the big, thick lead of a Number 2 pencil. We must do it so every kid in America can see it./7

The point is not whether the President can prevail, but whether truth can prevail. We need to cease the cannibalizing of Members of Congress. We need to cease the attacks on the President and his family because, friends, this is not about the President of the United States. He is not the injured party. Our country is./8

In this moment, our children's future is more important than our future. If our country looks the other way, our country will lose its way./9

Speech Against Impeachment   Rep. Richard Gephardt

Mr. Speaker, I stood on this floor yesterday and implored all of us to say that the politics of slash and burn must end. I implored all of us that we must turn away from the politics of personal destruction and return to the politics of values./1

It is with that same passion that I say to all of you today that the gentleman from Louisiana (Mr. Bob Livingston) is a worthy and good and honorable man./2

I believe his decision to retire [after sexual indiscretions were revealed] is a terrible capitulation to the negative forces that are consuming our political system and our country, and I pray with all my heart that he will reconsider this decision./3

Our Founding Fathers created a system of government of men, not of angels. No one standing in this House today can pass the puritanical test of purity that some are demanding that our elected leaders take. If we demand that mere mortals live up to this standard, we will see our seats of government lay empty and we will see the best, most able people unfairly cast out of public service./4

We need to stop destroying imperfect people at the altar of an unobtainable morality. We need to start living up to the standards which the public in its infinite wisdom understands, that imperfect people must strive towards, but too often fall short./5

We are now rapidly descending into a politics where life imitates farce, fratricide dominates our public debate, and America is held hostage to tactics of smear and fear./6

Let all of us here today say no to resignation, no to impeachment, no to hatred, no to intolerance of each other and no to vicious self-righteousness./7

We need to start healing. We need to start binding up our wounds. We need to end this downward spiral which will culminate in the death of representative democracy./8

I believe this healing can start today by changing the course we have begun. This is exactly why we need this today to be bipartisan. This is why we ask the opportunity to vote on a bipartisan censure resolution, to begin the process of healing our Nation and healing our people./9

We are on the brink of the abyss. The only way we stop this insanity is through the force of our own will. The only way we stop this spiral is for all of us to finally say "enough."/10

Let us step back from the abyss and let us begin a new politics of respect and fairness and decency, which realizes what has come before./11

May God have mercy on this Congress, and may Congress have the wisdom and the courage and the goodness to save itself today./12

Structuring Persuasive Speeches

Persuasive speeches stop short of a call for direct action, but nonetheless they're still easily structured with the motivated sequence. The primary difference is in the action step. Sometimes, no action is called for because there are no acceptable action plans formulated; so, everyone wants to reform the medical system of this country, but agreement on actions can't be reached. At other times, you simply want people to change how they think, not how they act. Asking parents to think about high school education as a primary method for gaining discipline in their children's lives won't change how schools operate, but it might get them to redefine their relationship to schools. Sure, in the long run you might want them to support tax increases for schools, but at this point, those parents probably are not ready for such a request. Seek to change their attitudes and then later, perhaps, you can take them farther down the road to educational reform.

Notice how the action step in the outline that follows differs from the one built for an actuative speech.

SAMPLE OUTLINE FOR A PERSUASIVE SPEECH

Henri Mann Morton presented a keynote speech at the Northwest's Colville and Okanogan National Forest conference on cultural diversity on March 23, 1989. As a Native American woman, she was in an excellent position to comment on the issues related to gaining workforce parity for all peoples. During the speech, she differentiated the Native American experience from that of others in the hope of modifying her audience's beliefs about the values and interests of Native Americans. Given that her cultural commentary is still relevant in the American situation, look carefully at her structural strategies.

Strength Through Cultural Diversity

ATTENTION STEP

She thanks an audience of U.S. Forest Service people for listening.

I. "Thanks for honoring me with your gracious invitation to speak."

II. "We must never forget that American Indians were the first people to live in this beautiful country."

NEED STEP

The need analysis begins with a mini-lecture on sacred gendered and tribal beliefs.

I. The beliefs of the Native American are unique.
  A. They believe in "the dualities of life . . . sky-earth; sun/moon; love-hate; wisdom-ignorance."
  B. The most imporant duality is man-woman as together they are "part of the great sacred circle of life."

II. Tribal views also are unique—with different tribes holding different beliefs about women sacred.
  A. The Hopi believe in the Spider Grandmother who made the four races of people.
  B. The Iroquois give status to the Clan Mother.
  C. The Cherokee give status to the Beloved Woman.
  D. Each tribe grants respect to Indian women.

III. As a woman, I am part of that which has preceded me.
  A. "My grandmothers have been here for all time."
  B. "The land you strive to protect is my grandmother—my mother."

Then comes the transition to Americans' lack of respect for those beliefs—the need.

IV. Once the majority, we are now the "minority of minorities."
  A. We number less than one percent of the population.
  B. Due to our small number, policymakers are generally uninformed about our culture.
  C. "I would characterize American society as . . . 'culturally disrespectful.'"

V. Historically, American Indians have had three "agencies of oppression."

   A. Church: Christianize the pagans.

   B. Government: Assimilate them.

   C. Education: Civilize the "savages."

SATISFACTION STEP

I. Policymakers should acknowledge five basic truths.

   A. "Indians have been here for thousands of years."

   B. This is their homeland.

   C. Their own distinct cultures have evolved.

   D. We were not forced into abandoning our cultures.

   E. Assimilation and acculturation occur on individuals' terms.

II. The American Indian culture can contribute without changing.

   A. To the Iroquois, for example, "peace was the law."

      1. The same word is used for both *peace* and *law*.

      2. "Peace was a way of life."

   B. The allegory of the Great White Pine represents the unity of peace with law and land.

      1. For the Iroquois, the Tree symbolizes law.

      2. The Tree's branches symbolize shelter within the law.

      3. The Tree's roots symbolize the law's ability to stretch out and embrace all peoples.

Her plan calls for reorienting white America's thinking about Native Americans.

VISUALIZATION STEP

I. With recognition of the Indian's true nature and contribution can come change.

   A. Change is a cause for celebration.

   B. "With clarity of vision we can celebrate the natural diversity of our universe and our world."

II. The Indian values—patience, honesty, acceptance, respect—can serve as the foundation for good interpersonal relationships in a culturally diverse world.

She details the cultural values of Native Americans visually, using them as contact points between herself and white America.

ACTION STEP

I. I applaud your commitment to a culturally diverse workforce.

II. My tribute to you is to share with you a Cheyenne philosophical belief: "A nation is not conquered until the hearts of its women are on the ground. Then it is done, no matter how brave its warriors nor how strong its weapons."

   A. This is the power of women as equals.

   B. This is why the most powerful pairing is men and women working together.[8]

The action is a mental commitment at this point, in hopes that the U.S. Forest Service (among others) will act on that commitment later.

ASSESSING YOUR PROGRESS

Chapter Summary

1. Speeches to persuade and actuate have psychological and behavioral change as their primary goal.
2. Because need satisfaction is important to all human beings, the concept of motive need is central to an understanding of persuasion and actuation.
3. Keys to the achievement of persuasion are motivational appeals, which are verbally created visualizations that link an idea, entity, or course of action to a motive.
4. Occasionally motivational appeals are attached directly to other concepts in a verbal process known as attribution.
5. Commonly used motivational appeals can be grouped into three clusters: affiliation, achievement, and power.
6. Monroe's motivated sequence is an organizational pattern for actuative and persuasive speeches based on people's natural psychological tendencies.
7. The five steps in the motivated sequence are attention, need, satisfaction, visualization, and action. Each step can be developed by using appropriate rhetorical devices.

Key Terms

achievement motives (p. 261)

actuative speech (p. 257)

affiliation motives (p. 261)

attribution (p. 260)

desire (p. 258)

Monroe's motivated sequence (p. 266)

motivational appeal (p. 259)

motive cluster (p. 260)

motive need (p. 258)

need (p. 258)

power motives (p. 261)

persuasive speech (p. 256)

Assessment Activities

1. Present a five- to eight-minute actuative speech in which your primary goal is to get class members to actually *do* something: sign a petition, write a letter to an official, attend a meeting, give blood, or take some other personal action. Use the motivated sequence to create attention, lay out needs, propose a solution, visualize the results, and call for action. On a future "Actuative Speech Check-up Day," find out how many took the actions you suggested. How successful were you? Why?
2. In a brief persuasive speech, attempt to alter your classmates' impression or understanding of a particular concept. Analyze their current attitudes toward it and then prepare a speech reversing those attitudes. Sample topics might include: pesticides, recycling, United Nations peacekeeping operations, in vitro fertilization, animal rights, or genetic counseling for prospective parents.

3. What relevant motivational appeals might you use in addressing each of the following audiences? Be ready to discuss your choices in class.

   a. A group of farmers protesting the so-called Freedom to Farm Act.

   b. A meeting of liberal arts majors concerned about jobs.

   c. Women at a meeting to set up a campus evening escort service.

   d. A meeting of local elementary and secondary classroom teachers setting up a school system–wide media literacy program.

   e. A group gathered to restore an old cemetery.

References

1. For a fuller discussion of attribution, see Philip G. Zimbardo, *Psychology and Life,* 13th ed. (New York: Longman, 1994).

2. The clusters we're using develop out of the work of David McClelland. See Katharine Blick Hoyenga and Hermit T. Hoyenga, *Motivational Explanations of Behavior: Physiological and Cognitive Ideas* (Monterey, CA: Brooks/Cole Pub., 1984), ch. 1; Abigail J. Stewart, ed., *Motivation and Society: A Volume in Honor of David C. McClelland* (San Francisco: Jossey-Bass, 1982); and Janet T. Spence, ed., *Achievement and Achievement Motives* (San Francisco: W. H. Freeman, 1983).

3. See Hoyenga and Hoyenga, ch. 4 (n. 1). A classic work on affiliation is Stanley Schachter, *The Psychology of Affiliation: Experimental Studies of the Sources of Gregariousness* (Stanford, CA: Stanford University Press, 1959).

4. From an interview with Ron Mitscher, Vietnam veteran, for *Parallels: The Soldiers' Knowledge and the Oral History of Contemporary Warfare,* edited by J. T. Hansen, A. Susan Owen, and Michael Patrick Madden (New York: Aldine de Gruyter, 1992), 137.

5. Abraham Lincoln, "Gettysburg Address," speech delivered in 1863, reprinted in *Lincoln at Gettysburg: The Words That Remade America,* edited by Garry Wills (New York: Simon & Schuster, 1992), 261.

6. To see how Alan Monroe originally conceived of the motivated sequence—as much, then, a psychological theory as an organizational pattern—see especially the Foreword to Alan H. Monroe, *Principles and Types of Speech* (Chicago: Scott, Foresman, 1935), vii–x.

7. These paragraphs draw their material from Todd Ames, "The Silent Killer," *Winning Orations.* His materials were used by special arrangement with Larry Schnoor, Director, Interstate Oratorical Association, Mankato, MN.

8. The texts of Reps. Watts' and Gephardt's speeches on December 19, 1998, are from the *Congressional Record,* Proceedings and Debates of the 105th Congress, 2nd sess. (Washington, D.C.: U.S. Government Printing Office, 1998), 144, no. 155:H11973-4, H2031-2.

9. Outline drawn from materials in a speech by Henri Mann Morton, "Strength Through Cultural Diversity," *Native American Reader,* ed. Jerry D. Blancae (Juneau, AK: Denali Press, 1990), 400–474.

Chapter 15

Argumentation and Critical Thinking

The ability to think critically is central to your survival in the social world. You're constantly bombarded with requests, appeals, and pleas to change your beliefs or adopt new ways of doing things. Sorting through all those appeals to determine which are justified and whether you should alter your thoughts or actions requires analysis and evaluation skills and a cool head, not emotional responses. Before committing yourself, you've got to be able to analyze appeals, to determine if the reasons fit the claim being made. Skilled speakers, too, must be able not only to construct motivational appeals but also to work from data-based evidence to seemingly logical conclusions. You've got to use your head in reasonable ways, as Mario found out:

> "Boy," said Mario, "I'm really bummed out. My best friend and I had a big fight last night. He

yelled at me for not taking him seriously. I told him he was crazy for never eating meat. He got even angrier and then I got scared and told him I'd think about vegetarianism if it would make him feel better, and then he got even more mad. It was a bad argument." "No, it wasn't," another friend Romano replied. "You had a fight, not an argument." "So what's the difference?" queried Mario. "A lot," said Romano. "Arguments depend on your head. Fights depend on your volume."

Mario needs to develop what's called a critical spirit—the ability to analyze others' ideas and requests.[1] *Criticism* is a process of careful assessment, evaluation, and judgment of ideas and motives. It's also a matter of supporting your assessment, evaluation, and judgment with reasons. As you engage in evaluation—assessing reasons or offering counter-reasons—you become a critical thinker. You also develop critical skills when you advance a claim and then offer reasons why others ought to accept it. And finally, a critical spirit requires fair-mindedness, an important dimension of a person's credibility.[2] Critical thinkers inspire confidence in others, thus, by demonstrating both reasonableness and ethical commitments. Both speakers and listeners need to cultivate the critical spirit.

Argumentation is a process of advancing claims supported by good reasons and allowing others to test those claims and reasons or to offer counterarguments. Through argumentation, people hope to come to reasonable conclusions about matters of fact, value, and policy. The act of arguing does not consist merely of offering an opinion or stating information, and certainly not of screaming. An act of arguing

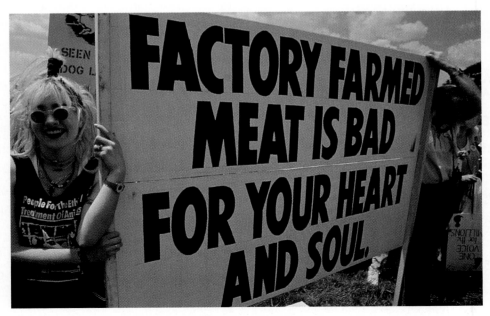

Different sorts of arguments appeal to different segments of your audience. Vegetarians argue that meat harms your body ("heart") for some people and that it is a sin against nature ("soul") for others.

is an act one step beyond the act of persuading by appealing to motives. It commits you to communicating by using good reasons.

You probably engage in argument in many ways. In public forums such as city council meetings, you might provide reasons your community should preserve a marshland rather than erect a dam or you might advocate better community regulation of local day care facilities. You might write a letter to the editor of a newspaper proposing a downtown pedestrian mall. In conversations with friends, you probably argue over sports teams and players. In each of these cases, you'll be more effective if your arguments are sound, with clearly identifiable reasons given for each claim you make. In this chapter, we'll examine the structure of arguments, then offer ways for you to critically evaluate the arguments of others. We'll finish with some tips to help you argue effectively.

RATIONAL THINKING AND TALKING: ARGUMENTATION

To turn rational thought into powerful talk, you've got to learn how to construct an argument. An **argument** is built out of three essential elements that must work together to compel belief in another person: (a) the claim or proposition you are defending, (b) the relevant evidence that you provide in support of that claim, and (c) the reasoning pattern that you use to connect the evidence with the claim. (See Figure 15.1.)

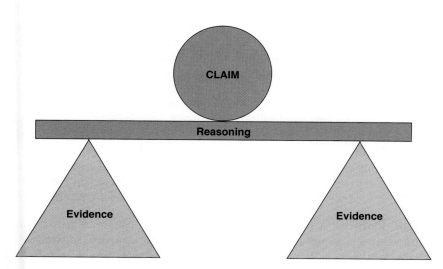

FIGURE 15.1   The Elements of Argument

Why are all three elements necessary for an argument?

Types of Claims

Most argumentative speeches assert that (a) something is or is not the case, (b) something is desirable or undesirable, or (c) something should or should not be done. Such judgments or assessments are the speaker's **claims** or propositions. Your first task as an arguer or listener is to determine the type of claim being argued.

Claims of Fact   A **claim of fact** asserts that something is or is not the case. If you're trying to convince listeners that "Using compact fluorescent light bulbs will reduce your utilities cost significantly," you're presenting a factual claim asserting that a given state of affairs exists. When confronted with this sort of claim, two questions can occur to the critically aware listener:

1. *How can the truth or accuracy of the claim be measured?* If you're asked to determine someone's height, you immediately look for a yardstick or other measuring tool. Similarly, listeners look for a standard by which to measure the accuracy of a factual claim. Before agreeing with your claim, the critical thinker asks what you mean by "reduce your utilities costs significantly." What percentage reduction in your electrical bill is being considered significant? Against what standard, precisely, is the accuracy of the claim to be judged? As a speaker, you need to build those judgments into your speeches.

2. *Do the facts of the situation fit the criteria?* Now then, to the replacement of light bulbs: how many have to be replaced to achieve the utility bill reduction you're after? First, get listeners to agree to certain standards of judgment, and then present evidence that a given state of affairs meets those standards. In these ways, you work to gain the assent of listeners to your factual claims.

Web Exploration

To compare claims of fact with claims of value go to

http://awl.com/german

Claims of Value   When your claim asserts that something is good or bad, desirable or undesirable, justified or unjustified, you're advancing a **claim of value**—a claim about the intrinsic worth of the belief or action in question. Here, too, it is always appropriate to ask (a) by what standards is something to be judged? and (b) how well does the item in question measure up to the standards specified?

For example, you can measure the quality of a college by the distinction of its faculty (intellectual value), the excellence of its building program (material value), the success of its graduates (practical value), the size of its endowment (monetary value), or the reputation that it enjoys according to surveys of educational excellence (educational value). You then can assess the worth of a particular college by each of these criteria to come up with a rating. In other words, value judgments are not mere assertions of personal preference—"I like Grand Valley State or Michigan State." Rather, they must be argued for, as if someone else is going to examine or challenge them.

Claims of Policy   A **claim of policy** recommends a course of action that you want the audience to approve. Typical examples are "State standards for welfare eligibility should be tightened," or "A test for English competency should be instituted as a graduation requirement." In both instances, you're asking your audience to endorse a proposed policy or course of action. Four questions are relevant to the judgments your listeners are being asked to make when analyzing a policy claim:

1. *Is there a need for such a policy or course of action?* If your listeners don't believe that a change is called for, they're not likely to approve your proposal. If, for example, students are already required to pass four English courses before graduation, is a test for English competency necessary?

2. *Is the proposal practical?* Can we afford the expense it would entail? Would it really solve the problem or remove the evil it is designed to correct? Does such a policy stand a reasonable chance of being adopted? If you can't show that your proposal meets these and similar tests, you can hardly expect it to be endorsed.

3. *Are the benefits your proposal will bring greater than its disadvantages?* People are reluctant to approve a proposal that promises to create conditions worse than the ones it is designed to correct. Burning a barn to the ground may be an effective way to get rid of rats, but it's hardly a desirable one. The benefits and disadvantages that will result from a plan of action must always be carefully weighed along with considerations of its basic workability. Would an English proficiency test, for example, be fair for international students?

4. *Is the proposal superior to the alternatives?* Listeners are hesitant to approve a policy if they have reason to believe that another course of action is more practical or more beneficial. A program of job training may be a better way to remove people from the welfare rolls than new qualifications tests.

Web Exploration

To evaluate claims of policy go to http://awl.com/german

Different types of claims make varying demands on you as an arguer. (See Table 15.1.) Further, arguers must tell audiences how to assess their claims. Articulating criteria or standards for judgment is essential for the person who tries to win

TABLE 15.1 Types of Claims

Notice how each type of claim can be analyzed.

Claim	Description	Analysis
Claim of fact	Assertion of truth or that something exists	1. By what criteria is the truth or accuracy of the claim measured? 2. Do the facts of the situation fit the criteria?
Claim of value	Assertion that something is good or bad; desirable or undesirable; justified or unjustified	1. By what standards is something to be judged? 2. How well does the thing measure up?
Claim of policy	Recommendation of a course of action	1. Is there a need for this policy or course of action? 2. Is the proposal practicable? 3. Are the benefits of the proposal greater than its disadvantages? 4. Is the proposal better than other courses of action?

an argument. If you think tuition waivers should be tied to financial need rather than academic performance, you must show your listeners why financial need is a better standard for waiving tuition.

Unless there are sound reasons for delay, you should announce your claim early in your speech. If listeners don't see where you're going in your argument, your strongest arguments may be lost on them. Take time to say something such as, "Today, I want to convince you that increases and decreases in student tuition should be coupled with the Consumer Price Index. If the Board of Regents takes this action, the cost of education will be more fairly distributed between the state and the students."³

Types of Evidence

As you discovered in Chapter 7, supporting materials clarify, amplify, and strengthen the ideas in your speech. They provide evidence for the acceptance of your central idea and its supporting points. Evidence is the base from which an argument builds. It can be presented in any of the forms of supporting materials with which you are already familiar: comparisons and contrasts, illustrations, specific instances, statistics, and testimony.

There's no single or easy rule for selecting relevant evidence. Supporting material that's relevant to one claim may be irrelevant to another, or it may provide logical proof but not compelling reasons for action. You should consider both the rational and the motivational characteristics of evidence as you select it: What does it prove? Whom does it affect?

Rationally Relevant Evidence   The type of evidence you choose should reflect your claim. For example, if you're defending the claim that controls on the content of Internet chat rooms violate the First Amendment guarantee of freedom of speech, you'll probably choose testimony by noted authorities or definitions of terms to advance your claim. On the other hand, examples, illustrations, and statistics work better for showing that a problem exists or a change is needed. For example, if you argue that the speed limit in your state should be lowered by 10 miles per hour on interstate highways and have statistics indicating that lives will be saved, you'll be showing that there is a compelling reason for a change. The claim you present requires rationally relevant type of evidence. As you plan your arguments, you should ask yourself, "What type of evidence is logically relevant in support of my claim?"

Motivationally Relevant Evidence   If you hope to convince listeners to adopt your attitudes or actions, your claim must be supported by more than logically relevant evidence. You must get your listeners emotionally involved, as we saw in Chapter 14. That is, your evidence must be motivationally relevant to them. So, you should ask two questions:

1. *What type of evidence will this audience demand?* If you want to argue that your city needs to build a new sewage plant, many people will demand that you demonstrate the problems with the present system, a financial plan that won't bankrupt the city, incentives that the new plant will provide for new jobs, and even a plan for laying the lines that won't paralyze neighborhoods. On the

other hand, if you're reviewing a new video release for friends, an example from the plot, an analogy to other videos like this one, or an illustration of dialogue would be more forceful as proof than statistical word counts, box office receipts, or testimony from published movie critics. Careful audience analysis, as we discussed earlier, will help you determine what type of evidence is needed to move your particular group of listeners psychologically.

2. *What specific evidence will generate the best response?* You should pose this question once you've determined the type of evidence required by your argument. For example, if you've decided to use expert testimony to support your argument, whom should you quote? Or if you're using an illustration, should you use a factual example or develop one of your own? Will listeners be more moved by a personalized story or a general illustration?

To answer these and similar questions about your listeners, you need to analyze them. A homogeneous audience of townspeople may be suspicious of outsiders. They might react best to local experts or illustrations from the local community or common range of experience: the mayor, a reference to a particular neighborhood, or the town's experience in the flood of 1993. A heterogeneous audience of college students who do not share experience and background, on the other hand, will not know those local experts and probably will prefer geographically varied examples. Such an audience will probably respond better to a nationally known expert and references to well-known communities across the country. You should consider your listeners' demographic or psychological characteristics in order to choose the most effective evidence for them.

Forms of Reasoning

Reasoning or inference is a process of connecting something that is known or believed (evidence) to a concept or idea (claim) that you wish others to accept. **Patterns of reasoning** are habitual ways in which a culture or society uses inferences to connect what is accepted to what it is being urged to accept. There are five generally accepted reasoning patterns: from examples, from generalization or axiom, from sign, from parallel case, and from causal relation.

Often called inductive reasoning, **reasoning from examples** involves examining a series of examples of known occurrences (evidence) and drawing a general conclusion (claim). The inference of this reasoning pattern is, "What is true of particular cases is true of the whole class." This inference represents a kind of mental inductive leap from specifics to generalities. For example, the National Cancer Institute has studied hundreds of individual case histories and discovered that people with high-fiber diets are less prone to develop cancers of the digestive tract. With an inductive leap, the Institute then moved to the factual claim, "High-fiber diets help control certain types of cancer." Commuters use a similar pattern of reasoning every time they drive during rush hour. After trial and error, they decide that a residential street is the best route to take home before 5:30 P.M. and the expressway after 5:30 P.M. In other words, after experiencing enough instances, they arrive at a generalization and act on it.

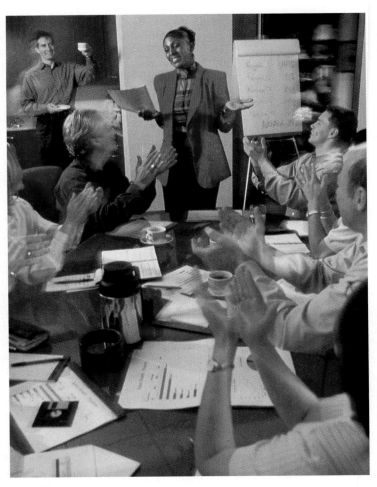

Both constructive and refutational arguments are usually necessary for argumentative victory.

Reasoning from generalization (sometimes called deduction) means applying a general truth to a specific situation. It is essentially the reverse of reasoning from examples or induction. In high school consumer education class, you may have learned that buying goods in large quantities saves money (the generalization). Now, you may shop at discount stores because they purchase goods in quantity, thereby saving money and passing those savings on to you (the claim deduced from the evidence). Or, you may believe that getting a college education is the key to a better future (the generalization). Therefore, if you get a college degree, you will get a better job (claim). This inference gathers power because of experience (you learned it through observation) or by definition (one of the characteristics of education is self-improvement). You ultimately accept this inference because of the uniformities you believe exist in the world.

Reasoning from sign uses an observable mark, or sign, as proof of the existence of a state of affairs. You reason from sign when you notice the tickle in your throat (the evidence) and decide that you're getting a cold (the claim). The tickle in your throat doesn't cause the condition; rather, it's a sign of the virus that does cause it. Detectives, of course, are experts at reasoning from sign. When they discover that a particular suspect had motive, means, and opportunity (the signs), they make the claim that he or she might be the murderer. Your doctor works the same way every time he or she examines your respiration and heart rhythms for signs of ailments. Reasoning from sign works well with natural occurrences (ice on the pond is always a sign that the temperature has been below 32° F). However, reasoning from sign can be troublesome in the world of human beings (as when some people take body weight as a sign of laziness or skin color as a sign of dishonesty). Signs, of course, are circumstantial evidence—and could be wrong. Just ask detectives and doctors. Yet, we often must use signs as indicators; otherwise, we couldn't project our economy, predict our weather, or forecast the success of political candidates.

Another common reasoning pattern, **reasoning from parallel case,** involves thinking solely in terms of similar things and events. You probably designed your first homecoming float by looking at others; they served as models of what people expect of homecoming floats in your area. Those floats functioned as evidence; the claim was that you should make a similar mark of pride and identification. The inference that linked the evidence and the claim was probably something such as, "What was acceptable as a homecoming float last year will be acceptable/expected this year." Your instructors might use parallel reasoning every time they tell you, "Study hard for this exam. The last exam was difficult; this one will be, too." Obviously this is not a generalization, since every exam will probably not be exactly the same. However,

TABLE 15.2   Kinds of Reasoning

Try to think of additional examples of each kind of reasoning.

Reasoning	Description	Examples
Reasoning from examples (inductive reasoning)	Drawing a general conclusion from instances or examples	I enjoy the music of Bach, Beethoven, and Brahms. I like classical music.
Reasoning from generalization or axiom (deductive reasoning)	Applying a general conclusion to a specific example	Irish Setters are friendly dogs. I think I'll get an Irish Setter puppy for my niece.
Reasoning from sign	Using an observable mark or symptom as proof of a state of affairs	The petunias are all dead. Someone forgot to water them.
Reasoning from parallel case	Asserting that two things or events share similar characteristics or patterns	North Korea is developing nuclear technology; South Korea won't be far behind.
Reasoning from causal relation	Concluding that an event that occurs first is responsible for a later event	The engine won't start because the carburetor is flooded with gasoline.

your instructors are asserting that the upcoming examinations and past examinations are similar cases—they have enough features in common to increase the likelihood that careful study habits will benefit you.

Finally, **reasoning from cause** is an important vehicle for reaching conclusions. The underlying assumption of causal reasoning is that events occur in a predictable, routine manner, with causes that account for occurrences. Reasoning from cause involves associating events that come before with events that follow. (See Table 15.2 on page 287.) When substance abuse appears to be increasing across the country, people scramble to identify causes: the existence of international drug cartels, corrupt foreign governments, organized crime inside our own borders, lower moral standards, the breakup of the nuclear family, and lax school discipline. What the arguer must do is assert causes that might reasonably be expected to produce the effects—to point to material connections between, for example, foreign governments' actual policies and the presence of drugs in Los Angeles or other American cities. Overall, the inference in causal reasoning is simple and constant: every effect has a cause.

EVALUATING ARGUMENTS

The reasoning process is the fulcrum on which argument pivots. You must test reasoning in order to protect yourself, both as a speaker and as a critical listener, from embarrassment when you're arguing and from faulty decisions when you're listening to others. For each kind of reasoning, there are special tests or questions that help you determine the soundness of arguments. Consider the following questions as you construct arguments and evaluate those of others:

Reasoning from Examples

1. *Have you looked at enough instances to warrant generalizing?* If you live in Idaho, you don't assume spring has arrived after experiencing one warm day in February.

2. *Are the instances fairly chosen?* You certainly hope that a teacher doesn't judge your speech skills by listening only to your first speech, when you were confused and nervous. You want to be judged only after being observed in several speaking situations.

3. *Are there important exceptions to the generalization or claim that must be considered?* While presidential elections show that, generally, "As Maine goes, so goes the nation," there have been enough exceptions to this rule to keep presidential candidates who lose in Maine campaigning hard.

Reasoning from Generalization

1. *Is the generalization true?* Women are more emotional than men; woolly caterpillars come out when winter's about to arrive; private universities provide better education than public universities. Each of these statements is a generalization. You need to determine if sufficient evidence exists to support the truth of the statement.

2. *Does the generalization apply to this particular case?* Usually, discount stores have lower prices, but if a small neighborhood store has a sale, it may offer better prices than a discount house. While the old saying "Birds of a feather flock together" certainly applies to birds, it may not apply to human beings.

Reasoning from Sign

1. *Is the sign fallible?* As we've noted, many signs are merely circumstantial. Be extremely careful not to confuse reasoning from sign with causal reasoning. If sign reasoning were infallible, the weather forecaster would never be wrong.

2. *Is the observation accurate?* Some of us see what we want to see, not what's there; children see ghosts at night and jealous lovers can interpret each other's acts in erroneous ways. Be sure that the observation is reliable.

Reasoning from Parallel Case

1. *Are there more similarities than differences between the two cases?* College A and College B may have many features in common—size, location, programs, and so on—yet they probably also have many different features, perhaps in the subgroups that make up their populations, the backgrounds of their faculty, and their historical development. Too many differences between two cases rationally destroy the parallel.

2. *Are the similarities you have pointed out the relevant and important ones?* There are two children in your neighborhood who are the same age, go to the same school, and wear the same kinds of clothes; are you therefore able to assume that one is well-behaved simply because the other is? Probably not, because more relevant similarities than their clothing and age would include their home lives, their relationships with siblings, and so forth. Comparisons must be based on relevant and important similarities.

Reasoning from Cause

1. *Can you separate causes and effects?* We often have a difficult time doing this. Does stress lead to a propensity to drink too much, or does excessive alcohol consumption lead to stress? Does a strained home life make a child misbehave, or is it the other way around?

2. *Are the causes strong enough to have produced the effect?* Did Bill Clinton's appearance on MTV really win the 1992 election for him, or was that an insufficient cause? There probably were much stronger and more important causes.

3. *Did intervening events or persons prevent a cause from having its normal effect?* If a gun is not loaded, you can't shoot anything, no matter how hard you pull the trigger. Even if Iraq cuts off the United States' oil supply, prices may not go up if enough oil's been stockpiled, if other producers offer competitive rates, or if U.S. consumer gas consumption drops.

4. *Could any other cause have produced the effect?* Although crime often increases when neighborhoods deteriorate, increased crime rates can be caused by any number of other changes—alterations in definitions of crime, increased reporting of crimes that have been going on for years, or closings of major

SPEAKING OF . . . *Skills*
Evaluating Arguments

Undoubtedly you'll participate in disputes or arguments many times as an advocate or a bystander. Often, you'll have to determine if your arguments or those of others were effective. Here are four questions you can ask to help discover the effectiveness of an argument:

1. *What was its effect?* Did the argument convince people to vote? to boycott? to donate canned goods? Clearly, if your argument results in a desired response, it was effective. However, this is only one way of judging the effectiveness of arguments. You must also ask the next three questions.
2. *Was the argument valid?* Did the arguer follow a logical order of development? Did he or she use supporting materials to prove the points? Were those supporting materials relevant to the claim advanced? If the argument was sound, it can be judged valid.
3. *Was the argument truthful?* Did it meet the test of reality? If an argument doesn't correspond to the way things really are, then it fails the truthfulness test.
4. *Was the argument ethical?* Did it advocate what is morally good? Did the arguer use ethical means to achieve results? This is an especially important test in this age of ethical malaise.

For additional development of these ideas, see J. Michael Sproule, *Argument: Language and Its Influence* (New York: McGraw-Hill, 1980), 22–24.

industries. We rationally must sort through all of the possible causes before championing one.

The heart of critical thinking is idea testing. You must learn to use what you have available—the evidence others have presented, your own experience, your wits, and sometimes a trip to the library when the decision's particularly important—to test the rationality and force of others' arguments.

SAMPLE OUTLINE FOR AN ARGUMENTATIVE SPEECH

The Dangers of Chewing Tobacco[4]

INTRODUCTION

I. When he was 12 years old, Ricky Bender tried his first plug of chewing tobacco. After all, he was a Little Leaguer and all his heroes in the major leagues chewed tobacco. Fourteen years later, Ricky found out he had oral cancer. The cancer cost him most of his tongue, half of his jaw, and the use of his right arm.

The speaker uses motivationally relevant evidence to gain attention.

II. Little Ricky Bender's case isn't an isolated one. Every day children like little Ricky Bender start using "spit tobacco." It's estimated that 10 percent of teenage males are regular users.

The growing scope of the problem is explained with rationally relevant evidence.

III. It's important that we recognize the dangers of this addictive drug because health problems related to its use are rising dramatically in this country.

Listeners' motivation to listen is developed.

IV. Let's examine the addictive nature of spit tobacco, the health problems it causes, and the myths that surround it.

The speech structure is previewed.

BODY

I. The addictive nature of spit tobacco.
   A. Spit tobacco is leaf tobacco that comes in two forms:

   The uses of spit tobacco are explained.

   1. Chewing tobacco comes in a pouch in a coarsely shredded form.
   2. More finely shredded snuff is packaged in a tin and is sometimes flavored.
   3. Both forms are put between the cheek and the gum. Nicotine is absorbed through the tissues of the mouth.
   B. Nicotine dependency results from the use of spit tobacco.

   Reasoning from parallel case establishes the similarities between cigarette and spit tobacco use.

   1. Studies reveal that nicotine blood levels for smokers and spit tobacco users are identical.
   2. Psychological dependency on tobacco results in both users.
   3. The only difference between the two forms is that nicotine enters the bloodstream more slowly when it is absorbed through the skin.

II. The health problems caused by spit tobacco.
   A. Dental problems are rampant among spit tobacco users.

   Causal reasoning is supported with statistical evidence.

   1. Habitual users injure the linings of their mouths where the tobacco is held.
      a. The first signs of deterioration are halitosis or bad breath and tooth discoloration.
      b. Then, teeth begin to decay and gingivitis sets in.
      c. Finally, users begin to lose their teeth prematurely.
   2. Statistics reveal the toll spit tobacco takes on dental health.
   B. The risk of oral cancer increases.

   Causal reasoning links nitrosamines to oral cancer.

   1. Nitrosamines, known carcinogenic agents, are formed when spit tobacco is manufactured.
   2. These carcinogens enter the user's bloodstream along with nicotine.
      a. The risk of oral cancer is four to six times higher than for non-users.
      b. The risk of oral cancer is higher than for cigarette and pipe smokers.

      c. There is also a risk from the expelled tobacco when it comes into contact with skin.

C. Heart disease increases with the use of spit tobacco.

Nicotine is identified as a cause of heart disease.

    1. Systemic problems result from spit tobacco use.

      a. Within minutes, nicotine causes blood pressure to increase.

      b. The heart is required to pump harder, increasing the heart rate.

    2. The strain on the cardiovascular system over a period of time leads to coronary problems and heart disease.

III. The myths surrounding spit tobacco.

A. It's often called "smokeless tobacco," fostering the perception that it is less harmful than smoking.

Reasoning from generalization applies overall rates of cancer to spit tobacco users.

    1. The fact is that spit tobacco is just as likely to cause cancer as cigarette smoking.

      a. Oral cancer rates are higher among spit tobacco users.

      b. Other cancers exceed the rates of non-users.

    2. Heart disease is another result of using spit tobacco.

Reasoning from sign uses advertising and peer pressure to explain spit tobacco use among teenagers.

B. Some people argue that there is less pressure among teens to use spit tobacco. The opposite is true, peer pressure spirals during the adolescent years.

    1. Companies spend millions of dollars advertising spit tobacco at sponsor rodeos, NASCAR, and other popular events.

    2. Potential users frequent these events.

    3. Studies reveal that peer pressure induced by pervasive advertising is the chief reason for the initial use of spit tobacco.

CONCLUSION

Return to introductory example reaches closure by reminding listeners of motivationally relevant example.

I. Remember little Ricky Bender? What started as an innocent attempt to emulate his major league heroes cost him most of his face and threatened to take his life.

II. The threat to young people, especially teenaged males, is on an upward spiral.

Listeners are warned about the lethal nature of spit tobacco.

III. It's important for us to recognize that spit tobacco is addictive—not only that, it kills.

DETECTING FALLACIES IN REASONING

Your primary job as a critical listener and arguer is to evaluate the claims, evidence, and reasoning of others. On one level, you're looking for ways that the ideas and reasoning of others are important to your own thinking; and, on another level, you're examining the logical soundness of others' thinking. A **fallacy** is a flaw in the rational properties of an argument or inference. There are many different fallacies. Let's look at eight common ones.

Web Exploration
To practice identifying different types of fallacies go to
http://awl.com/german

1. *Hasty generalization.* A **hasty generalization** is a claim made on the basis of too little evidence. You should ask, "Has the arguer really examined enough typical cases to make a claim?" If the answer is no, then a flaw in reasoning has occurred. Urging a ban on ibuprofen because some people have had liver problems with it and the closure of a pedestrian mall because of an armed robbery are examples of hasty generalization.

2. *Genetic fallacy.* A **genetic fallacy** occurs when someone assumes that the only "true" understanding of some idea, practice, or event is to be found in its origins—in its "genes," literally or metaphorically. People sometimes assume that if an idea has been around for a long time, it must be true. Many people who defended slavery in the nineteenth century referred to the biblical practices of slavery to support their claim. Studies of origins can help us understand a concept, but they're hardly proof of present correctness or justice.

3. *Appeal to ignorance.* People sometimes appeal to ignorance by arguing with double negatives: "You can't prove it won't work!" They may even attack an idea because information about it is incomplete. "We can't cure all varieties of AIDS so let's just stop therapies until we learn more." Both of these illogical claims **appeal to ignorance** because they depend on what we don't know. Sometimes we must simply act on the basis of the knowledge we have, despite the gaps in it. In countering such claims, you can cite parallel cases and examples. So, you might say:

   OK, so we don't have all of the answers to the AIDS puzzle. That doesn't mean we don't work with what we know. Consider the case of tuberculosis. The vaccines against it weren't developed until the 1950s, and yet thousands of lives were saved earlier in the century because TB sanitariums used the physical and pharmacological regimens they had available. Of course they couldn't save everyone, but they relieved suffering and even prevented the deaths of many with the partial knowledge they had. Give HIV-positive people the same chance—to use what we have now even while we're waiting for the miracle cure.

4. *Bandwagon Fallacy.* A frequent strategy is to appeal to popular opinion or to urge people to jump on the bandwagon. The **bandwagon fallacy** assumes that if everyone else is doing something, you should, too: "African Americans don't belong to the Republican Party!" or "But Dad, everyone else is going!" While these appeals may be useful in stating valuative claims, they're not the basis for factual claims. The world has witnessed hundreds of widely believed but false ideas, from the belief that night air causes tuberculosis to panic over an invasion by Martians.

5. *Sequential fallacy.* Often present in arguments based on evidence from causal relations, the **sequential fallacy** arises from the assumption that if one event follows another, the first event must cause the second. Thunder and lightning do not cause rain, although the phenomena often occur sequentially. Even if

you usually catch colds in the spring, the two occurrences are not causally related. The season of the year does not cause your cold—a virus does.

6. *Begging the question.* **Begging the question** is rephrasing an idea and then offering it as its own reason. This kind of reasoning is circular thought. If someone asserts, "Abortion is murder because it is taking the life of the unborn," he or she has committed a fallacy by rephrasing the claim (it is murder) to constitute the reason (it is taking life). Sometimes questions can be fallacious, such as "Have you quit smoking on weekends?" The claim, phrased as a question, assumes that you smoke during the week. Whatever your answer to the question, therefore, you're guilty. Claims of value are especially prone to begging the question.

7. *Appeal to authority.* **Appeal to authority** occurs when someone who is popular but not an expert urges the acceptance of an idea or a product. Television advertisers frequently ask consumers to purchase products because movie stars or sports heroes endorse them. Michael Jordan promotes everything from underwear to telephone services. The familiar figure provides name recognition but not expertise. You can detect this fallacy by asking, "Is he or she an expert on this topic?"

8. *Name-calling.* **Name-calling** is the general label for attacks on people instead of on their arguments. Name-calling may take the form of an attack on the special interests of a person: "Of course, you're voting for O'Casey, you're Irish." Or it may be an attack on a personal characteristic rather than on ideas: "You're just a dweeb (or nerd or retrograde male)." Even dweebs, nerds, and retrograde males sometimes offer solid claims. Claims ought to be judged on their own features, preferably their objective features, not on the characteristics of the person who makes them.

These are some of the fallacies that creep into argumentation. A good basic logic book can point out additional fallacies.[5] Armed with knowledge of such fallacies, you should be able to protect yourself against unscrupulous demagogues, sales personnel, and advertisers. The Roman phrase, *caveat emptor!*—"Buyer, beware!"—should be a part of your thinking as an audience member. You share with speakers the responsibility of cultivating the sort of critical spirit discussed in the opening of this chapter.

TIPS FOR DEVELOPING ARGUMENTATIVE SPEECHES

As you get ready to pull all of your claims, kinds of evidence, and reasoning patterns together into coherent argumentative speeches, consider the following pieces of advice:

1. *Place your strongest arguments first or last.* This strategy takes advantage of the **primacy-recency effects.** Arguments presented first set the agenda for what is to follow, and a strong opening argument often impresses an audience with its power, thereby heightening the credibility of the arguer (the primacy effect).

We also know that listeners tend to retain the most recently presented idea (the recency effect), so you might put your strongest argument at the end of your speech so that listeners will remember your best shot.[6] Decide which position will best help you with the particular audience you face, and then place your best argument there (but then, of course, summarize all of the arguments in your conclusion).

2. *Vary your evidence.* Different listeners are likely to prefer different kinds of evidence, and most listeners want supporting materials that are both logically relevant and psychologically motivating. For example, if you're arguing that more Americans must invest in solar power units for their home electrical needs, general statistics on energy savings and average reduction in costs of utilities are good, but a good, clear illustration with details on what it's like to live in a solar-assisted environment will more likely clinch the argument.

3. *Avoid personal attacks on opponents.* Maintain arguments on an appropriate intellectual level. This tactic enhances your credibility. If you can argue well without becoming vicious, you'll earn the respect—and perhaps the agreement—of your listeners; most know that the more someone screams, the weaker his or her arguments are. Hold your opponent accountable for arguments and reasoning, yes, but without name-calling and smear tactics (see "Speaking of . . . Ethics: Name-Calling").

4. *Know the potential arguments of your opponents.* The best advocates know their opponents' arguments as well as their opponents do; they have thought about those arguments and ways of responding to them ahead of time. Having

SPEAKING OF . . . *Ethics*
Name-Calling

Arguments often threaten to degenerate into fights, not always physical clawing and punching, but certainly into symbolic assaults: attacks on an opponent's intelligence, parentage (or lack thereof), associations, motives, appearance. Is that ethical? Where do you draw the line?

1. You're having a class argument about ways to control hate speech. You know that your opponent is gay—do you reveal that information in the debate?
2. Both Michael Dukakis in 1988 and Bill Clinton in 1992 were accused by the National Conservative Political Action Committee of being "card-carrying members of the American Civil Liberties Union." Is that a relevant issue in presidential politics?
3. "Well, you're over thirty, so how would you understand?" "You're a girl, so of course . . . ." "Now, you're black and so I'd expect you to . . . ." "When you lived in the ghetto, didn't you . . . ?" Is it ethical to make statements like these when arguing with someone?

Name-calling—*argumentum ad hominem* (arguments to the person)—has been used since Homer wrote *The Iliad*. But is it ethical? Anytime? Sometimes? When?

SPEAKING OF . . . *Skills*

Responding to Counterarguments

Constructing an argument is often not enough. You may have to respond to the objections of others who oppose your ideas. Here are some suggestions for developing an effective response:

1. Listen and take notes. You need to understand your opponent's position before you can refute it.
2. Decide whether to answer the objection. Many times people just want to vent frustration or be heard by others. Their comments may not be relevant to your argument.
3. Organize your response. Here's a four-step process to help:

   Restate your opponent's claim. "Mary said learning a foreign language is useless."

   Explain your objection to it. "I think learning a foreign language can be beneficial in your career and in your personal life."

   Offer evidence to support your position. "Studies show that . . ."

   Indicate the significance of your rebuttal. "If you want faster career advancement and more satisfying international travel experiences, take a foreign language."
4. Keep the exchange on an intellectual level. Name-calling or emotionally charged ranting harms your credibility.

thought through opposing positions early allows you to prepare a response and feel confident about your own position. Notice how presidential candidates are able to anticipate each other's positions in their debates.

5. *Practice constructing logical arguments and detecting fallacious ones.* Ultimately, successful argument demands skill in performing the techniques of public reasoning. You need to practice routinely constructing arguments with solid relationships between and among claims, evidence, and reasoning patterns; and you need to practice regularly detecting the fallacies in other people's proposals. Critically examine product advertisements, political claims, and arguments that your neighbors make in order to improve your communication skills—as both a sender and a receiver of argumentative messages.

ASSESSING YOUR PROGRESS

Chapter Summary

1. Argumentation is a process of advancing propositions or claims supported by good reasons.
2. Criticism is a process of careful assessment, evaluation, and judgment of ideas and motives.

3. Arguments are built from three elements—the claim, the evidence, and the reasoning pattern.

4. The types of claims common to arguments are claims of fact, claims of value, and claims of policy.

5. Evidence for arguments can be chosen to reflect the rational quality of the claim (rationally relevant evidence) or to stimulate audience involvement (motivationally relevant evidence).

6. Five forms of reasoning connect evidence and claims—reasoning from examples, reasoning from generalization, reasoning from sign, reasoning from parallel case, and reasoning from cause.

7. A fallacy is a flaw in the rational properties of an argument or inference.

8. Common fallacies are hasty generalization, genetic fallacy, appeal to ignorance, bandwagon fallacy, sequential fallacy, begging the question, appeal to authority, and name-calling.

9. In developing argumentative speeches (a) organize your arguments by putting the strongest first or last, (b) vary the evidence, (c) avoid personal attacks on opponents, (d) know the potential arguments of your opponents, and (e) practice constructing logical arguments and detecting fallacious ones.

Key Terms

appeal to authority (p. 294)

appeal to ignorance (p. 293)

argument (p. 281)

argumentation (p. 280)

bandwagon fallacy (p. 293)

begging the question (p. 294)

claim (p. 282)

claim of fact (p. 282)

claim of policy (p. 282)

claim of value (p. 282)

fallacy (p. 292)

genetic fallacy (p. 293)

hasty generalization (p. 293)

name-calling (p. 294)

patterns of reasoning (p. 285)

primacy-recency effects (p. 294)

reasoning (p. 285)

reasoning from cause (p. 287)

reasoning from examples (p. 285)

reasoning from generalization (p. 286)

reasoning from parallel case (p. 287)

reasoning from sign (p. 286)

sequential fallacy (p. 293)

Assessment Activities

1. Choose a controversial topic and phrase it as a question of policy, such as, "Should the federal government privatize Social Security?" or "Should all 18-year-olds be required to complete two years of military or domestic service?" As a class, think of arguments for and against the policy. Then, determine what rationally and motivationally relevant evidence would be required to develop each argument.

2. Fallacies are often present in assertions made by advertisers. Think of as many assertions made in current television and print advertisements as you can. Choose a member of the class to list them on the chalkboard and then assess the claims. What kinds of fallacies can you detect? Explain why the reasoning in the advertisement is flawed.

 ## Surfing the Web

1. Individuals and organizations often post their views on the Internet. Locate a Web page that develops an argument. Assess the argument. Is the claim clearly stated? Is supporting material provided to substantiate the claim? Is the supporting material rationally or motivationally relevant? What reasoning patterns are present in the argument? Are they logical?

2. Many argumentative exchanges are available through the Internet. Among other sites, the home page for the White House is a good place to locate practical uses of argument. Transcriptions of argumentative speeches including the second presidential debate in 1996 are available at this site.

References

1. Harvey Siegel, *Educating Reason: Rationality, Critical Thinking, and Education* (New York: Routledge, 1988), 1–47. The importance of critical thinking has been underscored in two national reports on higher education: The National Institute of Education, *Involvement in Learning: Realizing the Potential of American Higher Education,* 1984; and the Association of American Colleges, *Integrity in the College Curriculum: A Report to the Academic Community,* 1985. For a summary of research on critical thinking in the college setting, see James H. McMillan, "Enhancing College Students' Critical Thinking: A Review of Studies," *Research in Higher Education,* 26 (1987): 3–29.

2. Fairness or fair-mindedness is one dimension of a primary factor underlying positive source credibility, trustworthiness. See James B. Stiff, *Persuasive Communication* (New York: Guilford Press, 1994), esp. 90–92.

3. A full discussion of the logical grounding of claims in evidence and reasoning is presented in the classic book on argumentation: Douglas Ehninger and Wayne Brockriede, *Decision by Debate,* 2nd ed. (New York: Harper & Row, 1978).

4. Information for this sample outline was drawn from: The Johns Hopkins Health Information Web site (http://www.intelihealth.com/IH/ihtlH) and Marjike Rowland, "Man Without a Face to Talk on Dangers of Chewing Tobacco," *Modesto Bee* (2 February 1999).

5. See lrving M. Copi and Keith Cohen, *Informal Logic,* 10th ed. (Englewood Cliffs, NJ: Prentice Hall, 1998); and Frans H. Vaneemeren and Rob Grootendorst, *Argumentation, Communication, and Fallacies* (Hillsdale, NJ: Lawrence Erlbaum Associates, 1992).

6. The debate over primacy-recency effects continues. For the position that primacy and recency are equally potent, see Stephen W. Littlejohn and David M. Jabusch, *Persuasive Transactions* (Glenview, IL: Scott, Foresman, and Co., 1987), 235–236; for the arguments championing the primacy position, see Robert E. Denton, Jr., *Persuasion and Influence in American Life* (Prospect Heights, IL: Waveland Press, 1988), 299–300.

Appendix

Speaking at Community- and Group-Centered Events

Much has been made throughout this book about public speaking as both grounded in and governed by cultural understandings of public behavior. There are culturally based understandings at work in every society governing the ways in which people talk and listen publicly. Those understandings also form expectations. People come to expect speakers to talk, move, and even think in ways that are comprehensible and acceptable in the circumstances they find themselves. To be sure, speakers ought not to cave in to the temptation of simply saying what everyone wants or expects them to say. When that happens, public speakers are abandoning the service element of public talk; if you bring audiences nothing new, different, or useful, you're wasting their time.

Some situations—often called **special occasions**—do, however, call for speeches that are particularly sensitive to community or group needs and expectations. Such special occasions have a ritualistic air to them. Members of societies learn that there are generally acceptable—almost required—ways to speak at funerals, weddings, Veterans' Day ceremonies, academic conferences, or breakfasts honoring community leaders. A **community** is a group of people who think of themselves as bonded together—whether by blood, locale, nationality, race, occupation, gender, or other shared experiences or attributes. The phrase *who think of themselves* is the key here. Communities are bonded by shared characteristics or commitments, and those shared characteristics and commitments, often, are recognized—celebrated, probed, redefined—on "special occasions."

In this appendix, we will review some of the special occasions upon which various communities explore those characteristics or common beliefs that bind them together. Often, that exploration occurs through the examination of exemplary members of the community or even the introduction of someone new to the community. At other times, it occurs through the humorous exploration of the group's beliefs or actions; humor can be a gentle but effective way to offer criticism of groups. Not only, however, do groups explore their communities generally and particularly. They also seek to bring new knowledge to their members, through public discussions of issues or ideas, through problem-solving interactions, or through panel presentations at meetings such as conventions or monthly assemblies.

We will divide our discussion of such special occasions into two parts. **Community-based special occasion speeches** occur at times set aside to honor community membership or members themselves. We'll look in particular at speeches of introduction, speeches of courtesy (welcomes, responses, acceptances, toasts), and speeches to entertain (because the humorous exploration of group beliefs or attitudes often becomes the basis for changing member behavior). **Group-based special occasion speeches** are given at gatherings where groups want to learn more, solve problems, or explore each other's understandings. So, under this heading we'll examine group discussions, team presentations, and responding to questions and objections as some of the usual ways of getting group work done publicly.

COMMUNITY-BASED SPECIAL OCCASION SPEECHES

Let's now look at three types of special occasion talk: speeches of introduction, speeches of courtesy, and speeches to entertain. How do we live out *E pluribus unum* (Out of many, one)?

Speeches of Introduction

Speeches of introduction are usually given by members of the group that will hear the speech. They're designed to prepare the community (the audience) to accept the featured speaker and his or her message. In a way, a speech of introduction asks permission for an outsider to speak. The decision to grant that permission is based upon what the nonmember can contribute to the group: the group must *want* to hear the outsider before the featured speaker can be successful. Or if the speaker is a member of the group, the introduction may serve as a reminder of his or her role and accomplishments within the community or organization.

Purpose   If you're invited to give a speech of introduction, remember that your main objective is to create in others a desire to hear the speaker you're introducing. Everything else should be subordinate to this aim. Don't bore your audience with a long recital of the speaker's biography or with a series of anecdotes about your acquaintance with the person. Above all, don't air your own views on the subject of the speaker's message. You're only the speaker's advance agent; your job is to sell that person to the audience. Your goals should be (1) to arouse curiosity about the speaker and the subject in the minds of the listeners so that it will be easy to capture their attention and (2) to motivate the audience to like and respect the speaker so they'll tend to respond favorably to the forthcoming information or proposal.

Formulating the Content   Usually, the better-known or more respected a speaker is, the shorter your introduction needs to be; the less well-known the person is, the more you'll need to arouse interest in the speaker's subject and to build up the person's prestige. When presenting a speech of introduction:

1. *Be brief.* To say too much is often worse than to say nothing at all. For example, if you were to introduce the president, you might simply say, "Ladies and gentlemen, the president of the United States." The prestige of the person you introduce won't always be great enough for you to be so brief, but it's always better to say too little than to speak too long.

2. *Talk about the speaker.* Anticipate the audience's questions: "Who are you? What's your position in business, education, sports, or government? What experiences have you had that qualify you to speak on the announced subject?" Build up speakers' identities, tell what they know or have done, but do not praise their abilities as speakers. Let them demonstrate their own skills.

3. *Emphasize the importance of the speaker's subject.* For example, in introducing a speaker who'll talk about the oil industry, you might say, "In one way or another, the oil industry is in the news every day—Middle East concerns, the ups and downs of the cost of heating oil, gasohol research, tanker spills, our energy needs for the twenty-first century. To help us make sense of the industry and the ways it impacts our daily lives, today's speaker. . . ."

4. *Stress the appropriateness of the subject or the speaker.* If your town is considering a program to rebuild its Main Street area, a speech by a city planner is likely to be timely and appreciated. References to relevant aspects of a speaker's background or the topic can tie speaker and speech to the audience's interests.

5. *Use humor if it suits the occasion.* Nothing puts an audience at ease better than laughter. Take care, however, that the humor is in good taste and doesn't negatively affect the speaker's credibility. The best stories are usually those shared by the introducer and speaker and told to illustrate a positive character trait of the speaker.

SAMPLE INTRODUCTION

The four primary virtues of a speech of introduction are (1) tact, (2) brevity, (3) sincerity, and (4) enthusiasm. These virtues are illustrated in the following introduction.

Introducing a Classmate   Angela Vangelisti

A popular sport in the student union cafeteria is reading through lists of ingredients in prepared foods and candies, especially the chemical additives. One of the best players of this sport I've seen is our next speaker, Angela Vangelisti. Angela is amazing. Even with products like coffee whitener, which contains only one or two things I've even heard of, Angela can identify most of the emulsifiers, stabilizers, and flavor enhancers that make up fake food./1

While identifying chemical food additives passes the time in the cafeteria, there's also a serious side to the game. As Angela knows, there's a difference between blue dye nos. 1 and 2, and between good old yellow no. 5 and yellow no. 6; the cancer risk varies from one to the other. For example, the red dye no. 3 that you'll find in maraschino cherries is related to thyroid tumors. These are some of the reasons I was gratified to learn that Angela would share some of her technical knowledge as a nutrition major in a speech entitled, "How to Read Labels and Live Longer."/2

Speeches of Courtesy: Welcomes, Responses, Acceptances, and Toasts

Speeches of courtesy explicitly acknowledge the presence or qualities of the audience or of a member of the audience. When you extend a welcome to a political candidate who's visiting your class or when you accept an award, for example, you are giving speeches of courtesy.

Typical Situations   Speeches of courtesy fulfill social obligations such as welcoming visitors, responding to welcomes or greetings, accepting awards from groups, and toasting individuals with short speeches recognizing achievements.

Welcoming Visitors   When guests or visiting groups are present, someone extends a public greeting to them. For example, your basketball announcer might greet the opposing team or a fraternity chapter president might greet the representative from the national office who's visiting your campus. The speech of welcome is a way of introducing strangers into a group or organization, giving them group approval, and making them feel more comfortable.

Responding to a Welcome or Greeting   Responses are ways for outsiders to recognize their status as visitors and to express appreciation for acceptance by the group or organization. Thus, the representative from the national office who's visiting a fraternity might respond to a greeting, in turn, by thanking the group for its welcome or by recognizing its importance and accomplishments.

Accepting Awards   An individual who has received an award usually acknowledges the honor. Sometimes the award is made to an organization rather than to an individual, in which case someone is selected to respond for the group. In all cases, the acceptance of awards via a speech is a way of thanking the group and acknowledging the importance of the activity being recognized; for example, people who receive Academy Awards (if they do more than blubber) thank the American Academy of Motion Picture Arts and Sciences for the Oscar and often recognize the importance of making serious films on significant subjects.

Offering Toasts   While toasts offered to bridegrooms or others being toasted can become silly, the act of toasting is usually an important ritual. Toasts are acts of tribute: through them, a group recognizes the achievements of an individual and expresses the hope that the person will continue to achieve distinction. After negotiations, heads of state usually toast each other's positive personal qualities, accomplishments, and desire for future good relations. Ceremonially, toasts can unite separated peoples.

Purpose   The speech of courtesy has a double purpose. The speaker not only expresses a sentiment of gratitude or hospitality but also tries to create an aura of good feeling in the audience. Usually the success of such a speech depends on satisfying the listeners that the appropriate thing has been said.

Formulating the Content   The scope and content of a speech of courtesy should by guided by the following principles:

1. *Indicate for whom you're speaking.* When you act on behalf of a group, make clear that the greeting or acknowledgment comes from everyone and not from you alone.

2. *Present complimentary facts about the person or persons to whom you are extending the courtesy.* Review the accomplishments or qualities of the person or group you're greeting or whose gift or welcome you're acknowledging.

3. *Illustrate; don't argue.* Present incidents and facts that make clear the importance of the occasions, but don't be contentious. Avoid areas of disagreement. Don't use a speech for courtesy as an opportunity to air your own views on controversial subjects or to advance your own policies. Express concretely and vividly the thoughts that are already in the minds of your listeners.

These virtues are illustrated in William Faulkner's "On Accepting the Nobel Prize for Literature," reprinted in Chapter 10, pages 184–85. Faulkner clearly indicates he's speaking *as* a writer *to* future writers. He honors those young writers by taking their compositional problems seriously; his own difficulties as a writer, which come out in a flood of metaphors and images that make up the bulk of his speech, stand not as arguments but as illustrations of the struggle he finds at the core of all good writing.

Speeches of courtesy are more than merely polite talk. The courtesies extended in welcoming someone into your midst or in thanking someone for work done are statements of your group's rules for living—its guiding principles. In extending courtesies to others, you're acknowledging the culture you share with them.

What follows is a short toast offered to a retiring professor by those attending a spring dinner in his honor. Notice its conciseness, the qualities of the person that form the basis for the tribute, and the use of illustrations (the honoree's values) not only to celebrate the person but to suggest to those assembled the nature of the community standards for accomplishment.

A Toast to Leo Brecker

As we prepare to leave the dinner table, I'd like to offer a toast to the man we honor this evening—retiring Professor Leo Brecker./1

Leo, you've been a part of this university for 50 years: as an undergraduate student before and after World War II; as a graduate student; and as a professor of speech education, broadcasting, and mass communication. Your life is indistinguishable from the life of this university. You embody the values everyone else reaches for. You constantly pose what you call the "interesting questions" that are the essence of the scholar's life. You often say that no matter how crazy our students are, they're still the reason we come to work every day. You remind us weekly that we are not only *in* the world but are *of* the world; just as the world gives us the opportunity to study and teach, so do we owe it not only our thanks but our attention and good works./2

In living out the values that justify the very existence of the state university, Leo, you've been the flesh-and-blood example of all that is good in higher education. For that, I toast you—your vision, your daily life, and your ideals that will guide our future. In you, Professor Brecker, we see the best that we can be. I toast you in the hope that the best is indeed yet to come for all of us./3

Speeches to Entertain

Speeches to entertain present special challenges to speakers. As you may recall, in Chapter 2, we identified the speech to entertain as one of the three types embodying an independent general purpose. Discounting slapstick of the slipping-on-a-banana-peel type, most humor depends primarily upon a listener's sensitivities to the routines and morals of his or her own society. This is obvious if you've ever listened to someone tell jokes from a foreign country. Often, humor cannot be translated, in part because of language differences (puns, for example, don't translate well) and, in larger measure, because of cultural differences.

Purpose   Like most humor in general, speeches to entertain usually work within the cultural frameworks of a particular group or society. Such speeches may be "merely funny," as in comic monologues, but most are serious in their force or demand on audiences. After-dinner speeches, for example, are usually more than dessert; their topics are normally relevant to the group at hand, and the anecdotes they contain usually are offered to make a point. That point may be as simple as deflecting an audience's antipathy toward the speaker or making the people in the audience feel more like a group, or it may be as serious as offering a critique of society.

Speakers seeking to deflect an audience's antipathy often use humor to ingratiate themselves. For example, Henry W. Grady, editor of the *Atlanta Constitution,* expected a good deal of distrust and hostility when he journeyed to New York City in 1886 to tell the New England Society about "The New South." He opened the speech not only by thanking the society for the invitation, but also by telling stories about farmers, husbands and wives, and preachers. He praised Abraham Lincoln, a northerner, as "the first typical American" of the new age; told another humorous story about shopkeepers and their advertising; poked fun at the great Union General Sherman—"who is considered an able man in our hearts, though some people think he is a kind of careless man about fire"; and assured his audience that a New South, one very much like the old North, was arising from the ashes.[1] Through the use of humor, Henry Grady had his audience cheering every point he made about the New South that evening.

Group cohesiveness can also be created through humor. Especially when campaigning, politicians spend much time telling humorous stories about their opponents, hitting them with stinging remarks. In part, of course, biting political humor detracts from the opposition candidates and party; however, such humor also can make one's own party feel more cohesive. For example, Democrats collected Richard Nixon's 1972 bumper stickers that said, "Nixon Now," cut off the *w,* and put them on their own autos. Democrats did endless turns on the names Bush and Quayle in 1988. Similarly, Republicans poked fun at Michael Dukakis, laughing at a picture of him awkwardly driving a tank. Such zingers allow political party members to laugh at their opponents and to celebrate their membership in the "better" party.

Finally, speeches to entertain can be used not merely to poke fun at outsiders and to celebrate membership but even to critique one's society. Humor can be used to urge general changes and reform of social practices.

Formulating the Content   When arranging materials for speeches to entertain, develop a series of illustrations, short quotations or quips, and stories, each following another in fairly rapid succession. Most important, make sure that each touches on a central theme or point. An entertaining speech must be more than a comic monologue; it must be cohesive and pointed. The following sequence works well for speeches to entertain:

1. Relate a story or anecdote, present an illustration, or quote an appropriate passage.

2. State the main idea or point of view implied by your opening.

3. Follow with a series of additional stories, anecdotes, quips, or illustrations that amplify or illuminate your central idea; arrange those supporting materials so they're thematically connected.

4. Close with restatement of the central point you have developed; as in step 1, you can use a quotation or one final story that clinches and epitomizes your speech as a whole.

SAMPLE SPEECH TO ENTERTAIN

By organizing your speech materials in the pattern just suggested, you'll not only provide your listeners with entertainment but help them remember your central idea. The speech that follows illustrates the four steps.

A Case for Optimism[2]   Douglas Martini

Most of you probably have heard some version of this poem:

Twixt the optimist and pessimist
The difference is droll:
The optimist sees the doughnut,
The pessimist, the hole.

The longer I live, the more I'm convinced of the truth of that poem. Like a doughnut, life may seem full, rich, and enjoyable, or it can seem as empty as that hole in the middle. To the pessimist, the optimist seems foolish. But I'm here today to tell you it's the pessimist who's the foolish one./1

Another way of seeing the difference between an optimist and a pessimist is this way: an optimist looks at an oyster and expects a pearl; a pessimist looks at an oyster and expects ptomaine poisoning. Even if the pessimist is right—which is not very often—he probably won't enjoy himself either before or after he proves it. But the optimist is happy because he always has that expectation of a future reward./2

Pessimists are easy to recognize. They're the ones who go around asking "What's good about it?" when someone says "Good morning." If they looked around, they undoubtedly could find *something* good, as did the storekeeper after she was robbed. The day after the robbery she was asked about the loss. "Lose much?" her friend wanted to know. "Some," she said, "but then it would have been worse if the robbers had got in the night before. You see, yesterday I just finished marking everything down 20 percent."/3

There's another story about a happy-go-lucky shoemaker who left the gas heater in his shop turned on overnight, and upon arriving in the morning he struck a match to light it. There was a terrific explosion, and the shoemaker was blown out through the door to the middle of the street. A passerby rushed to help and asked if he were injured. The shoemaker got up slowly, jiggled his arms and legs, looked back at the burning shop, and said, "No, I'm not hurt, but I sure got out just in time, didn't I?"/4

Some writers have ridiculed this kind of outlook. The great French writer Voltaire made fun of optimism in *Candide.* "Optimism," he said, "is a mania for maintaining that all is well when things are going badly." A later writer, James Branch Cabell, did a turn on one of Voltaire's phrases when he quipped: "The optimist proclaims that we live in the best of all possible worlds; the pessimist fears this is true."/5

A lot of college professors, too, can't resist the urge to jab a little at optimists. But I, for one, refuse to take them seriously. I like the remark made by literary critic and journalist Keith Preston: "There's as much bunk among the busters as among the boosters."/6

Some may like the cynicism of Voltaire or *Doonesbury* cartoonist Gary Trudeau. But optimism is the philosophy I like to hear preached. There was a grandmother who complained about the weather. "But, Melissa," said her friend, "awful weather is better than no weather at all." So quit complaining. Change the bad things in the world that you can, to be sure, but then work within the rest. And stop expecting the worst. Be the optimist who cleans his glasses *before* he eats his grapefruit!/7

When you're tempted to grumble about your rotten future, remember the doughnut. And, as Elbert Hubbard advised:

As you travel through life, brother,

Whatever be your goal,

Keep your eye upon the doughnut

And not upon the hole.

GROUP-BASED SPECIAL OCCASION SPEECHES

There are many public speaking situations in which you'll be participating in a different role—as part of a group rather than as a single speaker addressing an audience. As a team member, you may present proposals to your employer, you may join a group filing a grievance against a city council, or you may be asked to justify your actions as part of an executive committee.

As a member of a group, you will participate in the discussion of ideas; you may also address an audience as a representative of the group. In either case, your role as a speaker will be changed by your relationship to others in your group. You will need to understand the functions of public group communication. It order to help you in this role, we will examine the responsibilities of participants in group discussions, panels, and symposia; provide guidelines for developing a discussion plan; and suggest ways to respond to audiences' questions and objections.

Group Discussions

Business people and professionals depend heavily on oral communication for their success. Businesses and professional organizations rely on committees, task forces, and more informal groups to formulate ideas, evaluate courses of action, and put proposals into effect. These exchanges are generally termed group discussions. A **group discussion** is a communication transaction in which a small group of people exchanges and evaluates ideas and information in order to solve a problem. Usually group discussions involve 4 to 6 people. As many as 12 people can join the discussion, but as the number of participants increases, the efficiency of the group normally declines.

There can be many different goals for small groups—amateurs gather to discuss art, literature, or coin collecting, for example. Book clubs, genealogical societies, and religious instruction classes function to educate their members. While these are important goals, we will focus on decision-making discussions.

In **decision-making discussions,** participants seek agreement on what the group should believe or do. These groups may also discuss ways of implementing their decisions. In discussions of this kind, participants examine conflicting facts and values, evaluate differences of opinion, and explore proposed courses of action for their practicality. The goal is to arrive at a consensus. A neighborhood homeowners' association may gather to evaluate a local sewer improvement project. A city council might plan for rezoning to control future growth. A subcommittee of a business can discuss how to expand markets. Once decisions are made, these groups may explore ways to implement their plans.

Responsibilities of Participants   When you participate in group communication, the most important requirement is that you be knowledgeable about the subject at hand. If you know what you're talking about, you're better prepared to contribute to the group process. For example, before you attend a discussion on locating a minimum-security prison in your neighborhood, you need to research the issue. You should find out how other neighborhoods have been affected by minimum-security prisons. You should investigate what measures will be taken to ensure the safety of neighborhood residents. You also will need to know what economic, environmental, and social impacts such a facility will have in your neighborhood. This information will help you contribute to the discussion.

It's equally important for you to practice good listening behavior as the discussion progresses. Unless you listen to what's going on, you'll forget what's already been said or lose track of the direction in which the group is moving. As a result, you may make redundant or irrelevant comments, require the restatement of points already settled, or misunderstand the positions taken by other participants. In any case, you won't be adding to the progress of the discussion. If you've seen a recent TV talk show, you've probably seen exactly how frustrated and angry people can become when they are ignored or misunderstood. Many times this frustration can be prevented if everyone listens carefully to the discussion.

You also should be aware of the dynamics of the group and its members. To the extent that you can acquaint yourself with group members' values and interests, you'll be able to judge more accurately the importance of their remarks. You'll also be able to determine the role you must play in order to make the group discussion profitable. If group members want to chat about the party last weekend instead of tackling the task at hand, you can remind them of the group's purpose; or if the atmosphere becomes tense or members show antagonism, you can relieve the strain by reminding everyone that the whole group will benefit from consensus or by redirecting the discussion until tempers have cooled.

The key to successful group communication experiences is interdependence. Even though discussions are sometimes competitive or hostile, they are ultimately a cooperative activity. You share with others; they share with you. Your ideas are deflected, reshaped, or accepted by others. In the end, they belong to everybody in the group. All group members leave parts of themselves in the final outcome. You are changed, even if just a little, by having worked as part of a team. When group members promote a sense of interdependence, the result is positive and productive.

Responsibilities of Leaders   Effective group leadership requires at least three basic talents. First, the leader of the group must keep the discussion moving. To do this, a leader should call attention to basic issues, remind members of what's on the floor, note common elements in diverse points of view, and strip controversial matters of their unnecessary complexity. It is important for a discussion leader periodically to summarize the results of the discussion. When the group has reached consensus, the leader might say, "Before we move on, let me summarize what I think we've decided." Such restatements will ensure that group members are in agreement and will reinforce the group decision for everyone.

Second, a discussion leader must be impartial. The leader needs to ensure that unpopular viewpoints are allowed expression. The leader must make sure that participants phrase questions and comments in neutral terms. Through the example of the leader, a spirit of cooperation and conciliation will be promoted among participants who may disagree. The leader may ask for opinions from individuals who have not yet contributed to the discussion or may remind the group there are several different interpretations of an idea.

Third and finally, a discussion leader should encourage active participation. At the beginning of a discussion, the leader may be required to present background information to frame the issues. If individuals are hesitant to state their opinions, the leader may stimulate them to participate by asking questions such as, "Mary, do you agree with John's position?" or "John, will you give us reasons to consider your viewpoint?" A leader whose manner conveys confidence in participants may encourage group members who have ideas to contribute.

Developing a Discussion Plan   A carefully developed discussion plan will prevent wasted time and effort. Ideally, the entire group will cooperate in determining the discussion plan, but sometimes a leader must take the responsibility for formulating it. The plan can be used in most situations or modified to meet special needs.

Decision-making discussions characteristically raise claims of policy: "What voice should students have in decision making in our department?" "How can our company meet competition from foreign imports?" "What should be done to control the escalating violence among American teenagers?" Answering such questions of policy requires answering secondary questions of fact and value.

The five steps in the following plan for decision-making discussions are adapted from John Dewey's analysis of reflective thinking.[3] This plan is one of several possible ways of deciding on a course of action and is intended to be suggestive rather than prescriptive. Any plan that's developed, however, probably should follow a problem-solution order.

Step 1: Defining the Problem   After the leader makes introductory remarks stating the general purpose of the discussion and its importance, the group should consider the following questions:

1. How can the problem for discussion be phrased as a question?
2. What terms or concepts should be defined?

If the question has not been phrased before the discussion begins, group members should start by developing it. The question should be specific yet allow for a variety of approaches. For example, it's better to phrase your discussion question, "What should be done to control the escalating violence among American teenagers?" than to phrase it, "Should we control violence among teenagers?" Clearly, you are encouraging many viewpoints when you ask, "What should be done?" Phrasing the question to require a yes or no answer limits the discussion.

To make the discussion flow smoothly, you will need to define the key terms in the discussion question. If your group is considering violence among teenagers, you will probably need to define *violence*. Will you consider vandalism as well as murder to be violence? Are you discussing both misdemeanors and felonies? Should you narrow your discussion to focus on assault with deadly weapons? Another term that probably requires definition is *teenager*. Will you focus on high school students, or will you expand your discussion to include 19-year-olds? As you define your terms, you may discover that the discussion question becomes clearer or even changes. It is easier to conduct a discussion if every group member understands what is meant by each of the key terms in the discussion question.

Step 2: Analyzing the Problem   This step involves evaluating the problem's scope and importance, discovering its causes, and setting up the basic requirements of an effective solution. The following questions are suggested for this step:

1. What evidence is there that a problem exists?
2. What are the causes of the problem?
3. What do we want a solution to accomplish?

First, your group must look closely at the problem to determine if it is real. Many factors could account for what seems to be an escalation of violent crime among teenagers. More careful record keeping, an expanded definition of violent crime, or computer access to violent material could all account for a bulge in the statistics.

If your group determines that a problem does exist, then you must identify its causes. Through research and discussion, you might decide that social and economic factors contribute to the problem. The increasing instability of the family, greater access to dangerous weapons, financially strapped schools, and computerization of violent entertainment among the young may all be identified as causes.

At this point in the discussion, it is obvious that teenage violence has many roots. Your group will want to narrow the discussion by limiting the scope of the solution. It isn't feasible to control all of the factors contributing to the problem with one solution. You should decide how much of the problem to solve. For example, you may want to consider only solutions involving the school system, such as confiscation of handguns or stress on teaching moral principles. You might set up budget limitations or focus on one aspect of the problem, such as control of neighborhood gangs. Whatever your group decides, it should develop parameters for evaluating the solution.

Step 3: Suggesting Solutions   In Step 3, group members suggest a wide range of possible solutions and ask the following questions:

1. What are the various ways in which the problem could be solved?
2. What is the exact nature of each proposed solution? That is, what cost, actions, or changes does it entail?

At this stage, it is helpful to list all solutions, preferably on a chalkboard. Group members should volunteer ideas, withholding criticism or judgment until all the possibilities have been listed. Some suggestions may trigger alternatives or other creative proposals. Other suggestions may come from policies or plans proposed by politicians, civic leaders, or friends.

After the proposed solutions have been listed, the group considers each in turn. Members expand upon each proposed solution, alter it, or investigate its ramifications. For example, bullet rationing may be suggested as a solution to teenage violence involving handguns. As this solution is considered, group members ask for development of the plan. How will bullets be rationed? How many bullets are now in circulation? How long will it take before bullet rationing makes handguns useless? Will the federal government control all bullet manufacturing? Can people manufacture their own bullets? Will some groups have unrestricted access to bullets? Will this create a black market in bullets? How will the armed services be treated? As you can see, there are a lot of questions to be answered about bullet rationing. The group proceeds through all the proposed solutions in this manner, asking questions and seeking full understanding of each proposal.

Step 4: Evaluating the Proposed Solutions   After your group has fully explored each solution, compare solutions and try to agree on a mutually satisfactory plan. Your group may consider the following questions:

1. What are the similarities and differences among the proposed solutions?
2. How well do the various solutions meet the criteria set up by the group?
3. Which solutions should be eliminated and which ones retained for further consideration?
4. Which solution or combination of solutions finally should be approved?

A group begins selecting its solution by finding the common elements among all of the suggested solutions. For example, your group may discover that each solution focuses on controlling violence through limiting access to handguns. In addition, you may realize that many of the solutions involve creating zones of safety for teenagers, such as schools or recreation centers. Finally, your group has called for stiffer penalties than teenagers currently receive for serious crimes such as murder.

Since cost is an important criterion for adopting a solution, your group can eliminate some solutions immediately. Training a national police force for patrolling schools is costly. As a result, your group will cross this idea off its list of realistic solutions. On the other hand, establishing a uniform code for sentencing teenagers is less expensive. It also meets your group's endorsement of stiffer penalties for teenage crime.

The group may choose its final solution from among the ones proposed by group members, or it may combine several ideas to form a desirable answer to teenage crime. For example, your group may decide to prohibit teenagers from possessing handguns, to install metal detectors in all high-crime areas frequented by teenagers, and to enforce stiffer penalties for crimes teenagers commit with handguns. This solution meets your group's criteria, and it uses the best features of several proposed solutions.

As soon as your group reaches an agreement, the leader sums up the principal features of the accepted plan. If your group has no authority to act, this statement normally concludes the discussion.

Step 5: Deciding How to Put the Solution into Operation When a group has the power to puts its solution into operation, the following additional questions are pertinent:

1. What is necessary to put the plan into effect? Does it require an official law, an appropriation of money, the formation of a committee, or other action?
2. When and where should the solution go into effect?

In this step, your group will discuss the procedures for implementing its solution. Sometimes your group will meet with other groups to iron out the details of the plan. For example, if you plan to place metal detectors in schools, you will need to estimate costs. You may require contractors to submit bids for the project. You must also arrange to start training school personnel to operate the equipment. When these matters have been decided, your group has finished its task.

Presentations in Teams: Panels and Symposia

When a group is too large for an effective discussion or when its members are not well informed on the topic, a **panel** of individuals may be selected to discuss the topic for the benefit of others, who then become an audience. Members of a panel may be particularly well informed on the subject or may represent divergent views. For example, your group may be interested in UFOs (unidentified flying objects) and hold a discussion for your classmates. Or your group might tackle the problems of tenants and landlords. Whatever your topic, the audience should learn the basic issues from your discussion.

Another type of audience-oriented discussion is the **symposium.** In a symposium format usually three to five speakers present short speeches on different facets of a subject or offer different solutions to a problem. This format is especially valuable when the speakers are recognized experts. The symposium is commonly used at large conferences and conventions. For example, if you attend a conference on education, you might learn from symposium speakers about careers for the next century or new technologies for teaching.

Various modifications of the panel and symposium formats are possible. Sometimes the two may be successfully combined. Frequently, the speeches of the symposium are followed by an informal exchange among the speakers. Then the meeting might be opened up for audience questions, comments, and reactions. The essential characteristic of both the panel and symposium is that a few people discuss a subject or problem for the benefit of a large audience.

Preparing for Panels and Symposia   As part of a panel or symposium team, it's important that you take others into account as you plan your remarks. The team approach involves several constraints that you don't face in other speaking situations. First, you have to fit your comments into a general theme. Suppose the theme of your panel is "Improving Health Care on Campus." This topic imposes certain substantial and stylistic limits on you. You'll be expected to talk about the current state of health care, requirements for good health care, personal responsibilities for improved health, and high-risk health practices.

Second, remember that you may be responsible for covering only a portion of a topic or theme. In most panels and symposia, speakers divide the topic into parts to avoid duplication. Doing so provides the audience with a variety of viewpoints. You might divide the responsibilities of a five-member panel as follows:

Speaker 1: The current status of health care on campus.

Speaker 2: Standards for effective health care.

Speaker 3: Changes needed in our campus health care system.

Speaker 4: Changing high-risk health behaviors among students.

Speaker 5: Paying for a campus health care system.

Third, the more you know about the subject under discussion, the better. You should be ready to discuss many facets of the topic in addition to the part of the discussion for which you are responsible. Analyze each aspect of the subject or implication of the problem you think may be discussed by following these four steps.

1. *Review the facts you already know.* Go over the information you've acquired through previous reading or personal experience and organize it in your mind. Prepare as if you were going to present a speech on every phase of the topic. You'll then be better qualified to discuss any part of it.

2. *Bring your knowledge up to date.* Find out if recent changes have affected the situation. Fit the newly acquired information into what you already know.

3. *Determine a tentative point of view on each of the important issues.* Decide what your attitude will be. Is health care on campus currently adequate? What changes are necessary? How will changes affect most students? What responsibilities

can students take for their own health? Stake out a tentative position on each issue that is likely to come before the group. Have the facts and reasons that support your view clearly in mind. Be ready to contribute to the group whenever it's most appropriate.

4. *Anticipate the effect of your ideas or proposals on the other members of the group or the organization.* Will your proposal require people to change their personal habits? What are the economic repercussions of changes in the health care system? Some forethought may enable you to adjust to possible opposition. The more thoroughly you relate your facts to the subject and to listeners, the more effective your contributions to the discussion will be.

Participating in Panels and Symposia   Present your point of view clearly and succinctly. Participation in a panel or symposium should always be guided by one underlying aim: to help group members think objectively and creatively so that they can analyze the subject or solve the problem at hand. To this end, present and organize your contributions in a way that will best stimulate people to think for themselves.

Your delivery will, of course, vary with the nature and purpose of the discussion and the degree of formality being observed. In general, however, speak in a direct, friendly, conversational style. As the discussion proceeds, differences of opinion may arise, tensions may increase, and some conflict may surface. You should be sensitive to the evolution of the discussion and adjust the way you voice your ideas and reactions. You might calm participants by using humor or by suggesting a compromise on a difficult issue, for example.

Clearly organized ideas are easiest to understand and should stimulate group members to think for themselves. Inquiry order or elimination order work well. Begin by stating the nature of the problem as you see it; next, outline the various hypotheses or solutions that occurred to you; then, tell why you rejected certain solutions; and finally, state your own opinion and explain the reasons for it. In this way, you give other group members a chance to examine your thinking and to add other ideas. At the same time, you'll be making your contribution in the most objective and rational manner possible.

Remain sincere, open-minded, and objective. Above all, remember that a serious discussion is not a stage for prima donnas or an arena for settling personal problems. When you have something to say, say it modestly and sincerely. Always maintain an open, objective attitude. Accept criticism with dignity and treat disagreement with an open mind. Your primary purpose is not to get your own view accepted but to work out the best group decision. The best result is a team effort.

Responding to Questions and Objections

Direct feedback from listeners is often a part of public group communication. In meetings, listeners are usually given a chance to ask questions. Panelists frequently direct questions to each other; professors ask students to clarify points made in classroom reports; club treasurers are often asked to justify particular expenditures; and spokespersons usually field questions about statements they've made.

Sometimes, questions require only a short response—a bit of factual material, a yes or no, or a reference to an authoritative source. But at other times, questions from listeners require more detailed responses. For example, some questions call for elaboration and explanation. After an oral report, you might be asked to elaborate on some statistical information you've presented. Other questions call for justification and defense. Politicians often must defend positions they've taken. In open hearings, school boards seeking to cut expenditures must justify their selection of school programs to be eliminated. University officials might be asked to defend specific campus facilities. In these special cases, the response to questions and objections calls for a brief speech.

Techniques for Responding to Questions Responses to questions that call for elaboration and explanation are, in many ways, equivalent to informative speeches. Think of your responses as short informative speeches in which you offer listeners ideas and information in response to their needs and interests. Consider the following points on how to turn your responses into effective informative speeches:

1. *Give a whole speech.* Your responses should include an introduction, a body, and a conclusion. Even though a response is an impromptu speech, you're still expected to structure ideas and to present information clearly. An elaborated remark might take the following form:

   a. *Introduction:* A rephrasing of the question to clarify it for the other audience members; an indication of why the question is a good one; a forecast of the steps you will take in answering it.

   b. *Body:* First point—often a brief historical review; second point—the information or explanation requested.

   c. *Conclusion:* A very brief summary (unless the answer was extraordinarily long); a direct reference to the questioner to see if further elaboration or explanation is required.

2. *Directly address the question as it has been asked.* Nothing is more frustrating to a questioner than an answer that misses the point or drifts from the query. Suppose that, after you have advocated a pass-fail grading system for all colleges, you are asked how graduate schools can evaluate potential candidates for advanced degrees. The questioner is calling for information and an explanation. If your response is a tirade against the inequities of letter grades or the cowardice of professors who refuse to give failing grades, you probably won't satisfy the questioner. A better response would include all of the factors—letters of recommendation, standardized tests, number of advanced courses taken, and so on—that graduate schools can use to evaluate candidates. If you're unsure what the point of the question is, ask before you attempt an answer.

3. *Be succinct.* While you certainly don't want to give a terse yes or no in response to a question calling for detail, neither should you talk for eight minutes when two minutes will suffice. If you really think that a long, complex answer is needed, you can say, "To understand why we should institute a summer orientation program at this school, you should know more about recruitment, student fears, problems with placement testing, and so on. I can go into these

topics if you'd like, but for now, in response to the particular question I was asked, I'd say that. . . ." In this way, you're able to offer a short answer, leaving other listeners an opportunity to ask additional questions.

4. *Be courteous.* During question periods, you may be amazed to hear a person ask a question that you answered during your talk. Or another person may ask for information so basic that you realize your whole presentation was probably too complex. In these situations, it's easy to become flip or overly patronizing. Avoid those temptations; don't embarrass a questioner by pointing out that you've already answered the question; don't insult your listeners. If you really think it would be a waste of the audience's time for you to review fundamental details, simply say that you're willing to answer questions after the meeting.

Techniques for Responding to Objections   A full response to an objection has two parts: (a) it answers the objection *(rebuttal)* and (b) it rebuilds the original ideas *(reestablishment).* Suppose that at an office meeting you propose that your division institute a management-by-objectives system of employee evaluation. With this approach, supervisors and employees plan goals together. You contend that this approach increases productivity, gives employees a voice in determining their own futures, and makes company expectations more concrete. During a question period, someone objects, saying that the approach means more busywork, that supervisors aren't really interested in involving employees in work decisions, and that job frustration rather than job satisfaction is the more likely result.

Your rebuttal rests on effective arguments. You can cite the results of studies at other companies similar to your own (reasoning from parallel case). You say that those studies conclude that paperwork doesn't increase, that supervisors like having concrete commitments from employees on paper, and that employee satisfaction probably increases because job turnover rates usually go down (reasoning from sign). Following your rebuttal, you reestablish your original arguments by reporting on the results of interviews with selected employees in your own company. They think the system would be a good one.

Responding successfully to objections involves the following communication techniques:

1. *Be constructive as well as destructive when responding to objections.* Don't simply tear down the other person's counterarguments; constructively bolster your original statements as well. Reestablishment rationally shores up your position and, consequently, increases your credibility.

2. *Answer objections in an orderly fashion.* If several objections are raised by a single questioner, answer them one at a time. You may need to jot down the objections as they are stated. This approach lets you respond to each objection and helps listeners sort out the issues raised.

3. *Attack each objection in a systematic fashion.* Refutation usually proceeds in a series of four steps:

   a. State the claim that you seek to rebut: "Joe has said that a management-by-objectives system won't work because supervisors don't want input from their subordinates."

    b. State your objection to it: "I don't agree with Joe because I know of three studies done at businesses much like ours, and these studies support my position."

    c. Offer evidence for your rebuttal: "The first study that reinforces my point was done at the XYZ Insurance Company in 1991. This study was duplicated by subsequent studies at several other companies in 1993 and 1994."

    d. Indicate the significance of your rebuttal: "If our company is similar to the three I've mentioned—and I think it is—then I believe our supervisors will likewise appreciate specific commitments from their subordinates, quarter by quarter. I think we will have to agree that my position is most feasible."

4. *Keep the exchange on an intellectual level.* Counterarguments and rebuttals can degenerate into name-calling exchanges. Little is settled in verbal battles. Effective decision making is more likely to occur when the calm voice of reason dominates than when group members squabble.

Answering questions and responding to objections are vital parts of the group communication process because they allow us to interact directly with others. We are made accountable for what we say by questioners and counterarguers. Through verbal exchanges we can discover flaws in logic, insufficient evidence, prejudices, and unfeasible plans of action. By testing our ideas in the give-and-take of the public forum, we ultimately contribute to the group process and its sense of community.

Key Terms

community (p. 300)

community-based special
    occasion speeches (p. 300)

decision-making discussions (p. 308)

group discussion (p. 308)

group-based special
    occasion speeches (p. 300)

panel (p. 312)

special occasions (p. 300)

speeches of courtesy (p. 302)

speeches of introduction (p. 300)

speeches to entertain (p. 304)

symposium (p. 313)

References

1. Henry W. Grady, "The New South," *American Public Addresses: 1740–1952,* edited by A. Craig Baird (New York: McGraw-Hill, 1956), 181–185.

2. Based in part on material taken from *Friendly Speeches* (Cleveland: National Reference Library, n.d.) and on material developed for earlier editions of this book.

3. See John Dewey, "Analysis of Reflective Thinking," *How We Think* (Boston: D. C. Heath, 1993), Chapter 7.

Credits

TEXT–Excerpt from *Cat's Eye* by Margaret Atwood, (c) 1989 by Bantam Books. Reprinted by permission of Doubleday, a division of Random House, Inc.; "The Geisha" by Joyce Chapman from *Communication Strategy: A Guide to Speech Preparation*. Copyright (c) 1981 by Scott Foresman-Addison Wesley. Reprinted by permission of Addison-Wesley Educational Publishers, Inc.; William Faulkner's speech on accepting the Nobel Prize for Literature, December 10, 1950. Copyright The Nobel Foundation. Reprinted by permission of The Nobel Foundation; Excerpt from *Hannibal* by Thomas Harris, (c) 1999 by Delacorte Press. Reprinted by permission of Dell Publishing, a division of Random House, Inc.; "Bill Veeck" by David Mellor from *Winning Orations*. Reprinted by permission of Larry Schnoor, Executive Secretary, Interstate Oratorical Association; Excerpt from "Common Ground and Common Sense" by Rev. Jesse Jackson from *Vital Speeches of the Day*, Vol. 54, August 15, 1988, p. 651. Copyright (c) 1988 by Jesse Jackson. Reprinted by permission of the author; Excerpt from "Strength Through Cultural Diversity" by Henri Mann Morton from *Native American Reader: Stories, Speeches and Poems*. Copyright (c) 1989. Reprinted by permission of Denali Press; Excerpt from speech at the Republican National Convention by Mary Fisher. Copyright (c) 1996 by Mary Fisher. Reprinted by permission of Mary Fisher; Illustration of parts and functions of Rollerblades. Copyright (c) Rollerblade, Inc. Reprinted by permission of Rollerblade, Inc.; "The Strangler" by Charles Schaillol from *Winning Orations*. Reprinted by permission of Larry Schnoor, Executive Secretary, Interstate Oratorical Association; Excerpt from "Have You Checked Lately?" by Deanna Sellnow from *Winning Orations*. Reprinted by permission of Larry Schnoor, Executive Secretary, Interstate Oratorical Association; "Line Graphs" from Smith Travel Research, as reported in *USA Today*, October 27, 1995, B1. Copyright (c) 1995 by *USA Today*. Reprinted by permission of *USA Today*; "Pie Graph" from Research Corp. for Fuji Computer Products, as reported in *USA Today*, October 27, 1995, B1. Copyright (c) 1995 by *USA Today*. Reprinted by permission of *USA Today*; "Pictographs" from Angus Reid Group for American Sensors, as reported in *USA Today*, October 27, 1995, B1. Copyright (c) 1995 by *USA Today*. Reprinted by permission of *USA Today*; Excerpt from *The Kandy-Kolored Tangerine-Flake Streamline Baby* by Tom Wolfe, (c) 1965. Reprinted by permission of Farrar, Straus & Giroux; Excerpt from "The Flood Gates of the Mind" by Michael Twitchell from *Winning Orations*. Reprinted by permission of Larry Schnoor, Executive Secretary, Interstate Oratorical Association.

PHOTOS–xxiv: Bob Daemmrich; 3: AP/Wide World Photos; 4: AP/Wide World Photos; 7: Will & Deni McIntyre/Photo Researchers, Inc.; 8: Joe Traver/Archive Photos/Reuters; 14: Steven Rubin/The Image Works; 25: Dave Schaefer/Monkmeyer Press; 28: Robert Ullmann/Monkeyer Press; 34: Bob Daemmrich; 37: Ramey/PhotoEdit; 41: Culver Pictures, Inc.; 48: Jeff Greenberg/PhotoEdit; 52: Dollarhide/Monkmeyer Press; 55: Jonathan Elderfield/Liaison Agency; 59: Bob Daemmrich/The Image Works; 68: Stephen Ferry/Liaison Agency; 76: Myleen Ferguson/PhotoEdit; 77: Bob Daemmrich; 88: Steve Mitchell/AP/Wide World Photos; 95: Bob Daemmrich; 106: Bob Daemmrich; 116: Bob Daemmrich/The Image Works; 126: Olympia/PhotoEdit; 136: John Curtis/The Stock Market; 144: Greg Gibson/AP/Wide World Photos; 160: Carol Halebian/Liaison Agency; 166: Bob Daemmrich; 168: Starr/Stock Boston, Inc.; 178: Bob Daemmrich/The Image Works; 182: Eascott/The

Image Works; 188: Michael Newman/PhotoEdit; 200: Rhoda Sidney/Stock Boston, Inc.; 201: Evan Agostini/Liaison Agency; 202: Mark Richards/PhotoEdit; 208: Carl J. Single/The Image Works; 212, top: Roller Blade Inc.; 212, bottom: Roller Blade Inc.; 212, bt right: Roller Blade Inc.; 223: Spencer Grant/PhotoEdit; 228: Steve Rubin/The Image Works; 231: J. Greenberg/The Image Works; 242: Matusow/Monkmeyer Press; 254: Paul Conklin/PhotoEdit; 257: Robert Brenner/PhotoEdit; 258: Dick Blume/The Image Works; 263: Levis Strauss & Company; 278: Mark Wilson/AP/Wide World Photos; 280: P.F. Gero/Corbis Sygma; 286: Andrew Yates PR/Image Bank.

Index